FIVE GO TO SMUGGLE[illegible]

FIVE GO OFF IN A CARAVAN

FIVE ON KIRRIN ISLAND AGAIN

Have you got them all?

- ☐ 1 FIVE ON A TREASURE ISLAND
- ☐ 2 FIVE GO ADVENTURING AGAIN
- ☐ 3 FIVE RUN AWAY TOGETHER
- ☐ 4 FIVE GO TO SMUGGLER'S TOP
- ☐ 5 FIVE GO OFF IN A CARAVAN
- ☐ 6 FIVE ON KIRRIN ISLAND AGAIN
- ☐ 7 FIVE GO OFF TO CAMP
- ☐ 8 FIVE GET INTO TROUBLE
- ☐ 9 FIVE FALL INTO ADVENTURE
- ☐ 10 FIVE ON A HIKE TOGETHER
- ☐ 11 FIVE HAVE A WONDERFUL TIME
- ☐ 12 FIVE GO DOWN TO THE SEA
- ☐ 13 FIVE GO TO MYSTERY MOOR
- ☐ 14 FIVE HAVE PLENTY OF FUN
- ☐ 15 FIVE ON A SECRET TRAIL
- ☐ 16 FIVE GO TO BILLYCOCK HILL
- ☐ 17 FIVE GET INTO A FIX
- ☐ 18 FIVE ON FINNISTON FARM
- ☐ 19 FIVE GO TO DEMON'S ROCKS
- ☐ 20 FIVE HAVE A MYSTERY TO SOLVE
- ☐ 21 FIVE ARE TOGETHER AGAIN

Enid Blyton

The Famous Five

FIVE GO TO SMUGGLER'S TOP

FIVE GO OFF IN A CARAVAN

FIVE ON KIRRIN ISLAND AGAIN

Hodder Children's Books

a division of Hachette Children's Books

This edition first published in Great Britain in 2009
by Hodder Children's Books

1

A Catalogue record for this book is available from the British Library

ISBN 978 1 444 90076 7

Printed and bound in Great Britain by
CPI Bookmarque Ltd, Croydon, Surrey

The paper and board used in this paperback by Hodder Children's Books are natural recyclable products made from wood grown in sustainable forests. The manufacturing processes conform to the environmental regulations of the country of origin.

Hodder Children's Books
a division of Hachette Children's Books
338 Euston Road, London, NW1 3BH
An Hachette UK Company
www.hachette.co.uk

FIVE GO TO SMUGGLER'S TOP

[1]

Back to Kirrin Cottage

One fine day, right at the beginning of the Easter holidays, four children and a dog travelled by train together.

'Soon be there now,' said Julian, a tall strong boy, with a determined face.

'Woof,' said Timothy the dog, getting excited, and trying to look out of the window too.

'Get down, Tim,' said Julian. 'Let Anne have a look.'

Anne was his younger sister. She put her head out of the window. 'We're coming into Kirrin Station!' she said. 'I do hope Aunt Fanny will be there to meet us.'

'Of course she will!' said Georgina, her cousin. She looked more like a boy than a girl, for she wore her hair very short, and it curled close about her head. She too had a determined face, like Julian. She pushed Anne away and looked out of the window.

'It's nice to be going home,' she said. 'I love school – but it will be fun to be at Kirrin Cottage and perhaps sail out to Kirrin Island and visit the castle there. We haven't been since last summer.'

'Dick's turn to look out now,' said Julian, turning to his younger brother, a boy with a pleasant face, sitting reading in a corner. 'We're just coming into sight of Kirrin, Dick. Can't you stop reading for a second?'

'It's such an exciting book,' said Dick, and shut it with a clap. 'The most exciting adventure story I've ever read!'

'Pooh! I bet it's not as exciting as some of the adventures *we've* had!' said Anne, at once.

It was quite true that the five of them, counting in Timmy the dog, who always shared everything with them, had had the most amazing adventures together. But now it looked as if they were going to have nice quiet holidays, going for long walks over the cliffs, and perhaps sailing out in George's boat to their island of Kirrin.

'I've worked jolly hard at school this term,' said Julian. 'I could do with a holiday!'

'You've gone thin,' said Georgina. Nobody called her that. They all called her George. She would never answer to any other name. Julian grinned.

'Well, I'll soon get fat at Kirrin Cottage, don't you worry! Aunt Fanny will see to that. She's a great one for trying to fatten people up. It will be nice to see your mother again, George. She's an awfully good sort.'

'Yes. I hope Father will be in a good temper these hols,' said George. 'He ought to be because he has just finished some new experiments, Mother says, which have been quite successful.'

George's father was a scientist, always working out new ideas. He liked to be quiet, and sometimes he flew into a temper when he could not get the peace he needed or things did not go exactly as he wanted them to. The children often thought that hot-tempered Georgina was very like her father! She too could fly into fierce tempers when things did not go right for her.

Aunt Fanny was there to meet them. The four children jumped out on the platform and rushed to hug her. George got there first. She was very fond of her gentle mother, who had so often tried to shield her when her father got angry with her. Timmy pranced round, barking in delight. He adored George's mother.

She patted him, and he tried to stand up and lick her face. 'Timmy's bigger than ever!' she said, laughing. 'Down, old boy! You'll knock me over.'

Timmy was certainly a big dog. All the children loved him, for he was loyal, loving and faithful. His brown eyes looked from one to the other, enjoying the children's excitement. Timmy shared in it, as he shared in everything.

But the person he loved most, of course, was his mistress, George. She had had him since he was a small puppy. She took him to school with her each term, for she and Anne went to a boarding-school that allowed pets. Otherwise George would most certainly have refused to go!

They set off to Kirrin in the pony-trap. It was very windy and cold, and the children shivered and pulled their coats tightly round them.

'It's awfully cold,' said Anne, her teeth beginning to chatter. 'Colder than in the winter!'

'It's the wind,' said her aunt, and tucked a rug round her. 'It's been getting very strong the last day or two. The fishermen have pulled their boats high up the beach for fear of a big storm.'

The children saw the boats pulled right up as they passed the beach where they had bathed so often. They did not feel like bathing now. It made them shiver even to think of it.

The wind howled over the sea. Great scudding clouds raced overhead. The waves pounded on the beach and made a terrific noise. It excited Timmy, who began to bark.

'Be quiet, Tim,' said George, patting him. 'You will have to learn to be a good quiet dog now we are home again, or Father will be cross with you. Is Father very busy, Mother?'

'Very,' said her mother. 'But he's going to do very little work now you are coming home. He thought he would like to go for walks with you, or go out in the boat, if the weather calms down.'

The children looked at one another. Uncle Quentin was not the best of companions. He had no sense of humour, and when the children went off into fits of laughter, as they did twenty times a day or more, he could not see the joke at all.

'It looks as if these hols won't be quite so jolly if Uncle Quentin parks himself on us most of the time,' said Dick in a low voice to Julian.

'Sh,' said Julian, afraid that his aunt would hear, and be hurt. George frowned.

'Oh Mother! Father will be bored stiff if he comes with us – and we'll be bored too.'

George was very outspoken, and could never learn to keep a guard on her tongue. Her mother sighed. 'Don't talk like that, dear. I daresay your father will get tired of going with you after a bit. But it does him good to have a bit of young life about him.'

'Here we are!' said Julian, as the trap stopped outside an old house. 'Kirrin Cottage! My word, how the wind is howling round it, Aunt Fanny!'

'Yes. It made a terrible noise last night,' said his aunt. 'You take the trap round to the back, Julian, when we've got the things out. Oh, here's your uncle to help!'

Uncle Quentin came out, a tall, clever-looking man, with rather frowning eyebrows. He smiled at the children and kissed George and Anne.

'Welcome to Kirrin Cottage!' he said. 'I'm quite glad your mother and father are away, Anne, because now we shall have you all here once again!'

Soon they were sitting round the table eating a big tea. Aunt Fanny always got ready a fine meal for their first one, for she knew they were very hungry after their long journey on the train.

Even George was satisfied at last, and leaned back in her chair, wishing she could manage just one more of her mother's delicious new-made buns.

Timmy sat close to her. He was not supposed to be fed at meal-times but it was really surprising how many tit-bits found their way to him under the table!

The wind howled round the house. The windows rattled, the doors shook, and the mats lifted themselves up and down as the draught got under them.

'They look as if they've got snakes wriggling underneath them,' said Anne. Timmy watched them and growled. He was a clever dog, but he did not know why the mats wriggled in such a strange way.

'I hope the wind will die down tonight,' said Aunt Fanny. 'It kept me awake last night. Julian dear, you look rather thin. Have you been working hard? I must fatten you up.'

The children laughed. 'Just what we thought

you'd say, Mother!' said George. 'Goodness, what's that?'

They all sat still, startled. There was a loud bumping noise on the roof, and Timmy put up his ears and growled fiercely.

'A tile off the roof,' said Uncle Quentin. 'How tiresome! We shall have to get the loose tiles seen to, Fanny, when the storm is over, or the rain will come in.'

The children rather hoped that their uncle would retire to his study after tea, as he usually did, but this time he didn't. They wanted to play a game, but it wasn't much good with Uncle Quentin there. He really wasn't any good at all, not even at such a simple game as snap.

'Do you know a boy called Pierre Lenoir?' Uncle Quentin suddenly asked, taking a letter from his pocket. 'I believe he goes to your school and Dick's, Julian.'

Oh you mean old Sooty,' said Julian. 'Yes – he's in Dick's form. Mad as a hatter.'

'Sooty! Now why do you call him that?' said

Uncle Quentin. 'It seems a silly name for a boy.'

'If you saw him you wouldn't think so,' said Dick, with a laugh. 'He's very dark! Hair as black as soot, eyes like bits of coal, eyebrows that look as if they've been put in with charcoal. And his name means "The black one", doesn't it? Le-noir – that's French for black.'

'Yes. Quite true. But what a name to give anyone – *Sooty*!' said Uncle Quentin. 'Well, I've been having quite a lot of correspondence with this boy's father. He and I are interested in the same scientific matters. In fact, I've asked him whether he wouldn't like to come and stay with me for a few days – and bring his boy, Pierre.'

'Oh really!' said Dick, looking quite pleased. 'Well it wouldn't be bad sport to have old Sooty here, Uncle. But he's quite mad. He never does as he's told, he climbs like a monkey, and he can be awfully cheeky. I don't know if you'd like him much.'

Uncle Quentin looked sorry he had asked Sooty after he had heard what Dick had to say.

He didn't like cheeky boys. Nor did he like mad ones.

'Hm,' he said, putting the letter away. 'I wish I'd asked you about the boy first, before suggesting to his father that he might bring him with him. But perhaps I can prevent him coming.'

'No, don't, Father,' said George, who rather liked the sound of Sooty Lenoir. 'Let's have him. He could come out with us and liven things up!'

'We'll see,' said her father, who had already made up his mind on no account to have the boy at Kirrin Cottage, if he was mad, climbed everywhere, and was cheeky. George was enough of a handful without a devil of a boy egging her on!

Much to the children's relief Uncle Quentin retired to read by himself about eight o'clock. Aunt Fanny looked at the clock.

'Time for Anne to go to bed,' she said. 'And you too, George.'

'Just one good game of Slap-Down Patience,

all of us playing it together, Mother!' said George. 'Come on – you play it too. It's our first evening at home. Anyway, I shan't sleep for ages, with this gale howling round! Come on, Mother – one good game, then we'll go to bed. Julian's been yawning like anything already!'

[2]

A shock in the night

It was nice to climb up the steep stairs to their familiar bedrooms that night. All the children were yawning widely. Their long train journey had tired them.

'If only this awful wind would stop!' said Anne, pulling the curtain aside and looking out into the night. 'There's a little moon, George. It keeps bobbing out between the scurrying clouds.'

'Let it bob!' said George, scrambling into bed. 'I'm jolly cold. Hurry, Anne, or you'll catch a chill at that window.'

'Don't the waves make a noise?' said Anne, still at the window. 'And the gale in the old ash tree is making a whistling, howling sound, and bending it right over.'

'Timmy, hurry up and get on my bed,'

commanded George, screwing up her cold toes. 'That's one good thing about being at home, Anne. I can have Timmy on my bed! He's far better than a hot water bottle.'

'You're not supposed to have him on your bed at home, any more than you're supposed to at school,' said Anne, curling up in bed. 'Aunt Fanny thinks he sleeps in his basket over there.'

'Well, I can't stop him coming on my bed at night, can I, if he doesn't want to sleep in his basket?' said George. 'That's right, Timmy darling. Make my feet warm. Where's your nose? Let me pat it. Goodnight, Tim. Goodnight, Anne.'

'Goodnight,' said Anne, sleepily. 'I hope that Sooty boy comes, don't you? He does sound fun.'

'Yes. And anyway Father would stay in with Mr Lenoir, the boy's father, and not come out with us,' said George. 'Father doesn't mean to, but he does spoil things somehow.'

'He's not very good at laughing,' said Anne. 'He's too serious.'

A loud bang made both girls jump. 'That's the bathroom door!' said George, with a groan. 'One of the boys must have left it open. That's the sort of noise that drives Father mad! There it goes again!'

'Well, let Julian or Dick shut it,' said Anne, who was now beginning to feel nice and warm. But Julian and Dick were thinking that George or Anne might shut it, so nobody got out of bed to see to the banging door.

Very soon Uncle Quentin's voice roared up the stairs, louder than the gale.

'Shut that door, one of you! How can I work with that noise going on?'

All four children jumped out of bed like a shot. Timmy leapt off George's bed. Everyone fell over him as they rushed to the bathroom door. There was a lot of giggling and scuffling. Then Uncle Quentin's footsteps were heard on the stairs and the five fled silently to their rooms.

The gale still roared. Uncle Quentin and Aunt Fanny came up to bed. The bedroom door flew out of Uncle Quentin's hand and slammed itself shut so violently that a vase leapt off a nearby shelf.

Uncle Quentin leapt too, startled. 'This wretched gale!' he said, fiercely. 'Never known one like it all the time we've been here. If it gets much worse the fishermen's boats will be smashed up, even though they've pulled them as high up the beach as possible.'

'It will blow itself out soon, dear,' said Aunt Fanny, soothingly. 'Probably by the time morning comes it will be quite calm.'

But she was wrong. The gale did not blow itself out that night. Instead it raged round the house even more fiercely, shrieking and howling like a live thing. Nobody could sleep. Timmy kept up a continuous low growling, for he did not like the shakes and rattles and howls.

Towards dawn the wind seemed in a fury. Anne thought it sounded as if it was in a horrible temper, out to do all the harm it could. She lay and trembled, half-frightened.

Suddenly there was a strange noise. It was a

loud and woeful groaning and creaking, like someone in great pain. The two girls sat up, terrified. What could it be?

The boys heard it too. Julian leapt out of bed and ran to the window. Outside stood the old ash tree, tall and black in the fitful moonlight. It was gradually bending over!

'It's the ash! It's falling!' yelled Julian, almost startling Dick out of his wits. 'It's falling, I tell you. It'll crash on the house! Quick, warn the girls!'

Shouting at the top of his voice, Julian raced out of his door on to the landing. 'Uncle! Aunt! George and Anne! Come downstairs quickly. The ash tree is falling!'

George jumped out of bed, snatched at her dressing-gown, and raced to the door, yelling to Anne. The little girl was soon with her. Timmy ran in front. At the door of Aunt Fanny's bedroom Uncle Quentin appeared, tall and amazed, wrapping his dressing-gown round him.

'What's all this noise? Julian, what's—?'

'Aunt Fanny! Come downstairs – the ash tree is falling! Listen to its terrible groans and creaks!' yelled Julian, almost beside himself with impatience. 'It'll smash in the roof and the bedrooms! Listen, here it comes!'

Everyone fled downstairs as, with an appalling wail, the great ash tree hauled up its roots and fell heavily on to Kirrin Cottage. There was a terrible crash, and the sound of tiles slipping to the ground everywhere.

'Oh dear!' said poor Aunt Fanny, covering her eyes. 'I knew something would happen! Quentin, we ought to have had that ash tree topped. I knew it would fall in a great gale like this. What has it done to the roof?'

After the great crash there had come other smaller noises, sounds of things falling, thuds and little smashing noises. The children could not imagine what was happening. Timmy was thoroughly angry, and barked loudly. Uncle Quentin slapped his hand angrily on the table, and made everyone jump.

'Stop that dog barking! I'll turn him out!' But

nothing would stop Timmy barking or growling that night, and George at last pushed him into the warm kitchen, and shut the door on him.

'I feel like barking or growling myself,' said Anne, who knew exactly what Timmy felt like. 'Julian, has the tree broken in the roof?'

Uncle Quentin took a powerful torch and went carefully up the stairs to the landing to see what damage had been done. He came down looking rather pale.

'The tree has crashed through the attic, smashed the roof in, and wrecked the girls' bedroom,' he said. 'A big branch has penetrated the boys' room too, but not badly. But the girls' room is ruined! They would have been killed if they had been in their beds.'

Everyone was silent. It was an awful thought that George and Anne had had such a narrow escape.

'Good thing I yelled my head off to warn them then,' said Julian, cheerfully, seeing how white Anne had gone. 'Cheer up, Anne – think what a tale you'll have to tell at school next term.'

'I think some hot cocoa would do us all good,' said Aunt Fanny, pulling herself together, though she felt very shaken. 'I'll go and make some. Quentin, see if the fire is still alight in your study. We want a little warmth!'

The fire was still alight. Everyone crowded round it. They welcomed Aunt Fanny when she came in with some steaming milk-cocoa.

Anne looked curiously round the room as she sat sipping her drink. This was where her uncle did his work, his very clever work. He wrote his difficult books here, books which Anne could not understand at all. He drew his weird diagrams here, and made many strange experiments.

But just at the moment Uncle Quentin did not look very clever. He looked rather ashamed, somehow. Anne soon knew why.

'Quentin, it is a mercy none of us was hurt or killed,' said Aunt Fanny, looking at him rather sternly. 'I told you a dozen times you should get that ash tree topped. I knew it was too big and heavy to withstand a great gale. I was always afraid it would blow down on the house.'

'Yes, I know, my dear,' said Uncle Quentin, stirring his cup of cocoa very vigorously. 'But I was so busy these last months.'

'You always make that an excuse for not doing urgent things,' said Aunt Fanny, with a sigh. 'I shall have to manage things myself in the future. I can't risk our lives like this!'

'Well, a thing like this would only happen once in a blue moon!' cried Uncle Quentin, getting angry. Then he calmed down, seeing that Aunt Fanny was really shocked and upset, very near to tears. He put down his cocoa and slipped his arm round her.

'You've had a terrible shock,' he said. 'Don't you worry about things. Maybe they won't be so bad when morning comes.'

'Oh, Quentin – they'll be much worse!' said his wife. 'Where shall we sleep tonight, all of us, and what shall we do till the roof and upstairs rooms are repaired? The children have only just come home. The house will be full of workmen for weeks! I don't know how I'm going to manage.'

'Leave it all to me!' said Uncle Quentin. 'I'll settle everything. Don't worry. I'm sorry about this, very sorry, particularly as it's my fault. But I'll straighten things out for everyone, you just see!'

Aunt Fanny didn't really believe him, but she was grateful for his comforting. The children listened in silence, drinking their hot cocoa. Uncle Quentin was so very clever, and knew so many things – but it was so like him to neglect something urgent like cutting off the top of the old ash tree. Sometimes he didn't seem to live in this world at all!

It was no use going up to bed! The rooms upstairs were either completely ruined, or so messed up with bits and pieces, and clouds of dust, that it was impossible to sleep there. Aunt Fanny began to pile rugs on sofas. There was one in the study, a big one in the sitting-room and a smaller one in the dining-room. She found a camp bed in a cupboard and, with Julian's help, put that up too.

'We'll just have to do the best we can,' she said. 'There isn't much left of the night, but we'll get a little sleep if we can! The gale is not nearly so wild now.'

'No – it's done all the damage it can, so it's satisfied,' said Uncle Quentin, grimly. 'Well, we'll talk things over in the morning.'

The children found it very difficult to go to sleep after such an excitement, tired though they were. Anne felt worried. How could they all stay at Kirrin Cottage now? It wouldn't be fair on Aunt Fanny. But they couldn't go home because her father and mother were both away and the house was shut up for a month.

'I hope we shan't be sent back to school,' thought Anne, trying to get comfortable on the sofa. 'It would be too awful, after having left there, and starting off so cheerfully for the holidays.'

George was afraid of that, too. She felt sure that they would all be packed back to their schools the next morning. That would mean that she and Anne wouldn't see Julian and Dick any more these holidays, for the boys, of course, went to a different school.

Timmy was the only one who didn't worry about things. He lay on George's feet, snoring a little, quite happy. So long as he was with George he didn't really mind *where* he went!

[3]

Uncle Quentin has an idea

Next morning the wind was still high, but the fury of the gale was gone. The fishermen on the beach were relieved to find that their boats had suffered very little damage. But word soon went round about the accident to Kirrin Cottage, and a few sightseers came up to marvel at the sight of the great, uprooted tree, lying heavily on the little house.

The children rather enjoyed the importance of relating how nearly they had escaped with their lives. In the light of day it was surprising what damage the big tree had done. It had cracked the roof of the house like an eggshell, and the rooms upstairs were in a terrible mess.

The woman who came up from the village to help Aunt Fanny during the day exclaimed at the sight: 'Why, it'll take weeks to set that right!' she said. 'Have you got on to the builders? I'd get them up here right away and let them see what's to be done.'

'*I'm* seeing to things, Mrs Daly,' said Uncle Quentin. 'My wife has had a great shock. She is not fit to see to things herself. The first thing to do is to decide what is to happen to the children. They can't remain here while there are no usable bedrooms.'

'They had better go back to school, poor things,' said Aunt Fanny.

'No. I've a better idea than that,' said Uncle Quentin, fishing a letter out of his pocket. 'Much better. I've had a letter from that fellow Lenoir this morning – you know, the one who's interested in the same kind of experiments as I am. He says – er, wait a minute, I'll read you the bit. Yes here it is.'

Uncle Quentin read it out: 'It is most kind of you to suggest my coming to stay with you and bringing my boy Pierre. Allow me to extend hospitality to you and your children also. I do not know how many you have, but all are welcome here in this big house. My Pierre will be glad of company, and so will his sister, Marybelle.'

Uncle Quentin looked up triumphantly at his wife. 'There you are! I call that a most generous invitation! It couldn't have come at a better time. We'll pack the whole of the children off to this fellow's house.'

'But Quentin – you can't possibly do that! Why, we don't know anything about him or his family!' said Aunt Fanny.

'His boy goes to the same school as Julian and Dick, and I know Lenoir is a remarkable, clever fellow,' said Uncle Quentin, as if that was all that really mattered. 'I'll telephone him now. What's his number?'

Aunt Fanny felt helpless in the face of her husband's sudden determination to settle everything himself. He was ashamed because it was his forgetfulness that had brought on the accident to the house. Now he was going to show that he *could* see to things if he liked. She heard him telephoning, and frowned. How could they possibly send off the children to a strange place like that?

Uncle Quentin put down the receiver, and went to find his wife, looking jubilant and very pleased with himself.

'It's all settled,' he said. 'Lenoir is delighted, most delighted. Says he loves children about the place, and so does his wife, and his two will be thrilled to have them. If we can hire a car today, they can go at once.'

'But Quentin – we *can't* let them go off like that to strange people! They'll hate it! I shouldn't be surprised if George refuses to go,' said his wife.

'Oh – that reminds me. She's not to take Timothy,' said Uncle Quentin. 'Apparently Lenoir doesn't like dogs.'

'Well, then, you know George won't go!' said his wife. 'That's foolish, Quentin. George won't go anywhere without Timmy.'

'She'll have to, this time,' said Uncle Quentin, quite determined that George should not upset all his marvellous plans. 'Here are the children.

I'll ask them what *they* feel about going, and see what they say!'

He called them into his study. They came in, feeling sure that they were to hear bad news – probably they were all to return to school!

'You remember that boy I spoke to you about last night?' began Uncle Quentin. 'Pierre Lenoir. You had some absurd name for him.'

'Sooty,' said Dick and Julian together.

'Ah yes, Sooty. Well, his father has kindly invited you all to go and stay with him at Smuggler's Top,' said Uncle Quentin.

The children were astonished.

'*Smuggler's Top!*' said Dick, his fancy caught by the peculiar name. 'What's Smuggler's Top?'

'The name of his house,' said Uncle Quentin. 'It's very old, built on the top of a strange hill surrounded by marshes over which the sea once flowed. The hill was once an island, but now it's just a tall hill rising up from the marsh. Smuggling went on there in the old days. It's a very peculiar place, so I've heard.'

All this made the children feel excited. Also

Julian and Dick had always liked Sooty Lenoir. He was quite mad, but awfully good fun. They might have a first-rate time with him.

'Well – would you like to go? Or would you rather go back to school for the holidays?' asked Uncle Quentin impatiently.

'Oh *no* – not back to school!' said everyone at once.

'I'd *love* to go to Smuggler's Top,' said Dick. 'It sounds a thrilling place. And I always liked old Sooty, especially since he sawed half-way through one of the legs of our form-master's chair. It gave way at once when Mr Toms sat down!'

'Hm. I don't see that a trick like that is any reason for liking someone,' said Uncle Quentin, beginning to feel a little doubtful about Master Lenoir. 'Perhaps, on the whole, school would be best for you.'

'Oh no, no!' cried everyone. 'Let's go to Smuggler's Top! Do, do let's!'

'Very well,' said Uncle Quentin, pleased at their eagerness to follow his plan. 'As a matter of fact, I have already settled it. I telephoned a few minutes ago. Mr Lenoir was very kind about it all.'

'Can I take Timmy?' asked George, suddenly.

'No,' said her father. 'I'm afraid not. Mr Lenoir doesn't like dogs.'

'Then I shan't like *him*,' said George, sulkily. 'I won't go without Timmy.'

'You'll have to go back to school, then,' said her father, sharply. 'And take off that sulky expression, George. You know how I dislike it.'

But George wouldn't. She turned away. The others looked at her in dismay. Surely old George wasn't going to get into one of her moods, and spoil everything! It would be fun to go to Smuggler's Top. But, of course, it certainly wouldn't be so much fun without Timmy. Still – they couldn't all go back to school just because George wouldn't go anywhere without her dog.

They all went into the sitting-room. Anne put her arm through George's. George shook it off.

'George! You simply *must* come with us,' said Anne. 'I can't bear to go without you – it would be awful to see you going back to school all alone.'

'I shouldn't be all alone,' said George. 'I should have Timmy.'

The others pressed her to change her mind, but she shook them off. 'Leave me alone,' she said. 'I want to think. How are we supposed to get to Smuggler's Top, and where is it? Which road do we take?'

'We're going by car, and it's right up the coast somewhere, so I expect we'll take the coast-road,' said Julian. 'Why, George?'

'Don't ask questions,' said George. She went out with Timmy. The others didn't follow her. George was not very nice when she was cross.

Aunt Fanny began to pack for them, though it was impossible to get some of the things from the girls' room. After a time George came back, but Timmy was not with her. She looked more cheerful.

'Where's Tim?' asked Anne, at once.

'Out somewhere,' said George.

'Are you coming with us, George?' asked Julian, looking at her.

'Yes. I've made up my mind to,' said George, but for some reason she wouldn't look Julian in the eyes. He wondered why.

Aunt Fanny gave them all an early lunch, and then a big car came for them. They packed themselves inside. Uncle Quentin gave them all sorts of messages for Mr Lenoir, and Aunt Fanny kissed them goodbye. 'I do hope you have a nice time at Smuggler's Top,' she said. 'Mind you write at once and tell me all about it.'

'Aren't we going to say goodbye to Timmy?' said Anne, her eyes opening wide in amazement at George, forgetting. 'George, surely you're not going without saying goodbye to old Timmy!'

'Can't stop now,' said Uncle Quentin, afraid that George might suddenly become awkward again. 'Right, driver! You can go off now. Don't drive too fast, please.'

Waving and shouting the children drove away from Kirrin Cottage, sad when they looked back and saw the smashed roof under the fallen tree. Never mind – they had not been sent back to school. That was the main thing. Their spirits rose as they thought of Sooty and his oddly-named home, Smuggler's Top.

'Smuggler's Top! It sounds too exciting for words!' said Anne. 'I can picture it, an old house right on the top of a hill. Fancy being an island once. I wonder why the sea went back and left marshes instead.'

George said nothing for a while, and the car sped on. The others glanced at her once or twice, but came to the conclusion that she was grieving about Timmy. Still she didn't look very sad!

The car went over a hill and sped down to the bottom. When they got there George leaned forward and touched the driver's arm.

'Would you stop a moment, please? We have to pick somebody up here.'

Julian, Dick and Anne stared at George in

surprise. The driver, also rather surprised, drew the car to a standstill. George opened the car door and gave a loud whistle.

Something shot out of the hedge and hurled itself joyfully into the car. It was Timmy! He licked everyone, trod on everyone's toes, and gave the little short barks that showed he was excited and happy.

'Well,' said the driver, doubtfully, 'I don't know if you're supposed to take that dog in. Your father didn't say anything about him.'

'It's all right,' said George, her face red with joy. 'Quite all right. You needn't worry. Start the car again, please.'

'You *are* a monkey!' said Julian, half-annoyed with George, and half-pleased because Timmy was with them after all. 'Mr Lenoir may send him back, you know.'

'Well, he'll have to send *me* back too,' said George, defiantly. 'Anyhow, the main thing is, we've got Timmy after all, and I am coming with you.'

'Yes – that's fine,' said Anne, and gave first

George and then Timmy a hug. '*I* didn't like going without Tim either.'

'On to Smuggler's Top!' said Dick, as the car started off again. 'On to Smuggler's Top. I wonder if we shall have any adventures there!'

[4]

Smuggler's Top

The car sped on, mostly along the coast, though it sometimes went inland for a few miles. But sooner or later it was in sight of the sea again. The children enjoyed the long drive. They were to stop somewhere for lunch, and the driver told them he knew of a good inn.

At half past twelve he drew up outside an old inn, and they all trooped in. Julian took charge, and ordered lunch. It was a very good one, and all the children enjoyed it. So did Timmy. The innkeeper liked dogs, and put down such a piled-up plate for Timmy that the dog hardly liked to begin on his meal in case it was not for him!

He looked up at George and she nodded to him. 'It's your dinner, Timmy. Eat it up.'

So he ate it, hoping that if they were going to

stay anywhere they might be staying at the inn. Meals like this did not arrive every day for a hungry dog!

But after lunch the children got up. They went to find the driver, who was having his lunch in the kitchen with the innkeeper and his wife. They were old friends of his.

'Well, I hear you're going to Castaway,' said the innkeeper, getting up. 'You be careful there!'

'Castaway!' said Julian. 'Is that what the hill is called, where Smuggler's Top is?'

'That's its name,' said the innkeeper.

'Why is it called that?' said Anne. 'What a funny name! Were people cast away on it once, when it was an island?'

'Oh no. The old story goes that the hill was once joined to the mainland,' said the innkeeper. 'But it was the haunt of bad people, and one of the saints became angry with the place, and cast it away into the sea, where it became an island.'

'And so it was called Castaway,' said Dick.

'But perhaps it has got good again, because the sea has gone away from it, and you can walk from the mainland to the hill, can't you?'

'Yes. There's one good road you can take,' said the innkeeper. 'But you be careful of wandering away from it, if you go walking on it! The marsh will suck you down in no time if you set foot on it!'

'It does sound a most exciting place,' said George. 'Smuggler's Top on Castaway Hill! Only one road to it!'

'Time to get on,' said the driver, looking at the clock. 'You've got to be there before tea, your uncle said.'

They got into the car again, Timmy clambering over legs and feet to a comfortable place on George's lap. He was far too big and heavy to lie there but just occasionally he seemed to want to, and George never had the heart to refuse him.

They drove off once more. Anne fell asleep, and the others felt drowsy too. The car purred on and on. It began to rain, and the countryside looked rather dreary.

The driver turned round after a while and spoke to Julian. 'We're coming near to Castaway Hill. We'll soon be leaving the mainland, and taking the road across the marsh.'

Julian woke Anne. They all sat up expectantly. But it was very disappointing after all! The marshes were full of mist! The children could not pierce through it with their eyes, and could only see the flat road they were on, raised a little higher than the surrounding flat marsh. When the mist shifted a little now and again the children saw a dreary space of flat marsh on either side.

'Stop a minute,' said Julian. 'I'd like to see what the marsh is like.'

'Well, don't step off the road,' warned the driver stopping the car. 'And don't you let that dog out. Once he runs off the road and gets into the marsh he'll be gone for good.'

'What do you mean – gone for good?' said Anne, her eyes wide.

'He means the marsh will suck down Timmy at once,' said Julian. 'Shut him in the car, George.'

So Timmy, much to his disgust, was shut safely in the car. He pawed at the door, and tried to look out of the window. The driver turned and spoke to him. 'It's all right. They'll be back soon, old fellow!'

But Timmy whined all the time the others were out of the car. He saw them go to the edge of the road. He saw Julian jump down the couple of feet that raised the road above the marsh.

There was a line of raised stones running in the marsh alongside the road. Julian stood on one of these peering at the flat marsh.

'It's mud,' he said. 'Loose, squelchy mud! Look, when I touch it with my foot it moves! It would soon suck me down if I trod heavily on it.'

Anne didn't like it. She called to Julian. 'Come up on the road again. I'm afraid you'll fall in.'

Mists were wreathing and swirling over the salty marshes. It was a weird place, cold and damp. None of the children liked it. Timmy began to bark in the car.

'Tim will scratch the car to bits if we don't get back,' said George. So they all went back, rather silent. Julian wondered how many travellers had been lost in that strange sea-marsh.

'Oh, there're many that've never been heard of again,' said the driver, when they asked him. 'They say there're one or two winding paths that go to the hill from the mainland, that were used before the road was built. But unless you know every inch of them you're off them in a second, and find your feet sinking in the mud.'

'It's horrid to think about,' said Anne. 'Don't let's talk about it any more. Can we see Castaway Hill yet?'

'Yes. There it is, looming up in the mist,' said the driver. 'The top of it is out of the mist, see? Strange place, isn't it?'

The children looked in silence. Out of the slowly moving mists rose a tall, steep hill, whose rocky sides were as steep as cliffs. The hill seemed to swim in the mists, and to have no roots in the earth. It was covered with buildings which even at that distance looked old and quaint. Some of them had towers.

'That must be Smuggler's Top, right at the summit,' said Julian, pointing. 'It's like an old building of centuries ago – probably is! Look at the tower it has. What a wonderful view you'd get from it.'

The children gazed at the place where they were to stay. It looked exciting and picturesque, certainly – but it also looked rather forbidding.

'It's sort of – sort of *secret*, somehow,' said Anne, putting into words what the others were thinking. 'I mean – it looks as if it had kept all kinds of strange secrets down the centuries. I guess it could tell plenty of tales!'

The car drove on again, quite slowly, because the mists came down thickly. The road had a line of sparkling round buttons set all along the middle, and when the driver switched on his fog-lamp, they shone brightly and guided him well. Then as they neared Castaway Hill the road began to slope upwards.

'We go through a big archway soon,' said the driver. 'That used to be where the city gate once was. The whole town is surrounded by wall still, just as it used to be in olden times. It's wide enough to walk on, and if you start at a certain place, and walk long enough, you'll come round to the place you started at!'

All the children made up their minds to do this without fail. What a view they would have all round the hill, if they chose a fine day!

The road became steeper, and the driver put the engine into a lower gear. It groaned up the hill. Then it came to an archway, from which old gates were fastened back. It passed through, and the children were in Castaway.

'It's almost as if we've gone back through the centuries, and come to somewhere that existed ages ago!' said Julian, peering at the old houses and shops, with their cobbled streets, their diamond-paned windows, and stout old doors.

They went up the winding high street, and

came at last to a big gateway, set with wrought-iron gates. The driver hooted and they opened. They swept into a steep drive, and at last stopped before Smuggler's Top.

They got out, feeling suddenly shy. The big old house seemed to frown down at them. It was built of brick and timber, and its front door was as massive as that of a castle.

Weird gables jutted here and there over the diamond-paned windows. The house's one tower stood sturdily at the east side of the house, with windows all round. It was not a square tower, but a rounded one, and ended in a point.

'Smuggler's Top!' said Julian. 'It's a good name for it somehow. I suppose lots of smuggling went on here in the old days.'

Dick rang the bell. To do this he had to pull down an iron handle, and a jangling at once made itself heard in the house.

There was the sound of running feet, and the door was opened. It opened slowly, for it was heavy.

Beyond it stood two children, one a girl of about Anne's age, and the other a boy of Dick's age.

'Here you are at last!' cried the boy, his dark eyes dancing. 'I thought you were never coming!'

'This is Sooty,' said Dick to the girls, who had not met him before. They stared at him.

He was certainly very, very dark. Black hair, black eyes, black eyebrows, and a brown face. In contrast to him the girl beside him looked pale and delicate. She had golden hair, blue eyes and her eyebrows were so faint they could hardly be seen.

'This is Marybelle, my sister,' said Sooty. 'I always think we look like Beauty and the Beast!'

Sooty was nice. Everyone liked him at once. George found herself twinkling at him in a way quite strange to her, for usually she was shy of strangers, and would not make friends for some time. But who could help liking Sooty with his dancing black eyes and his really wicked grin?

'Come in,' said Sooty. 'Driver, you can take the car round to the next door, and Block will take in the luggage for you and give you tea.'

Suddenly Sooty's face lost its smile and grew very solemn. He had seen Timmy!

'I say! I say – that's not your dog, is it?' he said.

'He's mine,' said George, and she laid a protecting hand on Timmy's head. 'I had to bring him. I can't go anywhere without him.'

'Yes, but – no dog's allowed at Smuggler's Top,' said Sooty, still looking very worried, and glancing behind him as if he was afraid someone might come along and see Timmy. 'My stepfather won't allow any dogs here. Once I brought in a stray one and he licked me till I couldn't sit down – my stepfather licked me, I mean, not the dog.'

Anne gave a frightened little smile at the poor joke. George looked stubborn and sulky.

'I thought – I thought maybe we could hide him somewhere while we were here,' she said.

'But if that's how you feel, I'll go back home with the car. Goodbye.'

She turned and went after the car, which was backing away. Timmy went with her. Sooty stared, and then he yelled after her. 'Come back, stupid! We'll think of *some*thing!'

[5]

Sooty Lenoir

Sooty ran down the steps that led to the front door, and tore after George. The others followed. Marybelle went too, shutting the big front door behind her carefully.

There was a small door in the wall just where George was. Sooty caught hold of her and pushed her roughly through the door, holding it open for the others.

'Don't shove me like that,' began George, angrily. 'Timmy will bite you if you push me about.'

'No, he won't,' said Sooty, with a cheerful grin. 'Dogs like me. Even if I boxed your ears your dog would only wag his tail at me.'

The children found themselves in a dark passage. There was a door at the farther end. 'Wait here a minute and I'll see if the coast is clear,' said Sooty. 'I know my stepfather is in, and I tell you, if he sees that dog he'll pack you all into the car again, and send you back! And I don't want him to do that because I can't tell you how I've looked forward to having you all!'

He grinned at them, and their hearts warmed towards him again, even George's, though she still felt angry at being so roughly pushed. She kept Timmy close beside her.

All the same everyone felt a bit scared of Mr Lenoir. He sounded rather a fierce sort of person!

Sooty tiptoed to the door at the end of the passage and opened it. He peeped into the room there, and then came back to the others.

'All clear,' he said. 'We'll take the secret passage to my bedroom. No one will see us then, and once we're there we can make plans to hide the dog. Ready?'

A secret passage sounded thrilling. Feeling rather as if they were in an adventure story, the children went quietly to the door and into the room beyond. It was a dark, oak-panelled room, evidently a study of some sort, for there was a big desk there, and the walls were lined with books. There was no one there.

Sooty went to one of the oak panels in the wall, felt along it deftly, and pressed in a certain place. The panel slid softly aside. Sooty put in his hand and pulled at something. A much larger panel below slid into the wall, and left an opening big enough for the children to pass through.

'Come on,' said Sooty in a low voice. 'Don't make a noise.'

Feeling excited, the children all passed through the opening. Sooty came last, and did something that shut the opening and slid the first panel back into its place again.

He switched on a small torch, for it was pitch dark where the children were standing.

They were in a narrow stone passage, so narrow that two people could not possibly have passed one another unless both were as thin as rakes. Sooty passed his torch along to Julian, who was in front.

'Keep straight on till you come to stone steps,' he said. 'Go up them, turn to the right at the top, and keep straight on till you come to a blank wall, then I'll tell you what to do.'

Julian led the way, holding up the torch for the others. The narrow passage ran straight, and came to some stone steps. It was not only very narrow but rather low, so that Anne and Marybelle were the only ones who did not have to bend their heads.

Anne didn't like it very much. She never liked being in a very narrow enclosed space. It reminded her of dreams she sometimes had of being somewhere she couldn't get away from. She was glad when Julian spoke. 'The steps are here. Up we go, everyone.'

'Don't make a noise,' said Sooty, in a low voice. 'We're passing the dining-room now. There's a way into this passage from there too.'

Everyone fell silent, and tried to walk on tiptoe, though this was unexpectedly difficult when heads had to be bent and shoulders stooped.

They climbed up fourteen steps, which were quite steep, and curved round half-way. Julian turned to the right at the top. The passage ran upwards then, and was as narrow as before. Julian felt certain that a very fat person could not possibly get along it.

He went on until, with a start, he almost bumped into a blank stone wall! He flashed his torch up and down it. A low voice came from the back of the line of children.

'You've got to the blank wall, Julian. Shine your torch up to where the roof of the passage meets the wall. You will see an iron handle there. Press down on it hard.'

Julian flashed his torch up and saw the handle. He put his torch into his left hand, and grasped the thick iron handle with his right. He pressed down as hard as he could.

And, quite silently, the great stone in the middle of the wall slid forward and sideways, leaving a gaping hole.

Julian was astonished. He let go of the iron

handle and flashed his torch into the hole. There was nothing but darkness there!

'It's all right. It leads into a big cupboard in my bedroom!' called Sooty from the back. 'Get through, Julian, and we'll follow. There won't be anyone in my room.'

Julian crawled through the hole and found himself in a spacious cupboard, hung with Sooty's clothes. He groped his way through them and bumped against a door. He opened it and at once daylight flooded into the cupboard, lighting up the way from the passage into the room.

One by one the others clambered through the hole, lost themselves in clothes for a moment and then went thankfully into the room through the cupboard door.

Timmy, puzzled and silent, followed close beside George. He had not liked the dark, narrow passage very much. He was glad to be in daylight again!

Sooty, coming last, carefully closed the opening into the passage by pressing the stone back.

It worked easily, though Julian could not imagine how. There must be some sort of pivot, he thought.

Sooty joined the others in his bedroom, grinning. George had her hand on Timmy's collar. 'It's all right George,' said Sooty. 'We're quite safe here. My room and Marybelle's are separate from the rest of the house. We're in a wing on our own, reached by a long passage!'

He opened the door and showed the others what he meant. There was a room next to his, which was Marybelle's. Beyond stretched a stone-floored, stone-walled passage, laid with mats. At the end of it a big window let in light. There was a door there, a great oak one, which was shut.

'See? We're quite safe here, all by ourselves,' said Sooty. 'Timmy could bark if he liked, and no one would know.'

'But doesn't anyone ever come?' said Anne surprised. 'Who keeps your rooms tidy, and cleans them?'

'Oh, Sarah comes and does that every

morning,' said Sooty. 'But usually no one else comes. And anyway, I've got a way of knowing when anyone opens that door!'

He pointed to the door at the end of the passage. The others stared at him.

'How *do* you know?' said Dick.

'I've rigged up something that makes a buzzing noise here, in my room, as soon as that door is opened,' said Sooty, proudly. 'Look, I'll go along and open it, while you stay here and listen.'

He sped along the passage and opened the heavy door at the end. Immediately a low buzzing noise sounded somewhere in his room, and made everyone jump. Timmy was startled too, pricked up his ears, and growled fiercely.

Sooty shut the door and ran back. 'Did you hear the noise? It's a good idea, isn't it? I'm always thinking of things like that.'

The others thought they had come to rather a strange place! They stared round Sooty's bedroom, which was quite ordinary in its furnishings, and in its general untidiness. There was a big diamond-paned window, and Anne went to look out of it.

She gave a gasp. She had not expected to look down such a precipice! Smuggler's Top was built at the summit of the hill, and, on the side where Sooty's bedroom was, the hill fell away steeply, down and down to the marsh below!

'Oh look!' she said. 'Look how steep it is! It really gives me a very funny feeling to look down there!'

The others crowded round and looked in silence, for it certainly was strange to gaze down such a long way.

The sun was shining up on the hill-summit, but all around, as far as they could see, mists hid the marsh and the far-off sea. The only bit of the marsh that could be seen was far down below, at the bottom of the steep hill.

'When the mists are away, you can see over the flat marshes to where the sea begins,' said Sooty. 'That's quite a fine sight. You can hardly tell where the marsh ends and sea begins except when the sea is very blue. Fancy, once upon a time, the sea came right up and around this hill, and it was an island.'

'Yes. Father and the innkeeper told us that,' said George. 'Why did the sea go back and leave it?'

'I don't know,' said Sooty. 'People say it's going back farther and farther. There's a big scheme afoot to drain the marsh, and turn it into fields, but I don't know if that will ever happen.'

'I don't like that marsh,' said Anne, with a shiver. 'It looks wicked, somehow.'

Timmy whined. George remembered that they must hide him, and make plans for him. She turned to Sooty.

'Did you mean what you said about hiding Tim?' she asked. 'Where shall we put him? And can he be fed? And how can we exercise him? He's a big dog, you know.'

'We'll plan it all,' said Sooty. 'Don't you worry. I love dogs, and I shall be thrilled to have Timmy here. But I do warn you that if my stepfather ever finds out we shall probably all get a jolly good telling off, and you'll be sent home in disgrace.'

'But why doesn't your father like dogs?' said Anne puzzled. 'Is he afraid of them?'

'No, I don't think so. It's just that he won't have them here in the house,' said Sooty. 'I think he must have a reason for it, but I don't know what it is. He's an odd sort of man, my stepfather!'

'How is he odd?' asked Dick.

'Well – he seems full of secrets,' said Sooty. 'Strange people come here, and they come secretly without anyone knowing. I've seen lights shining in our tower on certain nights, but I don't know who puts them there or why. I've tried to find out, but I can't.'

'Do you think – do you think your father is a smuggler?' said Anne, suddenly.

'I don't think so,' said Sooty. 'We've got one smuggler here, and everyone knows him! See that house over there to the right, lower down the hill? Well, that's where he lives. He's as rich as can be. His name is Barling. Even the police know his goings-on, but they can't stop him! He is very rich and very powerful, so he does what he likes – and he won't let anyone play the same game as he plays! No one else would dare to do any smuggling in Castaway, while *he* does it!'

'This seems rather an exciting place,' said Julian. 'I have a kind of feeling there might be an adventure somewhere about!'

'Oh no,' said Sooty. 'Nothing happens, really. It's only just a feeling you get here, because the place is so old, so full of secret ways and pits and passages. Why, the whole hill is mined with passages in the rock, used by the smugglers of olden times!'

'Well,' began Julian, and stopped very suddenly. Everyone stared at Sooty. His secret buzzer had suddenly barked from its hidden corner! Someone had opened the door at the end of the passage!

[6]

Sooty's stepfather and mother

'Someone's coming!' said George, in a panic. 'What shall we do with Tim? Quick!'

Sooty took Timmy by the collar and shoved him into the old cupboard, and shut the door on him. 'Keep quiet!' he commanded, and Timmy stood still in the darkness, the hairs at the back of his neck standing up, his ears cocked.

'Well,' began Sooty, in a bright voice, 'perhaps I'd better show you where your bedrooms are now!'

The door opened and a man came in. He was dressed in black trousers and a white linen coat. He had a peculiar face. 'It's a shut face,' thought Anne to herself. 'You can't tell a bit what he's like inside, because his face is all shut and secret.'

'Oh hallo, Block,' said Sooty, airily. He turned to the others. 'This is Block, my stepfather's man,' he said. 'He's deaf, so you can say what you like, but it's better not to, because though he doesn't hear he seems to sense what we say.'

'Anyway, I think it would be beastly to say things we wouldn't say in front of him if he wasn't deaf,' said George, who had very strict ideas about things of that sort.

Block spoke in a curiously monotonous voice. 'Your stepfather and your mother want to know why you have not brought your friends to see them,' he said. 'Why did you rush up here like this?'

Block looked all round as he spoke – almost as if he knew there was a dog, and wondered where he had gone to, George thought, in alarm. She did hope the car-driver had not mentioned Timmy.

'Oh – I was so pleased to see them I took them straight up here!' said Sooty. 'All right, Block. We'll be down in a minute.'

The man went, his face quite impassive. Not a smile, not a frown! 'I don't like him,' said Anne. 'Has he been with you long?'

'No – only about a year,' said Sooty. 'He suddenly appeared one day. Even Mother didn't know he was coming! He just came, and, without a word, changed into that white linen coat, and went to do some work in my stepfather's room. I suppose my stepfather was expecting him – but he didn't say anything to my mother, I'm sure of that. She seemed so surprised.'

'Is she your real mother, or a stepmother, too?' asked Anne.

'You don't have a stepmother *and* a stepfather!' said Sooty, scornfully. 'You only have one or the other. My mother is my real mother, and she's Marybelle's mother, too. But Marybelle and I are only half-brother and sister, because my stepfather is her *real* father.'

'It's rather muddled,' said Anne, trying to sort it out.

'Come on – we'd better go down,' said Sooty,

remembering. 'By the way, my stepfather is always being very affable, always smiling and joking – but it isn't real, somehow. He's quite likely to fly into a furious temper at any moment.'

'I hope we shan't see very much of him,' said Anne, uncomfortably. 'What's your mother like, Sooty?'

'Like a frightened mouse!' said Sooty. 'You'll like her, all right. She's a darling. But she doesn't like living here; she doesn't like this house, and she's terrified of my stepfather. She wouldn't say so herself, of course, but I know she is.'

Marybelle, who was too shy to have joined in any talking until then, nodded her head.

'I don't like living here, either,' she said. 'I shall be glad when I go to boarding-school, like Sooty. Except that I shall leave Mother all alone then.'

'Come on,' said Sooty, and led the way. 'We'd better leave Timmy in the cupboard till we come back, just in case Block does a bit of snooping. I'll lock the cupboard door and take the key.'

Feeling rather unhappy at leaving Timmy locked up in the cupboard, the children followed Sooty and Marybelle down the stone passage to the oak door. They went through, and found themselves at the top of a great flight of stairs, wide and shallow. They went down into a big hall.

At the right was a door, and Sooty opened it. He went in and spoke to someone.

'Here they all are,' he said. 'Sorry I rushed them off to my bedroom like that, Father, but I was so excited to see them all!'

'Your manners still need a little polishing, Pierre,' said Mr Lenoir, in a deep voice. The children looked at him. He sat in a big oak chair, a neat, clever-looking man, with fair hair brushed upwards, and eyes as blue as Marybelle's. He smiled all the time, but with his mouth, not his eyes.

'What cold eyes!' thought Anne, when she went forward to shake hands with him. His hand was cold, too. He smiled at her, and patted her on the shoulder.

'What a nice little girl!' he said. 'You will be a good companion for Marybelle. Three boys for Sooty, and one girl for Marybelle. Ha ha!'

He evidently thought George was a boy, and she did look rather like one – she was wearing jeans and jersey as usual, and her curly hair was very short.

Nobody said that George wasn't a boy. Certainly George was not going to! She, Dick and Julian shook hands with Mr Lenoir. They had not even noticed Sooty's mother!

She was there, though, sitting lost in an armchair, a tiny woman like a doll, with mouse-coloured hair and grey eyes. Anne turned to her.

'Oh, how small you are!' she said, before she could stop herself.

Mr Lenoir laughed. He laughed no matter what anyone said. Mrs Lenoir got up and smiled. She was only as tall as Anne, and had the smallest hands and feet that Anne had ever seen on a grown-up. Anne liked her. She shook hands, and said, 'It's so nice of you to have us all here like this. You know, I expect, that a tree fell on the roof of our house and smashed it.'

Mr Lenoir's laugh came again. He made some kind of joke, and everyone smiled politely.

'Well, I hope you'll have a good time here,' he said. 'Pierre and Marybelle will show you the old town, and, if you promise to be careful, you can walk along the road to the mainland to go to the cinema there.'

'Thank you,' said everyone, and Mr Lenoir laughed his curious laugh again.

'Your father is a very clever man,' he said, suddenly turning to Julian, who guessed that he had mistaken him for George. 'I am hoping he will come here to fetch you home again when you go, and then I shall have the pleasure of talking with him. He and I have been doing the same kind of experiments, but he has got further than I have.'

'Oh!' said Julian, politely. Then the doll-like Mrs Lenoir spoke in her soft voice.

'Block will give you all your meals in Marybelle's schoolroom, then you will not disturb my husband. He does not like talk at meal-times, and that would be rather hard on six children.'

Mr Lenoir laughed again. His cold blue eyes looked intently at all the children. 'By the way, Pierre,' he said suddenly, 'I forbid you to wander about the catacombs in this hill, as I have forbidden you before, and I also forbid you to do any of your dare-devil climbing, nor will I have you acting about on the city wall now that you have others here. I will not have them taking risks. Will you promise me this?'

'I don't act about on the city wall,' protested Sooty. 'I don't take risks, either.'

'You play the fools always,' said Mr Lenoir, and the tip of his nose turned quite white. Anne looked at it with interest. She did not know that it always did this when Mr Lenoir got angry.

'Oh, sir – I was top of my form last term,'

said Sooty, in a most injured tone. The others felt certain that he was trying to lead Mr Lenoir away from his request – he was not going to promise him what he had asked!

Mrs Lenoir now joined in. 'He really did do well last term,' she said. 'You must remember—'

'Enough!' snapped Mr Lenoir, and the smiles and laughs he had so freely lavished on everyone vanished, entirely. 'Get out, all of you!'

Rather scared, Julian, Dick, Anne and George hurried from the room, followed by Marybelle and Sooty. Sooty was grinning as he shut the door.

'I didn't promise!' he said. 'He wanted to take all our fun away. This place isn't any fun if you don't explore it. I can show you heaps of strange places.'

'What are catacombs?' asked Anne, with a vague picture of cats and combs in her head.

'Winding, secret tunnels in the hill,' said Sooty. 'Nobody knows them all. You can get lost in them easily, and never get out again. Lots of people have.'

'Why are there so many secret ways and things here?' wondered George.

'Easy!' said Julian. 'It was a haunt of smugglers, and there must have been many a time when they had to hide not only their goods, but themselves! And, according to old Sooty, there still *is* a smuggler here! What did you say his name was – Barling, wasn't it?'

'Yes,' said Sooty. 'Come on upstairs and I'll show you your rooms. You've got a good view over the town.'

He took them to two rooms set side by side, on the opposite side of the big staircase from his bedroom and Marybelle's. They were small but well-furnished, and had, as Sooty said, a marvellous view over the quaint roofs and towers of Castaway Hill. They also had a remarkably good view of Mr Barling's house.

George and Anne were to sleep in one room, and Julian and Dick in the other. Evidently Mrs Lenoir had taken the trouble to remember that there were two girls and two boys, not one girl and three boys, as Mr Lenoir imagined!

'Nice cosy rooms,' said Anne. 'I like these dark oak panels. Are there any secret passages in our rooms, Sooty?'

'You wait and see!' grinned Sooty. 'Look, there are your things, all unpacked from your suitcases. I expect Sarah did that. You'll like Sarah. She's a good sort, fat and round and jolly – not a bit like Block!'

Sooty seemed to have forgotten all about Tim. George reminded him.

'What about Timmy? He'll have to be near me, you know. And we must arrange to feed him and exercise him. Oh, I do hope he'll be all right, Sooty. I'd rather leave straight away than have Timmy unhappy.'

'He'll be all right!' said Sooty. 'I'll give him the free run of that narrow passage we came up to my bedroom by, and we'll smuggle him out by a secret tunnel that opens half-way down the town, and give him plenty of exercise each morning. Oh, we'll have a grand time with Timmy!'

George wasn't so sure. 'Can he sleep with me

at night?' she asked. 'He'll howl the place down if he can't.'

'Well – we'll try and manage it,' said Sooty, rather doubtfully. 'You've got to be jolly careful, you know. We don't want to land in serious trouble. You don't know what my stepfather can be like!'

They could guess, though. Julian looked curiously at Sooty. 'Was your own father's name Lenoir, too?' he asked.

Sooty nodded. 'Yes. He was my stepfather's cousin, and was as dark as all the Lenoirs usually are. My stepfather is an exception – he's fair. People say the fair Lenoirs are no good – but don't tell my stepfather that!'

'As if we should!' said George. 'Gracious, he'd cut off our heads or something! Come on – let's go back to Tim.'

[7]

The hidden pit

The children were all very glad to think that they were going to have meals by themselves in the old schoolroom. Nobody wanted to have much to do with Mr Lenoir! They felt sorry for Marybelle because she had such a peculiar father.

They soon settled down at Smuggler's Top. Once George was satisfied that Timmy was safe and happy, though rather puzzled about everything, she settled down too. The only difficulty was getting Timmy to her room at night. This had to be done in darkness. Block had a most tiresome way of appearing silently and suddenly, and George was terrified of him catching a glimpse of the big dog.

Timmy had a strange sort of life the next few days! While the children were indoors, he had to stay in the narrow secret passage, where he wandered about, puzzled and lonely, pricking his ears for a sound of the whistle that meant he was to come to the cupboard and be let out.

He was fed very well, for Sooty raided the larder every night. Sarah, the cook, was amazed at the way things like soup-bones disappeared. She could not understand it. But Timmy devoured everything that was given to him.

Each morning he was given good exercise by the children. The first morning this had been really very exciting!

George had reminded Sooty of his promise to take Timmy for walks each day. 'He simply must have exercise, or he'll be terribly miserable!' she said. 'But how can we manage it? We can't possibly take him through the house and out of the front door! We'd be certain to walk into your father!'

'I told you I knew a way that came out halfway down the hill, silly,' said Sooty. 'I'll show you. We shall be quite safe once we are down there, because even if we met Block or anyone else that knew us, they wouldn't know it was our dog. They would think it was just a stray we had picked up.'

'Well – show us the way,' said George, impatiently. They were all in Sooty's bedroom, and Timmy was lying on the mat beside George. They felt really safe in Sooty's room because of the buzzer that warned them when anyone opened the door at the end of the long passage.

'We'll have to go into Marybelle's room,' said Sooty. 'You'll get a shock when you see the way that leads down the hill, I can tell you!'

He looked out of the door. The door at the end of the passage was shut. 'Marybelle, slip along and peep through the passage door,' said Sooty. 'Warn us if anyone is coming up the stairs. If not, we'll all slip quickly into your room.'

Marybelle ran to the door at the end of the passage. She opened it, and at once the warning buzzer sounded in Sooty's room, making Timmy growl fiercely. Marybelle looked through the doorway to the stair. Then she signalled to the others that no one was coming.

They all rushed out of Sooty's room into Marybelle's, and Marybelle came to join them. She was a funny little mouse of a girl, shy and timid. Anne liked her, and once or twice teased her for being so shy.

But Marybelle did not like being teased. Her eyes filled with tears at once, and she turned away. 'She'll be better when she goes to school,' Sooty said. 'She can't help being shy, shut up all the year round in this strange house. She hardly ever sees anyone of her own age.'

They crowded into the little girl's bedroom and shut the door. Sooty turned the key in the lock. 'Just in case friend Block comes snooping,' he said with a grin.

Sooty began to move the furniture in the room to the sides, near the walls. The others watched in surprise and then helped. 'What's the idea of the furniture removal?' asked Dick, struggling with a heavy chest.

'Got to get this heavy carpet up,' panted Sooty.

'It's put there to hide the trap-door below At least, that's what I've always thought.'

Once the furniture stood by the walls, it was easy to drag up the heavy carpet. There was a felt lining under it too, and that had to be pulled aside as well. Then the children saw a trap-door, let flat into the floor, with a ring-handle to pull it up.

They felt excited. Another secret way! This house seemed full of them. Sooty pulled at the ring and the heavy door came up quite easily. The children peered down, but they could see nothing. It was pitch-dark.

'Are there steps down?' asked Julian, holding Anne back in case she fell.

'No,' said Sooty, reaching out for a big torch he had brought in with him. 'Look!'

He switched on his torch, and the children gave a gasp. The trap-door led down to a pit, far, far below!

'Why! It's miles below the foundations of the house, surely!' said Julian, surprised. 'It's just a hole down to a big pit. What's it for?'

'Oh, it was probably used to hide people – or to get rid of them!' said Sooty. 'Nice little place, isn't it? If you fell down there you'd land with an awful bump!'

'But – how in the world could we get Timmy down there – or get down ourselves?' said George. '*I'm* not going to fall down it, that's certain!'

Sooty laughed. 'You won't have to,' he said. 'Look here.' He opened a cupboard and reached up to a wide shelf. He pulled something down, and the children saw that it was a rope-ladder, fine but very strong.

'There you are! We can all get down by that,' he said.

'Timmy can't,' said George at once. 'He couldn't possibly climb up or down a ladder.'

'Oh, couldn't he?' said Sooty. 'He seems such a clever dog – I should have thought he could easily have done a thing like that.'

'Well, he can't,' said George, decidedly. 'That's a silly idea.'

'I know,' said Marybelle, suddenly, going red

at her boldness in breaking in on the conversation. 'I think I know! We could get the laundry basket and shut Timmy in it. And we would tie it with ropes, and let him down – and pull him up the same way!'

The others stared at her. 'Now that really *is* a brainwave!' said Julian, warmly. 'Good for you, Marybelle. Timmy would be quite safe in a basket. But it would have to be a big one.'

'There's a very big one in the kitchen,' said Marybelle. 'It's never used except when we have lots of people to stay, like now. We could borrow it.'

'Oh *yes*!' said Sooty. 'Of course we could. I'll go and get it now.'

'But what excuse will you give?' shouted Julian after him. Sooty had already unlocked the door and shot out! He was a most impatient person, and could never put off anything for a single minute.

Sooty didn't answer. He sped down the passage. Julian locked the door after him. He didn't want anyone coming in and seeing the carpet up and the yawning hole!

Sooty was back in two minutes, carrying a very heavy wicker laundry basket on his head. He banged on the door, and Julian unlocked it.

'Good!' said Julian. 'How did you get it? Did anyone mind?'

'Didn't ask them,' grinned Sooty. 'Nobody there to ask. Block's with Father, and Sarah has gone out shopping. I can always put it back if any awkward questions are asked.'

The rope-ladder was shaken out down the hole. It slipped like an uncoiling snake, down and down, and reached the pit at the bottom. Then Timmy was fetched from Sooty's room. He came in wagging his tail, overjoyed at being with everyone again. George hugged him.

'Darling Timmy! I hate you being hidden away like this. But never mind, we're all going out together this morning!'

'I'll go down first,' said Sooty. 'Then you'd better let Timmy down. I'll tie his basket round with this rope. It's nice and strong, and there's plenty to let down. Better tie the other end to the end of the bed, then when we come up again we can easily pull him up.'

Timmy was made to get inside the big basket and lie down. He was surprised and barked a little. But George put her hand over his mouth.

'Sh! You mustn't say a word, Timmy,' she said. 'I know all this is very astonishing. But never mind, you'll have a marvellous walk at the end of it.'

Timmy heard the word 'Walk' and was glad. That was what he wanted – a really nice long walk in the open air and sunshine!

He didn't at all like having the lid shut down on him, but as George seemed to think he must put up with all these strange happenings, Timmy did so, with a very good grace.

'He's really a marvellous dog,' said Marybelle. 'Sooty, get down the hole now, and be ready for when we let him down.'

Sooty disappeared down the dark hole, holding his torch between his teeth. Down and down he went, down and down. At last he stood safely at the bottom, and flashed his torch upwards. His voice came to them, sounding rather strange and far away.

'Come on! Lower Timmy down!'

The laundry basket, feeling extraordinarily heavy now, was pushed to the edge of the hole. Then down it went, knocking against the sides here and there. Timmy growled. He didn't like this game!

Dick and Julian had hold of the rope between them. They lowered Timmy as smoothly as they could. He reached the bottom with a slight bump, and Sooty undid the basket. Out leapt Timmy, barking! But his bark sounded very small and distant to the watchers at the top.

'Now come on down, one by one!' shouted up Sooty, waving his torch. 'Is the door locked, Julian?'

'Yes,' said Julian. 'Look out for Anne. She's coming now.'

Anne climbed down, a little frightened at first, but as her feet grew used to searching for and finding the rungs of the rope-ladder, she went down quite quickly.

Then the others followed, and soon they were all standing together at the bottom of the hole, in the enormous pit. They locked round curiously. It had a musty smell, and its walls were damp and greenish. Sooty swung his torch round, and the children saw various passages leading off here and there.

'Where do they all lead to?' asked Julian, in amazement.

'Well, I told you this hill was full of tunnels,' said Sooty. 'This pit is down in the hill and these tunnels lead into the catacombs. There are miles and miles of them. No one explores them now, because so many people have been lost in them and never heard of again. There used to be an old map of them, but it's lost.'

'It's weird!' said Anne, and shivered. 'I wouldn't like to be down here alone.'

'What a place to hide smuggled goods in,' said Dick. 'No one would ever find them here.'

'I guess the old-time smugglers knew every

inch of these passages,' said Sooty. 'Come on! We'll take the one that leads out of the hillside. We'll have to do a bit of climbing when we get there. I hope you don't mind.'

'Not a bit,' said Julian. 'We're all good climbers. But I say, Sooty – you're sure you know the way? We don't want to be lost for ever down here!'

''Course I know the way! Come on!' said Sooty, and, flashing his torch in front of him, he led the way into the dark and narrow tunnel.

[8]

An exciting walk

The tunnel ran slightly downwards, and smelt nasty in places. Sometimes it opened out into pits like the one they themselves had come from. Sooty flashed his torch up them.

'That one goes into Barling's house somewhere,' he said. 'Most of the old houses hereabouts have openings into pits, like ours. Jolly well hidden some of them are, too!'

'There's daylight or something in front!' said Anne, suddenly. 'Oh good! I hate this tunnel.'

Sure enough, it was daylight, creeping in through a kind of cave-entrance in the hillside. The children crowded there, and looked out.

They were outside the hill, and outside the town, somewhere on the steep cliff-side that ran down to the marsh. Sooty climbed out on to a ledge. He put his torch into his pocket.

'We've got to get to that path down there,' he said, pointing. 'That will lead us to a place where the city wall is fairly low, and we can climb over it. Is Timmy sure-footed? We don't want him tumbling into the marsh down there!'

The marsh lay a good way below, looking ugly and flat. George sincerely hoped Timmy would never fall into it. Still, he was very sure-footed, and she didn't think he would slip. The path was steep and rocky, but quite passable.

They all went down it, clambering over rocks now and again. The path led them to the city wall, which, as Sooty had said, was fairly low just there. He climbed up to the top. He was like a cat for climbing!

'No wonder he's got such a name for climbing about everywhere at school!' said Dick to Julian. 'He's had good practice here. Do you remember how he climbed up to the roof of the school the term before last? Everyone was scared he'd slip and fall, but he didn't. He tied the Union Jack to one of the chimney-pots!'

'Come on!' called Sooty. 'The coast is clear.

This is a lonely bit of the town, and no one will see us climbing up.'

Soon they were all over the wall, Timmy too. They set off for a good walk, swinging down the hill, enjoying themselves. The mist began to clear after a while, and the sun felt nice and warm.

The town was very old. Some of the houses seemed almost tumble-down, but there were people living in them, for smoke came from the chimneys. The shops were quaint, with their long narrow windows, and overhanging eaves. The children stopped to look into them.

'Look out – here's Block!' said Sooty suddenly in a low voice. 'Don't take any notice of Timmy at all. If he comes around licking us or jumping up, pretend to try and drive him off as if he were a stray.'

They all pretended not to see Block, but gazed earnestly into the window of a shop. Timmy, feeling rather out of it, ran up to George and pawed at her, trying to make her take notice of him.

'Go away, dog!' said Sooty, and flapped at the surprised Timmy. 'Go away! Following us about like this! Go home, can't you?'

Timmy thought this was some sort of a game. He barked happily, and ran round Sooty and George, giving them an occasional lick.

'Home, dog, home!' yelled Sooty, flapping hard again.

Then Block came up to them, no expression on his face at all. 'The dog bothers you?' he said. 'I will throw a stone at him and make him go.'

'Don't you dare!' said George, immediately. 'You go home yourself! I don't mind the dog following us. He's quite a nice one.'

'Block's deaf, silly,' said Sooty. 'It's no good talking to him.' To George's horror Block picked up a big stone, meaning to throw it at Timmy. George flew at him, punched him hard on the arm, and made him drop the stone.

'How dare you throw stones at a dog!' yelled the little girl in a fury. 'I'll – I'll tell the police.'

'Now, now,' said a voice nearby. 'What's all this about? Pierre, what's the trouble?'

The children turned and saw a tall man standing near them, wearing his hair rather long. He had long, narrow eyes, a long nose and a long chin. 'He's long everywhere!' thought Anne, looking at his long thin legs and long narrow feet.

'Oh, Mr Barling! I didn't see you,' said Sooty, politely. 'Nothing's the matter, thanks. It's only that this dog is following us, and Block said he'd make it go away by chucking a stone at it. And George here is fond of dogs and got angry about that.'

'I see. And who are all these children?' said Mr Barling, looking at each one of them out of his long, narrow eyes.

'They've come to stay with us because their uncle's house has been damaged in a gale,' explained Sooty. 'George's father's house, I mean. At Kirrin.'

'Ah – at Kirrin?' said Mr Barling, and seemed to prick up his long ears. 'Surely that is where that very clever scientist friend of Mr Lenoir's lives?'

'Yes. He's my father,' said George. 'Why, do you know him?'

'I have heard of him – and of his very interesting experiments,' said Mr Barling. 'Mr Lenoir knows him well, I believe?'

'Not awfully well,' said George, puzzled. 'They just write to one another, I think. My father telephoned to Mr Lenoir to ask him if he could have us to stay while our own house is being mended.'

'And Mr Lenoir, of course, was only too delighted to have the whole company of you! said Mr Barling. '*Such* a good, generous fellow, your father, Pierre!'

The children stared at Mr Barling, thinking that it was strange of him to say nice things in such a nasty voice. They felt uncomfortable. It was plain that Mr Barling did not like Mr Lenoir at all. Well, neither did they, but they didn't like Mr Barling any better!

Timmy saw another dog and darted happily after him. Block had now disappeared, going up the steep high street with his basket. The children said goodbye to Mr Barling, not wanting to talk to him any more.

They went after Timmy, talking eagerly as soon as they had left Mr Barling behind.

'Goodness – that was a narrow escape from Block!' said Julian. 'Old beast – going to throw that enormous stone at Timmy. No wonder you flew at him, George! But you very nearly gave the game away, though.'

'I don't care,' said George. 'I wasn't going to have Timmy's leg broken. It was a bit of bad luck meeting Block our very first morning out.'

'We'll probably never meet him again when we take Timmy out,' said Sooty, comfortingly. 'And if we do we'll simply say the dog always joins us when it meets us. Which is perfectly true.'

They enjoyed their walk. They went into a quaint old coffee shop and had steaming cups of delicious creamy coffee and jammy buns. Timmy had two of the buns and gobbled them greedily. George went off to buy some meat for him at the butcher's, choosing a shop that

Sooty said Mrs Lenoir did not go to. She did not want any butcher telling Mrs Lenoir that the children had been buying dog-meat!

They went back the same way as they had come. They made their way up the steep cliff-path, and in at the tunnel-entrance, back through the winding tunnel to the pit, and there was the rope-ladder waiting for them. Julian and Dick went up first, while George packed the surprised Timmy into the basket again and tied the rope firmly round it. Then up went the whining Timmy, bumping against the sides of the hole, until the two panting boys pulled the basket into Marybelle's room and undid it.

It was ten minutes before the dinner-hour. 'Just time to shut the trap-door, pull back the carpet and wash our hands,' said Sooty. 'And I'll put old Timmy back into the secret passage behind the cupboard in my room, George. Where is that meat you bought? I'll put that in the passage too. He can eat it when he likes.'

'Did you put him a nice warm rug there, and

a dish of fresh water?' asked George, anxiously, for the third or fourth time.

'You know I did. I keep telling you,' said Sooty. 'Look, we won't put back all the furniture except the chairs. We can say we want it left back because we like to play a game on the carpet. It'll be an awful bore if we have to move chests and things every time we exercise Tim.'

They were just in time for their dinner. Block was there to serve it, and so was Sarah. The children sat down hungrily, in spite of having had coffee and buns. Block and Sarah ladled out hot soup on to their plates.

'I hope you got rid of the unpleasant dog,' said Block in his monotonous voice. He gave George a rather nasty look. Evidently he had not forgotten how she had flown at him.

Sooty nodded. It was no good speaking an answer, for Block would not hear. Sarah bustled round, taking away the soup-plates and preparing to give them their second course.

The food was very good at Smuggler's Top. There was plenty of it, and the hungry visitors and Sooty ate everything put before them. Marybelle hadn't much appetite, but she was the only one. George tried to secrete tit-bits and bones whenever she could, for Timmy.

Two or three days went by, and the children fell into their new life quite happily. Timmy was taken out each morning for a long walk. The children soon got used to slipping down the rope-ladder, and making their way with Timmy to the cliff-side.

In the afternoons they went to either Sooty's room or Marybelle's, and played games or read. They could have Timmy there, because the buzzer always warned them if anyone was coming.

At night it was always an excitement to get Timmy to George's room without being seen. This was usually done when Mr and Mrs Lenoir were sitting at their dinner, and Block and Sarah were serving them. The children had a light supper first, and Mr and Mrs Lenoir had their dinner an hour later. It was quite the best time to smuggle Timmy along to George's room.

Timmy seemed to enjoy the smuggling. He ran silently beside George and Sooty, stopped at every corner, and scampered gladly into George's room as soon as he got there. He lay quietly under the bed till George was in bed herself, and then he came out to lie on her feet.

George always locked their door at night. She didn't want Sarah or Mrs Lenoir coming in and finding Timmy there! But nobody came, and as night after night went by, George grew more easy about Timmy.

Taking him back to Sooty's room in the morning was a bit of a nuisance, because it had to be done early, before anyone was up. But George could always wake herself at any time she chose, and each morning about half past six the little girl slipped through the house with Timmy. She went in at Sooty's door, and he jumped out of bed to deal with Timmy. He was always awakened by the buzzer that sounded when George opened the door at the end of the passage.

'I hope you are all enjoying yourselves,' Mr Lenoir said to the children, whenever they met him in the hall or on the stairs. And they always replied politely, 'Oh yes, Mr Lenoir, thank you.'

'It's quite a peaceful holiday after all,' said Julian. 'Nothing happens at all!'

And then things *did* begin to happen and once they had begun they never stopped!

[9]

Who is in the tower?

One night Julian was awakened by someone opening his door. He sat up at once. 'Who is it?' he said.

'Me, Sooty,' said Sooty's voice, very low. 'I say, I want you to come and see something.'

Julian woke Dick, and the two of them put on their dressing-gowns. Sooty led them quietly out of the room and took them to a peculiar little room, tucked away in an odd wing of the house. All kinds of things were kept here, trunks and boxes, old toys, chests of old clothes, broken vases that had never been mended, and many other worthless things.

'Look,' said Sooty, taking them to the window. They saw that the little room had a view of the tower belonging to the house. It was the only room in the house that did, for it was built at a strange angle.

The boys looked – and Julian gave an exclamation. Someone was signalling from the tower! A light there flashed every now and again. In and out – pause – flash, flash, in and out – pause. The light went regularly on and off in a certain rhythm.

'Now – who's doing that?' whispered Sooty.

'Your father?' wondered Julian.

'Don't think so,' said Sooty. 'I think I heard him snoring away in his room. We could go and find out though – see if he really is in his bedroom.'

'Well – for goodness' sake don't let's get caught,' said Julian, not at all liking the idea of prying about in his host's house.

They made their way to where Mr Lenoir had his room. It was quite plain he was there, for a regular low snoring came from behind the closed door.

'It may be Block up in the tower,' said Dick. 'He looks full of secrets. I wouldn't trust him an inch. I bet it's Block.'

'Well – shall we go to his room and see if it's empty?' whispered Sooty. 'Come on. If it's Block signalling, he's doing it without Father knowing.'

'Oh, your father might have told him to,' said Julian, who felt that he wouldn't trust Mr Lenoir much further than he would trust Block.

They went up the back-stairs to the wing where the staff slept. Sarah slept in a room there with Harriet the kitchen-maid. Block slept alone.

Sooty pushed open Block's door very softly and slowly. When he had enough room to put in his head, he did so. The room was full of moonlight. By the window was Block's bed. And Block was there! Sooty could see the humpy shape of his body, and the black round patch that was his head.

He listened, but he could not catch Block's breathing. He must sleep very quietly.

He withdrew his head, and pushed the other two boys quietly down the back-stairs.

'Was he there?' whispered Julian.

'Yes. So it can't be him, signalling up in our tower,' said Sooty. 'Well – who can it be then? I don't like it. It couldn't possibly be Mother or Sarah or Harriet. Is there a stranger in our house, someone we don't know, living here in secret?'

'Can't be!' said Julian, a little shiver running down his back. 'Look here – what about us going up to the tower and trying to peep through the door or something? We'd soon find out who it was then. Perhaps we ought to tell your father.'

'No. Not yet. I want to find out a whole lot more before I say anything to anyone,' said Sooty, sounding obstinate. 'Let's creep up to the tower. We shall have to be jolly careful though. You get to it by a spiral staircase, rather narrow. There's nowhere much to hide if anyone suddenly came down out of the tower.'

'What's in the tower?' whispered Dick, as they made their way through the dark and silent house, thin streaks of moonlight coming in here and there through the crack of the closed curtains.

'Nothing much. Just a table and a chair or two, and a bookcase of books,' said Sooty. 'We use it on hot summer days when the breeze gets in strongly through the windows there, and we can see a long way all round us.'

They came to a little landing. From this a winding, narrow stairway of stone went up to the rounded tower. The boys looked up. Moonlight fell on the stairway from a slit-like window in the wall.

'We'd better not all go up,' said Sooty. 'We should find it so difficult to hurry down, three of us, if the person in the tower suddenly came out. I'll go. You stay down here and wait. I'll see if I can spy anything through the crack in the door or the keyhole.'

He crept softly up the stairway, soon lost to view as he rounded the first spiral. Julian and Dick waited in the shadows at the bottom. There was a thick curtain over one of the windows there, and they got behind it, wrapping its folds round them for warmth.

Sooty crept up to the top. The tower-room had a stout oak door, studded and barred. It was shut! It was no use trying to look through the crack, because there wasn't one. He bent down to peer through the keyhole.

But that was stuffed up with something, so he could not see through that either. He pressed his ear to it and listened.

He heard a series of little clicks. Click – click – click – click – click. Nothing else at all.

'That's the click of the light they're using,' thought Sooty. 'Still signalling like mad! What for? Who to? And who is in our tower-room, using it as a signalling-station? How I wish I knew!'

Suddenly the clicking stopped. There was the sound of someone walking across the stone floor of the tower. And almost at once the door opened!

Sooty had no time to hurry down the stairs. All he could do was to squeeze into a niche, and hope that the person would not see him or touch him as he went by. The moon went behind a cloud at that moment, and Sooty was thankful to know he was hidden in black shadow. Someone came down the stairs and actually brushed against Sooty's arm.

Sooty jumped almost out of his skin, expecting to be hauled out of his niche. But the person did not seem to notice, and went on down the spiral stairway, walking softly.

Sooty did not dare to go down after him, for he was afraid the moon would come out, and cast his shadow down for the signaller to see.

So he stayed squeezed in his niche, hoping that Julian and Dick were well-hidden, and would not think it was he, Sooty, who was walking down the stairs!

Julian and Dick heard the soft footsteps coming, and thought at first it was Sooty. Then, not hearing his whisper, they stiffened behind the curtains, guessing that it was the signaller himself who was walking by!

'We'd better follow him!' whispered Julian to Dick. 'Come on. Quiet, now!'

But Julian got muddled up with the great curtains, and could not seem to find his way out. Dick, however, slipped out easily enough, and padded after the disappearing person. The moon was now out again, and Dick could catch glimpses of the signaller as he went past the moonlight streaks. Keeping well in the shadows himself, he darted quietly after him. Where was he going?

He followed him across the landing to a passage. Then across another landing and up the back-stairs! But those led to the staff bedrooms. Surely the man was not going there?

Dick, to his enormous surprise, saw the person disappear silently into Block's bedroom. He crept to the door, which had been left a little ajar. There was no light in the room except that of the moon. There was no sound of talking. Nothing at all except a creak which might have come from the bed.

Dick peeped in, full of the most intense

curiosity. Would he see the man waking up Block? Would he see him climbing out of the window?

He stared round the room. There was no one there at all, except Block lying in bed. The moonlight lit up the corners, and Dick could quite plainly see that the room was empty. Only Block lay there, and, as Dick watched, he heard him give a sigh and roll over in bed.

'Well! That's the strangest thing I ever saw,' thought Dick, puzzled. 'A man goes into a room and completely disappears, without a single sound! Where can he have gone?'

He went back to find the others. Sooty by this time had crept down the spiral staircase and had found Julian, who had explained that Dick had gone to follow the peculiar signaller.

They went to find Dick, and suddenly bumped into him, creeping along quietly in the darkness. They all jumped violently, and Julian almost cried out, but stifled his voice just in time.

'Golly! You gave me a scare, Dick!' he whispered. 'Well, did you see who it was and where he went?'

Dick told them of his strange experience. 'He simply went into Block's room and vanished,' he said. 'Is there any secret passage leading out of Block's room, Sooty?'

'No, none,' said Sooty. 'That wing is much newer than the rest of the house, and hasn't any secrets in at all. I simply can't imagine what happened to the man. How very odd! Who is he, and why does he come, and where on earth does he go?'

'We really must find out,' said Julian. 'It's such a mystery! Sooty, how did you know there was signalling going on from the tower?'

'Well, some time ago I found it out, quite by accident,' said Sooty. 'I couldn't sleep, and I went along to that funny little box-room place, and ferreted about for an old book I thought I'd seen there. And suddenly I looked up at the tower, and saw a light flashing there.'

'Funny,' said Dick.

'Well, I went along there at night a good

many times after that, to see if I could see the signals again,' said Sooty, 'and at last I did. The first time I had seen them there was a good moon, and the second time there was, too. So, I thought, next time there's a moon, I'll creep along to that old box-room and see if the signaller is at work again. And sure enough he was!'

'Where does that window look out on, that we saw the light flashing from?' asked Julian, thoughtfully. 'The seaward side – or the landward?'

'Seaward,' said Sooty at once. 'There's something or someone out at sea that receives those signals. Goodness knows who.'

'Some kind of smugglers, I suppose,' said Dick. 'But it can't be anything to do with your father, Sooty. I say – let's go up into the tower, shall we? We might find something there – or see something.'

They went back to the spiral staircase and climbed up to the tower-room. It was dark, for the moon was behind a cloud. But it came out after a while, and the boys looked out of the seaward window.

There was no mist at all that night. They could see the flat marshes stretching away to the sea. They gazed down in silence. Then the moon went in and darkness covered the marsh.

Suddenly Julian clutched the others, making them jump. 'I can see something!' he whispered. 'Look beyond there. What is it?'

They all looked. It seemed like a tiny line of very small dots of light. They were so far away that it was difficult to see if they stayed still or moved. Then the moon came out again, flooding everywhere with silvery light, and the boys could not see anything except the moonshine.

But when the moon went in again, there was the line of tiny, pricking lights again! 'A bit nearer, surely!' whispered Sooty. 'Smugglers – coming over a secret path from the sea to Castaway Hill! Smugglers!'

[10]

Timmy makes a noise

The three girls were very excited the next day when the boys told them their adventure of the night before.

'Gracious!' said Anne, her eyes wide with surprise. 'Who can it be signalling like that? And wherever did he go to? Fancy him going into Block's room, with Block there in bed!'

'It's very peculiar,' said George. 'I wish you had come and told me and Anne.'

'There wasn't time – and anyway, we couldn't have Timmy about at night. He might have flown at the signaller,' said Dick.

'The man must have been signalling to the smugglers,' said Julian, thoughtfully. 'Let me see – probably they came over from France in a ship – came as near to the marsh as they could – waited for a signal to tell them that the coast was clear – probably the signal from the tower – and then waded across a path they knew through the marsh. Each man must have carried a torch to prevent himself from leaving the path and falling into the marsh. No doubt there was someone waiting to receive the goods they brought – someone at the edge of the marsh below the hill.'

'But who?' said Dick. 'It can't have been Mr Barling, who, Sooty says, is known to be a smuggler. Because the signal lights came from *our* house, not his. It's all very puzzling.'

'Well, we'll do our best to solve the mystery,' said George. 'There's some peculiar game going on in this very house, without your father's knowledge, Sooty. We'll keep a jolly good lookout and see if we can find out what it is.'

They were at breakfast alone, when they discussed the night's adventure. Block came in to see if they had finished at that moment. Anne did not notice him.

'What does Mr Barling smuggle?' she asked Sooty. Immediately she got a hard kick on her ankle, and started in pain and surprise. 'Why did you—?' she began, and got another kick, harder still. Then she saw Block.

'But he's deaf,' she said. 'He can't hear anything we say.'

Block began to clear away, his face as usual showing no expression. Sooty glared at Anne. She was upset and cross, but said no more. She rubbed her bruised ankle hard. As soon as Block went out of the room she turned on Sooty.

'You mean thing! You hurt my ankle like anything! Why shouldn't I say things in front of Block? He's quite deaf!' said Anne, her face very red.

'I know he's supposed to be,' said Sooty. 'And I think he is. But I saw a funny look come over his face when you asked me what Mr Barling smuggled – almost as if he had heard what you said, and was surprised.'

'You imagined it!' said Anne, crossly, still rubbing her ankle. 'Anyway, don't kick me so hard again. A gentle push with your toe would have been enough. I won't talk in front of Block if you don't want me to, but it's quite plain he's as deaf as a post!'

'Yes, he's deaf all right,' said Dick. 'I dropped a plate off the table yesterday, by accident, just behind him, and it smashed to bits, if you remember. Well, he didn't jump or turn a hair, as he would have done if he could have heard.'

'All the same – I never trust Block, deaf or not,' said Sooty. 'I always feel he might read our lips or something. Deaf people can often do that, you know.'

They went off to take Timmy for his usual morning walk. Timmy was quite used to being shut in the laundry basket by now, and lowered into the pit. In fact, he always jumped straight into the basket as soon as the lid was opened, and lay down.

That morning they again met Block, who stared with great interest at the dog. He plainly recognised it as the same dog as before.

'There's Block,' said Julian, in a low voice. 'Don't drive Timmy off this time. We'll pretend he's a stray who always meets us each morning.'

So they let Timmy run round them, and when Block came up, they nodded to him, and made as if to go on their way. But the man stopped them.

'That dog seems to be a friend of yours,' he said, in his curious monotone of a voice.

'Oh yes. He goes with us each morning now,' said Julian, politely. 'He quite thinks he's our dog! Nice fellow, isn't he?'

Block stared at Timmy, who growled. 'Mind you do not bring that dog into the house,' said Block. 'If you do, Mr Lenoir will have him killed.'

Julian saw George's face beginning to turn red with fury. He spoke hurriedly. 'Why should we bring him to the house, Block? Don't be silly!'

Block, however, did not appear to hear. He gave Timmy a nasty look, and went on his way, occasionally turning round to look at the little company of children.

'Horrid fellow!' said George, angrily. 'How dare he say things like that?'

When they got back to Marybelle's bedroom that morning, they pulled Timmy up from the pit, and let him out of the basket. 'We'll put him into the secret passage as usual,' said George, 'and I'll put some biscuits in with him. I got some nice ones for him this morning, the sort he likes, all big and crunchy.'

She went to the door – but just as she was about to unlock it and take Timmy into Sooty's room next door, Timmy gave a small growl.

George took her hand away from the door at once. She turned to look at Timmy. He was standing stiffly, the hackles on his neck rising up, and he was staring fixedly at the door. George put her hand to her lips warningly, and whispered: 'Someone's outside. Timmy knows. He's smelt them. Will you all talk loudly, and pretend to be playing a game? I'll pop Timmy into the cupboard where the rope-ladder is kept.'

At once the others began to talk to one

another, while George swiftly dragged Timmy to the cupboard, patted him to make him understand he was to be quiet, and shut him in.

'My turn to deal,' said Julian loudly, and took a pack of snap cards from the top of the chest. 'You won last time, Dick. Bet I'll win this time.'

He dealt swiftly. The others, still talking loudly, saying anything that came into their heads, began to play snap. They yelled 'snap' nearly all the time, pretending to be very jolly and hilarious. Anyone listening outside the door would never guess it was all pretence.

George, who was watching the door closely, saw that the handle was gradually turning, very slowly indeed. Someone meant to open the door without being heard, and come in unexpectedly. But the door was locked!

Soon the person outside, whoever it was, realised that the door was locked, and the handle slowly turned the other way again. Then it was still. There came no other sound. It was impossible to know if anyone was still outside the door or not.

But Timmy would know! Signing to the others to carry on with their shouting and laughing, George let Timmy out of the cupboard. He ran to the door of the room, and stood there, sniffing quietly. Then he turned and looked at George, his tail wagging.

'It's all right,' said George to the others. 'There's no one there now. Timmy always knows. We'd better quickly take him into your room, Sooty, while the coast is clear. Who could it have been, do you think, snooping outside?'

'Block, I should say,' said Sooty. He unlocked the door and peered out. There was no one in the passage. Sooty tiptoed to the door at the end and looked out there also. He waved to George to tell her it was all right to take Timmy into his room.

Soon Timmy was safely in the secret passage, crunching up his favourite biscuits. He had got quite used to his peculiar life now, and did not mind at all. He knew his way about the passage, and had explored other passages that led from it. He was quite at home in the maze of secret ways!

'Better go and have our dinner now,' said Dick. 'And mind, Anne – don't go and say anything silly in front of that horrid Block, in case he reads your lips.'

'Of course I shan't,' said Anne, indignantly. 'I wouldn't have before, but I never thought of him reading my lips. If he does, he's very clever.'

Soon they were all sitting down to lunch. Block was there, waiting to serve them. Sarah was out for the day and did not appear. Block served them with soup, and then went out.

Suddenly, to the children's intense surprise and fright, they heard Timmy barking loudly! They jumped violently.

'Listen! That's Timmy!' said Julian. 'He must be somewhere near here, in that secret passage. How weird it sounds, his bark coming muffled and distant like that. But anyone would know it was a dog barking.'

'Don't say anything at all about it in front of

Block,' said Sooty. 'Not a word. Pretend not to hear at all, if Timmy barks again. What on earth is he barking for?'

'It's the bark he uses when he's excited and pleased,' said George. 'I expect he's chasing a rat. He always goes right off his head when he sees a rat or a rabbit. There he goes again. Oh, dear, I hope he catches the rat quickly and settles down!'

Block came back at that moment. Timmy had again just stopped barking. But, in a moment or two, his doggy voice could be heard once more, very muffled. 'Woof! Woof-woof!'

Julian was watching Block closely. The man went on serving the meat. He said nothing, but looked round at the children intently, as if he wanted to see each child's expression, or see if they said anything.

'Jolly good soup that was today,' said Julian, cheerfully, looking round at the others. 'I must say Sarah is a wonderful cook.'

'I think her ginger buns are gorgeous,' said

Anne. 'Especially when they are all hot from the oven.'

'Woof-woof,' said Timmy's voice from far away behind the walls.

'George, your mother makes the most heavenly fruit cake I ever tasted,' said Dick to George, wishing Timmy would be quiet. 'I do wonder how they're all getting on at Kirrin Cottage, and if they've started mending the roof yet.'

'Woof!' said Timmy, joyfully chasing his rat down another bit of passage.

Block served everyone and then silently disappeared. Julian went to the door to make sure he had gone and was not outside.

'I hope old Block *is* as deaf as a post!' he said. 'I could have sworn I saw a surprised look come into those cold eyes of his, when Timmy barked.'

'Well, if he *could* hear him, which I don't believe,' said George, 'he must have been jolly surprised to see us talking away and not paying any attention to a dog's barking at all!'

The others giggled. They kept a sharp ear for Block's return. They heard footsteps after a time, and began to pile their plates together for him to take away.

The schoolroom door opened. But it was not Block who came in. It was Mr Lenoir! He came in, smiling as usual, and looked round at the surprised children.

'Ah! So you are enjoying your dinner, and eating it all up, like good children,' he said. He always irritated the children because he spoke to them as if they were very small. 'Does Block wait on you properly?'

'Oh yes, thank you,' said Julian, standing up politely. 'We are having a very nice time here. We think Sarah is a wonderful cook!'

'Ah, that's good, that's good,' said Mr Lenoir. The children waited impatiently for him to go. They were so afraid that Timmy would bark again. But Mr Lenoir seemed in no hurry.

And then Timmy barked again! 'Woof, woof, woof!'

[11]

George is worried

Mr Lenoir cocked his head on one side almost like a startled dog, when he heard the muffled barking. He looked at the children. But they made no sign of having heard anything. Mr Lenoir listened a little while, saying nothing. Then he turned to a drawing-book, belonging to Julian, and began to look at the sketches there.

The children felt somehow that he was doing it for the sake of staying in the schoolroom a little longer. Into Julian's mind came the quick suspicion that somehow Mr Lenoir must have been told of Timmy's barking and come to investigate it for himself. It was the first time he had ever come to the schoolroom!

Timmy barked again, a little more distantly. Mr Lenoir's nose grew white at the tip. Sooty and Marybelle knew the danger-sign, and glanced at one another. That white-tipped nose usually meant a storm of temper!

'Do you hear that noise?' said Mr Lenoir, snapping out the words.

'What noise?' asked Julian, politely.

Timmy barked again.

'Don't be foolish! There's the noise again!' said Mr Lenoir. At that moment a gull called outside the window, circling in the sea-breeze.

'Oh – that gull? Yes, we often hear the gulls,' said Dick, brightly. 'Sometimes they seem to mew like a cat.'

'Pah!' said Mr Lenoir, almost spitting out the word. 'I suppose you will say they also bark like a dog?'

'Well, they might, I suppose,' agreed Dick, looking faintly surprised. 'After all, if they can mew like cats, there's no reason why they shouldn't bark like dogs.'

Timmy barked again very joyfully. Mr Lenoir faced the children, in a very bad temper indeed now.

'Can't you hear that? Tell me what *that* noise is!'

The children all put their heads on one side, and pretended to listen very carefully. 'I can't hear anything,' said Dick. 'Not a thing.'

'I can hear the wind,' said Anne.

'I can hear the gulls again,' said Julian, putting his hand behind one ear.

'I can hear a door banging. Perhaps that's the noise you mean,' said Sooty, with a most innocent expression. His stepfather gave him a poisonous look. He could really be very unpleasant.

'And there's a window rattling,' said Marybelle, eager to do her bit too, though she felt very frightened of her father, for she knew his sudden rages very well.

'I tell you, it's a dog, and you know it!' snapped Mr Lenoir, the tip of his nose so white now that it looked very strange indeed. 'Where's the dog? Whose is he?'

'What dog?' began Julian, frowning as if he were very puzzled indeed. 'There's no dog here that I can see.'

Mr Lenoir glared at him, and clenched his fingers. It was quite clear that he would have liked to box Julian's ears. 'Then listen!' he hissed. 'Listen and say what you think could make that barking, if not a dog?'

They were all forced to listen, for by now they felt scared of the angry man. But fortunately Timmy made no sound at all. Either he had let the rat escape, or was now gobbling it up. Anyway, there was not a single sound from him!

'Sorry, but *really* I can't hear a dog barking,' said Julian, in rather an injured tone.

'Nor can I!' said Dick, and the others joined in, saying the same. Mr Lenoir knew that this time they were speaking the truth, for he too could not hear anything.

'When I catch that dog I will have him poisoned,' he said, very slowly and clearly. 'I will not have dogs in my house.'

He turned on his heel and went out quickly, which was a very good thing, for George was quite ready to fly into one of *her* rages, and then there would have been a real battle! Anne put her hand on George's arm to stop her shouting after Mr Lenoir.

'Don't give the game away!' she whispered. 'Don't say anything, George!'

George bit her lip. She had gone first red with rage and then white. She stamped her foot.

'How dare he, how dare he?' she burst out.

'Shut up, silly,' said Julian. 'Block will be back in a minute. We must all pretend to be awfully surprised that Mr Lenoir thought there was a dog, because, if Block can read our lips, he mustn't know the truth.'

Block came in with the pudding at that moment, his face as blank as ever. It was the most curious face the children had ever seen, for there was never any change of expression on it at all. As Anne said, it might have been a wax mask!

'Funny how Mr Lenoir thought there was a dog barking!' began Julian, and the others backed him up valiantly. If Block could indeed read their lips he would be puzzled to know whether there *had* been a dog barking or not!

The children escaped to Sooty's room afterwards, and held a council of war. 'What are we to do about Timmy?' said George. 'Does your stepfather know the secret way behind the walls of Smuggler's Top, Sooty? Could he possibly get in and find Timmy? Timmy might fly at him, you know.'

'Yes, he might,' said Sooty, thoughtfully. 'I don't know if Father does know about the secret passages. I mean, I expect he knows, but I don't know if he's guessed where the entrances are. I found them out quite by accident.'

'I'm going home,' said George, suddenly. 'I'm not going to risk Timmy being poisoned.'

'You can't go home alone,' said Julian. 'It would look funny. If you do, we'll all have to, and then we won't have a chance to solve this mystery with Sooty.'

'No, for goodness' sake don't go and leave me just now,' said Sooty, looking quite alarmed. 'It would make my father furious, simply furious.'

George hesitated. She didn't want to make

trouble for Sooty, whom she liked very much. But, on the other hand, she certainly was not going to risk danger to Timmy.

'Well – I'll telephone my father and say I'm homesick and want to go back,' said George. 'I'll say I miss Mother. It's quite true. I do miss her. You others can stay on here and solve the mystery. It wouldn't be fair of you to try and keep me and Timmy here when you know I'd worry every moment in case someone got into the secret passage and put down poisoned meat for him to eat.'

The others hadn't thought of this. That would be terrible. Julian sighed. He would have to let George have her own way after all.

'All right. You telephone your father,' he said. 'There's a phone downstairs. Do it now if you like. There won't be anyone about now, I don't suppose.'

George slipped down the passage, out of the door there, and down the stairs to where the telephone was enclosed in a dark little cupboard. She dialled the number she wanted.

There was a long wait. Then she heard the buzzing noise – brr – brr – brr – that told her that the telephone bell at Kirrin Cottage was ringing. She began to plan what she should say to her father. She must, she really must go home with Timmy. She didn't know how she was going to explain about Timmy – perhaps she needn't explain at all. But she meant to go home that day or the next!

'Brr – brr – brr – brr' said the bell at the other end. It went on and on, and nobody answered it. She did not hear her father's familiar voice – only the bell that went on ringing. Why did nobody answer?

The operator at the exchange spoke to her. 'I'm sorry, there's no reply.'

George put down the receiver miserably. Perhaps her parents were out? She would have to try again later on.

Poor George tried three times, but each time with the same result. No reply. As she was coming out of the telephone cupboard for the third time, Mrs Lenoir saw her.

'Have you been trying to telephone your home?' she said. 'Haven't you heard any news?'

'I haven't had a letter yet,' said George. 'I've tried three times to telephone Kirrin Cottage but each time there is no reply.'

'Well, we heard this morning that it is impossible to live in Kirrin Cottage while the men are hammering and knocking everywhere,' said Mrs Lenoir, in her gentle voice. 'We heard from your mother. She said that the noise was driving your father mad, and they were going away for a week or so, till things were better. But Mr Lenoir at once wrote and asked them here. We shall know tomorrow, because we have asked them to telephone a reply. We could not get them on the telephone today, of course, any more than you could, because they have gone away already.'

'Oh,' said George, surprised at all this news, and wondered why her mother had not written to tell her too.

'Your mother said she had written to you,' said Mrs Lenoir. 'Maybe the letter will come by the next post. The posts are often most peculiar here. It will be a pleasure to have your parents if they can come. Mr Lenoir particularly wants to meet your clever father. He thinks he is quite a genius.'

George said no more but went back to the others, her face serious. She opened Sooty's door, and the others saw at once that she had had news of some sort.

'I can't go home with Timothy,' said George. 'Mother and Father can't stand the noise the workmen make, and they have both gone away!'

'Bad luck!' said Sooty. 'All the same, I'm glad you'll have to stay here, George. I should hate to lose you or Timmy.'

'Your father has written to ask my mother and father to come and stay here too,' said George. 'What I shall do about Timmy I don't know! And they are sure to ask questions about him too. I can't tell a downright lie and say I left him with Alf the fisher-boy, or anything like that. I can't think *what* to do!'

'We'll think of something,' promised Sooty. 'Perhaps I can get one of the villagers to look after him for us. That would be a very good idea.'

'Oh yes!' said George, cheering up. 'Why didn't I think of that before? Let's ask someone quickly, Sooty.'

But it was impossible to do anything that day because Mrs Lenoir asked them to go down into the drawing-room after tea, and have a game with her. So none of them could go out to find someone to look after Timmy. 'Never mind,' thought George. 'He'll be safe tonight on my bed! Tomorrow will be soon enough.'

It was the first time that Mrs Lenoir had asked them down to be with her. 'You see, Mr Lenoir is out tonight on important business,' she explained. 'He has had to go to the mainland with the car. He doesn't like his evenings disturbed when he is at home, so I haven't been able to see as much of you all as I should have liked. But tonight I can.'

Julian wondered if Mr Lenoir had gone to the

mainland on smuggling business! Somehow the smuggled goods must be taken across to the mainland and if all that signalling business the other night had to do with Mr Lenoir's smuggling then maybe he had now gone to dispose of the goods!

The telephone bell rang shrilly. Mrs Lenoir got up. 'I expect that is your mother or father on the phone,' she said to George. 'Maybe I shall have news for you! Perhaps your parents will be arriving here tomorrow.'

She went out into the hall. The children waited anxiously. Would George's parents come or not?

[12]

Block gets a surprise

Mrs Lenoir came back after a time. She smiled at George.

'That was your father,' she said. 'He is coming tomorrow, but not your mother. They went to your aunt's, and your mother says she thinks she must stay and help her, because your aunt is not very well. But your father would like to come, because he wants to discuss his latest experiments with Mr Lenoir, who is very interested in them. It will be very nice to have him.'

The children would very much rather have had Aunt Fanny instead of Uncle Quentin, who could be very difficult at times. But still, he would probably be talking with Mr Lenoir most of the time, so that would be all right!

They finished their game with Mrs Lenoir and went up to bed. George was to get Timmy to take him to her room. Sooty went to see that the coast was clear. He could not see Block anywhere. His stepfather was still away from the house. Sarah was singing in the kitchen and the little kitchen-maid, Harriet, was knitting there in a corner.

'Block must be out,' thought Sooty, and went to tell George that the coast was clear. As he went across the landing to the long passage that led to his own room, the boy noticed two black lumps sticking out at the bottom of the thick curtains drawn across the landing window. He looked at them in surprise, and then recognised them. He grinned.

'So old Block suspects we have a dog, and he thinks it sleeps in George's room or Julian's, and he's posted himself there to watch!' he thought. 'Aha! I'll give friend Block a nasty shock!'

He ran to tell the others. George listened, alarmed. But Sooty, as usual, had a plan.

'We'll give Block an awful shock!' he said. 'I'll get a rope, and we'll all go down to the landing. I'll suddenly yell out that there's a robber hiding behind the curtains and I'll pounce on Block, and give him a few good punches. Then, with your help, Julian and Dick, I'll fold him up well in the curtains – a good jerk will bring them down on top of him as well!'

The others began to laugh. It would be fun to play a trick on Block. He really was such an unpleasant fellow. A good lesson would do him no harm.

'While all the excitement is beginning I'll slip by with Timmy,' said George. 'I only hope he won't want to join in! He might give Block a good nip!'

'Well, hold on to Timmy firmly,' said Julian. 'Get him into your room quickly. Now – are we ready?'

They were. Feeling excited they crept down the long passage that led to the door which opened out on to the landing where Block was hiding. They saw the curtains move very slightly as they came along. Block was watching.

George waited with Timmy at the passage door, not showing herself at all. Then, with a yell from Sooty, a really blood-curdling yell that made both George and Timmy jump, things began to happen!

Sooty flung himself on the hidden Block with all his might. 'A robber! Help, a robber hiding here!' he shouted.

Block jumped, and began to struggle. Sooty got in two or three well-aimed punches. Block had often got him into trouble with his father, and now Sooty was getting a bit of his own back! Julian and Dick rushed to help.

A violent tug at the curtains brought them down on Block's head! Not only that, the curtain pole descended on him too, and knocked him sideways. Poor Block – he was completely taken by surprise, and could do nothing against the three determined boys. Even Anne gave a hand, though Marybelle stood apart, enjoying the fun though not daring to take part in it.

Just as it all began George slipped by with

Timmy. But Timmy could not bear to miss the fun. He dragged behind George, and would not go with her.

She tried to force him, her hand on his collar. But Timmy had seen a nice fat leg waving about near him, protruding from the curtain. He pounced on it.

There was an agonised yell from Block. Certainly Timmy could nip hard with his sharp white teeth. He worried at the kicking leg for a few seconds, and then had a sharp slap from George. Shocked, Timmy let go of the leg and humbly followed his mistress. She never slapped him! She must indeed be angry with him. With tail well down Timmy followed her into the bedroom and got under the bed at once. He poked his head out and looked beseechingly at George with big brown eyes.

'Oh, Timmy – I *had* to slap you!' said George, and she knelt down by the big dog and patted his head. 'You see, you might have spoilt everything if you'd been seen. As it is I'm sure you bit Block and I don't know how we're going to explain that! Lie quietly now, old fellow. I'm going out to join the others.'

Timmy's tail thumped softly on the floor. George ran out of the room and joined the others on the landing. They were having a fine game with Block, who was yelling and wriggling and struggling for all he was worth. He was wrapped up in the curtains like a caterpillar inside a cocoon. His head was completely covered and he could see nothing.

Suddenly Mr Lenoir appeared in the hall below, with a very scared Mrs Lenoir beside him. 'What's all this?' thundered Sooty's stepfather. 'Have you gone mad? How dare you behave like this at this time of night?'

'We've caught a robber and tied him up,' panted Sooty.

Mr Lenoir ran up the stairs two steps at a time, amazed. He saw the kicking figure on the ground well tied up in the heavy curtains. 'A robber! Do you mean a burglar? Where did you find him?'

'He was hiding behind the curtains!' said

Julian. 'We managed to get hold of him and tie him up before he could escape. Could you call the police?'

An anguished voice came from inside of the curtains. 'Let me go! I've been bitten! Let me go!'

'Good heavens! You've got Block tied up there!' said Mr Lenoir, in amazement and anger. 'Untie him, quickly.'

'But – it can't be Block. He was hiding behind those curtains at the window,' protested Sooty.

'Do as you're told,' commanded Mr Lenoir, getting angry. Anne looked at the tip of his nose. Yes, it was turning white, as usual.

The boys reluctantly undid the ropes. Block angrily parted the curtains that enfolded him, and looked out, his usually blank face crimson with rage and fright.

'I won't stand this sort of thing!' he raged. 'Look here, at my leg, sir! I've been bitten. Only a dog could have done that. See my leg?'

Sure enough there were the marks of teeth on his leg, slowly turning purple. Timmy had taken a good nip, and almost gone through the skin.

'There's no dog here,' said Mrs Lenoir, coming timidly up the stairs at last. 'You couldn't have been bitten by a dog, Block.'

'Who bit him, then?' demanded Mr Lenoir, turning fiercely on poor Mrs Lenoir.

'Do you think *I* could have bitten him, in my excitement?' suddenly said Sooty, to the enormous surprise of the others, and to their immense amusement. He spoke very seriously with a worried look on his face. 'When I lose my temper, I hardly know what I do. Do you think I bit him?'

'Pah!' said Mr Lenoir, in disgust. 'Don't talk nonsense, boy! I'll have you punished if I think you go about biting people. Get up, Block. You're not badly hurt.'

'My teeth do feel a bit funny, now I come to think of it,' said Sooty, opening and shutting his mouth as if to see if they were all right. 'I think I'd better go and clean them. I feel as if I've got the taste of Block's ankle in my mouth. And it isn't nice.'

Mr Lenoir, driven to fury by Sooty's impudence, reached out swiftly to box the boy's ears. But Sooty dodged and ran back up the passage. 'Just going to clean my teeth!' he called, and the others tried to keep from laughing. The idea of Sooty biting anyone was absurd. It was quite obvious, however, that neither Mr nor Mrs Lenoir guessed what had bitten Block.

'Go to bed, all of you,' ordered Mr Lenoir. 'I hope I shall not have to complain about you to your father tomorrow when he comes – or your uncle, as it may be. I don't know which of you are his children, and which not. I'm surprised at you making such a nuisance of yourselves in somebody else's house. Tying up my servant! If he leaves, it will be your fault!'

The children hoped fervently that Block *would* leave. It would be marvellous to have the blank-faced fellow out of the house. He was on the watch for Timmy, they felt sure. He would snoop about till he got Timmy or one of them into trouble.

But Block was still there next morning. He

came into the schoolroom with the breakfast, his face almost as blank as usual. He gave Sooty an evil look.

'You look out for yourself,' he said, in a curiously soft voice. 'You look out. Something's going to happen to you one of these days. Yes – and that dog too! I know you've got a dog, see? You can't deceive *me*.'

The children said nothing, but looked at one another. Sooty grinned, and rapped out a cheerful little tune on the table with his spoon.

'Dark, dire, dreadful threats!' he said. 'You look out for yourself too, Block. Any more snooping about, and you'll find yourself tied up again – yes, and I might bite you again too. You never know. My teeth feel quite ready for it this morning.'

He bared his teeth at Block, who made no reply at all, but merely looked as if he had not heard a word. The man went out, and closed the door softly behind him.

'Nasty bit of work, isn't he?' said Sooty. But George felt rather alarmed. She feared Block.

There was something cold and clever and bad about those narrow eyes of his. She longed with all her heart to get Timmy out of the house.

She got a terrible shock that morning! Sooty came to her, looking agitated. 'I say! What do you think? Your father's going to have *my* room. I've got to sleep with Julian and Dick. Block is taking all my things from my room to theirs this very minute, with Sarah. I hope we shall have a chance to get Timmy out all right, before your father comes!'

'Oh Sooty!' said George, in despair. 'I'll go and see if I can get him at once.'

She went off, pretending to go to Marybelle's room for something. But Block was still in Sooty's room. And there he stayed, cleaning it all morning!

George was very worried about Timmy. He would wonder why she hadn't fetched him. He would miss his walk. She hovered about the passage all morning, getting into Sarah's way as she carried clothes from Sooty's old room to Julian's.

Block gave George some curious looks. He walked with a limp to show that his leg was bad from the bite. He left the room at last and George darted in. But Block returned almost at once and she dashed into Marybelle's room. Again Block left and went down the passage, and again the desperate little girl rushed into Sooty's room.

But Block was back before she could even open the cupboard door. 'What are you doing in this room?' he said, roughly. 'I haven't cleaned it all morning to have children in here messing it up again! Clear out of it!'

George went – and then once more waited for Block to go. He would have to see to the luncheon soon! He went at last. George rushed to the door of Sooty's room, eager to get poor Timmy.

But she couldn't open the door. It was locked – and Block had taken the key!

[13]

Poor George!

By now George was in despair. She felt as if she was in a nightmare. She went to find Sooty. He was in Julian's room, next to hers, washing his hands ready for lunch.

'Sooty! I shall have to get into the secret passage the way you first took us in,' she said. 'Through that little study-room of your father's – you know, where the sliding panels are.'

'We can't,' said Sooty, looking rather alarmed. 'He uses it now, and he'd half-kill anyone who went in there. He's got the records of all his experiments there, and he's put them ready to show your father.'

'I don't care,' said George, desperately. 'I've got to get in there somehow. Timmy may starve!'

'Not Timmy! He'll live on the rats in the

passages!' said Sooty. 'Timmy could always look after himself, I bet!'

'Well, he'd die of thirst then,' said George, obstinately. 'There's no water in those secret passages. You know that!'

George could hardly eat any lunch because she was so worried. She made up her mind somehow to get into that little study-room, and see if she could open the entrance into the wall behind the panels. Then she would slip in and get Timmy. She didn't care what happened; she was going to get Timmy.

'I shan't tell the others, though,' she thought. 'They would only try and stop me, or offer to do it themselves, and I don't trust anyone but myself to do this. Timmy's my dog, and *I'm* going to save him!'

After lunch, everyone went to Julian's room to discuss things. George went with them. But after a few minutes she left them. 'Back in a minute,' she said. They took no notice and went on discussing how to rescue Timmy. It really did seem as if the only way was to raid the study, and try and get into the secret passage without being seen.

'But my stepfather works there now,' said Sooty. 'And I shouldn't be surprised if he locks the door when he leaves the room.'

George didn't come back. After about ten minutes Anne grew puzzled.

'What can George be doing? It must be about ten minutes since she went.'

'Oh, she's probably gone to see if my old room is unlocked yet,' said Sooty, getting up. 'I'll peep out and see if she's about.'

She wasn't. She didn't seem to be anywhere! She wasn't in the passage that led to Sooty's old room; she couldn't be in that room because it was still locked, and she wasn't in Marybelle's room.

Sooty peeped in George's own room, the one she shared with Anne. But that was empty too. He went downstairs and snooped around a bit. No George!

He went back to the others, puzzled.

'I can't find her anywhere,' he said. 'Where can she be?'

Anne looked alarmed. This was such a strange house, with strange happenings. She wished George would come.

'She's not gone into that little study-room, has she?' said Julian, suddenly. 'It would be just like George to try and get into the lion's den!'

'I didn't think of that,' said Sooty. 'Silly of me. I'll go and see.'

He went down the stairs. He made his way cautiously to his father's study. He stood quietly outside the shut door. There was no sound from inside. Was his father there or not?

Sooty debated whether to open the door and peep in or whether to knock. He decided to knock. Then, if his father answered he could rush back upstairs before the door could be opened, and his father would not know whom to scold for the interruption.

So he knocked, very smartly, rap-rap.

'Who's that?' came his stepfather's irritable voice. 'Come in! Am I to have no peace?'

Sooty fled upstairs at once. He went to the others. 'George can't be in the study,' he said.

'My stepfather's there, and he didn't sound in too good a temper either.'

'Then *where* can she be?' said Julian, looking worried. 'I do wish she wouldn't go off without telling us where she's going. She must be somewhere about. She wouldn't go very far from Timmy.'

They all had a good hunt over the house, even going into the kitchen. Block was there, reading a paper. 'What do you want?' he said. 'You won't get it, whatever it is.'

'We don't want anything from *you*,' said Sooty. 'How's your poor bad bitten leg?'

Block looked so unpleasantly at them that they all retreated from the kitchen in a hurry. Sooty put Julian and Dick on guard, and went up to the staff bedrooms to see if by any chance George had gone there. A silly idea, he knew, but George must be somewhere!

She wasn't there, of course. The children went back gloomily to Julian's room. 'This beastly house!' said Julian. 'I can't say I like it. Sorry to say so, Sooty, but it's a weird place with a funny feeling about it.'

Sooty was not hurt at all. 'Oh, I agree with you,' he said. 'I've always thought the same myself. So has Mother, and so has Marybelle. It's my stepfather that likes it.'

'Where *is* George?' said Anne. 'I keep on and on trying to think. There's only one place I'm certain she's not in – and that's your step-father's study, Sooty. Even George wouldn't dare to go there while your stepfather was there.'

But Anne was wrong. The study was the very place where George was at that very moment! The little girl had made up her mind that it was best to try and get in there, and wait for a chance to open the sliding panel. So she had slipped downstairs, gone across the hall, and tried the door of the study. It was locked.

'Blow!' said George, desperately. 'Everything is against me and Timmy. How can I get in? I must, I must!'

She slipped out of the side-door near the

study and went into the little yard on to which the study-window looked. Could she get in there?

But the window was barred! So that was no good either. She went back again, wishing she could find the key to unlock the door. But it was nowhere to be seen.

Suddenly she heard Mr Lenoir's voice in the room across the hall. In a panic George lifted up the lid of a big wooden chest nearby, and climbed hurriedly into it. She closed the lid over her, and knelt there, waiting, heart beating fast.

Mr Lenoir came across the hall. He was going to his study. 'I shall get everything ready to show my visitor when he comes,' he called to his wife. 'Don't disturb me at all. I shall be very busy indeed.'

George heard the sound of a key being put into the study door. It turned. The door opened and shut with a click.

But it was not locked again from the inside. George knelt in the dark chest and considered matters. She meant to get into that study. She meant to get through the entrance into the secret passage, where Tim was. That passage led from the study to Sooty's old bedroom, and somewhere in that passage was Timmy.

What she was going to do once she had Timmy she didn't quite know. Perhaps Sooty would take him to someone who could look after him for her, someone on Castaway Hill.

She heard the sound of Mr Lenoir coughing. She heard the shuffling of papers. Then she heard the click of a cupboard being opened and shut. Mr Lenoir was evidently busy!

Then he gave an exclamation of annoyance. He said something in an irritable voice that sounded like 'Now where did I put that?'

Then the door opened very suddenly and Mr Lenoir came out. George had just time to close down the lid, which she had opened to let in fresh air. She knelt in the chest, trembling, as Mr Lenoir passed there and went on across the hall.

George suddenly knew that this was her

chance. Mr Lenoir might be gone for a few minutes and give her time to open that panel in the wall! She lifted the lid of the chest, and jumped out quickly. She ran into the study, and went to the place where Sooty had pressed the panelling.

But before she could even run her fingers over the smooth brown oak, she heard returning footsteps! Mr Lenoir had hardly been half a minute. He was coming back at once.

In a panic poor George looked round for somewhere to hide. There was a large sofa against one wall. George crawled behind it, finding just room to crouch there without being seen. She was hardly there before Mr Lenoir entered the room, shut the door, and sat down at his desk. He switched on a big lamp over it, and bent to look at some documents.

George hardly dared to breathe. Her heart bumped against her ribs and seemed to make a terrible noise. It was very uncomfortable behind the sofa, but she did not dare to move.

She could not think what in the world to do.

It would be terrible to be there for hours! What would the others think? They would soon be looking for her.

They were. Even at that moment Sooty was outside the study door, pondering whether to go in or to knock. He knocked smartly – rap-rap – and George almost jumped out of her skin!

She heard Mr Lenoir's impatient voice. 'Who's that? Come in! Am I to have no peace?'

There was no answer. No one came in. Mr Lenoir called again. 'Come in, I say!'

Still no answer. He strode to the door and flung it open angrily. No one was there. Sooty had fled upstairs at once.

'Those tiresome children, I suppose,' muttered Mr Lenoir. 'Well, if any of them comes and knocks again and goes away, I'll punish them properly. Bed and bread and water for them!'

He sounded fierce. George wished she was anywhere but in his study. What would he say if he knew she was only three or four feet away from him?

Mr Lenoir worked for about half an hour, and poor George got stiffer and stiffer, and more and more uncomfortable. Then she heard Mr Lenoir yawn, and her heart felt lighter. Perhaps he would have a nap! That would be good luck. She might creep out then, and try to get into the secret passage.

Mr Lenoir yawned again. Then he pushed his papers aside and went to the sofa. He lay down on it and pulled the rug there over his knees. He settled himself down as if for a good sleep.

The sofa creaked under him. George tried to hold her breath again, afraid that now he was so near to her he would certainly hear her.

Soon a small snore came to her ears. Then another and another. Mr Lenoir was asleep! George waited for a few minutes. The snores went on, a little louder. Surely it would be safe now to creep from her hiding-place?

George began to move, very cautiously and quietly. She crept to the end of the sofa. She squeezed out from behind it. Still the snores went on.

She stood upright and went on tiptoe to the panel that had slid aside. She began to press here and there with her fingers, trying to find the spot that would move the panel to one side.

She couldn't seem to find it. She grew red with anxiety. She cast a glance at the sleeping Mr Lenoir, and worked feverishly at the panel. Where was the spot to press, oh, where was it?

Then a stern voice came from behind her, making her jump almost out of her skin.

'And what exactly do you think you are doing, my boy? How dare you come into my study and mess about like this?'

George turned round and faced Mr Lenoir. He always thought she was a boy! She didn't know what to say. He looked very angry indeed, and the tip of his nose was already white.

George was frightened. She ran to the door, but Mr Lenoir caught her before she opened it. He shook her hard.

'What were you doing in my study? Was it you who knocked and ran away? Do you think it is funny to play tricks like that? I'll soon teach you that it isn't!'

He opened the door and called loudly. 'Block! Come here! Sarah, tell Block I want him.'

Block appeared from the kitchen, his face as blank as usual. Mr Lenoir wrote something down quickly on a piece of paper and gave it to him to read. Block nodded.

'I've told him to take you to your room, lock you in, and give you nothing but bread and water for the rest of the day,' said Mr Lenoir, fiercely. 'That will teach you to behave yourself in the future.'

'My father won't be very pleased when he hears you're punishing me like this,' began George in a trembling voice. But Mr Lenoir sneered.

'Pah! Wait till he hears from me how you have misbehaved yourself, and I am sure he will agree with me. Now go, and you will not be allowed out of your room till tomorrow. I will make your excuses to your father, when he comes.'

Poor George was propelled upstairs by Block, who was only too delighted to be punishing one of the children. As she came to the door of the room George shouted to the others who were in Julian's room next door.

'Julian! Dick! Help me! Quick, help me!'

[14]

A very puzzling thing

Julian, Dick, and the others rushed out at once, just in time to see Block shove George roughly into her room and shut the door. There was a click as he locked it.

'Here! What are you doing?' cried Julian, indignantly.

Block took no notice, but turned to go. Julian caught hold of his arm, and yelled loudly in his ear. 'Unlock that door at once! Do you hear?'

Block gave no sign whether he had or not. He shook off Julian's hand, but the boy put it back again at once, getting angry.

'Mr Lenoir gave me orders to punish that girl,' said Block, looking at Julian out of his cold, narrow eyes.

'Well, you jolly well unlock that door,' commanded Julian, and he tried to snatch the key from Block. With sudden vicious strength the man lifted his hand and struck Julian, sending him half across the landing. Then he went swiftly downstairs to the kitchen.

Julian looked after him, a little scared. 'The brute!' he said. 'He's as strong as a horse. George, George, whatever's happened?'

George answered angrily from the locked bedroom. She told the others everything, and they listened in silence. 'Bad luck, George,' said Dick. 'Poor old girl! Just as you were feeling for the opening to the passage too!'

'I must apologise for my stepfather,' said Sooty. 'He has such a terrible temper. He wouldn't have punished you like this if he had thought you were a girl. But he keeps thinking you're a boy.'

'I don't care,' said George. 'I don't care about any punishment. It's only that I'm so worried about Timmy. Well, I suppose I'll have to stay here now, till I'm let out tomorrow. I shan't eat anything that Block brings me, you can tell him. I don't want to see his horrid face again!'

'How shall I go to bed tonight?' wailed Anne. 'All my things are in your room, George.'

'You'll have to sleep with me,' said little Marybelle, who looked very frightened. 'I can lend you a nightie. Oh dear – what will George's father say when he comes? I hope he will say that George is to be set free at once.'

'Well, he won't,' said George, from behind the locked door. 'He'll just think I've been in one of my bad moods, and he won't mind my being punished at all. Oh dear – I wish Mother was coming too.'

The others were very upset about George, as well as about Timmy. Things seemed to be going very wrong indeed. At tea-time they went to the schoolroom to have tea, wishing they could take George some of the chocolate cake set ready for them.

George felt lonely when the others had gone to tea. It was five o'clock. She was hungry. She wanted Timmy. She was angry and miserable, and longed to escape. She went to the window and looked out.

Her room looked straight down the cliff-side, just as Sooty's old room did. Below was the city wall that ran round the town, going unevenly up and down as it followed the contours of the hillside.

George knew that she could not jump down to the wall. She might roll off it and fall straight down to the marsh below. That would be horrible. Then she suddenly remembered the rope-ladder that they used when they got down into the pit each day.

It had at first been kept in Marybelle's room, on the shelf in the cupboard, but since the children had been scared by knowing that someone had tried the handle of the door one morning, they had decided to keep the ladder in George's room for safety. They were afraid that perhaps Block might go snooping round Marybelle's room and find it. So George had smuggled it to her own room, and hidden it in her suitcase, which she had locked.

Now, her hands shaking a little with excitement, she unlocked her suitcase and took out the rope-ladder. She might perhaps escape out of the window with it. She looked out again, the rope in her hands.

But windows overlooked the city wall just there. The kitchen too must be just below, and maybe Block would see her climbing down. That would never do. She must wait till it was twilight.

When the others came back she told them what she was going to do, speaking in a low voice through the door.

'I'll get down on the wall, walk along it for some way, and then jump down and creep back,' she said. 'You get some food for me somehow, and I'll have it. Then tonight, when everyone has gone to bed I'll get into the study again and find the way through to the secret passage. Sooty can help me. Then I can get Timmy.'

'Right,' said Sooty. 'Wait till it's fairly dark before you go down the ladder, though. Block has gone to his room with a bad headache, but Sarah and Harriet are in the kitchen, and you don't want to be seen.'

So, when the twilight hung like a soft purple curtain over the house, George slid down the rope-ladder out of the window. She only needed to let about a quarter of it out for it was far too long for such a short distance.

She fastened it to the legs of her heavy little oak bed. Then she climbed out of the window and slid quietly down the rope-ladder.

She passed the kitchen window, which fortunately had its blinds drawn down now. She landed squarely on the old wall. She had brought a torch with her so that she could see.

She debated with herself what to do. She did not want to run any risk of coming up against either Block or Mr Lenoir. Perhaps it would be best to walk along the wall till she came to some part of the town she knew. Then she could jump off and make her way cautiously back up the hill, looking out for the others.

So she began to walk along the broad top of the old wall. It was very rough and uneven in places, and many stones were missing. But her torch showed a steady light and she did not miss her footing.

The wall ran round some stables, then round the backs of some quaint old shops. Then it ran round a big yard belonging to some house, and then round the house itself. Then down it went, around some more houses.

George could look into those windows that were not curtained. Lights shone out from them now. It was strange being able to see into the windows without being seen. A little family sat at a meal in one room, their faces cheerful and happy. An old man sat alone in another, reading and smoking.

A woman sat listening to a radio, knitting, as George silently walked on the wall outside her window. Nobody heard her. Nobody saw her.

Then she came to another house, a big one. The wall ran close against it, for it was built where the cliff ran steeply down to the marsh just there.

There was a lit window there. George

glanced in as she passed. Then she stood still in great surprise.

Surely, surely that was Block in there! He had his back to her, but she could have sworn it was Block. The same head, the same ears, the same shoulders!

Who was he talking to? George tried to see – and all at once she knew. He was talking to Mr Barling, whom everyone said was a smuggler – *the* smuggler of Castaway Hill!

But wait a minute – could it be Block? Block was deaf, and this man evidently wasn't. He was listening to Mr Barling, that was plain, and was answering him, though George could not hear the words, of course.

'I oughtn't to be snooping like this,' said George to herself. 'But it's very strange, very puzzling and very interesting. If only the man would turn round I'd know at once if it was Block!'

But he didn't turn. He just sat in his chair, his back to George. Mr Barling, his long face lit up by the nearby lamp, was talking animatedly, and Block, if it *was* Block, was listening intently and nodding his head in agreement every now and again.

George felt puzzled. If she only knew for certain that it was Block! But why should he be talking to Mr Barling – and wasn't he stone deaf after all then?

George jumped down from the wall into a dark little passage and made her way through the town, up to Smuggler's Top. Outside the front door, hiding in the shadows was Sooty. He laid his hand on George's arm, making her jump.

'Come on in. I've left the side door open. We've got a fine spread for you!'

The two slipped in at the side door, tiptoed past the study, across the hall, and up to Julian's bedroom. Truly there was a spread there!

'I went and raided the larder,' said Sooty, with satisfaction. 'Harriet was out, and Sarah had run along to the post. Block has gone to bed for a rest, because, he said, he had such an awful headache.'

'Oh,' said George, 'then it couldn't have been Block I saw. And yet I'm as certain as certain can be that it was!'

'Whatever do you mean?' asked the others, in surprise. George sat down on the floor and began to gobble up cakes and tarts, for she was terribly hungry. Between her mouthfuls she told them how she had got out of the window, walked along the city wall, and found herself unexpectedly by Mr Barling's house.

'And I looked into a lit window there, and saw Block talking to Mr Barling – and listening to him and answering him!' she said.

The others could not believe this. 'Did you see his face?' asked Julian.

'No,' said George. 'But I'm *certain* it was Block. Go and peep into his room and see if he's there, Sooty. He wouldn't be back yet from Mr Barling's, because he had a glass full of something or other, which would take him some time to drink. Go and peep.'

Sooty vanished. He came back quickly. 'He's in bed!' he said. 'I could see the shape of his body and the dark patch of his head. Are there *two* Blocks then? Whatever does this mean?'

[15]

Strange happenings

It certainly was very puzzling – most of all to George, who felt so certain it had been Block talking to the well-known smuggler. The others did not feel so certain, especially as George admitted that she had not seen his face.

'Is my father here yet?' asked George, suddenly, remembering that he was supposed to come that evening.

'Yes. Just arrived,' said Sooty. 'Just before you came. I nearly got run over by the car! Just hopped aside in time. I was out there waiting for you.'

'What are our plans?' asked George. 'I'll have to get Timmy tonight, or he'll be frantic. I think I'd better go and climb back through my window again now, in case Block comes along and finds I've disappeared. I'll wait till everyone is in bed and then I'll slip out of the window again, and you must let me into the house, Sooty, please. Then I'll go to the study with you and you must open the secret way for me. Then I'll find Timmy and everything will be all right.'

'I don't see that everything will be all right,' said Sooty, doubtfully. 'But anyway, your plan is the only one to follow. You'd better get back into your room now, if you've had enough to eat.'

'I'll take a few buns back with me,' said George, stuffing them into her pocket. 'Sooty, come and knock at my door when everyone is in bed and I'll know then that it's safe for me to slip out of the window, and come into the house again.'

It wasn't long before George was back in her room once more – just in time too, for Block appeared a little while after with a plate of dry bread and a glass of water. He unlocked the door and put them on the table.

'Your supper,' he said. George looked at his

blank face and disliked it so much that she felt she must do something about it. So she took up the water and threw it deftly at the back of his head. It dripped down his neck and made him jump. Block took a step towards her, his eyes gleaming – but Julian and Dick were by the door, and he did not dare to strike her.

'I'll pay you back for that,' he said. 'See? You will never get that dog of yours back again!'

He went out and locked the door. Julian called through as soon as he had gone.

'What did you do that for, you idiot? He's a bad enemy to make.'

'I know. I just couldn't help it somehow,' said George, forlornly. 'I wish I hadn't now.'

The others had to go down to see Mr Lenoir. They left George feeling lonely. It was horrid to be locked up like this, even though she could escape through the window whenever she wanted to. She listened for the others to come back.

They soon did, and reported their meeting with George's father.

'Uncle Quentin is awfully tired and a bit cross, and frightfully annoyed with you for misbehaving,' said Julian, through the door. 'He said you were to be locked up the whole of tomorrow too, if you don't apologise.'

George didn't mean to apologise. She couldn't bear Mr Lenoir, with his false smiles and laughter, and his sudden odd rages. She said nothing.

'We've got to go and have our supper now,' said Sooty. 'We'll save you some of it as soon as Block goes out of the room. Look out for a knocking on your door tonight. It'll be me, telling you everyone's in bed.'

George lay on her bed, thinking. Many things puzzled her. She couldn't get them straight somehow. The signaller in the tower – the peculiar man, Block – Mr Barling's talk to a man who looked so like Block; but Block was all the time in his bed at home. As she lay thinking, her eyes closed, and she fell asleep.

Anne went up to bed with Marybelle, and came to whisper goodnight to her. The boys all went into the next room, for Sooty was now to share Julian's and Dick's bedroom. George woke up enough to say goodnight and then slept again.

At midnight she awoke with a jump. Someone was knocking softly and impatiently on her door. It was Sooty.

'Coming!' whispered George through the door, and took up her torch. She went to the window and was soon safely down the rope-ladder. She jumped down from the wall, and went to the side door of the house. Sooty was there. She slipped in thankfully.

'Everyone's gone to bed,' whispered Sooty. 'I thought your father and my stepfather were never going. They stayed talking in the study for ages!'

'Come on. Let's go there,' said George, impatiently. They went to the study door, and Sooty turned the handle.

It was locked again! He pushed hard, but it wasn't a bit of good. It was well and truly locked!

'We might have thought of that,' said George, in despair. 'Blow, blow, blow! What are we to do now?'

Sooty thought for a few moments. Then he spoke in a low voice, in George's ear.

'There's only one thing left to do, George. I must creep into your father's room – my old bedroom – when he is asleep – and I must get into the cupboard there, open the entrance to the secret passage, and slip in that way. I'll find Timmy and bring him back the same way, hoping that your father won't wake!'

'Oh! Would you really do that for me?' said George gratefully. 'You *are* a good friend, Sooty! Would you rather I did it?'

'No. I know the way up and down that passage better than you do,' said Sooty. 'It's a bit frightening to be all alone there at midnight too. I'll go.'

George went with Sooty up the stairs, across the wide landing, to the door at the end of the passage that led to Sooty's old room, where

George's father was now sleeping. When they got there, George pulled his arm.

'Sooty! The buzzer will go as soon as you open the door – and it will wake my father and warn him.'

'Idiot! I disconnected it as soon as I knew my room was to be changed,' said Sooty, scornfully. 'As if I wouldn't think of that!'

He opened the door that led into the passage. He crept up to his old room. The door was shut. He and George listened intently.

'Your father sounds a bit restless,' said Sooty. 'I'll wait my chance to creep in, George, and then, as soon as possible, I'll slip into the cupboard and open the secret passage to find Tim. As soon as I've got Timmy I'll bring him along to you. You could wait in Marybelle's room if you liked. Anne's there too.'

George crept into the room next door, where Anne and Marybelle lay fast asleep. She left the door open, so that she might hear when Sooty returned. How lovely it would be to have dear old Timmy again! He would lick her and lick her.

Sooty crept into the room where George's father lay, half-asleep. He made no sound. He knew every creaking board and avoided them. He made his way quietly to a big chair, meaning to hide behind it till he was certain George's father was sound asleep.

For some time the man in the bed tossed and turned. He was tired with his long journey, and his mind was excited with his talk with Mr Lenoir. He muttered now and again, and Sooty began to feel he would never be sound asleep! He grew sleepy himself, and yawned silently.

At last George's father grew quiet and peaceful. No more creaks came from the bed. Sooty cautiously moved out from behind the chair.

Then suddenly something startled him. He heard a sound over by the window! But what could it be? It was a very small sound, like a tiny creak of a door.

The night was rather dark, but the window, its curtains pulled right back, could easily be seen as a square of grey. Sooty fixed his eyes on it. Was someone opening the window?

No. The window did not move. But something strange was happening under it, near the sill.

A big window-seat was built in under the window, wide and comfortable. Sooty knew it well! He had sat on it hundreds of times to look out of the window. Now, what was happening to it?

It looked as if the top, or lid, of the seat was slowly moving upwards, bit by bit. Sooty was puzzled. He had never known it could be opened like that. It had always been screwed down, and he had thought it was just a seat and nothing else. But now it looked as if someone had unscrewed the top, and had hidden himself inside, lifting up the top like a lid when he thought it was safe.

Sooty stared at the upward-moving lid, quite fascinated. Who was in there? Why had he hidden? It was rather frightening, seeing the lid move slowly, bit by bit.

At last the lid was wide open and rested against the window-pane. A big figure cautiously and slowly got out, not making the slightest sound. Sooty felt his hair rising up on his head. He was afraid, terribly afraid. He could not utter a sound.

The figure tiptoed over to the bed. He made a quick and sudden movement, and there was a stifled sound from George's father. Sooty guessed he had been gagged, so that he could not cry out. Still the boy could not move or speak. He had never been so scared in all his life.

The intruder lifted the limp body from the bed, and went to the window-seat. He put George's father into the darkness there. What he had done to make him unable to struggle Sooty didn't know. He only knew that poor George's father was being put down in the window-seat, and couldn't seem to move a hand to help himself!

The boy suddenly found his voice. 'Hi!' he yelled. 'Hi! What are you doing? Who are you?'

He remembered his torch and switched it on. He saw a face he knew, and cried out in surprise. 'Mr Barling!'

Then someone hit him a hard blow on the head and he remembered nothing more at all. He did not know that he was lifted into the window-seat too. He did not know that the intruder followed after him. He knew nothing.

George, awake in the next room, suddenly heard Sooty's voice crying out. 'Hi!' she heard. 'Hi! What are you doing? Who are you?' And then, as she slipped off the couch, she heard the next cry. 'Mr Barling!'

George was extremely startled. What was going on next door? She fumbled about for her torch. Anne and Marybelle were still asleep. George could not find her torch. She fell over a chair and banged her head.

When at last she had found her torch she tiptoed, trembling, to the door. She shone her torch and saw that the door next to hers was a little ajar, just as Sooty had left it, when he had crept inside. She listened. There was absolutely no sound at all now. She had heard a small bumping noise after Sooty's last cry, but she didn't know what it was.

She suddenly put her head round the door of her father's room, and shone her torch again. She stared in surprise. The bed was empty. The room was empty. There was no one there at all! She flashed her torch all round. She opened the cupboard door fearfully. She looked under the bed. She was, in fact, extremely brave.

At last she sank down on the window-seat, frightened and puzzled. Where was her father? Where was Sooty? Whatever had been happening here that night?

[16]

Next morning

As George sat by the window, on the very seat into which everyone had unaccountably disappeared, though she did not know it, she heard a faint sound from the passage.

Quick as lightning the girl slipped under the bed. Someone was creeping down the long passage! George lay silently on the floor, lifting the valance a little to try and see who it was. What strange things were going on tonight!

Someone came in at the door. Someone stopped there, as if to look and listen. Then someone crept over to the window-seat.

George watched and listened, straining her eyes in the darkness. She dimly saw the someone outlined against the grey square of the window. He was bent over the window-seat.

He showed no light at all. But he made some

curious little sounds. First came the sound of his fingers tapping about on the closed lid of the seat. Then came the clink of something metallic, and a very faint squeaking. George could not imagine what the man – if it was a man – was doing.

For about five minutes the somone worked away at his task in the darkness. Then, as quietly as he had come, he went away. George couldn't help thinking it was Block, though his outline against the dark-grey of the window was too dim to recognise. But he had once given a little cough exactly like Block so often gave. It *must* be Block! But whatever was he doing in her father's room at night, on the window-seat?

George felt as if she was in a bad dream. The strangest things happened and kept on happening, and they didn't seem to make sense at all. Where was her father? Had he left his room and gone wandering over the house? Where was Sooty, and why had he called out? He wouldn't have shouted out like that, surely, if her father had been asleep in the room!

George lay under the bed, shivering, for a little while longer. Then she rolled out softly and went out of the door. She crept down the long passage to the end. She opened the door there and peeped out. The whole house was in darkness. Little sounds came to George's ears – a window rattling faintly, the creak of some bit of furniture – but nothing else.

She had only one thought in her mind, and that was to get to the boys' room and tell them the mysterious things that had happened. Soon she was across the landing, and had slipped through the door of Julian's bedroom. He and Dick were awake, of course, waiting for Sooty to come with Timmy and George.

But only George arrived. A scared George, with a very very curious story to tell. She wrapped herself in the eiderdown on Julian's bed, and told what had happened, in whispers.

They were amazed. Uncle Quentin gone! Sooty disappeared! Someone creeping into the room and fiddling about on the window-seat! What did it all mean?

'We'll come to Uncle Quentin's room with you, straight away now,' said Julian, pulling on a dressing-gown, and hunting about for his slippers. 'I've got a feeling that things are getting pretty serious.'

They all padded off to the other rooms. They went into Marybelle's room and woke her and Anne. Both little girls felt scared. Soon all five children were in the next room, from which George's father and Sooty had so strangely vanished.

Julian shut the door, drew the curtains and switched on the light. At once they all felt better. It was so horrid to grope about in the dark with torches.

They looked round the silent room. There was nothing there to show them how the others had disappeared. The bed was crumpled and empty. On the floor lay Sooty's torch, where it had fallen.

George repeated again what she had thought she had heard Sooty call out, but it made no sense to anyone. 'Why call out Mr Barling's name, when there was only your father in the room?' said Julian. 'Surely Mr Barling wasn't hiding here – that would be nonsense. He has nothing to do with your father, George.'

'I know. But I'm sure it *was* Mr Barling's name that I heard Sooty call out,' said George. 'Do you think – oh yes, do you think Mr Barling could possibly have crept through the secret opening in the cupboard, meaning to do some dirty work or other – and have gone back the same way, taking the others with him because they discovered him?'

This seemed a likely explanation, though not a very good one. They all went to the cupboard and opened it. They groped between the clothes for the secret opening. But the little iron handle set there to pull on the stone at the back was gone! Someone had removed it – and now the secret passage could not be entered, for there was no way of opening it just there!

'Look at that!' said Julian in astonishment. 'Someone's been tampering with that too. No,

George, the midnight visitor, whoever he was, didn't go back that way.'

George looked pale. She had been hoping to go and fetch Timmy, by slipping through the secret opening in the cupboard. Now she couldn't. She longed for Timmy with all her heart, and felt that if only the big faithful dog were with her things would seem much brighter.

'I'm sure Mr Lenoir is at the bottom of all this!' said Dick. 'And Block too. I bet that *was* Block you saw in here tonight, doing something in the dark, George. I bet he and Mr Lenoir are hand in glove with each other over something.'

'Well, then – we can't possibly go and tell them what has happened!' said Julian. 'If they are at the bottom of all these weird happenings it would be foolish to go and tell them what we know. And we can't tell your mother, Marybelle, because she would naturally go to your father about it. It's a puzzle to know what to do!'

Anne began to cry. Marybelle, frightened

and puzzled, at once began to sob too. George felt tears pricking the backs of her eyelids, but she blinked them away. George never cried!

'I want Sooty,' wept Marybelle, who adored her cheeky, daring brother. 'Where's he gone? I'm sure he's in danger. I do want Sooty.'

'We'll rescue him tomorrow, don't you worry,' said Julian, kindly. 'We can't do anything tonight, though. There's nobody at Smuggler's Top we can possibly get advice or help from, as things are. I vote we go to bed, sleep on it, and make plans in the morning. By that time Sooty and Uncle Quentin may have turned up again. If they haven't, Mr Lenoir will have to be told by someone, and we'll see how he behaves! If he's surprised and upset, we'll soon know if he has had anything to do with this mystery or not. He'll have to do something – go to the police, or have the house turned upside down to find the missing people. We'll soon see what happens.'

Everyone felt a little comforted after this long speech. Julian sounded cheerful and firm, though he didn't feel at all happy, really. He knew, better than any of the others, that something very strange, and probably dangerous, was going on at Smuggler's Top. He wished the girls were not there.

'Now listen,' he said. 'George, you go and sleep with Anne and Marybelle next door. Lock your door and keep the light on. Dick and I will sleep here, in Sooty's old room, also with the light on, so you'll know we are quite nearby.'

It was comforting to know that the two boys were so near. The three girls went at last into Marybelle's room, tired out. Anne and Marybelle got into bed again, and George lay down again on the small but comfortable couch, pulling a thick rug over her. In spite of all the worry and excitement the girls were soon asleep, quite exhausted.

The boys talked a little, as they lay in Sooty's old bed, where their Uncle Quentin had been asleep some time before. Julian did not think anything more would happen that night. He and Dick fell asleep, but Julian was ready to wake at the slightest noise.

Next morning they were awakened by a most surprised Sarah, who had come in to draw the curtains and bring George's father a pot of early-morning tea. She could not believe her eyes when she saw the two boys in the visitor's bed – and no visitor!

'What's all this?' said Sarah, gaping. 'Where's your uncle? Why are you here?'

'Oh, we'll explain later,' said Julian, who did not want to enter into any details with Sarah, who was a bit of a chatterbox. 'You can leave the tea, Sarah. *We'd* like it!'

'Yes, but where's your uncle? Is he in *your* room?' said the puzzled Sarah. 'What's up?'

'You can go and look in our room if you like and see if he's there,' said Dick, wanting to get rid of the amazed woman. She disappeared, thinking that the household must be going mad. She left the hot tea behind, though, and the boys at once took it into the girls' room. George unlocked the door for them. They took it in turns to sip the hot tea from the one cup.

Presently Sarah came back, with Harriet and Block. Block's face was as blank as usual.

'There's nobody in your room, Julian,' began Sarah. Then Block gave a sudden exclamation and stared at George angrily. He had thought she was locked in her room – and here she was in Marybelle's room, drinking tea!

'How did you get out?' he demanded. 'I'll tell Mr Lenoir. You're in disgrace.'

'Shut up,' said Julian. 'Don't you dare to speak to my cousin like that. I believe you're mixed up in this curious business. Clear out, Block.'

Whether Block heard or not, he gave no sign of going. Julian got up, his face set.

'Clear out of this room,' he said, narrowing his eyes. 'Do you hear? I have a feeling that the police might be interested in you, Block. Now clear out!'

Harriet and Sarah gave little shrieks. The sudden mystery was too much for them. They gazed at Block and began to back out of the room. Fortunately Block went too, casting an evil look at the determined Julian.

'I shall go to Mr Lenoir,' said Block, and disappeared.

In a few minutes along came Mr and Mrs Lenoir to Marybelle's room. Mrs Lenoir looked scared out of her life. Mr Lenoir looked puzzled and upset.

'Now, what's all this?' he began. 'Block has been to me with a most curious tale. Says your father has disappeared, George, and—'

'And so has Sooty,' suddenly wailed Marybelle, bursting into tears again. 'Sooty's gone. He's gone too.'

Mrs Lenoir gave a cry. 'What do you mean? How can he have gone? Marybelle, what do you mean?'

'Marybelle, I think I had better take charge of the telling,' said Julian, who was not going to let the little girl give away all the things they knew. After all, Mr Lenoir was probably at the bottom of everything, and it would be foolish to tell him what they suspected about him.

'Julian – tell me what has happened. Quickly!' begged Mrs Lenoir, looking really upset.

'Uncle Quentin disappeared from his bed last night, and Sooty has vanished too,' said Julian, shortly. 'They may turn up, of course.'

'Julian! You are keeping back something,' said Mr Lenoir, suddenly, watching the boy sharply. 'You will tell us *everything*, please. How dare you keep anything back at a moment like this?'

'Tell him, Julian, tell him,' wailed Marybelle. Julian looked obstinate, and glared at Marybelle.

The tip of Mr Lenoir's nose went white. 'I am going to the police,' he said. 'Perhaps you will talk to *them*, my boy. They will knock some sense into you!'

Julian was surprised. 'Why – I shouldn't have thought *you* would want to go to the police!' he blurted out. 'You've got too many secrets to hide!'

[17]

More and more puzzling

Mr Lenoir stared in the utmost amazement at Julian. There was a dead silence after this remark. Julian could have kicked himself for making it, but he couldn't unsay it now.

Mr Lenoir opened his mouth to say something at last, when footsteps came to the door. It was Block.

'Come in, Block!' said Mr Lenoir. 'There seem to have been peculiar happenings here.'

Block did not appear to hear, and remained outside the door. Mr Lenoir beckoned him in impatiently.

'No,' said Julian, firmly. 'What we have to say is not to be said in front of Block, Mr Lenoir. We don't like him and we don't trust him.'

'What do you mean?' cried Mr Lenoir,

angrily. 'What do *you* know about my servants? I've known Block for years before he came into my service, and he's a most trustworthy fellow. He can't help being deaf, and that makes him irritable at times.'

Julian remained obstinate. He caught an angry gleam in Block's cold eyes, and glared back.

'Well, this is incredible!' said Mr Lenoir, trying not to lose his temper. 'I can't think what's come over everybody – disappearing like this – and now you children talking to me as if I wasn't master in my own house. I insist that you tell me all you know.'

'I'd rather tell it to the police,' said Julian, his eye on Block. But Block showed no trace of expression on his face.

'Go away, Block,' said Mr Lenoir at last, seeing that there was no hope of getting anything out of Julian while the servant was there. 'You'd better all come down to my study. This is getting more and more mysterious. If the police have got to know, you may as well tell me first. I don't want to look a complete idiot in my own house in front of them.'

Julian couldn't help feeling a bit puzzled. Mr Lenoir was not behaving as he had thought he might behave. He seemed sincerely puzzled and upset, and he was evidently planning to get the police in himself. Surely he wouldn't do that if he had had a hand in the disappearances? Julian was lost in bewilderment again.

Mrs Lenoir was now crying quietly, with Marybelle sobbing beside her. Mr Lenoir put an arm round his wife and kissed Marybelle, suddenly appearing very much nicer than he had ever seemed before. 'Don't worry,' he said, in a gentle voice. 'We'll soon get to the bottom of this, if I have to get the whole of the police force in. I think I know who's at the bottom of it all!'

That surprised Julian even more. He and the others followed Mr Lenoir down to his study. It was still locked. Mr Lenoir opened it and pushed aside a great pile of papers that were on his desk.

'Now – what do you know?' he said to Julian quietly. The children noticed that the top of his nose was no longer white. Evidently he had got over his burst of temper.

'Well, I think this is a strange house, with a lot of strange things happening in it,' said Julian, not quite knowing how to begin. 'I'm afraid, you won't like me telling the police all I know.'

'Julian, don't speak in riddles!' said Mr Lenoir, impatiently. 'You act as if I were a criminal, in fear of the police. I'm not. What goes on in this house?'

'Well – the signalling from the tower, for instance,' said Julian, watching Mr Lenoir's face.

Mr Lenoir gaped. It was clear that he was immensely astonished. He stared at Julian, and Mrs Lenoir cried out suddenly: 'Signalling! What signalling?'

Julian explained. He told how Sooty had discovered the light-flashing first, and then how he and Dick had gone with him to the tower when they had seen the flashing again. He described the line of tiny, pricking lights across the marsh from the seaward side.

Mr Lenoir listened intently. He asked questions about dates and times. He heard how the boys had followed the signaller to Block's room, where he had disappeared.

'Got out of the window, I suppose,' said Mr Lenoir. 'Block's got nothing to do with this, you can rest assured of that. He is most faithful and loyal, and has been a great help to me while he has been here. I have an idea that Mr Barling is at the bottom of all this. He can't signal from his house to the sea because it's not quite high enough up the hill, and is in the wrong position. He must have been using *my* tower to signal from – coming himself to do it too! He knows all the secret ways of this house, better than I do! It would be easy for him to come here whenever he wanted to.'

The children thought at once that probably Mr Barling *had* been the signaller! They stared at Mr Lenoir. They were all beginning to think that he really and truly had nothing to do with the strange goings-on after all.

'I don't see why Block shouldn't know all this,' said Mr Lenoir, getting up. 'It's plain to me that Barling could explain a lot of the odd things that have been happening. I'll see if Block has ever suspected anything.'

Julian pursed his lips together. If Mr Lenoir was going to tell everything to Block, who certainly must be in the plot somehow, he wasn't going to tell him anything more!

'I'll see what Block thinks about everything, and then if we can't solve this mystery ourselves, we'll get in the police,' said Mr Lenoir, going out of the room.

Julian did not want to say anything much in front of Mrs Lenoir. So he changed the subject completely.

'What about breakfast?' he said. 'I'm feeling hungry!'

So they all went to have breakfast, though Marybelle could eat nothing at all, because she kept thinking of poor Sooty.

'I think,' said Julian, when they were alone at the table, 'I rather think we'll do a little mystery-solving ourselves. I'd like a jolly good look round that room of your father's, George, to begin with. There must be some other way of getting out of there, besides the secret passage we know.'

'What do you think happened there last night?' said Dick.

'Well, I imagine that Sooty went there and hid, to wait until it was safe to try and get into the secret passage as soon as Uncle Quentin was asleep,' said Julian, thoughtfully. 'And while he was hiding, someone came into that room from somewhere, to kidnap Uncle Quentin. Why, I don't know, but that's what I think. Then Sooty yelled out in surprise, and got knocked on the head or something. Then he and Uncle Quentin were kidnapped together, and taken off through some secret way we don't know.'

'Yes,' said George. 'And it was Mr Barling who kidnapped them! I distinctly heard Sooty yell out "Mr Barling". He must have switched on his torch and seen him.'

'They are quite probably hidden somewhere in Mr Barling's house,' said Anne, suddenly.

'Yes!' said Julian. 'Why didn't I think of that? Why, that's just where they would be, of course. I've a jolly good mind to go down and have a look!'

'Oh, let me come too,' begged George.

'No,' said Julian. 'Certainly not. This is rather a dangerous adventure, and Mr Barling is a bad and dangerous man. You and Marybelle are certainly not to come. I'll take Dick.'

'You are absolutely *mean*!' began George, her eyes flashing. 'Aren't I as good as a boy? I'm going to come.'

'Well, if you're as good as a boy, which I admit you are,' said Julian, 'can't you stay and keep an eye on Anne and Marybelle for us? We don't want them kidnapped too.'

'Oh, don't go, George,' said Anne. 'Stay here with us.'

'I think it's mad to go, anyhow,' said George.

'Mr Barling wouldn't let you in. And if you did get in you wouldn't be able to find all the secret places in his house. There must be as many, and more, as there are here.'

Julian couldn't help thinking George was right. Still, it was worth trying.

He and Dick set out after breakfast, and went down the hill to Mr Barling's. But when they got there they found the whole house shut up. Nobody answered their knocking and ringing. The curtains were drawn across the closed windows, and no smoke came from the chimney.

'Mr Barling's gone away for a holiday,' said the gardener who was working in the next-door flower-beds. 'Went this morning, he did. In his car. All his servants have got a holiday too.'

'Oh!' said Julian, blankly. 'Was there anyone with him in the car – a man and a boy, for instance?'

The gardener looked surprised at this question, and shook his head.

'No. He was alone, and drove off himself.'

'Thanks,' said Julian, and walked back with Dick to Smuggler's Top. This was most odd. Mr Barling had shut up the house and gone off without his captives! Then what had he done with them? And why on earth had he kidnapped Uncle Quentin? Julian remembered that Mr Lenoir had not put forward any reason for that. Did he know one, and hadn't wanted to say what it was? It was all most puzzling.

Meantime George had been doing a little snooping round on her own. She had slipped into Uncle Quentin's room, and had had a really good look round everywhere to see if by chance there was another secret passage Sooty hadn't known about.

She had tapped the walls. She had turned back the carpet and examined every inch of the floor. She had tried the cupboard again, and wished she could get through into the secret passage there and find Timmy. The study door downstairs was again locked, and she did not dare to tell Mr Lenoir about Timmy and ask his help.

George was just about to leave the quiet room when she noticed something on the floor near the window. She bent to pick it up. It was a small screw. She looked round. Where had it come from?

At first she couldn't see any screws of the same size at all. Then her eyes slid down to the window-seat. There were screws there, screwing down the top oaken plank to the under ones that supported it.

Had the screw come out of the window-seat? Why should it, anyway? The others there were all screwed down tightly. She examined one. Then she gave a low cry.

'One's missing. The one in the middle of this side. Now just let me think.'

She remembered last night. She remembered how someone had crept in, while she had hidden under the bed, and had fiddled about by the window, bending over the polished window-seat. She remembered the little noises – the metallic clinks and the tiny squeaks. It was screws being screwed into the seat!

'Someone screwed down the window-seat last night – and in the darkness, dropped one of the little screws,' thought George, beginning to feel excited. 'Why did he screw it down? To hide something? What's in this window-seat? It sounds hollow enough. It never lifted up. I know that. It was always screwed down, because I remember looking for a cupboard under it, like the one we have at home, and there wasn't one.'

George began to feel certain there was some secret about the window-seat. She rushed off to get a screwdriver. She found one and hurried back.

She shut the door and locked it behind her in case Block should come snooping around. Then she set to work with the screwdriver. What would she find in the window-seat? She could hardly wait to see!

[18]

Curious discoveries

Just as she had unscrewed almost the last screw there came a tapping at the door. George jumped and stiffened. She did not answer, afraid that it was Block, or Mr Lenoir.

Then, to her great relief, she heard Julian's voice. 'George! Are you in here?'

The little girl hurried across to the door and unlocked it. The boys came in, looking surprised, followed by Anne and Marybelle. George shut the door and locked it again.

'Mr Barling's gone away and shut up the house,' said Julian. 'So that's that. What on earth are you doing, George?'

'Unscrewing this window-seat,' said George, and told them about the screw she had found on the floor. They all crowded round her, excited.

'Good for you, George!' said Dick. 'Here, let me finish the unscrewing.'

'No, thanks. This is *my* job!' said George. She took out the last screw. Then she lifted the edge of the window-seat. It came up like a lid.

Everyone peered inside, rather scared. What would they see? To their great surprise and disappointment they saw nothing but an empty cupboard! It was as if the window-seat was a box, with the lid screwed down for people to sit on.

'Well – what a disappointment!' said Dick. He shut down the lid. 'I don't expect you heard anyone screwing down the lid, really, George. It might have been your imagination.'

'Well, it wasn't,' said George, shortly. She opened the lid again. She got right into the box-like window-seat and stamped, and pressed with her feet.

And quite suddenly, there came a small creaking noise, and the bottom of the empty window-seat fell downwards like a trap-door on a hinge!

George gasped and clutched at the side. She kicked about in mid-air for a moment and then scrambled out. Everyone looked down in silence.

They looked down a straight yawning hole, which, however, came to an end only about eight feet down. There it appeared to widen out, and, no doubt, entered a secret passage which ran into one of the underground tunnels with which the whole hill was honeycombed. It might even run to Mr Barling's house.

'Look at that!' said Dick. 'Who would have thought of that? I bet even old Sooty didn't know about this.'

'Shall we go down?' said George. 'Shall we see where it goes to? We might find old Timmy.'

There came the noise of someone trying the handle of the door. It was locked. Then there was an impatient rapping, and a cross voice called out sharply:

'Why is this door locked? Open it at once! What are you doing in there?'

'It's Father!' whispered Marybelle, with wide eyes. 'I'd better unlock the door.'

George shut the lid of the window-seat down at once, quietly. She did not want Mr Lenoir to see their latest discovery. When the door was opened Mr Lenoir saw the children standing about, or sitting on the window-seat.

'I've had a good talk to Block,' he said, 'and, as I thought, he doesn't know a thing about all the goings-on here. He was most amazed to hear about the signalling from the tower. But he doesn't think it's Mr Barling. He thinks it may be a plot of some sort against *me*.'

'Oh!' said the children, who felt that *they* would not believe Block so readily as Mr Lenoir appeared to.

'It's quite upset Block,' said Mr Lenoir. 'He feels really sick, and I've told him to go and have a rest till we decide what to do next.'

The children felt that Block would not be so easily upset as all that. They all suspected at once that he would not really go to rest, but would probably sneak out on business of his own.

'I've some work to attend to for a little while,' said Mr Lenoir. 'I've rung up the police, but unluckily the Inspector is out. He will ring me directly he comes back. Now can you keep out of mischief till I've finished my work?'

The children thought that was a silly question. They made no reply. Mr Lenoir gave one of his sudden smiles and little laughs, and went.

'I'm going to pop along to Block's room and see if he really *is* there,' said Julian, as soon as Mr Lenoir was out of sight.

He went to the wing where the staff bedrooms were, and stopped softly outside Block's. The door was a little ajar, and Julian could see through the crack. He saw the shape of Block's body in the bed, and the dark patch that was his head. The curtains were drawn across the window to keep out the light, but there was enough to see all this.

Julian sped back to the others. 'Yes, he's in bed all right,' he said. 'Well, he's safe for a bit. Shall we have a shot at getting down to the window-seat hole? I'd dearly like to see where it leads to!'

'Oh yes!' said everyone. But it was not an easy job to drop eight feet down without being terribly jolted! Julian went first and was very much jarred. He called up to Dick: 'We'll have to get a bit of rope and tie it to something up there, and let it hang down the hole – it's an awful business to let yourself drop down.'

But just as Dick went to find a rope, Julian called up again. 'Oh, it's all right! I've just seen something. There are niches carved into the sides of the hole – niches you can put foot or hand into. I didn't see them before. You can use them to help you down.'

So down went everyone, one after another, feeling for the niches and finding them. George missed one or two, clawed wildly at the air, and dropped down the last few feet, landing with rather a bump, but she was not hurt.

As they had thought, the hole led to another secret passage in the house, but this one went straight downwards by means of steps, so that very soon they went well below the level of the house. Then they came into the maze of tunnels that honeycombed the hill. They stopped.

'Look here – we can't possibly go any farther,' said Julian. 'We shall get lost. We haven't got Sooty with us now, and Marybelle isn't any good at finding the way. It would be dangerous to wander about.'

They could hear the hollow sound of footsteps coming from a tunnel to the left of them. They all shrank back into the shadows, and Julian switched off his torch.

'It's *two* people!' whispered Anne, as two figures came out of the nearby tunnel. One was very tall and long. The other – yes, surely the other was Block! If it wasn't Block it was someone the exact image of him.

The men were talking in low voices, answering one another. How could it be Block, though, if he could hear as well as that? Anyway, Block was asleep in bed. It was hardly ten minutes since Julian had seen him there. Were there two Blocks, then? thought George, as she had thought once before.

The men disappeared into another tunnel, and the bright light of their lanterns disappeared gradually. The muffled rumble of their voices echoed back.

'Shall we follow them?' said Dick.

'Of course not,' said Julian. 'We might lose them – and lose ourselves too! And supposing they suddenly turned back and found us following them? We should be in a horrid fix.'

'I'm sure the first man was Mr Barling,' said Anne, suddenly. 'I couldn't see his face because the light of the lantern wasn't on it – but he seemed just like Mr Barling – awfully tall and long everywhere!'

'But Mr Barling's gone away,' said Marybelle.

'*Supposed* to have gone away!' said George. 'It looks as if he's come back, if it *was* him. I wonder where those two have gone – to see my father and Sooty, do you think?'

'Quite likely,' said Julian. 'Come on, let's get

back. We simply *daren't* wander about by ourselves in these old tunnels. They run for miles, Sooty said, and cross one another, and go up and down and round about – even right down to the marsh. We should never, never find our way out if we got lost.'

They turned to go back. They came to the end of the steps they had been climbing, and found themselves at the bottom of the window-seat hole. It was quite easy to pull themselves up by the niches in the sides of the hole.

Soon they were all in the room again, glad to see the sunshine streaming in at the window. They looked out. The marshes were beginning to be wreathed in mist once more, though up here the hill was golden with sunlight.

'I'm going to put the screws back into the window-seat again,' said Julian, picking up the screwdriver and shutting down the lid. 'Then if Block comes here he won't guess we've found this new secret place. I'm pretty certain that he unscrewed the seat so that Mr Barling could get into this room, and then screwed it down again so that no one would guess what had happened.'

He quickly put in the screws. Then he looked at his watch.

'Almost dinner-time, and I'm jolly hungry. I wish old Sooty was here – and Uncle Quentin. I do hope they're all right – and Timmy too,' said Julian. 'I wonder if Block is still in bed – or wandering about the tunnels. I'm going to have a peep again.'

He soon came back, puzzled. 'Yes, he's there all right, safe in bed. It's jolly funny.'

Block did not appear at lunch-time. Sarah said he had asked not to be disturbed, if he did not appear.

'He does get the most awful sick headaches,' she said. 'Maybe he'll be all right this afternoon.'

She badly wanted to talk about everything, but the children had decided not to tell her anything. She was very nice and they liked her, but somehow they didn't trust anyone at Smuggler's Top. So Sarah got nothing out of them at all, and retired in rather a huff.

Julian went down to speak to Mr Lenoir after the meal. He felt that even if the Inspector of Police was not at the police station, somebody else must be informed. He was very worried about his uncle and Sooty. He couldn't help wondering if Mr Lenoir had made up the bit about the Inspector being away, to put off time.

Mr Lenoir was looking cross when Julian knocked at his study door. 'Oh, it's you!' he said to Julian. 'I was expecting Block. I've rung and rung for him. The bell rings in his room and I can't imagine why he doesn't come. I want him to come to the police station with me.'

'Good!' thought Julian. Then he spoke aloud. 'I'll go and hurry him up for you, Mr Lenoir. I know where his room is.'

Julian ran up the stairs and went to the little landing up which the back-stairs went to the staff bedrooms. He pushed open Block's door.

Block was apparently still asleep in bed! Julian called loudly, then remembered that Block was deaf. So he went over to the bed and put his hand rather roughly on the hump of the shoulder between the clothes.

But it was curiously soft! Julian drew his hand away, and looked down sharply. Then he got a real shock.

There was no Block in the bed! There was a big ball of some sort, painted black to look like a head almost under the sheets – and, when Julian threw back the covers, he saw instead of Block's body, a large lumpy bolster, cleverly moulded to look like a curved body!

'*That's* the trick Block plays when he wants to slip off anywhere, and yet pretend he's still here!' said Julian. 'So it *was* Block we saw in the tunnel this morning – and it *must* have been Block that George saw talking to Mr Barling yesterday, when she looked through the window. He's not deaf, either. He's a very clever – sly – double-faced – deceitful ROGUE!'

[19]

Mr Barling talks

Meantime, what was happening to Uncle Quentin and Sooty? Many strange things!

Uncle Quentin had been gagged, and drugged so that he could neither struggle nor make any noise, when Mr Barling had crept so unexpectedly into his room. It was easy to drop him down the hole in the window-seat. He fell with a thud that bruised him considerably.

Then poor Sooty had been dropped down too, and after them had come Mr Barling, climbing deftly down by the help of the niches in the sides.

Someone else was down there, to help Mr Barling. Not Block, who had been left to screw down the window-seat so that no one might guess where the victims had been taken, but a hard-faced servant belonging to Mr Barling.

'Had to bring this boy, too – it's Lenoir's son,' said Mr Barling. 'Snooping about in the room. Well, it will serve Lenoir right for working against me!'

The two were half-carried, half-dragged down the long flight of steps and taken into the tunnels below. Mr Barling stopped and took a ball of string from his pocket. He tossed it to his servant.

'Here you are. Tie the end to that nail over there, and let the string unravel as we go. I know the way quite well, but Block doesn't, and he'll be coming along to bring food to our couple of prisoners tomorrow. Don't want him to lose his way! We can tie the string up again just before we get to the place I'm taking them to, so that they won't see it and use it to escape by.'

The servant tied the string to the nail that Mr Barling pointed out, and then as he went along he let the ball unravel. The string would then serve as a guide to anyone not knowing the way. Otherwise it would be very dangerous to wander about in the underground tunnels. For some of them ran for miles.

After about eight minutes the little company came to a kind of rounded cave, set in the side of a big, but rather low tunnel. Here had been put a bench with some rugs, a box to serve as a table, and a jug of water. Nothing else.

Sooty by now was coming round from his blow on the head. The other prisoner, however, still lay unconscious, breathing heavily.

'No good talking to him,' said Mr Barling. 'He won't be all right till tomorrow. We'll come and talk to him then. I'll bring Block.'

Sooty had been put on the floor. He suddenly sat up, and put his hand to his aching head. He couldn't imagine where he was.

He looked up and saw Mr Barling, and then suddenly he remembered everything. But how had he got there, in this dark cave?

'Mr Barling!' he said. 'What's all this? What did you hit me for? Why have you brought me here?'

'Punishment for a small boy who can't keep his nose out of things that don't concern him!' said Mr Barling, in a horrid sarcastic voice. 'You'll be company for our friend on the bench there. He'll sleep till the morning, I'm afraid. You can tell him all about it, then, and say I'll be back to have a little heart-to-heart talk with him! And see here, Pierre – you do know, don't you, the foolishness of trying to wander about these old passages? I've brought you to a little-known one, and if you want to lose yourself and never be heard of again, well, try wandering about, that's all!'

Sooty looked pale. He did know the danger of wandering about those lost old tunnels. This one he was in he was sure he didn't know at all. He was about to ask a few more questions when Mr Barling turned quickly on his heel and went off with his servant. They took the lantern with them and left the boy in darkness. He yelled after them.

'Hi, you beasts! Leave me a light!'

But there was no answer. Sooty heard the

footfalls going farther and farther away, and then there was silence and darkness.

The boy felt in his pocket for his torch, but it wasn't there. He had dropped it in his bedroom. He groped his way over to the bench, and felt about for George's father. He wished he would wake up. It was so horrid to be there in the darkness. It was cold, too.

Sooty crept under the rugs and cuddled close to the unconscious man. He longed with all his heart for him to wake up.

From somewhere there sounded the drip-drip-drip of water. After a time Sooty couldn't bear it. He knew it was only drops dripping off the roof of the tunnel in a damp place, but he felt he couldn't bear it. Drip-drip-drip. Drip-drip-drip. If only it would stop!

'I'll have to wake George's father up!' thought the boy, desperately. 'I *must* talk to someone!'

He began to shake the sleeping man, wondering what to call him, for he did not know his surname. He couldn't call him 'George's father'! Then he remembered that the others called him Uncle Quentin, and he began yelling the name in the drugged man's ear.

'Uncle Quentin! Uncle Quentin! Wake up! Do wake up! Oh, won't you please wake up!'

Uncle Quentin stirred at last. He opened his eyes in the darkness, and listened to the urgent voice in his ear, feeling faintly puzzled.

'Uncle Quentin! Wake up and speak to me. I'm scared!' said the voice. 'UNCLE QUENTIN!'

The man thought vaguely that it must be Julian or Dick. He put his arm round Sooty and dragged him close to him. 'It's all right. Go to sleep,' he said. 'What's the matter, Julian? Or is it Dick? Go to sleep.'

He fell asleep again himself, for he was still half-drugged. But Sooty felt comforted now. He shut his eyes, feeling certain that he couldn't possibly go to sleep. But he did, almost at once! He slept soundly all through the night, and was only awakened by Uncle Quentin moving on the bench.

The puzzled man was amazed to find his bed

so unexpectedly hard. He was even more amazed to find someone in bed with him, for he remembered nothing at all. He stretched out his hand to switch on the reading-lamp which had been beside his bed the night before.

But it wasn't there! Strange! He felt about and touched Sooty's face. What was this beside him? He began to feel extremely puzzled. He felt ill, too. What *could* have happened?

'Are you awake?' said Sooty's voice. 'Oh, Uncle Quentin, I'm so glad you're awake. I hope you don't mind me calling you that, but I don't know your surname. I only know you are George's father and Julian's uncle.'

'Well – who are you?' said Uncle Quentin, in wonder.

Sooty began to tell him everything. Uncle Quentin listened in the utmost amazement. 'But *why* have we been kidnapped like this?' he said, astonished and angry. 'I never heard of such a thing in my life!'

'I don't know why Mr Barling has kidnapped *you* but I know he took me because I happened to see what he was doing,' said Sooty. 'Anyway, he's coming back this morning, with Block, and he said he would have a heart-to-heart talk with you. We'll have to wait here, I'm afraid We can't possibly find our way to safety in the darkness, through this maze of tunnels.'

So they waited – and in due course Mr Barling did come, bringing Block with him. Block carried some food, which was very welcome to the prisoners.

'You beast, Block!' said Sooty, at once, as he saw the servant in the light of the lantern. 'How dare you help in this? You wait till my step-father hears about it! Unless he's in it too!'

'Hold your tongue!' said Block.

Sooty stared at him. 'So you *can* hear!' he said. 'All this time you've been pretending you can't! What a sly fellow you are! What a lot of secrets you must have learnt, pretending to be deaf, and overhearing all kinds of things not meant for you. You're sly, Block, and you're worse things than that!'

'Whip him, Block, if you like,' said

Mr Barling, sitting down on the box. 'I've no time for rude boys myself.'

'I will,' said Block, grimly, and he undid a length of rope from round his waist. 'I've often wanted to, cheeky little worm!'

Sooty felt alarmed. He leapt off the bench and put up his fists.

'Let me talk to our prisoner first,' said Mr Barling. 'Then you can give Pierre the hiding he deserves. It will be nice for him to wait for it.'

Uncle Quentin was listening quietly to all this. He looked at Mr Barling, and spoke sternly.

'You owe me an explanation for your strange behaviour. I demand to be taken to Smuggler's Top. You shall answer to the police for this!'

'Oh no, I shan't,' said Mr Barling, in a curiously soft voice. 'I have a very generous proposal to make to you. I know why you have come to Smuggler's Top. I know why you and Mr Lenoir are so interested in each other's experiments.'

'How do you know?' said Uncle Quentin. 'Spying, I suppose!'

'Yes – I bet Block's been spying and reading letters!' cried Sooty, indignantly.

Mr Barling took no notice of the interruption. 'Now, my dear sir,' he said to Uncle Quentin, 'I will tell you very shortly what I propose. I know you have heard that I am a smuggler. I am. I make a lot of money from it. It is easy to run a smuggling trade here, because no one can patrol the marshes, or stop men using the secret path that only I and a few others know. On favourable nights I send out a signal – or rather Block here does so, for me, using the convenient tower of Smuggler's Top—'

'Oh! So it *was* Block!' cried Sooty.

'Then when the goods arrive,' said Mr Barling, 'and again at a favourable moment I – er – dispose of them. I cover my tracks very carefully, so that no one can possibly accuse me because they never have any real proof.'

'Why are you telling me all this?' said

Uncle Quentin scornfully. 'It's of no interest to me. I'm only interested in a plan for draining the marshes, not in smuggling goods across them!'

'Exactly, my dear fellow!' said Mr Barling, amiably. 'I know that. I have even seen your plans and read about your experiments and Mr Lenoir's. But the draining of the marsh means the end of my own business! Once the marsh is drained, once houses are built there, and roads made, once the mists have gone, my business goes too! A harbour may be built out there, at the edge of the marshes – my ships can no longer creep in unseen, bringing valuable cargoes! Not only will my money go, but all the excitement, which is more than life to me, will go too!'

'You're mad!' said Uncle Quentin, in disgust.

Mr Barling *was* a little mad. He had always felt a great satisfaction in being a successful smuggler in days when smuggling was almost at an end. He loved the thrill of knowing that his little ships were creeping in the mist towards the treacherous marshes. He liked to know that men were making their way over a small and narrow path over the misty marsh to the appointed meeting-place, bringing smuggled goods.

'You should have lived a hundred years or more ago!' said Sooty, also feeling that Mr Barling was a little mad. 'You don't belong to nowadays.'

Mr Barling turned on Sooty, his eyes gleaming dangerously in the light of the lantern.

'Another word from you and I'll drop you in the marshes!' he said. Sooty felt a shiver go down his back. He suddenly knew that Mr Barling really did mean what he said. He was a dangerous man. Uncle Quentin sensed it too. He looked at Mr Barling warily.

'How do I come into this?' he asked. 'Why have you kidnapped me?'

'I know that Mr Lenoir is going to buy your plans from you,' said Mr Barling. 'I know he is going to drain the marsh by using your very excellent ideas. You see, I know all about them! I know, too, that Mr Lenoir hopes to make a lot of money by selling the land once it is drained. It is all his, that misty marsh – and no use to anyone now except to me! But that marsh is not going to be drained – I am going to buy your plans, not Mr Lenoir!'

'Do *you* want to drain the marsh, then?' said Uncle Quentin, in surprise.

Mr Barling laughed scornfully. 'No! Your plans, and the results of your experiments, will be burnt! They will be mine, but I shall not want to use them. I want the marsh left as it is, secret, covered with mist, and treacherous to all but me and my men. So, my dear sir, you will please name your price to me, instead of to Mr Lenoir, and sign this document, which I have had prepared, making over all your plans to me!'

He flourished a large piece of paper in front of Uncle Quentin. Sooty watched breathlessly.

Uncle Quentin picked up the paper. He tore

it into small pieces. He threw them into Mr Barling's face and said, scornfully, 'I don't deal with madmen, nor with rogues, Mr Barling!'

[20]

Timmy to the rescue

Mr Barling went very pale. Sooty gave a loud crow of delight. 'Hurrah! Good for *you*, Uncle Quentin!'

Block gave a loud exclamation, and darted to the excited boy. He took him by the shoulder, and raised the rope to thrash him.

'That's right,' said Mr Barling, in a funny kind of hissing voice. 'Deal with him first, Block, and then with this – this – stubborn – obstinate – fool! We'll soon bring them to their senses. A good thrashing now and again, a few days here in the dark, without any food – ah, that will make them more biddable!'

Sooty yelled at the top of his voice. Uncle Quentin leapt to his feet. The rope came down and Sooty yelled again.

Then there suddenly came the pattering of

quick feet, and something flung itself on Block. Block gave a scream of pain and turned. He knocked the lantern over by accident, and the light went out. There was a sound of fierce growling. Block staggered about trying to keep off the creature that had fastened itself on to him.

'Barling! Help me!' he shouted.

Mr Barling went to his aid, but was attacked in his turn. Uncle Quentin and Sooty listened in amazement and fear. What creature was this that had suddenly arrived? Would it attack them next? Was it a giant rat – or some fierce wild animal that haunted these tunnels?

The fierce animal suddenly barked. Sooty cheered.

'TIMMY! It's you, Timmy! Oh, good dog, good dog! Go for him, then, go for him! Bite him, Timmy, hard.'

The two frightened men could do nothing against the angry dog. Soon they were running down the tunnel as fast as they could go, feeling for the string for fear of being lost. Timmy chased them with much enjoyment, and then returned to Sooty and George's father, rather pleased with himself.

He had a tremendous welcome. George's father made a great fuss of him, and Sooty put his arms round the big dog's neck.

'How did you come here? Did you find your way out of the secret passage you've been in? Are you half-starved? Look, here's some food.'

Timmy ate heartily. He had managed to devour a few rats, but otherwise had had no food at all. He had licked the drops that here and there he had found dripping from the roof, so he had not been thirsty. But he had certainly been extremely puzzled and worried. He had never before been so long away from his beloved mistress!

'Uncle Quentin – Timmy could take us safely back to Smuggler's Top, couldn't he?' said Sooty, suddenly. He spoke to Timmy. 'Can you take us home, old boy? Home, to George?'

Timmy listened, with his ears cocked up. He ran down the passage a little way, but soon came back. He did not like the idea of going down there. He felt that enemies were waiting for them all. Mr Barling and Block were not likely to give in quite so easily!

But Timmy knew other ways about the tunnels that honeycombed the hillside. He knew, for instance, the way down to the marsh! So he set off in the darkness, with Uncle Quentin's hand on his collar, and Sooty following close behind, holding on to Uncle Quentin's coat.

It wasn't easy or pleasant. Uncle Quentin wondered at times if Timmy really did know where he was going. They went down and down, stumbling over uneven places, sometimes knocking their heads against an unexpected low piece of roof. It was not a pleasant journey for Uncle Quentin, for he had no shoes on his feet, and was dressed only in pyjamas and rugs.

After a long time they came out on the edge of the marsh itself, at the bottom of the hill! It was a desolate place, and the mists were over it, so that neither Sooty nor Uncle Quentin knew which way to turn!

'Never mind,' said Sooty, 'we can easily leave it to Timmy. He knows the way all right. He'll take us back to the town, and once there we'll know the way home ourselves!'

But suddenly, to their surprise and dismay, Timmy stopped dead, pricking up his ears, whined and would go no farther. He looked thoroughly miserable and unhappy. What could be the matter?

Then, with a bark, the big dog left the two by themselves, and galloped back into the tunnel they had just left. He disappeared completely!

'Timmy!' yelled Sooty. 'Timmy! Come here! Don't leave us! TIMMY!'

But Timmy was gone; why, neither Sooty nor Uncle Quentin knew. They stared at one another.

'Well – I suppose we'd better try to make our way over this marshy bit,' said Uncle Quentin, doubtfully, putting a foot out to see if the ground was hard. It wasn't! He drew back his foot at once.

The mists were so thick that it was really

impossible to see anything. Behind them was the opening to the tunnel. A steep rocky cliff rose up about it. There was no path that way, it was certain. Somehow they had to make their way round the foot of the hill to the main road that entered the town – but the way lay over marshy ground!

'Let's sit down and wait for a bit to see if Timmy comes back,' said Sooty. So they sat down on a rock at the entrance to the tunnel and waited.

Sooty began to think of the others. He wondered what they had thought when they had discovered that both he and Uncle Quentin were missing. How astonished they must have been!

'I wonder what the others are doing?' he said, aloud. 'I'd love to know!'

The others, as we know, had been doing plenty. They had found the opening in the window-seat where Mr Barling had taken the captives, and they had gone down it and actually seen Mr Barling and Block on their way to talk to Uncle Quentin and Sooty!

They had found out, too, that Block hadn't been in his bed – he had left a dummy there instead. Now everyone was talking at once, and Mr Lenoir was suddenly convinced that Block had been a spy, put in his house by Mr Barling, and not the good servant he had appeared!

Once Julian felt that he was convinced of this he spoke to him more freely, and told him of the way through the window-seat, and of how they had seen Mr Barling and Block that very day, in the underground tunnels!

'Good heavens!' said Mr Lenoir, now looking thoroughly alarmed. 'Barling must be mad! I've always thought he was a bit strange – but he must be absolutely mad to kidnap people like this – and Block must be, too. This is a plot! They've heard what I've been planning with your uncle – and they've made up their minds to stop it because it will interfere with their smuggling. Goodness knows what they'll do now! This is serious!'

'If only we had Timmy!' suddenly said George.

Mr Lenoir looked astonished.

'Who's Timmy?'

'Well, you might as well know everything now,' said Julian, and he told Mr Lenoir about Timmy, and how they had hidden him.

'Very foolish of you,' said Mr Lenoir, shortly, looking displeased. 'If you'd told me I would have had someone in the town look after him. I can't help not liking dogs. I detest them, and never will have them in the house. But I would willingly have arranged for him to be boarded out, if I'd known you'd brought him.'

The children felt sorry and a little ashamed. Mr Lenoir was an odd, hot-tempered person, but he didn't seem nearly as horrid as they had thought he was.

'I'd like to go and see if I can find Timmy,' said George. 'You'll get the police in now, I suppose, Mr Lenoir, and perhaps we could go and find Timmy? We know the way into the secret passage from your study.'

'Oh – so *that's* why you were hiding there in the afternoon yesterday,' said Mr Lenoir. 'I thought you were a very bad boy. Well, go and try and find him if you like, but don't let him come anywhere near me. I really cannot bear dogs in the house.'

He went to telephone the police station again. Mrs Lenoir, her eyes red with crying, stood by him. George slipped away to the study, followed by Dick and Julian and Anne. Marybelle stayed beside her mother.

'Come on – let's get into that secret passage and try and find old Timmy,' said George. 'If we all go, and whistle and shout and call, he's sure to hear us!'

They found the way into the passage, by doing the things they had done before. The panel slid back, and then another, larger opening came as before. They all squeezed through it, and found themselves in the very narrow passage that led from the study up to Sooty's bedroom.

But Timmy was not there! The children were surprised, but George soon thought why.

'Do you remember Sooty telling us there was a way into this passage from the dining-room, as well as from the study and Sooty's bedroom? Well, I believe I saw a door or something there, as we passed where the dining-room must be, and it's likely Timmy may have pushed through it, and gone into another passage somewhere.'

They went back, one by one. They came to the dining-room – or rather, they walked behind the dining-room wall. There they saw the door that George had noticed as they passed – a door, small and set quite flat to the wall, so that it was difficult to see. George pushed it. It opened easily, and then flapped shut, with a little click. It could be opened from one side but not from the other.

'That's where Timmy's gone!' said George, and she pushed the door open again. 'He pushed against the door and it opened – he went through, and the door fastened itself so that he couldn't get back. Come on, we must find him.'

They all went through the small door. It was

so low that they had to bend their heads to go through, even Anne. They found themselves in a passage rather like the one they had just left, but not quite so narrow. It suddenly began to go downwards. Julian called back to the others.

'I believe it goes down to the passages where we used to take Timmy when we let him down into that pit to go for a walk! Yes, look – we've come to where the pit itself is!'

They went on, calling Timmy, and whistling loudly, but no Timmy came. George began to feel worried.

'Hallo! – Surely this is where we came out when we climbed down all those steps from the window-seat passage!' said Dick, suddenly. 'Yes, it is. Look, there's the tunnel where we saw Block and Mr Barling going!'

'Oh – do you think they've done something to Timmy?' said George, in a frightened voice. 'I never thought of that!'

Everyone felt alarmed. It was strange that Block and Mr Barling could go about unmolested by Timmy if Timmy was somewhere near! Could they have harmed him in any way? They had no idea that Timmy was at that very minute with George's father and Sooty!

'Look at this!' said Julian, suddenly, and he shone his torch on to something to show the others. 'String! String going right down this tunnel. Why?'

'It's the tunnel that Mr Barling and Block took!' said George. 'I believe it leads to where they've taken my father and Sooty! They're keeping them prisoners down here! I'm going to follow the string and find them! Who's coming with me?'

[21]

A journey through the hill

'I'm coming!' said everyone at once. As if they would let George go alone!

So down the dark tunnel they went, feeling the string and following it. Julian ran it through his fingers, and the others followed behind, holding hands. It would not do for anyone to get lost.

After about ten minutes they came to the rounded cave where Sooty and George's father had been the night before. They were not there now, of course – they were on their way down to the marsh!

'Hallo, look! This is where they must have been!' cried Julian, shining his torch round. 'A bench – with tumbled rugs – and an over-turned lamp. And look here, scraps of paper torn into bits! Something's been happening here!'

Quick-witted George pieced it together in her

mind. 'Mr Barling took them here and left them. Then he came back with some sort of proposal to Father, who refused it! There must have been a struggle of some sort and the lamp got broken. Oh – I do hope Father and Sooty got away all right.'

Julian felt gloomy. 'I hope to goodness they haven't gone wandering about these awful tunnels. Even Sooty doesn't know a quarter of them. I wish I knew what's happened.'

'Someone's coming!' suddenly said Dick. 'Snap out the light, Ju.'

Julian snapped off the torch he carried. At once they were all in darkness. They crouched at the back of the cave, listening.

Yes – footsteps were coming. Rather cautious footsteps. 'Sound like two or three people,' whispered Dick. They came nearer. Whoever was coming was plainly following the tunnel where the string was.

'Mr Barling perhaps – and Block,' whispered George. 'Come to have another talk with Father! But he's gone!'

A brilliant light flashed suddenly round the cave – and picked out the huddled children. There was a loud exclamation of astonishment.

'Good heavens! Who's here? What's all this?'

It was Mr Barling's voice. Julian stood up, blinking in the bright light.

'We came to look for my uncle and Sooty,' he said. 'Where are they?'

'Aren't they here?' said Mr Barling, seeming surprised. 'And is that horrible brute of a dog gone?'

'Oh – was Timmy here?' cried George, joyfully. 'Where is he?'

There were two other men with Mr Barling. One was Block. The other was his servant. Mr Barling put down the lantern he was carrying.

'Do you mean to say you don't know where the others are?' he said, uneasily. 'If they've gone off on their own, they'll never come back.'

Anne gave a little scream. 'It's all your fault, you horrid man!'

'Shut up, Anne!' said Julian. 'Mr Barling,' he

said, turning to the angry smuggler, 'I think you'd better come back with us and explain things. Mr Lenoir is now talking to the police.'

'Oh, *is* he?' said Mr Barling. 'Then I think it would be as well for us all to stay down here for a while! Yes, you too! I'll make Mr Lenoir squirm! I'll hold you all prisoners – and this time you shall be bound so that you don't go wandering off like the others! Got some rope, Block?'

Block stepped forward with the other man. They caught hold of George first, very roughly.

She screamed loudly. 'Timmy! Timmy! Where are you? Timmy, come and help! Oh, TIMMY!'

But no Timmy came. She was soon in a corner with her hands tied behind her. Then they turned to Julian.

'You're mad,' Julian said to Mr Barling, who was standing nearby, holding the lantern. 'You *must* be mad to do things like this.'

'Timmy!' shouted George, trying to free her hands. 'Timmy, Timmy, Timmy!'

Timmy didn't hear. He was too far away. But the dog suddenly felt uneasy. He was with George's father and Sooty at the edge of the marsh, about to lead them round the hill to safety. But he stopped and listened. He could hear nothing of course. But Timmy knew that George was in danger. He knew that his beloved little mistress needed him.

His ears did not tell him, nor did his nose. But his heart told him. George was in danger!

He turned and fled back into the tunnel. He tore up the winding passages at top speed, panting.

And, quite suddenly, just as Julian was angrily submitting to having his hands tied tightly together, a furry thunderbolt arrived! It was Timmy!

He smelt his enemy, Mr Barling, again! He smelt Block. Grrrrrrrrr-rrrrrr!

'Here's that awful dog again!' yelled Block, and leapt away from Julian. 'Where's your gun, Barling?'

But Timmy didn't worry about guns. He

leapt at Mr Barling and got him on the floor. He gave him a nip in the shoulder that made him yell. Then he leapt at Block, and got him down, too. The other man fled.

'Call your dog off. Call him off, or he'll kill us!' cried Mr Barling, struggling up, his shoulder paining him terribly. But nobody said a word. Let Timmy do what he liked!

It wasn't long before all three of the men had gone into the dark tunnel, staggering about without a light, trying to find their way back. But they missed the string, and went wandering away in the darkness, groaning and terrified.

Timmy came running back very pleased with himself. He went to George and, whining with joy, he licked his little mistress from head to foot. And George, who never cried, was most astonished to find the tears pouring down her cheeks. 'But I'm glad, not sad!' she said. 'Oh, somebody undo my hands! I can't pat Timmy!'

Dick undid her hands and Julian's. Then they all had a marvellous time making a fuss of Timmy. And what a fuss he made of them too! He whined and barked, he rolled over and over, he licked them and butted them all with his head. He was wild with delight.

'Oh Timmy – it's lovely to have you again,' said George, happily. 'Now you can lead us to the others. I'm sure you know where Father is, Timmy, and Sooty.'

Timmy did, of course. He set off, his tail wagging, George's hand on his collar, and the others behind in a line, holding hands.

They had the lantern with them and two torches, so they could see the way easily. But they would never have taken the right tunnels if Timmy hadn't been with them. The dog had explored them all thoroughly, and his sense of smell enabled him to go the right way without mistake.

'He's a marvellous dog,' said Anne. 'I think he's the best dog in the world, George.'

'Of course he is,' said George, who had always thought that ever since she had had Timmy as a puppy. 'Darling Tim – wasn't it wonderful when he came racing up and jumped at Block just as he was tying Julian's hands? He must have known we needed him!'

'I suppose he's taking us to wherever your father and Sooty are,' said Dick. 'He seems certain of the way. We're going steadily downhill. I bet we'll be at the marshes soon!'

When they at last came to the bottom of the hill, and emerged from the tunnel in the mists, George gave a yell. 'Look! There's Father – and Sooty too!'

'Uncle Quentin!' shouted Julian, Dick and Anne. 'Sooty! Hallo, here we are!'

Uncle Quentin and Sooty turned in the greatest surprise. They jumped up and went to meet the dog and the excited children.

'How *did* you get here?' said George's father, giving her a hug. 'Did Timmy go back for you? He suddenly deserted us and fled back into the tunnel.'

'What's happened?' asked Sooty, eagerly, knowing that the others would have plenty of news to tell him.

'Heaps,' said George, her face glowing. It

was so nice all to be together again, Timmy too. She and Julian and Dick began to tell everything in turn, and then her father told his tale, too, interrupted a little by Sooty.

'Well,' said Julian at last, 'I suppose we ought to be getting back, or the police will be sending out bloodhounds to trace us all! Mr Lenoir will be surprised to see us all turning up together.'

'I wish I wasn't in pyjamas,' said his uncle, drawing the rugs about him. 'I shall feel most peculiar walking the streets like this!'

'Never mind – it's awfully misty now,' said George, and she shivered a little, for the air was damp. 'Timmy – show us the way out of this place. I'm sure you know it.'

Timmy had never been out of the tunnel before, but he seemed to know what to do. He set off round the foot of the hill, the rest following, marvelling at the way Timmy found a dry path to follow. In the mist it was almost impossible to see which place was safe to walk on and which was not.

The treacherous marsh was all around them!

'Hurrah! There's the road!' cried Julian, suddenly, as they came in sight of the roadway built over the marsh, running up the hill from the salty stretches of mud. They picked their way to it, their feet soaked with wet mud. Timmy tried to take a flying leap on to it.

But somehow or other he slipped! He fell back into the marsh, tried to find a safe foothold and couldn't. He whined.

'Timmy! Oh look, he's in the mud – and he's sinking!' screamed George, in panic. 'Timmy, Timmy, I'm coming!'

She was about to step down into the marsh to rescue Tim, but her father pulled her back roughly. 'Do you want to sink in, too?' he cried. 'Timmy will get out all right.'

But he wasn't getting out. He was sinking. 'Do something, oh, do something!' shouted George, struggling to get away from her father's hold. 'Oh, save Timmy, quick!'

[22]

Things come right at last

But what could anyone do? In despair they all gazed at poor Timmy, who was struggling with all his might in the sinking mud. 'He's going down!' wept Anne.

Suddenly there came the sound of rumbling wheels along the road to the hill. It was a lorry carrying a load of goods – coal, coke, planks, logs, sacks of various things. George yelled to it.

'Stop, stop! Help us! Our dog's in the marsh.'

The lorry came to a stop. George's father ran his eye over the things it carried. In a trice he and Julian were dragging out some planks from the load. They threw these into the marsh, and, using them as stepping-stones, the two reached poor sinking Timmy.

The lorry-driver jumped down to help. Into

the marsh, crosswise on the other planks, went some more wood, to make a safe path. The first lot were already sinking in the mud.

'Uncle Quentin's got Timmy – he's pulling him up! He's got him!' squealed Anne.

George had sat down suddenly at the edge of the road, looking white. She saw that Timmy would now be rescued, and she felt sick with shock and relief.

It was a difficult business getting Timmy right out, for the mud was strong, and sucked him down as hard as it could. But at last he was out, and he staggered across the sinking planks, trying to wag a very muddy tail.

Muddy as he was, George flung her arms round him. 'Oh Timmy – what a fright you gave us all! Oh, how you smell – but I don't care a bit! I thought you were gone, poor, poor Timmy!'

The lorry-driver looked ruefully at his planks in the marsh. They were now out of sight beneath the mud. Uncle Quentin, feeling rather foolish in pyjamas and rugs, spoke to him.

'I've no money on me now, but if you'll call at Smuggler's Top sometime I'll pay you well for your lost planks and your help.'

'Well, I'm delivering some coal to the house next to Smuggler's Top,' said the man, eyeing Uncle Quentin's curious attire. 'Maybe you'd all like a lift? There's plenty of room at the back there.'

It was getting dark now, as well as being foggy, and everyone was tired. Thankfully they climbed up into the lorry, and it roared up the hill into Castaway. Soon they were at Smuggler's Top, and they all clambered down, suddenly feeling rather stiff.

'I'll be calling tomorrow, said the driver. 'Can't stop now. Good evening to you all!'

The little company rang the bell. Sarah came hurrying to the door. She almost fell over in surprise as she saw everyone standing there in the light of the hall-lamp.

'Lands' sakes!' she said. 'You're all back! My, Mr and Mrs Lenoir will be glad – they've got the police hunting everywhere for you! They've gone down secret passages, and they've been to Mr Barling's, and—'

Timmy bounced into the hall, the mud now drying on him, so that he looked most peculiar. Sarah gave a scream. 'What's that? Gracious, it can't be a dog!'

'Come here, Tim!' said George, suddenly remembering that Mr Lenoir detested dogs. 'Sarah, do you think you'd have poor Timmy in the kitchen with you? I really can't turn him out into the streets – you've no idea how brave he's been.'

'Come along, come along!' said her father, impatient with all this talk. 'Lenoir can put up with Timmy for a few minutes, surely!'

'Oh, *I'll* have him with pleasure!' said Sarah. 'I'll give him a bath. That's what he wants. Mr and Mrs Lenoir are in the sitting-room. Oh, shall I get you some clothes?'

The little party went in, and made their way to the sitting-room, while Timmy went docilely to the kitchen with the excited Sarah. Mr Lenoir heard the talking and flung open the sitting-room door.

Mrs Lenoir fell on Sooty, tears pouring down her cheeks. Marybelle pawed at him in delight, just as if she was a dog! Mr Lenoir rubbed his hands, clapped everyone on the back, and said, 'Well, well! Fine to see you all safe and sound. Well, well! What a tale you've got to tell, I'm sure!'

'It's a strange tale, Lenoir,' said George's father. 'Very strange. But I'll have to see to my feet before I tell it. I've walked miles in my bare feet, and they're very painful now!'

So, with bits of tales pouring out from everyone, the household bustled round and got hot water for bathing Uncle Quentin's feet, a dressing-gown for him, food for everyone, and hot drinks. It was really a most exciting time, and now that the thrills were all over, the children felt rather important to be able to relate so much.

Then the police came in, of course, and the Inspector at once asked a lot of questions.

Everyone wanted to answer them, but the Inspector said that only George's father, Sooty and George were to tell the tale. They knew most about everything.

Mr Lenoir was perhaps the most surprised person there. When he heard how Mr Barling had actually offered to buy the plans for draining the marsh, and how he had frankly admitted to being a smuggler, he sat back in his chair, unable to say a word.

'He's mad, of course!' said the Inspector of Police. 'Doesn't seem to live in this world at all!'

'That's just what I said to him,' said Sooty. 'I told him he ought to have lived a hundred years ago!'

'Well, we've tried to catch him in the smuggling business many and many a time,' said the Inspector, 'but he was too artful. Fancy him planting Block here as a spy, sir – that was a clever bit of work – and Block using your tower as a signalling place! Bit of nerve, that! And Block isn't deaf, after all? That was clever, too – sending him about, pretending he was stone-deaf, so that he could catch many a bit of knowledge not meant for his ears!'

'Do you think we ought to do something about Block and Mr Barling and the other man?' said Julian, suddenly. 'For all we know they're still wandering about in that maze of tunnels – and two of them are bitten by Timmy, we know.'

'Ah yes – that dog saved your lives, I should think,' said the Inspector. 'A bit of luck, that. Sorry you don't like dogs, Mr Lenoir, but I'm sure you'll admit it was a lucky thing for you all that he was wandering about!'

'Yes – yes, it was,' said Mr Lenoir. 'Of course, Block never wanted dogs here, either – he was afraid they might bark at his curious comings and goings, I suppose. By the way – where *is* this marvellous dog? I don't mind seeing him for a moment – though I do detest dogs, and always shall.'

'I'll get him,' said George. 'I only hope Sarah's done what she said, and bathed him. He was awfully muddy!'

She went out and came back with Timmy. But what a different Timmy! Sarah had given him a good hot bath, and had dried him well. He smelt sweet and fresh, his coat was springy and clean, and he had had a good meal. He was feeling very pleased with himself and everything.

'Timmy – meet a friend,' said George to him, solemnly. Timmy looked at Mr Lenoir out of his big brown eyes. He trotted straight up to him, and held up his right paw politely to shake hands, as George had taught him.

Mr Lenoir was rather taken aback. He was not used to good manners in dogs. He couldn't help putting out his hand to Timmy – and the two shook hands in a most friendly manner. Timmy didn't attempt to lick Mr Lenoir or jump up at him. He took away his paw, gave a little wuff as if to say 'How-do-you-do?' and then went back to George. He lay down quietly beside her. 'Well – he doesn't seem like a *dog*!' said Mr Lenoir, in surprise.

'Oh, he *is*,' said George, at once, very earnestly. 'He's a real, proper dog, Mr Lenoir – only much, much cleverer than most dogs are. Could I keep him, please, while we stay here, and get someone in the town to look after him?'

'Well – seeing he is such a very fine fellow – and seems so sensible – I'll let you have him here,' said Mr Lenoir, making a great effort to be generous. 'Only – please keep him out of my way. I'm sure a sensible boy like you will see to that.'

Everyone grinned when Mr Lenoir called George a boy. He never seemed to realise she was a girl. She grinned, too. She wasn't going to tell him she wasn't a boy!

'You'll never see him!' she said, joyfully. 'I'll keep him right out of your way. Thank you very much. It's awfully good of you.'

The Inspector liked Timmy, too. He looked at him and nodded across to George. 'When you want to get rid of him, sell him to me!' he said. 'We could do with a dog like that in our police force! Soon round up the smugglers for us!'

George didn't even bother to reply! As if she

would ever sell Timmy, or let him go into the police force!

All the same, the Inspector had to call on Timmy for help before long. When the next day came, and no one had found Mr Barling and his companions in the maze of tunnels, and they hadn't turned up anywhere, the Inspector asked George if she would let Timmy go down into the tunnels and hunt them out.

'Can't leave them there, lost and starving,' he said. 'Bad as they are we'll have to rescue them! Timmy is the only one who can find them.'

That was true, of course. So Timmy once more went underground into the hill, and hunted for his enemies. He found them after a while, lost in the maze of passages, hungry and thirsty, in pain and frightened.

He took them like sheep to where the police waited for them. And after that Mr Barling and his friends disappeared from public life for quite a long time!

'The police must be glad to have got them at last,' said Mr Lenoir. 'They have tried to stop this smuggling for a long time. They even suspected *me* at one time! Barling was a clever fellow, though I still think he was half mad. When Block found out my ideas about draining the marsh, Barling was afraid that once the mists and the marsh were gone, that would be the end of all his excitement – no more smuggling! No more waiting for his little ships to come creeping up in the fog – no more lines of men slipping across the secret ways of the marsh – no more signalling, no more hiding away of smuggled goods. Did you know that the police had found a cave full of them inside the hill?'

It was an exciting adventure to talk about, now that it was all over. The children felt sorry about one thing, though – they were sorry that they had thought Mr Lenoir so horrid. He was a strange man in many ways, but he could be kind and jolly too.

'Did you know we're leaving Smuggler's Top?' said Sooty. 'Mother was so terribly upset when I disappeared, that Father promised her he'd sell the place and leave Castaway, if I came back safe and sound. Mother's thrilled!'

'So am I,' said Marybelle. 'I don't like Smuggler's Top – it's so weird and secret and lonely!'

'Well, if it will make you all happy to leave it, I'm glad,' said Julian. 'But *I* like it! I think it's a lovely place, set on a hill-top like this, with mists at its foot, and secret ways all about it. I'll be sorry never to come here again, if you leave.'

'So will I,' said Dick, and Anne and George nodded.

'It's an adventurous place!' said George, patting Timmy. 'Isn't it, Timmy? Do *you* like it, Timmy? Have *you* enjoyed your adventure here?'

'Woof!' said Timmy, and thumped his tail on the floor. Of course he had enjoyed himself. He always did, so long as George was anywhere about.

'Well – now perhaps we'll have a nice peaceful time!' said Marybelle. 'I don't want any more adventures.'

'Ah, but *we* do!' said the others. So no doubt they will get them. Adventures always come to the adventurous, there's no doubt about that!

FIVE GO OFF IN A CARAVAN

[1]

The beginning of the holidays

'I do love the beginning of the summer hols,' said Julian. 'They always seem to stretch out ahead for ages and ages.'

'They go so nice and slowly at first,' said Anne, his little sister. 'Then they start to gallop.'

The others laughed. They knew exactly what Anne meant. 'Woof,' said a deep voice, as if someone else thoroughly agreed too.

'Timmy thinks you're right, Anne,' said George, and patted the big dog lying panting beside them. Dick patted him, too, and Timmy licked them both.

The four children were lying in a sunny garden in the first week of the holidays. Usually they went to their cousin Georgina's home for holidays, at Kirrin – but this time, for a change, they were all at the home of Julian, Dick and Anne.

Julian was the oldest, a tall, sturdy boy with a strong and pleasant face. Dick and Georgina came next. Georgina looked more like a curly-headed boy than a girl, and she insisted on being called George. Even the teachers at school called her George. Anne was the youngest, though, much to her delight, she was really growing taller now.

'Daddy said this morning that if we didn't want to stay here all the hols we could choose what we wanted to do,' said Anne. 'I vote for staying here.'

'We could go off somewhere just for two weeks, perhaps,' said Dick. 'For a change.'

'Shall we go to Kirrin, and stay with George's mother and father for a bit?' said Julian, thinking that perhaps George would like this.

'No,' said George at once. 'I went home at half-term, and Mother said Father was just beginning one of his experiments in something or other – and you know what *that* means. If we go there we'd have to walk about on tiptoe, and talk in whispers, and keep out of his way the whole time.'

'That's the worst of having a scientist for a father,' said Dick, lying down on his back and shutting his eyes. 'Well, your mother couldn't cope with us and with your father, too, in the middle of one of his experiments, at the same time. Sparks would fly.'

'I like Uncle Quentin, but I'm afraid of him when he's in one of his tempers,' said Anne. 'He shouts so.'

'It's decided that we won't go to Kirrin, then,' said Julian, yawning. 'Not these hols, anyhow. You can always go and see your mother for a week or so, George, when you want to. What shall we do, then? Stay here all the time?'

They were now all lying down on their backs in the sun, their eyes shut. What a hot afternoon! Timmy sat up by George, his pink tongue hanging out, panting loudly.

'Don't, Timmy,' said Anne. 'You sound as if

you have been running for miles, and you make me feel hotter than ever.'

Timmy put a friendly paw on Anne's middle and she squealed. 'Oh, Timmy – your paw's heavy. Take it off.'

'You know, I think if we were allowed to go off by ourselves somewhere, it would be rather fun,' said George, biting a blade of grass and squinting up into the deep blue sky. 'The biggest fun we've ever had was when we were alone on Kirrin Island, for instance. Couldn't we go off somewhere all by ourselves?'

'But where?' said Dick. 'And how? I mean we aren't old enough to take a car – though I bet I could drive one. It wouldn't be much fun going on bicycles, because Anne can't ride as fast as we can.'

'And somebody always gets a puncture,' said Julian.

'It would be jolly good fun to go off on horses,' said George. 'Only we haven't got even one.'

'Yes, we have – there's old Dobby down in

the field,' said Dick. 'He is ours. He used to draw the pony-cart, but we don't use it any more now he's turned out to grass.'

'Well, one horse wouldn't take four of us, silly,' said George. 'Dobby's no good.'

There was a silence, and everyone thought lazily about holidays. Timmy snapped at a fly, and his teeth came together with a loud click.

'Wish I could catch flies like that,' said Dick, flapping away a blue-bottle. 'Come and catch this one, Timmy, old thing.'

'What about a walking tour?' said Julian after a pause. There was a chorus of groans.

'What! In this weather! You're mad!'

We shan't be allowed to.'

'All right, all right,' said Julian. 'Think of a better idea, then.'

'I'd like to go somewhere where we could bathe,' said Anne. 'In a lake, for instance, if we can't go to the sea.'

'Sounds nice,' said Dick. 'My goodness, I'm sleepy. Let's hurry up and settle this matter, or I shall be snoring hard.'

But it wasn't easy to settle. Nobody wanted to go off to a hotel, or to rooms. Grown-ups would want to go with them and look after them. And nobody wanted to go walking or cycling in the hot July weather.

'Looks as if we'll have to stay at home all the hols, then,' said Julian. 'Well – I'm going to have a snooze.'

In two minutes they were all asleep on the grass except Timmy. If his family fell asleep like this, Timmy considered himself on guard. The big dog gave his mistress George a soft lick and sat up firmly beside her, his ears cocked, and his eyes bright. He panted hard, but nobody heard him. They were all snoozing deliciously in the sun, getting brown.

The garden sloped up a hillside. From where he sat Timmy could see quite a long way, both up and down the road that ran by the house. It was a wide road, but not a very busy one, for it was a country district.

Timmy heard a dog barking in the distance, and his ears twitched in that direction. He heard people walking down the road and his ears twitched again. He missed nothing, not even the robin that flew down to get a caterpillar on a bush not far off. He growled softly in his throat at the robin – just to tell it that he was on guard, so beware.

Then something came down the wide road, something that made Timmy shake with excitement, and sniff at the strange smells that came floating up to the garden. A big procession came winding up the road, with a rumble and clatter of wheels – a slow procession, headed by a very strange thing.

Timmy had no idea what it was that headed the procession. Actually it was a big elephant, and Timmy smelt its smelt, strange and strong, and didn't like it. He smelt the scent of the monkeys in their travelling cage, too, and he heard the barking of the performing dogs in their van.

He answered them defiantly. 'WOOF, WOOF, WOOF.'

The loud barking awoke all four children at

once. 'Shut up, Timmy,' said George crossly. 'What a row to make when we're all having a nap.'

'WOOF,' said Timmy obstinately, and pawed at his mistress to make her sit up and take notice. George sat up. She saw the procession at once and gave a yell.

'Hey, you others, There's a circus procession going by. Look.'

They all sat up, wide awake now. They stared down at the caravans going slowly along, and listened to an animal howling, and the dogs barking.

'Look at that elephant, pulling the caravan along,' said Anne. 'He must be jolly strong.'

'Let's go down to the gate of the drive and watch,' said Dick. So they all got up and ran down the garden, then round the house and into the drive that led to the road. The procession was just passing the gates.

It was a colourful sight. The caravans were painted in brilliant colours, and looked spick and span from the outside. Little flowery curtains hung at the windows. At the front of each caravan sat the man or woman who owned it, driving the horse that pulled it. Only the front caravan was pulled by an elephant.

'Golly – doesn't it look exciting?' said George. 'I wish I belonged to a circus that went wandering all over the place all the year. That's just the sort of life I'd like.'

'Fat lot of good you'd be in the circus,' said Dick rudely. 'You can't even turn a cartwheel.'

'What's a cartwheel?' said Anne.

'What that boy's doing over there,' said Dick. 'Look.'

He pointed to a boy who was turning cartwheels very quickly, going over and over on his hands and feet, turning himself like a wheel. It looked so easy, but it wasn't, as Dick very well knew.

'Oh, is he turning a cartwheel?' said Anne admiringly. 'I wish I could do that.'

The boy came up to them and grinned. He had two terrier dogs with him. Timmy growled and George put her hand on his collar.

'Don't come too near,' she called. 'Timmy isn't quite sure about you.'

'We won't hurt him!' said the boy, and grinned again. He had an ugly, freckled face, with a shock of untidy hair. 'I won't let my dogs eat your Timmy.'

'As if they could!' began George scornfully, and then laughed. The terriers kept close to the boy's heels. He clicked and both dogs rose at once on their hind legs and walked sedately behind him with funny little steps.

'Oh – are they performing dogs?' said Anne. 'Are they yours?'

'These two are,' said the boy. 'This is Barker and this is Growler. I've had them from pups – clever as anything they are!'

'Woof,' said Timmy, apparently disgusted at seeing dogs walk in such a peculiar way. It had never occurred to him that a dog could get up on his hind legs.

'Where are you giving your next show?' asked George eagerly. 'We'd like to see it.'

'We're off for a rest,' said the boy. 'Up in the

hills, where there's a blue lake at the bottom. We're allowed to camp there with our animals – it's wild and lonely and we don't disturb anybody. We just camp there with our caravans.'

'It sounds fine,' said Dick. 'Which is your caravan?'

'This one, just coming,' said the boy, and he pointed to a brightly painted van, whose sides were blue and yellow, and whose wheels were red. 'I live in it with my Uncle Dan. He's the chief clown of the circus. There he is, sitting on the front, driving the horse.'

The children stared at the chief clown, and thought that they had never seen anyone less like a clown. He was dressed in dirty grey flannel trousers and a dirty red shirt open at an equally dirty neck.

He didn't look as if he could make a single joke, or do anything in the least funny. In fact, he looked really bad-tempered, the children thought, and he scowled so fiercely as he chewed on an old pipe that Anne felt quite scared. He didn't look at the children at all, but called in a sharp voice to the boy:

'Nobby! You come on along with us. Get in the caravan and make me a cup of tea.'

The boy Nobby winked at the children and ran to the caravan. It was plain that Uncle Dan kept him in order all right! He poked his head out of the little window in the side of the caravan nearest to the children.

'Sorry I can't ask you to tea too!' he called. 'And the dog. Barker and Growler wouldn't half like to know him!'

The caravan passed on, taking the scowling clown with it, and the grinning Nobby. The children watched the others going by, too; it was quite a big circus. There was a cage of monkeys, a chimpanzee sitting in a corner of a dark cage, asleep, a string of beautiful horses, sleek and shining, a great wagon carrying benches and forms and tents, caravans for the circus folk to live in, and a host of interesting people to see, sitting on the steps of their vans or walking together outside to stretch their legs.

At last the procession was gone and the children went slowly back to their sunny corner in the garden. They sat down – and then George announced something that made them sit up straight.

'*I* know what we'll do these hols! We'll hire a caravan and go off in it by ourselves. Do let's! Oh, do let's!'

[2]

George's great idea

The others stared at George's excited face. She had gone quite red. Dick thumped on the ground.

'A jolly good idea! Why didn't we think of it before?'

'Oh, *yes*! A caravan to ourselves! It sounds too good to be true!' said Anne, and her eyes shone.

'Well, I must say it would be something we've never done before,' said Julian, wondering if it was really possible. 'I say – wouldn't it be gorgeous if we could go off into the hills – where that lake is that the boy spoke about? We could bathe there – and we could perhaps get to know the circus folk. I've always wanted to know about circuses.'

'Oh, *Julian*! That's a better idea still!' said

George, rubbing her hands together in delight. 'I liked that boy Nobby, didn't you!?'

'Yes,' said everyone.

'But I didn't like his uncle,' said Dick. 'He looked a nasty bit of work. I bet he makes Nobby toe the mark and do what he's told.'

'Julian, do you think we'd be allowed to go caravanning by ourselves?' asked Anne earnestly. 'It does seem to me to be the most marvellous idea we've ever had.'

'Well – we can ask and see,' said Julian. 'I'm old enough to look after you all.'

'Pooh!' said George. 'I don't want any looking after, thank you. And anyway, if we want looking after, Timmy can do that. I bet the grown-ups will be glad to be rid of us for a week or two. They always think the summer hols are too long.'

'We'll take Dobby with us to pull the caravan!' said Anne suddenly, looking down at the field where Dobby stood, patiently flicking away the flies with his long tail. 'Dobby would love that! I always think he must be lonely, living in that field all by himself, just being borrowed by people occasionally.'

'Of course – Dobby could come,' said Dick. 'That would be fine. Where could we get the caravan from? Are they easy to hire?'

'Don't know,' said Julian. 'I knew a chap at school – you remember him, Dick, that big fellow called Perry – he used to go caravanning every hols with his family. They used to hire caravans, I know. I might find out from him where he got them from.'

'Daddy will know,' said Anne. 'Or Mummy. Grown-ups always know things like that. I'd like a nice large caravan – red and blue – with a little chimney, and windows each side, and a door at the back, and steps to go up into the caravan, and—'

The others interrupted with their own ideas, and soon they were all talking excitedly about it – so loudly that they didn't see someone walking up and standing near by, laughing at the excitement.

'Woof,' said Timmy politely. He was the only

one who had ears and eyes for anything else at the moment. The children looked up.

'Oh, hallo, Mother!' said Julian. 'You've just come at the right moment. We want to tell you about an idea we've got.'

His mother sat down, smiling. 'You seem very excited about something,' she said. 'What is it?'

'Well, it's like this, Mummy,' said Anne, before anyone else could get a word in, 'we've made up our minds that we'd like to go off in a caravan for a holiday by ourselves! Oh, Mummy – it would be such fun!'

'By yourselves?' said her mother doubtfully. 'Well, I don't know about that.'

'Julian can look after us,' said Anne

'So can Timmy,' put in George at once, and Timmy thumped the ground with his tail. Of course he could look after them! Hadn't he done it for years, and shared all their adventures? Thump, thump, thump!

'I'll have to talk it over with Daddy,' said Mother. 'Now don't look so disappointed – I can't decide a thing like this all by myself in a hurry. But it may fit in quite well because I know Daddy has to go up north for a little while, and he would like me to go with him. So he might think a little caravanning quite a good idea. I'll talk to him tonight.'

'We could have Dobby to pull the caravan, Mummy,' said Anne, her eyes bright. 'Couldn't we? He'd love to come. He has such a dull life now.'

'We'll see, we'll see,' said her mother, getting up. 'Now you'd better all come in and wash. It's nearly tea-time. Your hair is terrible, Anne. What *have* you been doing?'

Everyone rushed indoors to wash, feeling distinctly cheerful. Mother hadn't said NO. She had even thought it might fit in quite well. Golly, to go off in a caravan all alone – doing their own cooking and washing – having Dobby for company, and Timmy as well, of course. How simply gorgeous.

The children's father did not come home until late that evening, which was a nuisance, for nobody felt that they could wait for very long to know whether they might or might not go. Everyone but Julian was in bed when he came home, and even when he, too, came to bed he had nothing to report.

He stuck his head into the girls' bedroom. 'Daddy's tired and he's having a late supper, and Mother won't bother him till he's feeling better. So we shan't know till morning, worse luck!'

The girls groaned. How could they possibly go to sleep with thoughts of caravans floating deliciously in their heads – not knowing whether or not they would be allowed to go!

'Blow!' said George. 'I shan't go to sleep for ages. Get off my feet, Timmy. Honestly, it's too hot to have you anywhere near me in this weather.'

In the morning good news awaited the four children. They sat down at the breakfast-table, all very punctual for once, and Julian looked expectantly at his mother. She smiled at him and nodded.

'Yes, we've talked it over,' she said. 'And Daddy says he doesn't see why you shouldn't have a caravan holiday. He thinks it would be good for you to go off and rough it a bit. But you will have to have two caravans, not one. We couldn't have all four of you, and Timmy too, living in one caravan.'

'Oh – but Dobby couldn't pull *two* caravans, Mummy,' said Anne.

'We can borrow another horse,' said Julian. 'Can't we, Mother? Thanks awfully, Daddy, for saying we can go. It's jolly good of you.'

'Absolutely super,' said Dick.

'Wizard!' said George, her fingers scratching Timmy's head excitedly. 'When can we go? Tomorrow?'

'Of course not!' said Julian. 'We've got to get the caravans – and borrow a horse – and pack – and all sorts of things.'

'You can go next week, when I take your mother up north with me,' said his father. 'That will suit us very well. We can give Cook a holiday, too, then. You will have to send us a card every single day to tell us how you are and where you are.'

'It does sound thrilling,' said Anne. 'I really don't feel as if I can eat any breakfast, Mummy.'

'Well, if that's the effect the idea of caravanning has on you, I don't think you'd better go,' said her mother. Anne hastily began to eat her shredded wheat, and her appetite soon came back. It was too good to be true – to have *two* caravans – and *two* horses – and sleep in bunks perhaps – and cook meals outside in the open air – and . . .

'You will be in complete charge, you understand, Julian,' said the boy's father. 'You are old enough now to be really responsible. The others must realise that you are in charge and they must do as you say.'

'Yes,' said Julian, feeling proud. 'I'll see to things all right.'

'And Timmy will be in charge, too,' said George. 'He's just as responsible as Julian.'

'Woof,' said Timmy, hearing his name, and thumping the floor with his tail.

'You're a darling, Timmy,' said Anne. 'I'll always do what *you* say, as well as what Julian says!'

'Idiot!' said Dick. He patted Timmy's head. 'I bet we wouldn't be allowed to go without you, Timothy. You are a jolly good guard for anyone.'

'You certainly wouldn't be allowed to go without Timmy,' said his mother. 'We know you'll be safe with him.'

It was all most exciting. The children went off to talk things over by themselves when breakfast was finished.

'I vote we go caravanning up into the hills that boy spoke of, where the lake lies at the bottom – and camp there,' said Julian. 'We'd have company then – jolly exciting company, too. We wouldn't live *too* near the circus camp – they might not like strangers butting in – but we'll live near enough to see the elephant going for his daily walk, and the dogs being exercised . . .'

'And we'll make friends with Nobby, won't

we?' said Anne eagerly. 'I liked him. We won't go near his uncle, though. I think it's strange that such a bad-tempered looking man should be the chief clown in a circus.'

'I wonder when and where Mother will get the caravans!' said Julian. 'Gosh, won't it be fun when we see them for the first time!'

'Let's go and tell Dobby!' said Anne. 'He is sure to be excited, too!'

'Baby! He won't understand a word you tell him!' said George. But off she went with Anne just the same, and soon Dobby was hearing all about the wonderful holiday plan. Hrrrrumph! So long as it included him, too, he was happy!

[3]

The caravans arrive

At last the great day came when the two caravans were due to arrive. The children stood at the end of the drive for hours, watching for them.

Mother had managed to borrow them from an old friend of hers. The children had promised faithfully to look after them well, and not to damage anything. Now they stood at the end of the drive, watching eagerly for the caravans to arrive.

'They are being drawn by cars today,' said Julian. 'But they are fitted up to be horse-drawn, too. I wonder what they are like – and what colour they are.'

'Will they be like travellers' caravans, on high wheels, do you think?' asked Anne. Julian shook his head.

'No, they're modern, Mother says. Streamlined and all that. Not too big either, because a horse can't draw too heavy a van.'

'They're coming, they're coming! I can see them!' suddenly yelled George, making them all jump. 'Look, isn't that them, far down the road?'

They all looked hard into the distance. No one had such good eyes as George, and all they could see was a blotch, a moving speck far away on the road. But George's eyes saw two caravans, one behind the other.

'George is right,' said Julian, straining his eyes. 'It's our caravans. They're each drawn by a small car.'

'One's red and the other's green,' said Anne. 'Bags I the red one. Oh, hurry up, caravans!'

At last they were near enough to see properly. The children ran to meet them. They certainly were very nice ones, quite modern and 'streamlined', as Julian had said, well built and comfortable.

'They almost reach the ground!' said Anne.

'And look at the wheels, set so neatly into the side of the vans. I do like the red one, bags I the red one.'

Each van had a little chimney, long, narrow windows down the two sides, and tiny ones in front by the driver's seat. There was a broad door at the back and two steps down. Pretty curtains fluttered at the open windows.

'Red curtains for the green caravan, and green ones for the red caravan!' said Anne. 'Oh, I want to go inside!'

But she couldn't because the doors were locked. So she had to be content to run with the others up the drive after the two caravans, shouting loudly:

'Mummy! They're here, the caravans are here.'

Her mother came running down the steps to see. Soon the doors were unlocked and the children went inside the caravans. Delighted shouts came from both vans.

'Bunks along one side – is that where we sleep? How gorgeous!'

'Look at this little sink – we can really wash up. And golly, water comes out of these taps!'

'There's a proper stove to cook on – but I vote we cook out of doors on a camp-fire. I say, look at the bright frying-pans – and all the cups and saucers hanging up!'

'It's like a proper little house inside. Doesn't it seem nice and *big*? Mother, isn't it beautifully planned? Don't you wish you were coming with us?'

'Hey, you girls! Do you see where the water comes from? Out of that tank on the roof. It must collect rainwater. And look at this gadget for heating water. Isn't it all super?'

The children spent hours examining their caravans and finding out all the secrets. They certainly were very well fitted, spotlessly clean, and very roomy. George felt as if she couldn't wait to start out. She really must get Dobby and set out at once!

'No, you must wait, silly,' said Julian. 'You know we've to get the other horse. He's not coming till tomorrow.'

The other horse was a sturdy little black fellow called Trotter. He belonged to the milkman, who often lent him out. He was a sensible little horse, and the children knew him very well and liked him. They all learnt riding at school, and knew how to groom and look after a horse, so there would be no difficulty over their managing Dobby and Trotter.

Mother was thrilled over the caravans, too, and looked very longingly at them. 'If I wasn't going with Daddy I should be most tempted to come with you,' she said. 'Don't look so startled, Anne dear – I'm not really coming!'

'We're jolly lucky to get such decent caravans,' said Julian. 'We'd better pack our things today, hadn't we, Mother – and start off tomorrow, now we've got the caravans.'

'You won't need to pack,' said his mother. 'All you have to do is to pop your things straight into the cupboards and drawers – you will only want clothes and books and a few games to play in case it's rainy.'

'We don't need any clothes except our night

things, do we?' said George, who would have lived in a jersey and jeans all day and every day if she had been allowed to.

'You must take plenty of jerseys, another pair of jeans each, in case you get wet, your rain-coats, bathing-things, towels, a change of shoes, night things, and some cool shirts or blouses,' said Mother. Everyone groaned.

'What a frightful lot of things!' said Dick. 'There'll never be room for all those.'

'Oh yes there will,' said Mother. 'You will be sorry if you take too few clothes, get soaked through, have nothing to change into, and catch fearful colds that will stop you from enjoying a lovely holiday like this.'

'Come on, let's get the things,' said Dick. 'Once Mother starts off about catching cold there's no knowing what else she'll make us take – is there, Mother?'

'You're a cheeky boy,' said his mother, smiling. 'Yes, go and collect your things. I'll help you to put them into the cupboards and drawers. Isn't it marvellous how everything folds so neatly into the walls of the caravans – there seems to be room for everything, and you don't notice the cupboards.'

'I shall keep everything very clean,' said Anne. 'You know how I like *playing* at keeping house, don't you, Mother – well, it will be real this time. I shall have two caravans to keep clean, all by myself.'

'All by yourself!' said her mother. 'Well, surely the boys will help you – and certainly George must.'

'Pooh, the boys!' said Anne. 'They won't know how to wash and dry a cup properly – and George never bothers about things like that. If I don't make the bunks and wash the crockery, they would never be made or washed, I know that!'

'Well, it's a good thing that one of you is sensible!' said her mother. 'You'll find that everyone will share in the work, Anne. Now off you go and get your things. Bring all the raincoats, to start with.'

It was fun taking things down to the caravans

and packing them all in. There were shelves for a few books and games, so Julian brought down snap cards, ludo, lexicon, happy families and dominoes, as well as four or five books for each of them. He also brought down some maps of the district, because he meant to plan out where they were to go, and the best roads to follow.

Daddy had given him a useful little book in which were the names of farms that would give permission to caravanners to camp in fields for the night. 'You must always choose a field where there is a stream, if possible,' said his father, 'because Dobby and Trotter will want water.'

'Remember to boil every drop of water you drink,' said the children's mother. 'That's very important. Get as much milk from the farms as they will let you have. And remember that there is plenty of ginger-beer in the locker under the second caravan.'

'It's all so thrilling,' said Anne, peering down to look at the locker into which Julian had put the bottles of ginger-beer. 'I can't believe we're really going tomorrow.'

But it was true. Dobby and Trotter were to be taken to the caravans the next day and harnessed. How exciting for them, too, Anne thought.

Timmy couldn't quite understand all the excitement, but he shared in it, of course, and kept his tail on the wag all day long. He examined the caravans thoroughly from end to end, found a rug he liked the smell of, and lay down on it. 'This is *my* corner,' he seemed to say. 'If you go off in these peculiar houses on wheels, this is my own little corner.'

'We'll have the red caravan, George,' said Anne. 'The boys can have the green one. They don't care what colour they have – but I love red. I say, won't it be fun to sleep in those bunks? They look jolly comfortable.'

At last tomorrow came – and the milkman brought the sturdy little black horse, Trotter, up the drive. Julian fetched Dobby from the field. The horses nuzzled one another and

Dobby went 'Hrrrumph' in a very civil horsy voice.

'They're going to like each other,' said Anne. 'Look at them nuzzling. Trotter, you're going to draw *my* caravan.'

The two horses stood patiently while they were harnessed. Dobby jerked his head once or twice as if he was impatient to be off and stamped a little.

'Oh, Dobby, I feel like that, too!' said Anne. 'Don't you, Dick, don't you, Julian?'

'I do rather,' said Dick with a grin. 'Get up there, Dobby – that's right. Who's going to drive, Julian – take it in turns, shall we?'

'I'm going to drive *our* caravan,' said George. 'Anne wouldn't be any good at it, though I'll let her have a turn at it sometimes. Driving is a man's job.'

'Well, you're only a girl!' said Anne indignantly. 'You're not a man, nor even a boy!'

George put on one of her scowls. She always

wanted to be a boy, and even thought of herself as one. She didn't like to be reminded that she was a girl. But not even George could scowl for long that exciting morning! She soon began to caper round and about again, laughing and calling out with the others:

'We're ready! Surely we're ready!'

'Yes. Do let's go! JULIAN! He's gone indoors, the idiot, just when we want to start.'

'He's gone to get the cakes that Cook has baked this morning for us. We've heaps of food in the larder. I feel hungry already.'

'Here's Julian. Do come on, Julian. We'll drive off without you. Goodbye, Mother! We'll send you a card every single day, we faithfully promise.'

Julian got up on the front of the green caravan. He clicked to Dobby. 'Get on, Dobby! We're off! Goodbye, Mother!'

Dick sat beside him, grinning with pure happiness. The caravans moved off down the drive. George pulled at Trotter's reins and the little horse followed the caravan in front. Anne, sitting beside George, waved wildly.

'Goodbye, Mother! We're off at last on another adventure. Hurrah! Three cheers! Hurrah!'

[4]

Away they go!

The caravans went slowly down the wide road. Julian was so happy that he sang at the top of his voice, and the others joined in the choruses. Timmy barked excitedly. He was sitting on one side of George and as Anne was on the other, George was decidedly squashed. But little things like that did not bother her at all.

Dobby plodded on slowly, enjoying the sunshine and the little breeze that raised the hairs on his mane. Trotter followed at a short distance. He was very much interested in Timmy, and always turned his head when the dog barked or got down for a run. It was fun to have two horses and a dog to travel with.

It had been decided that they should make their way towards the hills where they hoped to find the circus. Julian had traced the place on his map. He was sure it must be right because of the lake that lay in the valley at the foot of the hills.

'See?' he said to the others, pointing. 'There it is – Lake Merran. I bet we'll find the circus camp somewhere near it. It would be a very good place for all their animals – no one to interfere with the camp, plenty of water for both animals and men, and probably good farms to supply them with food.'

'We'll have to find a good farm ourselves tonight,' said Dick. 'And ask permission to camp. Lucky we've got that little book telling us where to go and ask.'

Anne thought with delight of the coming evening, when they would stop and camp, cook a meal, drowse over a camp-fire, and go to sleep in the little bunks. She didn't know which was nicer – ambling along down country lanes with the caravans – or preparing to settle in for the night. She was sure it was going to be the nicest holiday they had ever had.

'Don't you think so?' she asked George as

they sat together on the driving-seat, with Timmy, for once, trotting beside the caravan, and leaving them a little more room than usual. 'You know, most of our hols have been packed with adventures – awfully exciting, I know – but I'd like an *ordinary* holiday now, wouldn't you – not *too* exciting.'

'Oh, I like adventures,' said George, shaking the reins and making Trotter do a little trot. 'I wouldn't a bit mind having another one. But we shan't this time, Anne. No such luck!'

They stopped for a meal at half past twelve, all of them feeling very hungry. Dobby and Trotter moved towards a ditch in which long, juicy grass grew, and munched away happily.

The children lay on a sunny bank and ate and drank. Anne looked at George. 'You've got more freckles these hols, George, than you ever had in your life before.'

'That doesn't worry *me*!' said George, who never cared in the least how she looked, and was even angry with her hair for being too curly, and making her look too much like a girl.

'Pass the sandwiches, Anne – the tomato ones – golly, if we always feel as hungry as this we'll have to buy eggs and bacon and butter and milk at every farm we pass!'

They set off again. Dick took his turn at driving Dobby, and Julian walked to stretch his legs. George still wanted to drive, but Anne felt too sleepy to sit beside her with safety.

'If I shut my eyes and sleep I shall fall off the seat,' she said. 'I'd better go into the caravan and sleep there.'

So in she went, all by herself. It was cool and dim inside the caravan, for the curtains had been pulled across the window to keep the inside cool. Anne climbed on to one of the bunks and lay down. She shut her eyes. The caravan rumbled slowly on, and the little girl fell asleep.

Julian peeped in at her and grinned. Timmy came and looked, too, but Julian wouldn't let him go in and wake Anne by licking her.

'You come and walk with me, Tim,' he said. 'You're getting fat. Exercise will do you good.'

'He's *not* getting fat!' called George, indignantly. 'He's a very nice shape. Don't you listen to him, Timmy.'

'Woof,' said Timmy, and trotted along at Julian's heels.

The two caravans covered quite a good distance that day, even though they went slowly. Julian did not miss the way once. He was very good indeed at map-reading. Anne was disappointed that they could not see the hills they were making for, at the end of the day.

'Goodness, they're miles and miles away!' said Julian. 'We shan't arrive for at least four or five days, silly! Now, look out for a farm, kids. There should be one near here, where we can ask permission to camp for the night.'

'There's one, surely,' said George, after a few minutes. She pointed to where a red-roofed building, with moss-covered barns, stood glowing in the evening sun. Hens clucked about it, and a dog or two watched them from a gateway.

'Yes, that's the one,' said Julian, examining

his map. 'Longman's Farm. There should be a stream near it. There it is, look – in that field. Now, if we could get permission to camp just here, it would be lovely.'

Julian went to the farm to see the farmer, and Anne went with him to ask for eggs. The farmer was not there, but the farmer's wife, who liked the look of the tall polite Julian very much, gave them permission at once to spend the night in the field by the stream.

'I know you won't leave a lot of litter, or go chasing the farm animals,' she said. 'Or leave the gates open like some campers do. And what's that you want, Missy – some new-laid eggs? Yes, of course, you can have some – and you can pick the ripe plums off that tree, too, to go with your supper!'

There was bacon in the larder of the caravans, and Anne said she would fry that and an egg each for everyone. She was very proud of being able to cook them. She had taken a few lessons from Cook in the last few days, and was very anxious to show the others what she had learnt.

Julian said it was too hot to cook in the caravan, and he built her a fine fire in the field. Dick set the two horses free and they wandered off to the stream, where they stood knee-high in the cool water, enjoying it immensely. Trotter muzzled against Dobby, and then tried to nuzzle down to Timmy, too, when the big dog came to drink beside him.

'Doesn't the bacon smell lovely?' called Anne to George, who was busy getting plates and mugs out of the red caravan. 'Let's have ginger-beer to drink, George. I'm jolly thirsty. Watch me crack these eggs on the edge of this cup, everybody, so that I can get out the yolk and white and fry them.' Crack! The egg broke against the edge of the cup – but its contents unfortunately fell outside the cup instead of inside. Anne went red when everyone roared with laughter.

Timmy came and licked up the mess. He was very useful for that sort of thing. 'You'd make a good dustbin, Timmy,' said Anne. 'Here's a bit of bacon-rind, too. Catch!'

Anne fried the bacon and eggs really well. The others were most admiring, even George, and they all cleared their plates well, wiping the last bit of fat off with bread, so that they would be easy to wash.

'Do you think Timmy would like me to fry him a few dog-biscuits, instead of having them cold?' said Anne, suddenly. 'Fried things are so nice. I'm sure Timmy would like fried biscuits better than ordinary ones.'

'Well, he wouldn't,' said George. 'They would just make him sick.'

'How do you know?' said Anne. 'You can't possibly tell.'

'I always know what Timmy would really like and what he wouldn't,' said George. 'And he wouldn't like his biscuits fried. Pass the plums, Dick. They look super.'

They lingered over the little camp-fire for a long time, and then Julian said it was time for bed. Nobody minded, because they all wanted to try sleeping on the comfortable-looking bunks.

'Shall I wash at the stream or in the little sink where I washed the plates?' said Anne. 'I don't know which would be nicer.'

'There's more water to spare in the stream,' said Julian. 'Hurry up, won't you, because I want to lock your caravan door so that you'll be safe.'

'Lock our door!' said George, indignantly. 'You jolly well won't! Nobody's going to lock *me* in! I might think I'd like to take a walk in the moonlight or something.'

'Yes, but a tramp or somebody might—' began Julian. George interrupted him scornfully.

'What about Timmy? You know jolly well he'd never let anyone come *near* our caravans, let alone into them! I won't be locked in, Julian. I couldn't bear it. Timmy's better than any locked door.'

'Well, I suppose he is,' said Julian. 'All right, don't look so furious, George. Walk half the night in moonlight if you want to – though there won't be any moon tonight, I'm sure. Golly, I'm sleepy!'

They climbed into the two caravans, after washing in the stream. They all undressed and got into the inviting bunks. There was a sheet, one blanket and a rug – but all the children threw off both blanket and rug and kept only a sheet over them that hot night.

At first Anne tried sleeping in the lower bunk, beneath George – but Timmy would keep on trying to clamber up to get to George. He wanted to lie on her feet as usual. Anne got cross.

'George! You'd better change places with me. Timmy keeps jumping on me and walking all over me trying to get up to your bunk. I'll never get to sleep.'

So George changed places, and after that Timmy made no more noise, but lay contentedly at the end of George's bunk on the rolled-up blanket, while Anne lay in the bunk above, trying not to go to sleep because it was such a lovely feeling to be inside a caravan that stood by a stream in a field.

Owls hooted to one another, and Timmy

growled softly. The voice of the stream, contented and babbling, could be quite clearly heard now that everything was so quiet. Anne felt her eyes closing. Oh dear – she would simply *have* to go to sleep.

But something suddenly awoke her with a jump, and Timmy barked so loudly that both Anne and George almost fell out of their bunks in fright. Something bumped violently against the caravan, and shook it from end to end! Was somebody trying to get in?

Timmy leapt to the floor and ran to the door, which George had left open a little because of the heat. Then the voices of Dick and Julian were heard.

'What's up? Are you girls all right? We're coming!' And over the wet grass raced the two boys in their dressing-gowns. Julian ran straight into something hard and warm and solid. He yelled.

Dick switched on his torch and began to laugh helplessly. 'You ran straight into Dobby. Look at him staring at you! He must have lumbered all round our caravans making the bumps we heard. It's all right, girls. It's only Dobby.'

So back they all went again to sleep, and this time they slept till the morning, not even stirring when Trotter, too, came to nuzzle round the caravan and snort softly in the night.

[5]

The way to Merran Lake

The next three or four days were absolutely perfect, the children thought. Blue skies, blazing sun, wayside streams to paddle or bathe in, and two houses on wheels that went rumbling for miles down roads and lanes quite new to them – what could be lovelier for four children all on their own?

Timmy seemed to enjoy everything thoroughly, too, and had made firm friends with Trotter, the little black horse. Trotter was always looking for Timmy to run beside him, and he whinnied to Timmy whenever he wanted him. The two horses were friends, too, and when they were set free at night they made for the stream together, and stood in the water side by side, nuzzling one another happily.

'I like this holiday better than any we've ever

had,' said Anne, busily cooking something in a pan. 'It's exciting without being adventurous. And although Julian thinks he's in charge of us, *I* am really! You'd never get your bunks made, or your meals cooked, or the caravans kept clean if it wasn't for me!'

'Don't boast!' said George, feeling rather guilty because she let Anne do so much.

'I'm not boasting!' said Anne, indignantly. 'I'm just telling the truth. Why, you've never even made your own bunk once, George. Not that I mind doing it. I love having two houses on wheels to look after.'

'You're a very good little housekeeper,' said Julian. 'We couldn't possibly do without you!'

Anne blushed with pride. She took the pan off the camp-fire and put the contents on to four plates. 'Come along!' she called, in a voice just like her mother's. 'Have your meal while it's hot.'

'I'd rather have mine when it's cold, thank you,' said George. 'It doesn't seem to have got a bit cooler, even though it's evening-time.'

They had been on the road four days now, and Anne had given up looking for the hills where they hoped to find the circus folk camping. In fact she secretly hoped they wouldn't find them, because she was so much enjoying the daily wanderings over the lovely countryside.

Timmy came to lick the plates. The children always let him do that now because it made them so much easier to wash. Anne and George took the things down to a little brown brook to rinse, and Julian took out his map.

He and Dick pored over it. 'We're just about here,' said Julian, pointing. 'And if so, it looks as if tomorrow we ought to come to those hills above the lake. Then we should see the circus.'

'Good!' said Dick. 'I hope Nobby will be there. He would love to show us round, I'm sure. He would show us a good place to camp, too, perhaps.'

'Oh, we can find that ourselves,' said Julian, who now rather prided himself on picking excellent camping sites. 'Anyway, I don't want to be *too* near the circus. It might be a bit smelly. I'd rather be up in the hills some way above it. We'll get a place with a lovely view.'

'Right,' said Dick, and Julian folded up the map. The two girls came back with the clean crockery, and Anne put it neatly back on the shelves in the red caravan. Trotter came to look for Timmy, who was lying panting under George's caravan.

Timmy wouldn't budge, so Trotter tried to get under the caravan too. But he couldn't possibly, of course, for he was much too big. So he lay down on the shady side, as near to Timmy as he could get.

'Trotter's really a comic horse,' said Dick. 'He'd be quite good in a circus, I should think! Did you see him chasing Timmy yesterday – just as if they were playing "tag"?'

The word 'circus' reminded them of Nobby and his circus, and they began to talk eagerly of all the animals there.

'I liked the look of the elephant,' said George.

'I wonder what his name is. And wouldn't I like to hold a monkey!'

'I bet that chimpanzee's clever,' said Dick. 'I wonder what Timmy will think of him. I hope he'll get on all right with all the animals, especially the other dogs.'

'I hope we don't see much of Nobby's uncle,' said Anne. 'He looked as if he'd like to box anybody's ears if they so much as answered him back.'

'Well, he won't box *mine*,' said Julian. 'We'll keep out of his way. He doesn't look a very pleasant chap, I must say. Perhaps he won't be there.'

'Timmy, come out from under the caravan!' called George. 'It's quite cool and shady where we are. Come on!'

He came, panting. Trotter immediately got up and came with him. The little horse lay down beside Timmy and nuzzled him. Timmy gave his nose a lick and then turned away, looking bored.

'Isn't Trotter funny?' said Anne. 'Timmy,

what *will* you think of all the circus animals, I wonder! I do hope we see the circus tomorrow. Shall we get as far as the hills, Julian? Though really I shan't mind a bit if we don't; it's so nice being on our own like this.'

They all looked out for the hills the next day as the caravans rumbled slowly down the lanes, pulled by Trotter and Dobby. And, in the afternoon, they saw them, blue in the distance.

'There they are!' said Julian. 'Those must be the Merran Hills – and Merran Lake must lie at the foot. I say, I hope the two horses are strong enough to pull the caravans a good way up. There should be an absolutely marvellous view over the lake if we get up high enough.'

The hills came nearer and nearer. They were high ones, and looked lovely in the evening light. Julian looked at his watch.

'We shan't have time to climb them and find a camping site there tonight, I'm afraid,' he said. 'We'd better camp a little way on this evening, and then make our way up into the hills tomorrow morning.'

'All right,' said Dick. 'Anything you say, Captain! There should be a farm about two miles on, according to the book. We'll camp there.'

They came to the farm, which was set by a wide stream that ran swiftly along. Julian went as usual to ask permission to camp, and Dick went with him, leaving the two girls to prepare a meal.

Julian easily got permission, and the farmer's daughter, a plump, jolly girl, sold the boys eggs, bacon, milk, and butter, besides a little crock of yellow cream. She also offered them raspberries from the garden if they liked to pick them and have them with the cream.

'Oh, I say, thanks awfully,' said Julian. 'Could you tell me if there's a circus camping in those hills? Somewhere by the lake.'

'Yes, it went by about a week ago,' said the girl. 'It goes camping there every year, for a rest. I always watch the caravans go by – quite a treat in a quiet place like this! One year they had lions, and at nights I could hear them roaring away. That fair frizzled my spine!'

The boys said goodbye and went off, chuckling to think of the farm-girl's spine being 'fair frizzled' by the roars of the distant lions.

'Well, it looks as if we'll pass the circus camp tomorrow all right,' said Julian. 'I shall enjoy camping up in the hills, won't you, Dick? It will be cooler up there, I expect – usually there's a breeze on the hills.'

'I hope we shan't get our spines fair frizzled by the noise of the circus animals at night,' grinned Dick. 'I feel fair frizzled up by the sun today, I must say!'

The next morning the caravans set off again on what the children hoped would be the last lap of their journey. They would find a lovely camping-place and stay there till they had to go home.

Julian had remembered to send a postcard each day to his parents, telling them where he was, and that everything was fine. He had found out from the farm-girl the right address for that district, and he planned to arrange with the nearest post office to take in any letters for them that came. They had not been able to receive any post, of course, when they were wandering about in their caravans.

Dobby and Trotter walked sedately down the narrow country lane that led towards the hills. Suddenly George caught sight of something flashing blue between the trees.

'Look! There's the lake! Merran Lake!' she shouted. 'Make Dobby go more quickly, Ju. I'm longing to come out into the open and see the lake.'

Soon the lane ended in a broad cart-track that led over a heathery common. The common sloped right down to the edge of an enormous blue lake that lay glittering in the August sunshine.

'I say! Isn't it magnificent?' said Dick, stopping Dobby with a pull. 'Come on, let's get down and go to the edge, Julian. Come on, girls!'

'It's lovely!' said Anne, jumping down from the driving-seat of the red caravan. 'Oh, do let's bathe straight away!'

'Yes, let's,' said Julian, and they all dived into their caravans, stripped off jeans and shirts and pulled on bathing-things. Then, without even a towel to dry themselves on, they tore down to the lakeside, eager to plunge into its blue coolness.

It was very warm at the edge of the water, but further in, where it was deep, the lake was deliciously cold. All the children could swim strongly, and they splashed and yelled in delight. The bottom of the lake was sandy, so the water was as clear as crystal.

When they were tired they all came out and lay on the warm sandy bank of the lake. They dried at once in the sun. Then as soon as they felt too hot in they went again, squealing with joy at the cold water.

'What gorgeous fun to come down here every day and bathe!' said Dick. 'Get away, Timmy, when I'm swimming on my back. Timmy's enjoying the bathe as much as we are, George.'

'Yes, and old Trotter wants to come in, too,' shouted Julian. 'Look at him – he's brought the red caravan right down to the edge of the lake. He'll be in the water with it if we don't stop him!'

They decided to have a picnic by the lake, and to set the horses free to have a bathe if they wanted one. But all they wanted was to drink and to stand knee-high in the water, swishing their tails to keep away the flies that worried them all day long.

'Where's the circus camp?' said George suddenly as they sat munching ham and tomato sandwiches. 'I can't see it.'

The children looked all round the edge of the lake, which stretched as far as they could see. At last George's sharp eyes saw a small spire of smoke rising in the air about a mile or so round the lake.

'The camp must be in that hollow at the foot of the hills over there,' she said. 'I expect the road leads round to it. We'll go that way, shall we, and then go up into the hills behind?'

'Yes,' agreed Julian. 'We shall have plenty of time to have a word with Nobby, and to find a good camping-place before night comes – and to find a farm, too, that will let us have food. Won't Nobby be surprised to see us?'

They cleared up, put the horses into their harness again and set off for the circus camp. Now for a bit of excitement!

[6]

The circus camp and Nobby

It did not take the caravans very long to come in sight of the circus camp. As George had said, it was in a comfortable hollow, set at the foot of the hills – a quiet spot, well away from any dwelling-places, where the circus animals could enjoy a certain amount of freedom and be exercised in peace.

The caravans were set round in a wide circle. Tents had been put up here and there. The big elephant was tied by a thick rope to a stout tree. Dogs ran about everywhere, and a string of shining horses was being paraded round a large field nearby.

'There they all are!' said Anne, excitedly, standing up on the driving-seat to see better. 'Golly, the chimpanzee is loose, isn't he? No, he isn't – someone has got him on a rope. Is it Nobby with him?'

'Yes, it is. I say, fancy walking about with a live chimp like that!' said Julian.

The children looked at everything with the greatest interest as their caravans came nearer to the circus camp. Few people seemed to be about that hot afternoon. Nobby was there with the chimpanzee, and one or two women were stirring pots over small fires – but that seemed to be all.

The circus dogs set up a great barking as the red and green caravans drew nearer. One or two men came out of the tents and looked up the track that led to the camp. They pointed to the children's caravans and seemed astonished.

Nobby, with the chimpanzee held firmly by the paw, came out of the camp in curiosity to meet the strange caravans. Julian hailed him.

'Hi, Nobby! You didn't think you'd see *us* here, did you?'

Nobby was amazed to hear his name called. At first he did not remember the children at all. Then he gave a yell.

'Jumping Jiminy, it's you kids I saw away back on the road! What are *you* doing here?'

Timmy growled ominously and George called to Nobby. 'He's never seen a chimpanzee before. Do you think they'll be friends?'

'Don't know,' said Nobby doubtfully. 'Old Pongo likes the circus dogs all right. Anyway, don't you let your dog fly at Pongo, or he'll be eaten alive! A chimp is very strong, you know.'

'Could I make friends with Pongo, do you think?' asked George. 'If he would shake hands with me, or something, Timmy would know I was friends with him and he'd be all right. Would Pongo make friends with me?'

''Course he will!' said Nobby. 'He's the sweetest-tempered chimp alive – aren't you, Pongo? Now, shake hands with the lady.'

Anne didn't feel at all inclined to go near the chimpanzee, but George was quite fearless. She walked up to the big animal and held out her hand. The chimpanzee took it at once, raised it to his mouth and pretended to nibble it, making friendly noises all the time.

George laughed. 'He's nice, isn't he?' she said. 'Timmy, this is Pongo, a friend. Nice Pongo, good Pongo!'

She patted Pongo on the shoulder to show Timmy that she liked the chimpanzee, and Pongo at once patted her on the shoulder, too, grinning amiably. He then patted her on the head and pulled one of her curls.

Timmy wagged his tail a little. He looked very doubtful indeed. What was this strange creature that his mistress appeared to like so much? He took a step towards Pongo.

'Come on, Timmy, say how do you do to Pongo,' said George. 'Like this.' And she shook hands with the chimpanzee again. This time he wouldn't let her hand go, but went on shaking it up and down as if he was pumping water with a pump-handle.

'He won't let go,' said George.

'Don't be naughty, Pongo,' said Nobby in a stern voice. Pongo at once dropped George's hand and covered his face with a hairy paw as if he was ashamed. But the children saw that he was peeping through his fingers with wicked eyes that twinkled with fun.

'He's a real monkey!' said George, laughing.

'You're wrong – he's an ape!' said Nobby. 'Ah, here comes Timmy to make friends. Jumping Jiminy, they're shaking paws!'

So they were. Timmy, having once made up his mind that Pongo was to be a friend, remembered his manners and held out his right paw as he had been taught. Pongo seized it and shook it vigorously. Then he walked round to the back of Timmy and shook hands with his tail. Timmy didn't know what to make of it all.

The children yelled with laughter, and Timmy sat down firmly on his tail. Then he stood up again, his tail wagging, for Barker and Growler had come rushing up. Timmy remembered them, and they remembered him.

'Well, *they're* making friends all right,' said Nobby, pleased. 'Now they'll introduce Timmy to all the other dogs, and there'll be no trouble. Hey, look out for Pongo, there!'

The chimpanzee had stolen round to the

back of Julian and was slipping his hand into the boy's pocket. Nobby went to him and slapped the chimpanzee's paw hard.

'Naughty! Bad boy! Pickpocket!'

The children laughed again when the chimpanzee covered his face with his paws, pretending to be ashamed.

'You'll have to watch out when Pongo's about,' said Nobby. 'He loves to take things out of people's pockets. I say – do tell me – are those your caravans? Aren't they posh?'

'They've been lent to us,' said Dick. 'As a matter of fact, it was seeing your circus go by, with all its colourful caravans, that made us think of borrowing caravans, too, and coming away for a holiday.'

'And as you'd told us where you were going we thought we'd follow you and find you out, and get you to show us round the camp,' said Julian. 'Hope you don't mind.'

'I'm proud,' said Nobby, going a bright red. ''Tisn't often folks want to make friends with a circus fellow like me – not gentlefolk like you, I mean. I'll be proud to show you round – and you can make friends with every blessed monkey, dog and horse in the place!'

'Oh, thanks!' said all four at once.

'That's kind of you,' said Dick. 'Gosh, look at that chimp – he's trying to shake hands with Timmy's tail again. I bet he's funny in the circus ring, isn't he, Nobby?'

'He's a scream,' said Nobby. 'Brings the house down. You should see him act with my Uncle Dan. He's the chief clown, you know. Pongo is just as big a clown as my uncle is – it's a fair scream to see them act the fool together.'

'I wish we *could* see them,' said Anne. 'Acting in the ring, I mean. Will your uncle mind you showing us all the animals and everything?'

'Why should he?' said Nobby. 'Shan't ask him! But you mind and act polite to him, won't you? He's worse than a tiger when he's in a temper. They call him Tiger Dan because of his rages.'

Anne didn't like the sound of that at all – Tiger Dan! It sounded very fierce and savage.

'I hope he isn't about anywhere now,' she said nervously, looking round.

'No. He's gone off somewhere,' said Nobby. 'He's a lonesome sort of chap – got no friends much in the circus, except Lou, the acrobat. That's Lou over there.'

Lou was a long-limbed, loose-jointed fellow with an ugly face, and a crop of black shining hair that curled tightly. He sat on the steps of a caravan, smoking a pipe and reading a paper. The children thought that he and Tiger Dan would make a good pair – bad-tempered, scowling and unfriendly. They all made up their minds that they would have as little as possible to do with Lou the acrobat and Tiger Dan the clown.

'Is he a very good acrobat?' said Anne in a low voice, though Lou was much too far away to hear her.

'Fine. First class,' said Nobby with admiration in his voice. 'He can climb anything anywhere – he could go up that tree there like a monkey – and I've seen him climb a drainpipe straight up the side of a tall building just like a cat. He's a marvel. You should see him on the tight-rope, too. He can dance on it!'

The children gazed at Lou with awe. He felt their glances, looked up and scowled. 'Well,' thought Julian, 'he may be the finest acrobat that ever lived – but he's a jolly nasty-looking fellow. There's not much to choose between him and Tiger Dan!'

Lou got up, uncurling his long body like a cat. He moved easily and softly. He loped over to Nobby, still with the ugly scowl on his face.

'Who are these kids?' he said. 'What are they doing messing about here?'

'We're not messing about,' said Julian politely. 'We came to see Nobby. We've seen him before.'

Lou looked at Julian as if he was something that smelt nasty. 'Those your caravans?' he asked, jerking his head towards them.

'Yes,' said Julian.

'Posh, aren't you?' said Lou sneeringly.

'Not particularly,' said Julian, still polite.

'Any grown-ups with you?' asked Lou.

'No. I'm in charge,' said Julian, 'and we've got a dog that flies at people he doesn't like.'

Timmy clearly didn't like Lou. He stood near him, growling in his throat. Lou kicked out at him.

George caught hold of Timmy's collar just in time. 'Down Tim, down!' she cried. Then she turned on Lou, her eyes blazing.

'Don't you dare kick my dog!' she shouted. 'He'll have you down on the ground if you do. You keep out of his way, or he'll go for you now.'

Lou spat on the ground in contempt and turned to go. 'You clear out,' he said. 'We don't want any kids messing about here. And I'm not afraid of any dog. I've got ways of dealing with bad dogs.'

'What do you mean by that?' yelled George, still in a furious temper. But Lou did not bother to reply. He went up the steps of his caravan and slammed the door shut. Timmy barked angrily and tugged at his collar, which George was still holding firmly.

'Now you've torn it!' said Nobby dismally. 'If Lou catches you about anywhere he'll hoof you out. And you be careful of that dog of yours, or he'll disappear.'

George was angry and alarmed. 'Disappear! What do you mean? If you think Timmy would let anyone steal him, you're wrong.'

'All right, all right. I'm only telling you. Don't fly at me like that!' said Nobby. 'Jumping Jiminy, look at that chimp. He's gone inside one of your caravans!'

The sudden storm was forgotten as everyone rushed to the green caravan. Pongo was inside, helping himself liberally from a tin of sweets. As soon as he saw the children he groaned and covered his face with his paws – but he sucked hard at the sweets all the time.

'Pongo! Bad boy! Come here!' scolded Nobby. 'Shall I whip you?'

'Oh, no, don't,' begged Anne. 'He's a scamp, but I do like him. We've plenty of sweets to spare. You have some, too, Nobby.'

'Well, thank you,' said Nobby, and helped himself. He grinned round at everyone. 'Nice to have friends like you,' he said. 'Isn't it, Pongo?'

[7]

A tea-party – and a visit in the night

Nobody particularly wanted to see round the camp just then, as Lou had been so unpleasant. So instead they showed the admiring Nobby over the two caravans. He had never seen such beauties.

'Jumping Jiminy, they're like palaces!' he said. 'Do you mean to say those taps turn on and water comes out? Can I turn on a tap? I've never turned a tap in my life!'

He turned the taps on and off a dozen times, exclaiming in wonder to see the water come gushing out. He thumped the bunks to see how soft they were. He admired the colourful soft rugs and the shining crockery. He was, in fact, a very nice guest to have, and the children liked him more and more. They liked Barker and

Growler, too, who were both well-behaved, obedient, merry dogs.

Pongo, of course, wanted to turn the taps on and off, too, and he threw all the coverings off the two bunks to see what was underneath. He also took the kettle off the stove, put the spout to his thick lips and drank all the water out of it very noisily indeed.

'You're forgetting your manners, Pongo!' said Nobby in horror, and snatched the kettle away from him. Anne squealed with laughter. She loved the chimpanzee, and he seemed to have taken a great fancy to Anne, too. He followed her about and stroked her hair and made funny affectionate noises.

'Would you like to stay and have tea here with us?' asked Julian, looking at his watch. 'It's about time.'

'Coo – I don't have tea as a rule,' said Nobby. 'Yes, I'd like to. Sure you don't mind me staying, though? I haven't got your manners, I know, and I'm a bit dirty, and not your sort at all. But you're real kind.'

'We'd love to have you stay,' said Anne in delight. 'I'll cut some bread and butter and make some sandwiches. Do you like potted meat sandwiches, Nobby?'

'Don't I just!' said Nobby. 'And Pongo does, too. Don't you let him get near them or he'll finish up the lot.'

It was a pleasant and amusing little tea-party. They all sat out on the heather, on the shady side of the caravan. Barker and Growler sat with Timmy. Pongo sat beside Anne, taking bits of sandwich from her most politely. Nobby enjoyed his tea immensely, eating more sandwiches than anyone and talking all the time with his mouth full.

He made the four children yell with laughter. He imitated his Uncle Dan doing some of his clown tricks. He turned cartwheels all round the caravan while he was waiting for Anne to cut more sandwiches. He stood solemnly on his head and ate a sandwich like that, much to Timmy's amazement. Timmy walked round and round him, and sniffed at his face as if to say: 'Strange! No legs! Something's gone wrong.'

At last nobody could eat any more. Nobby stood up to go, suddenly wondering if he had stayed too long.

'I was enjoying myself so much I forgot the time,' he said awkwardly. 'Bet I've stayed too long and you've been too polite to tell me to get out. Coo, that wasn't half a good tea! Thanks awfully for all those delicious sandwiches. 'Fraid my manners aren't like yours, kids, but thanks for a very good time.'

'You've got very good manners indeed,' said Anne, warmly. 'You've been a splendid guest. Come again, won't you?'

'Well, thanks, I will,' said Nobby, forgetting his sudden awkwardness, and beaming round. 'Where's Pongo? Look at that chimp! He's got one of your hankies, and he's blowing his nose!'

Anne squealed in delight. 'He can keep it!' she said. 'It's only an old one.'

'Will you be here camping for long?' asked Nobby.

'Well, not just exactly *here*,' said Julian. 'We thought of going up higher into the hills. It will be cooler there. But we might camp here just for tonight. We meant to go up higher this evening, but we might as well stay here and go tomorrow morning now. Perhaps we could see round the camp tomorrow morning.'

'Not if Lou's there you can't,' said Nobby. 'Once he's told people to clear out he means it. But it will be all right if he's not. I'll come and tell you.'

'All right,' said Julian. 'I'm not afraid of Lou – but we don't want to get *you* into any trouble, Nobby. If Lou's there tomorrow morning, we'll go on up into the hills, and you can always signal to us if he's out of the camp, and we can come down any time. And mind you come up and see us when you want to.'

'And bring Pongo,' said Anne.

'You bet!' said Nobby. 'Well – so long!'

He went off with Barker and Growler at his heels and with Pongo held firmly by the paw.

Pongo didn't want to go at all. He kept pulling back like a naughty child.

'I do like Nobby and Pongo,' said Anne. 'I wonder what Mummy would say if she knew we'd made friends with a chimpanzee. She'd have a fit.'

Julian suddenly looked rather doubtful. He was wondering if he had done right to follow the circus and let Anne and the others make friends with such strange folk and even stranger animals. But Nobby was so nice. He was sure his mother would like Nobby. And they could easily keep away from Tiger Dan and Lou the acrobat.

'Have we got enough to eat for supper tonight and breakfast tomorrow?' he asked Anne. 'Because there doesn't seem to be a farm near enough to go to just here. But Nobby says there's one up on the hill up there – the circus folk get their supplies from it, too – what they don't get from the nearest town. Apparently somebody goes in each day to shop.'

'I'll just see what we've got in the larder,

Julian,' said Anne, getting up. She knew perfectly well what there was in the larder – but it made her feel grown-up and important to go and look. It was nice to feel like that when she so often felt small and young, and the others were big and knew so much.

She called back to them: 'I've got eggs and tomatoes and potted meat, and plenty of bread, and a cake we bought today, and a pound of butter.'

'That's all right then,' said Julian. 'We won't bother about going to the farm tonight.'

When darkness fell that night, there were clouds across the sky for the first time. Not a star showed and there was no moon. It was pitch-black, and Julian, looking out of the window of his caravan, before clambering into his bunk, could not even see a shimmer of water from the lake.

He got into his bunk and pulled the covers up. In the other caravan George and Anne were asleep. Timmy was, as usual, on George's feet. She had pushed him off them once or twice, but now that she was asleep he was undisturbed, and lay heavily across her ankles, his head on his paws.

Suddenly his ears cocked up. He raised his head cautiously. Then he growled softly in his throat. He had heard something. He sat there stiffly, listening. He could hear footsteps from two different directions. Then he heard voices – cautious voices, low and muffled.

Timmy growled again, more loudly. George awoke and reached for his collar. 'What's the matter?' she whispered. Timmy listened and so did she. They both heard the voices.

George slipped quietly out of the bunk and went to the half-open door of the caravan. She could not see anything outside at all because it was so dark. 'Don't make a noise, Tim,' she whispered.

Timmy understood. He did not growl again, but George could feel the hairs rising all along the back of his neck.

The voices seemed to come from not very far away. Two men must be talking together,

George thought. Then she heard a match struck, and in its light she saw two men lighting their cigarettes from the same match. She recognised them at once – they were Nobby's Uncle Dan and Lou the acrobat.

What were they doing there? Had they got a meeting-place there – or had they come to steal something from the caravans? George wished she could tell Julian and Dick – but she did not like to go out of her caravan in case the men heard her.

At first she could not hear anything the men said. They were discussing something very earnestly. Then one raised his voice.

'Okay, then – that's settled.' Then came the sound of footsteps again, this time towards George's caravan. The men walked straight into the side of it, exclaimed in surprise and pain, and began to feel about to find out what they had walked into.

'It's those posh caravans!' George heard Lou exclaim. 'Still here! I told those kids to clear out!'

'What kids?' asked Tiger Dan, in surprise. Evidently he had come back in the dark and did not know they had arrived.

'Some kids Nobby knows,' said Lou in an angry voice. He rapped loudly on the walls of the caravan, and Anne woke up with a jump. George, just inside the caravan with Timmy, jumped in fright, too. Timmy barked in rage.

Julian and Dick woke up. Julian flashed on his torch and went to his door. The light picked out the two men standing by George's caravan.

'What are you doing here at this time of night?' said Julian. 'Making a row like that! Clear off!'

This was quite the wrong thing to have said to Dan and Lou, both bad-tempered men who felt that the whole of the camping-ground around belonged to them and the circus.

'Who do you think you're talking to?' shouted Dan angrily. 'You're the ones to clear off! Do you hear?'

'Didn't I tell you to clear out this afternoon?' yelled Lou, losing his temper, too. 'You do as you're told, you young rogue, or I'll set the dogs on you and have you chased for miles.'

Anne began to cry. George trembled with rage. Timmy growled. Julian spoke calmly but determinedly.

'We're going in the morning, as we meant. But if you're suggesting we should go now, you can think again. This is as much our camping-ground as yours. Now get off, and don't come disturbing us again.'

'I'll give you a leathering, you young cockerel!' cried Lou, and began to unfasten the leather belt from round his waist.

George let go her hold of Timmy's collar. 'Go for them, Timmy,' she said. 'But don't bite. Just worry them!'

Timmy sprang down to the ground with a joyful bark. He flung himself at the two men. He knew what George wanted him to do, and although he longed to snap at the two rogues with his sharp teeth, he didn't. He pretended to, though, and growled so fiercely that they were scared out of their wits.

Lou hit out at Timmy, threatening to kill him. But Timmy cared for no threats of that kind. He got hold of Lou's right trouser-leg, pulled, and ripped it open from knee to ankle.

'Come on – the dog's mad!' cried Dan. 'He'll have us by the throat if we don't go. Call him off, you kids. We're going. But mind you clear out in the morning, or we'll see you do! We'll pay you out one day.'

Seeing that the men really meant to go, George whistled to Timmy. 'Come here, Tim. Stand on guard till they're really gone. Fly at them if they come back.'

But the men soon disappeared – and nothing would have made either of them come back and face Timmy again that night!

[8]

Up in the hills

The four children were upset and puzzled by the behaviour of the two men. George told how Timmy had woken her by growling and how she had heard the men talking together in low voices.

'I don't really think they had come to steal anything,' she said. 'I think they were just meeting near here for a secret talk. They didn't know the caravans were here and walked straight into ours.'

'They're bad-tempered brutes,' said Julian. 'And I don't care what you say, George, I'm going to lock your caravan door tonight. I know you've got Timmy – but I'm not running any risk of these men coming back, Timmy or no Timmy.'

Anne was so scared that George consented to

let Julian lock the red caravan door. Timmy was locked in with them. The boys went back to their own caravan, and Julian locked his door, too, from the inside. He wanted to be on the safe side.

'I'll be glad to get away from here up into the hills,' he said. 'I shan't feel safe as long as we are quite so near the camp. We'll be all right up in the hills.'

'We'll go first thing after breakfast,' said Dick, settling down to his bunk again. 'Gosh, it's a good thing the girls had Timmy tonight. Those fellows looked as if they meant to go for you properly, Ju.'

'Yes. I shouldn't have had much chance against the two of them either,' said Julian. 'They are both hefty, strong fellows.'

The next morning all the four awoke early. Nobody felt inclined to lie and snooze – all of them were anxious to get off before Lou and Dan appeared again.

'You get the breakfast, Anne and George, and Dick and I will catch the horses and put them in the caravan shafts,' said Julian. 'Then we shall be ready to go off immediately after breakfast.'

They had breakfast and cleared up. They got up on to the driving-seats and were just about to drive away when Lou and Dan came down the track towards them.

'Oh, you're going, are you?' said Dan, with an ugly grin on his face. 'That's right. Nice to see kids so obedient. Where are you going?'

'Up into the hills,' said Julian. 'Not that it's anything to do with you where we go.'

'Why don't you go round the foot of the hills, instead of over the top?' said Lou. 'Silly way to go – up there, with the caravans dragging the horses back all the way.'

Julian was just about to say that he didn't intend to go right up to the top of the hills and over to the other side, when he stopped himself. No – just as well not to let these fellows know that he meant to camp up there, or they might come and worry them all again.

He clicked to Dobby. 'We're going the way

we want to go,' he said to Lou in a curt voice. 'And that's up the hill. Get out of the way, please.'

As Dobby was walking straight at them, the men had to jump to one side. They scowled at the four children. Then they all heard the sound of running footsteps and along came Nobby, with Barker and Growler at his heels as usual.

'Hey, what are you going so early for?' he yelled. 'Let me come part of the way with you.'

'No, you don't,' said his uncle, and gave the surprised boy an unexpected cuff. 'I've told these kids to clear out, and they're going. I won't have any meddling strangers round this camp. And don't you kid yourself they want to make friends with you, see! Go and get out those dogs and exercise them, or I'll give you another box on the ears that'll make you see all the stars in the sky.'

Nobby stared at him, angry and afraid. He knew his uncle too well to defy him. He turned on his heel sullenly and went off back to the camp. The caravans overtook him on the way. Julian called to him in a low voice:

'Cheer up, Nobby. We'll be waiting for you up in the hills – don't tell Lou and your uncle about it. Let them think we've gone right away. Bring Pongo up sometime!'

Nobby grinned. 'Right you are!' he said. 'I can bring the dogs up to exercise them, too – but not today. I daren't today. And as soon as those two are safely out for the day I'll bring you down to the camp and show you round, see? That all right?'

'Fine,' said Julian, and drove on. Neither Lou nor Dan had heard a word, or even guessed that this conversation was going on, for Nobby had been careful to walk on all the time and not even turn his face towards the children.

The road wound upwards into the hills. At first it was not very steep, but wound to and fro across the side of the hill. Half-way up the caravans crossed a stone bridge under which a very swift stream flowed.

'That stream's in a hurry!' said George,

watching it bubble and gurgle downwards. 'Look – is that where it starts from – just there in the hillside?'

She pointed some way up the hill, and it seemed as if the stream really did suddenly start just where she pointed.

'But it can't suddenly start here – not such a big fast stream as this!' said Julian, stopping Dobby on the other side of the bridge. 'Let's go and see. I'm thirsty, and if there's a spring there, it will be very cold and clear – lovely to drink from. Come on, we'll go and see.'

But there was no spring. The stream did not 'begin' just there, but flowed out of a hole in the hillside, as big and as fast as it was just under the stone bridge. The children bent down and peered into the water-filled hole.

'It comes out from inside the hill,' said Anne, surprised. 'Fancy it running around in the hill itself. It must be glad to find a way out!'

They didn't like to drink it as it was not the clear, fresh spring they had hoped to find. But, wandering a little farther on, they came to a real spring that gushed out from beneath a stone, cold and crystal clear. They drank from this and voted that it was the nicest drink they had ever had in their lives. Dick followed the spring-water downwards and saw that it joined the little rushing stream.

'I suppose it flows into the lake,' he said. 'Come on. Let's get on and find a farm, Julian. I'm sure I heard the crowing of a cock just then, so one can't be far away.'

They went round a bend of the hill and saw the farm, a rambling collection of old buildings sprawling down the hillside. Hens ran about, clucking. Sheep grazed above the farm, and cows chewed the cud in fields nearby. A man was working not far off, and Julian hailed him. 'Good morning! Are you the farmer?'

'No. Farmer's over yonder,' said the man, pointing to a barn near the farmhouse. 'Be careful of the dogs.'

The two caravans went on towards the farm. The farmer heard them coming and came out with his dogs. When he saw that there were only children driving the two caravans he looked surprised.

Julian had a polite, well-mannered way with him that all the grown-ups liked. Soon he was deep in a talk with the man, with most satisfactory results. The farmer was willing to supply them with any farm produce they wanted, and they could have as much milk as they liked at any time. His wife, he was sure, would cook them anything they asked her to, and bake them cakes, too.

'Perhaps I could arrange payment with her?' said Julian. 'I'd like to pay for everything as I buy it.'

'That's right, son,' said the farmer. 'Always pay your way as you go along, and you won't come to any harm. You go and see my old woman. She likes children and she'll make you right welcome. Where are you going to camp?'

'I'd like to camp somewhere with a fine view over the lake,' said Julian. 'We can't see it from just here. Maybe a bit farther on we'll get just the view I want.'

'Yes, you go on about half a mile,' said the farmer. 'The track goes that far – and when you come to a clump of fine birch trees you'll see a sheltered hollow, set right in the hillside, with a wonderful fine view over the lake. You can pull your caravans in there, son, and you'll be sheltered from the winds.'

'Thanks awfully,' said all the children together, thinking what a nice man this old farmer was. How different from Lou and Dan, with their threats and rages!

'We'll go and see your wife first,' said Julian. 'Then we'll go on and pull into the hollow you suggest. We'll be seeing you again some time, I expect.'

They went to see the farmer's wife, a fat, round-cheeked old woman, whose little curranty eyes twinkled with good humour. She made them very welcome, gave them hot buns from the oven and told them to help themselves to the little purple plums on the tree outside the old farmhouse.

Julian arranged to pay on the spot for

anything they bought each day. The prices the farmer's wife asked seemed very low indeed, but she would not hear of taking any more money for her goods.

'It'll be a pleasure to see your bonny faces at my door!' she said. 'That'll be part of my payment, see? I can tell you're well-brought-up children by your nice manners and ways. You'll not be doing any damage or foolishness on the farm, *I* know.'

The children came away laden with all kinds of food, from eggs and ham to scones and ginger cakes. She pushed a bottle of raspberry syrup into Anne's hand when the little girl said goodbye. But when Julian turned back to pay her for it she was quite annoyed.

'If I want to make a present to somebody I'll do it!' she said. 'Go on with you . . . paying for this and paying for that. I'll have a little something extra for you each time, and don't you dare to ask to pay for it, or I'll be after you with my rolling pin!'

'Isn't she awfully nice?' said Anne as they

made their way back to the caravans. 'Even Timmy offered to shake hands with her without you telling him to, George – and he hardly ever does that to anyone, does he?'

They packed the things away into the larder, got up into the driving-seats, clicked to Dobby and Trotter and set off up the track again.

Just over half a mile away was a clump of birch trees. 'We'll find that sheltered hollow near them,' said Julian.

'Yes, look – there it is – set back into the hill, a really cosy place! Just right for camping in – and oh, what a magnificent view!'

It certainly was. They could see right down the steep hillside to the lake. It lay spread out, flat and smooth, like an enchanted mirror. From where they were they could now see right to the opposite banks of the lake – and it was indeed a big stretch of water.

'Isn't it blue?' said Anne, staring. 'Bluer even than the sky. Oh, won't it be lovely to see this marvellous view every single day we're here?'

Julian backed the caravans into the hollow.

Heather grew there, like a springy purple carpet. Harebells, pale as an evening sky, grew in clumps in crevices of the hill behind. It was a lovely spot for camping in.

George's sharp ears caught the sound of water and she went to look for it. She called back to the others. 'What do you think? There's another spring here, coming out of the hill. Drinking and washing water laid on! Aren't we lucky?'

'We certainly are,' said Julian. 'It's a lovely place – and nobody will disturb us here!'

But he spoke too soon!

[9]

An unpleasant meeting

It really was fun settling into that cosy hollow. The two caravans were backed in side by side. The horses were taken out and led to a big field where the farmer's horses were kept when they had done their day's work. Trotter and Dobby seemed very pleased with the green, sloping field. It had a spring of its own that ran into a stone trough and out of it, keeping it always filled with fresh cold water. Both horses went to take a long drink.

'Well, that settles the two horses all right,' said Julian. 'We'll tell the farmer he can borrow them if he wants to – he'll be harvesting soon and may like to have Dobby and Trotter for a few days. They will enjoy hobnobbing with other horses again.'

At the front of the hollow was a rocky ledge,

hung with heathery tufts. 'This is the front seat for Lake View!' said Anne. 'Oh, it's warm from the sun! How lovely!'

'I vote we have all our meals on this ledge,' said George, sitting down too. 'It's comfortable and roomy – and flat enough to take our cups and plates without spilling anything – and honestly the view from here is too gorgeous for words. Can anyone see anything of the circus from up here?'

'There's a spire or two of smoke over there,' said Dick, pointing. 'I should think that's where the camp is. And look – there's a boat pushing out on the lake – doesn't it look tiny?'

'Perhaps Nobby is in it,' said Anne. 'Haven't we brought any field-glasses, Julian? I thought we had.'

'Yes – we have,' said Julian, remembering. 'I'll get them.' He went to the green caravan, rummaged about in the drawers, and came out with his field-glasses swinging on the end of their straps.

'Here we are!' he said, and set them to his

eyes. 'Yes – I can see the boat clearly now – and it *is* Nobby in it – but who's with him? Golly, it's Pongo!'

Everyone had to look through the glasses to see Nobby and Pongo in the boat. 'You know, we could always get Nobby to signal to us somehow from his boat when he wanted to tell us that Lou and his uncle were away,' said Dick. 'Then we should know it was safe, and we could pop down to the camp and see round it.'

'Yes. Good idea,' said George. 'Give me the glasses, Dick. Timmy wants to have a turn at seeing, too.'

'He can't see through glasses like these, idiot,' said Dick, handing them to George. But Timmy most solemnly glued his eyes to the glasses, and appeared to be looking through them very earnestly indeed.

'Woof,' he remarked, when he took his eyes away at last.

'He says he's seen Nobby and Pongo, too,' said George, and the others laughed. Anne half-believed that he had. Timmy was such an extraordinary dog, she thought, as she patted his smooth head.

It was a terribly hot day. Too hot to do anything – even to walk down to the lake and bathe! The children were glad they were up in the hills, for at least there was a little breeze that fanned them now and again. They did not expect to see Nobby again that day, but they hoped he would come up the next day. If not they would go down and bathe in the lake and hope to see him somewhere about there.

Soon the rocky ledge got too hot to sit on. The children retreated to the clump of birch trees, which at least cast some shade. They took books with them, and Timmy came along, too, panting as if he had run for miles. He kept going off to the little spring to drink. Anne filled a big bowl with the cold water, and stood it in a breezy place near by, with a cup to dip into it. They were thirsty all day long, and it was pleasant to dip a cup into the bowl of spring-water and drink.

The lake was unbelievably blue that day, and lay as still as a mirror. Nobby's boat was no longer in the water. He and Pongo had gone. There was not a single movement to be seen down by the lake.

'Shall we go down to the lake this evening, when it's cooler, and bathe there?' said Julian, at tea-time. 'We haven't had much exercise today, and it would do us good to walk down and have a swim. We won't take Timmy in case we happen to come across Lou or Dan. He'd certainly fly at them today. We can always keep an eye open for those two and avoid them ourselves – but Timmy would go for them as soon as he spotted them. We might be in the water and unable to stop him.'

'Anyway, he'll guard the caravans for us,' said Anne. 'Well, I'll just take these cups and plates and rinse them in the stream. Nobody wants any more to eat, do they?'

'Too hot,' said Dick, rolling over on to his back. 'I wish we were by the lake at this moment – I'd go straight into the water now!'

At half past six it was cooler, and the four children set off down the hill. Timmy was angry and hurt at being left behind.

'You're to be on guard, Timmy,' said George firmly. 'See? Don't let anyone come near our caravans. On guard, Timmy!'

'Woof,' said Timmy dismally, and put his tail down. On guard! Didn't George know that the caravans wouldn't walk off by themselves, and that he wanted a good splash in the lake?

Still, he stayed behind, standing on the rocky ledge to see the last of the children, his ears cocked to hear their voices and his tail still down in disgust. Then he went and lay down beneath George's caravan, and waited patiently for his friends to return.

The children went down the hill with their bathing-things, taking short cuts, and leaping like goats over the steep bits. It had seemed quite a long way up when they had gone so slowly in the caravans with Dobby and Trotter – but it wasn't nearly so far when they could go on their own legs, and take rabbit-paths and short cuts whenever they liked.

There was one steep bit that forced them back on to the track. They went along it where the track turned a sharp corner round a cliff-like bend – and to their surprise and dismay they walked almost straight into Lou and Tiger Dan!

'Take no notice,' said Julian, in a low voice. 'Keep together and walk straight on. Pretend that Timmy is somewhere just behind us.'

'Tim, Tim!' called George, at once.

Lou and Dan seemed just as surprised to see the children as they had been to see the two men. They stopped and looked hard at them, but Julian hurried the others on.

'Hey, wait a minute!' called Dan. 'I thought you had gone off – over the hill-top!'

'Sorry we can't stop!' called back Julian. 'We're in rather a hurry!'

Lou looked round for Timmy. He wasn't going to lose his temper and start shouting in case that mad dog came at him again. He spoke to the children loudly, forcing himself to appear good-tempered.

'Where are your caravans? Are you camping up here anywhere?'

But the children still walked on, and the men had to go after them to make them hear.

'Hey! What's the matter? We shan't hurt you! We only want to know if you're camping here. It's better down below, you know.'

'Keep on walking,' muttered Julian. 'Don't tell them anything. Why do they tell us it's better to camp down below when they were so anxious for us to clear out yesterday? They're mad!'

'Timmy, Timmy!' called George, again, hoping that the men would stop following them if they heard her calling for her dog.

It did stop them. They gave up going after the children, and didn't shout any more. They turned angrily and went on up the track.

'Well, we've thrown them off all right,' said Dick, with relief. 'Don't look so scared, Anne. I wonder what they want up in the hills. They don't look the sort that would go walking for pleasure.'

'Dick – we're not going to have another adventure, are we?' said Anne suddenly, looking very woebegone. 'I don't want one. I just want a nice ordinary, peaceful holiday.'

''Course we're not going to have an adventure!' said Dick, scornfully. 'Just because we meet two bad-tempered fellows from a circus camp you think we're in for an adventure, Anne! Well, *I* jolly well wish we were! Every hols we've been together so far we've had adventures – and you must admit that you love talking about them and remembering them.'

'Yes, I do. But I don't like it much when I'm in the *middle* of one,' said Anne. 'I don't think I'm a very adventurous person, really.'

'No, you're not,' said Julian, pulling Anne over a very steep bit. 'But you're a very nice little person, Anne, so don't worry about it. And, anyway, you wouldn't like to be left out of any of our adventures, would you?'

'Oh *no*,' said Anne. 'I couldn't bear it. Oh,

look – we're at the bottom of the hill – and there's the lake, looking icy-cold!'

It wasn't long before they were all in the water – and suddenly there was Nobby too, waving and yelling. 'I'm coming in! Lou and my uncle have gone off somewhere. Hurray!'

Barker and Growler were with Nobby, but not Pongo the chimpanzee. Nobby was soon in the water, swimming like a dog, and splashing George as soon as he got up to her.

'We met Lou and your uncle as we came down,' called George. 'Shut up, Nobby, and let me talk to you. I said, we met Lou and your uncle just now – going up into the hills.'

'Up into the hills?' said Nobby, astonished. 'Whatever for? They don't go and fetch things from the farm. The women do that, early each morning.'

'Well, we met those two,' said Dick swimming up. 'They seemed jolly surprised to see us. I hope they aren't going to bother us any more.'

'I've had a bad day,' said Nobby, and he showed black bruises on his arms. 'My uncle hit me like anything for making friends with you. He says I'm not to go talking to strangers any more.'

'Why ever not?' said Dick. 'What a surly, selfish fellow he is! Well, you don't seem to be taking much notice of him now!'

''Course not!' said Nobby. 'He's safe up in the hills, isn't he? I'll have to be careful he doesn't see me with you, that's all. Nobody else at the camp will split on me – they all hate Lou and Tiger Dan.'

'We saw you out in your boat with Pongo,' said Julian, swimming up to join in the conversation. 'We thought that if ever you wanted to signal to us you could easily do it by going out in your boat, and waving a handkerchief or something. We've got field-glasses, and we can easily see you. We could come along down if you signalled. We'd know it would be safe.'

'Right,' said Nobby. 'Come on, let's have a race. Bet you I'm on the shore first!'

He wasn't, of course, because he didn't swim

properly. Even Anne could race him. Soon they were all drying themselves vigorously.

'Golly, I'm hungry!' said Julian. 'Come on up the hill with us, Nobby, and share our supper!'

[10]

A curious change of mind

Nobby felt very much tempted to go and have a meal up in the hills with the children. But he was afraid of meeting Lou and his uncle coming back from their walk.

'We can easily look out for them and warn you if we see or hear them,' said Dick, 'and you can flop under a bush and hide till they go past. You may be sure we'll be on the look-out for them ourselves, because *we* don't want to meet them either!'

'Well, I'll come,' said Nobby. 'I'll take Barker and Growler too. They'll like to see Timmy.'

So all five of them, with the two dogs, set off up the hill. They climbed up short cuts at first, but they were soon panting, and decided to take the track, which, although longer, was easier to follow.

They all kept a sharp look-out for the two men, but they could see no sign of them. 'We shall be at our caravans soon,' said Julian. Then he heard Timmy barking in the distance. 'Hallo! What's old Tim barking for? I wonder if those fellows have been up to our caravans?'

'Good thing we left Timmy on guard if so,' said Dick. 'We might have missed something if not.'

Then he went red, remembering that it was Nobby's uncle he had been talking of. Nobby might feel upset and offended to hear someone speaking as if he thought Tiger Dan would commit a little robbery.

But Nobby wasn't at all offended. 'Don't you worry about what you say of my uncle,' he said, cheerfully. 'He's a bad lot. I know that. Anyway, he's not really my uncle, you know. When my father and mother died, they left a little money for me – and it turned out that they had asked Tiger Dan to look after me. So he took the money, called himself my uncle, and I've had to be with him ever since.'

'Was he in the same circus, then?' asked Julian.

'Oh yes. He and my father were both clowns,' said Nobby. 'Always have been clowns, in my family. But wait till I'm old enough, and I'll do a bunk – clear off and join another circus, where they'll let me look after the horses. I'm mad on horses. But the fellow at our circus won't often let me go near them. Jealous because I can handle them, I suppose!'

The children gazed at Nobby in wonder. He seemed an extraordinary boy to them – one who walked about with a tame chimpanzee, exercised hordes of performing dogs, lived with the chief clown in the circus, could turn the most marvellous cartwheels, and whose only ambition was to work with horses! What a boy! Dick half-envied him.

'Haven't you ever been to school?' he asked Nobby.

The boy shook his head. 'Never! I can't write. And I can only read a bit. Most circus folk are like that, so nobody minds. Jumping

Jiminy, I bet *you're* all clever, though! I bet even little Anne can read a book!'

'I've been able to read for *years*,' said Anne. 'And I'm up to fractions now in numbers.'

'Coo! What fractions?' said Nobby, impressed.

'Well – quarters and halves and seven-eighths, and things like that,' said Anne. 'But I'd rather be able to turn a cartwheel like you can, Nobby, than know how to do fractions.'

'Whatever *is* Timmy barking for?' said George as they came near the clump of birch trees. Then she stopped suddenly, for she had seen two figures lying down in the grass below the trees. Lou – and Tiger Dan!

It was too late for Nobby to hide. The men saw him at once. They got up and waited for the children to come near. George felt thankful that Timmy was within whistling distance. He would come at the first call or whistle, she knew.

Julian looked at the men. To his surprise they appeared to be quite amiable. A faint scowl came over Tiger Dan's face when he caught sight of Nobby, but it passed at once.

'Good evening,' said Julian curtly, and would have passed on without another word, but Lou stepped up to him.

'We see you're camping up by here,' said Lou, and smiled showing yellow teeth. 'Aren't you going over the hill?'

'I don't need to discuss my affairs with either you or your friend,' said Julian, sounding extremely grown-up. 'You told us to clear out from down below, and we have. What we do now is nothing to do with you.'

'Ho yes, it is,' said Tiger Dan, sounding as if he was being polite with great difficulty. 'We've come up here tonight to plan a place for some of our animals, see? And we don't want you to be in any danger.'

'We shan't be,' said Julian, scornfully. 'And there is plenty of room on these hills for you and your animals and for us, too. You won't scare us off, so don't think it. We shall stay here as long as we want to – and if we want help there's the farmer and his men quite near by – to say nothing of our dog.'

'Did you leave that there dog on guard?' asked Lou, as he heard Timmy barking again. 'He ought to be destroyed, that dog of yours. He's dangerous.'

'He's only dangerous to rogues and scamps,' said George, joining in at once. 'You keep away from our caravans when Timmy's on guard. He'll maul you if you go near.'

Lou began to lose his temper. 'Well, are you going or aren't you?' he said. 'We've told you we want this here bit of the hill. You can come down and camp by the lake again if you want to.'

'Yes – you come,' said Tiger Dan to the children's growing astonishment. 'You come, see? You can bathe in the lake every day, then – and Nobby here can show you round the camp, and you can make friends with all the animals, see?'

Now it was Nobby's turn to look amazed. 'Jumping Jiminy! Didn't you beat me black and blue for making friends with these kids?' he demanded. 'What's the game, now? You've never had animals up in the hills before. You've—'

'Shut up,' said Tiger Dan in such a fierce voice that all the children were shocked. Lou nudged Dan, and he made an effort to appear pleasant again.

'We didn't want Nobby to make friends with posh folk like you,' he began again. 'But it seems as if you want to pal up with him – so it's okay with us. You come on down and camp by the lake, and Nobby'll show you everything in the circus. Can't say fairer than that.'

'You've got other reasons for making all these suggestions,' said Julian, scornfully. 'I'm sorry – but our plans are made, and I am not going to discuss them with you.'

'Come on,' said Dick. 'Let's go and find Timmy. He's barking his head off because he can hear us, and it won't be long before he comes flying along here. Then we shall find it difficult to keep him off these two fellows.'

The four children began to move off. Nobby looked doubtfully at his uncle. He didn't know whether to go with them or not. Lou nudged Dan again.

'You go, too, if you want to,' said Tiger Dan, trying to grin amiably at the surprised Nobby. 'Keep your fine friends, see! Much good may they do you!' The grin vanished into a scowl, and Nobby skipped smartly out of reach of his uncle's hand. He was puzzled and wondered what was behind his uncle's change of mind.

He tore after the children. Timmy came to meet them, barking his head off, waving his plumy tail wildly in joy.

'Good dog, good dog!' said George, patting him. 'You keep on guard beautifully. You know I would have whistled for you if I'd wanted you, didn't you, Timmy? Good dog!'

'I'll get you some supper,' said Anne to everyone. 'We're all famished. We can talk while we eat. George, come and help. Julian, can you get some ginger-beer? And, Dick, do fill up the water-bowl for me.'

The boys winked at one another. They always thought that Anne was very funny when she took command like this, and gave her orders. But everyone went obediently to work.

Nobby went to help Anne. Together they boiled ten eggs hard in the little saucepan. Then Anne made tomato sandwiches with potted meat and got out the cake the farmer's wife had given them. She remembered the raspberry syrup, too – how lovely!

Soon they were all sitting on the rocky ledge, which was still warm, watching the sun go down into the lake. It was a most beautiful evening, with the lake as blue as a cornflower and the sky flecked with rosy clouds. They held their hard-boiled eggs in one hand and a piece of bread and butter in the other, munching happily. There was a dish of salt for everyone to dip their eggs into.

'I don't know why, but the meals we have on picnics always taste so much nicer than the ones we have indoors,' said George. 'For instance, even if we had hard-boiled eggs and bread and butter indoors, they wouldn't taste as nice as these.'

'Can everyone eat two eggs?' asked Anne. 'I did two each. And there's plenty of cake – and more sandwiches and some plums we picked this morning.'

'Best meal I've ever had in my life,' said Nobby, and picked up his second egg. 'Best company I've ever been in, too!'

'Thank you,' said Anne, and everyone looked pleased. Nobby might not have their good manners, but he always seemed to say just the right thing.

'It's a good thing your uncle didn't make you go back with him and Lou,' said Dick. 'Funny business – changing his mind like that!'

They began to talk about it. Julian was very puzzled indeed, and had even begun to wonder if he hadn't better find another camping site and go over the hill.

The others raised their voices scornfully.

'Julian! We're not cowards. We'll jolly well stay here!'

'What, leave now – why should we? We're in nobody's way, whatever those men say!'

'*I'm* not moving *my* caravan, whatever *anyone* says!' That was George, of course.

'No, don't you go,' said Nobby. 'Don't you take any notice of Lou and my uncle. They can't do anything to you at all. They're just trying to make trouble for you. Stay and let me show you over the camp, see?'

'It isn't that I *want* to give in to those fellows' ideas,' said Julian. 'It's just that – well, I'm in charge of us all – and I *don't* like the look of Lou and Tiger Dan – and, well . . .'

'Oh, have another egg and forget about it,' said Dick. 'We're going to stay here in this hollow, however much Dan and Lou want us out of it. And, what's more, I'd like to find out why they're so keen to push us off. It seems jolly strange to me.'

The sun went down in a blaze of orange and red, and the lake shimmered with its fiery reflection. Nobby got up regretfully, and Barker and Growler, who had been hobnobbing with Timmy, got up, too.

'I'll have to go,' said Nobby. 'Still got some jobs to do down there. What about you coming down tomorrow to see the animals? You'll like Old Lady, the elephant. She's a pet. And Pongo will be pleased to see you again.'

'Your uncle may have changed his mind again by tomorrow, and not want us near the camp,' said Dick.

'Well – I'll signal to you,' said Nobby. 'I'll go out in the boat, see? And wave a hanky. Then you'll know it's all right. Well – so long! I'll be seeing you.'

[11]

Fun at the circus camp

Next morning, while Anne cleared up the breakfast things with George, and Dick went off to the farm to buy whatever the farmer's wife had ready for him, Julian took the field-glasses and sat on the ledge to watch for Nobby to go out on the lake in his boat.

Dick sauntered along, whistling. The farmer's wife was delighted to see him, and showed him two big baskets full of delicious food.

'Slices of ham I've cured myself,' she said, lifting up the white cloth that covered one of the baskets. 'And a pot of brawn I've made. Keep it in a cool place. And some fresh lettuces and radishes I pulled myself this morning early. And some more tomatoes.'

'How gorgeous!' said Dick, eyeing the food in delight. 'Just the kind of things we love!

Thanks awfully, Mrs Mackie. What's in the other basket?'

'Eggs, butter, milk, and a tin of shortbread I've baked,' said Mrs Mackie. 'You should do all right till tomorrow, the four of you! And in that paper there is a bone for the dog.'

'How much do I owe you?' asked Dick. He paid his bill and took up the baskets. Mrs Mackie slipped a bag into his pocket.

'Just a few home-made sweets,' she said. That was her little present. Dick grinned at her.

'Well, I won't offer to pay you for them because I'm afraid of that rolling-pin of yours,' he said. 'But thank you very, very much.'

He went off delighted. He thought of Anne's pleasure when she came to unpack the baskets. How she would love to put the things in the little larder – and pop the butter in a dish set in a bowl of cold water – and set the eggs in the little rack!

When he got back Julian called to him: 'Nobby's out in his boat. Come and look. He's waving something that can't possibly be a hanky. It must be the sheet off his bed!'

'Nobby doesn't sleep in sheets,' said Anne. 'He didn't know what they were when he saw them in our bunks. Perhaps it's a table-cloth.'

'Anyway, it's something big, to tell us that it's absolutely all right to come down to the camp,' said Julian. 'Are we ready?'

'Not quite,' said Anne, unpacking the baskets Dick had brought. 'I must put away these things – and do you want to take a picnic lunch with you? Because if so I must prepare it. Oh – look at all these gorgeous things!'

They all came back to look. 'Mrs Mackie is a darling,' said Anne. 'Honestly, these things are super – look at this gorgeous ham. It smells heavenly.'

'Here's her little present – home-made sweets,' said Dick, remembering them and taking them out of his pocket. 'Have one!'

Anne had everything ready in half an hour. They had decided to take a picnic lunch with them for themselves and for Nobby as well. They took their bathing-things and towels, too.

'Are we going to take Timmy or not?' said George. 'I want to. But as these two men seem rather interested in our caravans, perhaps we had better leave him on guard again. We don't want to come back and find the caravans damaged or half the things stolen.'

'I should think not!' said Dick. 'They're not our things, nor our caravans. They belong to somebody else and we've got to take extra good care of them. I think we ought to leave Timmy on guard, don't you, Ju?'

'Yes, I do,' said Julian at once. 'These caravans are too valuable to leave at the mercy of any passing tramp – though I suppose we could lock them up. Anyway – we'll leave Timmy on guard today – poor old Timmy, it's a shame, isn't it?'

Timmy didn't answer. He looked gloomy and miserable. What! They were all going off without him again? He knew what 'on guard' meant – he was to stay here with these houses on wheels till the children chose to come back. He badly wanted to see Pongo again. He stood with his ears and tail drooping, the picture of misery.

But there was no help for it. The children felt that they couldn't leave the caravans unguarded while they were still so uncertain about Lou and Tiger Dan. So they all patted poor Timmy and fondled him, and then said goodbye. He sat down on the rocky ledge with his back to them and wouldn't even watch them go.

'He's sulking,' said George. 'Poor Timothy!'

It didn't take them very long to get down to the camp, and they found Nobby, Pongo, Barker and Growler waiting for them. Nobby was grinning from ear to ear.

'You saw my signal all right?' he said. 'Uncle hasn't changed his mind – in fact, he seems quite to have taken to you, and says I'm to show you all round and let you see anything you want to. That was his shirt I waved. I thought if I waved something enormous you'd know things were absolutely safe.'

'Where shall we put the bathing-things and the picnic baskets while we see round the camp?' asked Anne. 'Somewhere cool, if possible.'

'Put them in my caravan,' said Nobby, and led them to a caravan painted blue and yellow, with red wheels. The children remembered having seen it when the procession passed by their house a week or two before.

They peeped inside. It wasn't nearly so nice as theirs. It was much smaller, for one thing, and very untidy. It looked dirty, too, and had a nasty smell. Anne didn't like it very much.

'Not so good as yours!' said Nobby. 'I wish I had a caravan like yours. I'd feel like a prince. Now what do you want to see first? The elephant? Come on, then.'

They went to the tree to which Old Lady the elephant was tied. She curled her trunk round Nobby and looked at the children out of small, intelligent eyes.

'Well, Old Lady!' said Nobby. 'Want a bathe?'

The elephant trumpeted and made the children jump. 'I'll take you later on,' promised Nobby. 'Now then – hup, hup, hup!'

At these words the elephant curled her trunk tightly round Nobby's waist and lifting him bodily into the air, placed him gently on her big head!

Anne gasped.

'Oh! Did she hurt you, Nobby?'

''Course not!' said Nobby. 'Old Lady wouldn't hurt anyone, would you, big one?'

A small man came up. He had bright eyes that shone as if they had been polished, and a very wide grin. 'Good morning,' he said. 'How do you like my Old Lady? Like to see her play cricket?'

'Oh, *yes*!' said everyone, and the small man produced a cricket bat and held it out to Old Lady. She took it in her trunk and waved it about. Nobby slipped deftly off her head to the ground.

'I'll play with her, Larry,' he said, and took the ball from the small man. He threw it to Old

Lady and she hit it smartly with the bat. It sailed over their heads!

Julian fetched the ball. He threw it at the elephant, and again the great creature hit the ball with a bang. Soon all the children were playing with Old Lady and enjoying the game very much.

Some small camp children came up to watch. But they were as scared as rabbits as soon as Julian or George spoke to them and scuttled off to their caravans at once. They were dirty and ragged, but most of them had beautiful eyes and thick curly hair, though it wanted brushing and washing.

Nobby went to fetch Pongo, who was dancing to and fro in his cage, making anguished sounds, thinking he was forgotten. He was simply delighted to see the children again, and put his arm right round Anne at once. Then he pulled George's hair and hid his face behind his paws, peeping out mischievously.

'He's a caution, aren't you, Pongo?' said Nobby. 'Now you keep with me, Pongo, or I'll put you back into your cage, see?'

They went to see the dogs and let them all out. They were mostly terrier dogs, or mongrels, smart, well-kept little things who jumped up eagerly at Nobby, and made a great fuss of him. It was clear that they loved him and trusted him.

'Like to see them play football?' asked Nobby. 'Here, Barker – fetch the ball. Go on, quick!'

Barker darted off to Nobby's caravan. The door was shut, but the clever little dog stood on his hind legs and jerked the handle with his nose. The door opened and in went Barker. He came out dribbling a football with his nose. Down the steps it went and into the camp field. All the dogs leapt on it with howls of delight.

'Yap-yap-yap! Yap-yap!' They dribbled the football to and fro, while Nobby stood with his legs open to make a goal for them.

It was Barker's job and Growler's to score the goals, and the task of the other dogs to stop them. So it was a most amusing game to watch. Once, when Barker scored a goal by hurling himself on the ball and sending it rolling fast between Nobby's arched legs, Pongo leapt into the fray, picked up the ball and ran off with it.

'Foul, foul!' yelled Nobby and all the dogs rushed after the mischievous chimpanzee. He leapt on to the top of a caravan and began to bounce the ball there, grinning down at the furious dogs.

'Oh, this is such fun!' said Anne, wiping the tears of laughter from her eyes. 'Oh, dear! I've got such a pain in my side from laughing.'

Nobby had to climb up to the roof of the caravan to get the ball. Pongo jumped down the other side, but left the ball balanced neatly on the chimney. He was really a most mischievous chimpanzee.

Then they went to see the beautiful horses. All of them had shining satiny coats. They were being trotted round a big field by a slim, tall young fellow called Rossy, and they obeyed his slightest word.

'Can I ride Black Queen, Rossy?' asked Nobby eagerly. 'Do let me!'

'Okay,' said Rossy, his black hair shining like the horses' coats. Then Nobby amazed the watching children, for he leapt on to a great black horse, stood up on her back and trotted all round the field like that!

'He'll fall!' cried Anne. But he didn't, of course. Then he suddenly swung himself down on to his hands and rode Black Queen standing upside down.

'Good, good!' cried Rossy. 'You are good with horses, young one! Now ride Fury!'

Fury was a small, fiery-looking little horse, whose gleaming eyes showed a temper. Nobby ran to her and leapt on her, bare-backed. She rose up, snorting, and tried to throw him off. But he wouldn't be thrown off. No matter what she did, Nobby clung on like a limpet to a rock.

At last Fury tired of it, and began to canter round the field. Then she galloped – and suddenly she stopped absolutely dead, meaning to fling Nobby over her head!

But the boy was waiting for that trick and threw himself backwards at once. 'Good,

good!' cried Rossy. 'She will soon eat out of your hand, Nobby! Good boy.'

'Nobby, Nobby, you're terribly clever!' yelled Anne. 'Oh, I wish I could do the things you do! I wish I could.'

Nobby slid off Fury's back, looking pleased. It was nice to show off a little to his 'posh' friends. Then he looked round and about. 'I say – where's that chimp? Up to some mischief, I'll be bound! Let's go and find him.'

[12]

A lovely day – with a horrid end

They soon saw Pongo. He was coming round one of the caravans, looking exceedingly pleased with himself. He went to Anne and held out his paw to her, making little affectionate noises.

Anne took what he held. She looked at it. 'It's a hard-boiled egg! Oh, Nobby, he's been at the picnic baskets!'

So he had! Two of the eggs were gone, and some of the tomatoes! Nobby smacked the chimpanzee and took him back to his cage. He was very sad and made a noise as if he was crying, hiding his face in his paws. Anne was upset.

'Is he really crying? Oh, do forgive him, Nobby. He didn't mean to be naughty.'

'He's not crying. He's only pretending,' said Nobby. 'And he *did* mean to be naughty. I know him!'

The morning soon went in visiting the circus animals. It was dinner-time before they had had time to see the monkeys. 'We'll see them afterwards,' said Nobby. 'Let's have a meal now. Come on. We'll go and have it by the lake.'

The children hadn't seen Lou or Tiger Dan at all, much to their joy. 'Where are they?' asked Julian. 'Gone out for the day?'

'Yes, thank goodness,' said Nobby. 'Gone out on one of their mysterious jaunts. You know, when we're on the road, going from place to place, my uncle sometimes disappears at night. I wake up – and he's not there.'

'Where does he go?' asked George.

'I wouldn't dare to ask,' said Nobby. 'Anyway, he and Lou are out of the way today. I don't expect they'll be back till night.'

They had their meal by the lake. It glittered at their feet, calm and blue, and looked very inviting.

'What about a swim?' asked Dick, when they had eaten as much as they could. Julian looked at his watch.

'Can't swim directly after a good meal,' he said. 'You know that, Dick. We'll have to wait a bit.'

'Right,' said Dick and lay down. 'I'll have a snooze – or shall we go and see the monkeys?'

They all had a short nap and then got up to go and see the monkeys. When they got back to the camp they found it alive with people, all excited and yelling.

'What's up?' said Nobby. 'Jumping Jiminy, the monkeys are all loose!'

So they were. Wherever they looked the children saw a small brown monkey, chattering to itself, on the roof of a caravan or tent!

A brown-faced woman with sharp eyes came up to Nobby. She caught him by the shoulder and shook him. 'See what that chimp of yours has done!' she said. 'You put him in his cage and couldn't have locked it properly. He got out and let all the monkeys loose. Drat that chimp – I'll take a broomstick to him if ever I catch him!'

'Where's Lucilla then?' asked Nobby, dragging himself away from the cross woman. 'Can't she get them in?'

'Lucilla's gone to the town,' scolded the woman. 'And fine and pleased she'll be to hear this when she comes back!'

'Aw, let the monkeys be!' said Nobby. 'They won't come to any harm. They'll wait for Lucilla all right!'

'Who's Lucilla?' asked Anne, thinking that life in a circus camp was very exciting.

'She owns the monkeys,' said Nobby. 'Hi, look – there's Lucilla coming back! Now we'll be all right!'

A little wizened old woman was hurrying towards the camp. She really looked rather like a monkey herself, Anne thought. Her eyes were bright and sharp, and her tiny hands clutched a red shawl round her. They looked like brown paws.

'Your monkeys are out!' yelled the camp children. 'Lucilla! Your monkeys are out.'

Lucilla heard and, raising her voice, she scolded everyone in sight fully and shrilly. Then she stood still and held out her arms. She spoke some soft words in a language the children didn't know – magic words, Anne said afterwards.

One by one the wandering monkeys came scampering over to her, flinging themselves down from the caravan roofs, making little chattering sounds of love and welcome. They leapt on to Lucilla's shoulders and into her arms, cuddling against her like tiny brown children. Not one monkey was left out – all went to Lucilla as if drawn by some enchantment.

She walked slowly towards their cage, murmuring her soft words as she went. Everyone watched in silence.

'She's an odd one,' said the brown-faced woman to Nobby. 'She doesn't love anybody but her monkeys – and nobody loves her but them. You mind she doesn't go for that chimp of yours, letting out her precious monkeys!'

'I'll take him and Old Lady down to bathe,' said Nobby, hastily. 'By the time we're back, Lucilla will have forgotten.'

They fetched Old Lady and discovered where naughty Pongo was hiding under a caravan. As quickly as possible they went back to the lake, Old Lady stepping out well, looking forward to her bathe.

'I suppose things like that are always happening in a circus camp,' said Anne. 'It's not a bit like real life.'

'Isn't it?' said Nobby, surprised. 'It's real life all right to *me*!'

It was cool in the lake and they all enjoyed themselves very much, swimming and splashing. Pongo wouldn't go in very far, but splashed everyone who came within reach, laughing and cackling loudly. He gave Old Lady a shock by leaping up on to her back, and pulling one of her big ears.

She dipped her trunk into the lake, sucked up

a lot of water, turned her trunk over her back, and squirted the water all over the startled chimpanzee! The children yelled with laughter, and roared again to see Pongo falling in fright off Old Lady's back. Splash! He went right in and got himself wet from head to foot – a thing he hated doing.

'Serves you right, you scamp!' shouted Nobby. 'Hey, Old Lady, stop it! Don't squirt at me!'

The elephant, pleased with her little joke, didn't want to stop it. So the children had to keep well away from her, for her aim was very good.

'I've never had such a lovely time in my life!' said Anne, as she dried herself. 'I shall dream all night of monkeys and elephants, horses, dogs and chimpanzees!'

Nobby turned about twenty cartwheels by the edge of the lake from sheer good spirits – and Pongo at once did the same. He was even better at it than Nobby. Anne tried and fell down flop immediately.

They went back to the camp. 'Sorry I can't

offer you any tea,' said Nobby, 'but we never seem to have tea, you know – we circus folk, I mean. Anyway, I'm not hungry after that enormous lunch. Are you?'

Nobody was. They shared out Mrs Mackie's homemade toffees, and gave one to Pongo. It stuck his teeth together and he looked so comically alarmed when he found that he couldn't open his mouth that the children roared at him.

He sat down, swayed from side to side, and began to groan dismally. But the toffee soon melted away, and he found that he could open his mouth after all. He sucked the rest of the sweet noisily, but wouldn't have another.

They wandered round the camp, looking at the different caravans. Nobody took much notice of them now. They were just Nobby's 'posh' friends – that was all. Some of the smaller children peeped out and stuck out their little red tongues – but at Nobby's roar they vanished.

'Got no manners at all!' said Nobby. 'But they're all right really.'

They came to where big wagons stood, stored with all kinds of circus things. 'We don't bother to unpack these when we're resting in camp like this,' said Nobby. 'Don't need them here. One of my jobs is to help to unpack this stuff when we're camping to give a show. Have to get out all those benches and set them up in the big top – that's the circus tent, you know. We're pretty busy then, I can tell you!'

'What's in *this* cart?' asked Anne, coming to a small wagon with a tightly-fitting hood of tarpaulin.

'Don't know,' said Nobby. 'That cart belongs to my uncle. He won't ever let me unpack it. I don't know what he keeps there. I've wondered if it was things belonging to my dad and mum. I told you they were dead. Anyway, I thought I'd peep and see one day, but Uncle Dan caught me and half-killed me!'

'But if they belonged to your parents, they ought to be yours!' said George.

'Funny thing is, sometimes that cart's crammed full,' said Nobby. 'And sometimes it isn't. Maybe Lou puts some of his things there too.'

'Well, nobody could get anything else in there at the moment!' said Julian. 'It's full to bursting!'

They lost interest in the little wagon and wandered round to see the 'props' as Nobby called them. Anne pictured these as clothes-props, but they turned out to be gilt chairs and tables, the shining poles used for the tight-rope, gaily-painted stools for the performing dogs to sit on, and circus 'props' of that kind.

'*Prop*erties, Anne,' said Julian. 'Circus *prop*erties. Props for short. Look here, isn't it about time we went back? My watch has stopped. Whatever time is it?'

'Golly, it's quite late!' said Dick, looking at his watch. 'Seven o'clock. No wonder I feel jolly hungry. Time we went back. Coming with us, Nobby? You can have supper up there if you like. I bet you could find your way back in the dark.'

'I'll take Pongo with me, and Barker and Growler,' said Nobby, delighted at the invitation. 'If *I* lose the way back, *they* won't!'

So they all set off up the hill, tired with their long and exciting day. Anne began to plan what she would give the little company for supper. Ham, certainly – and tomatoes – and some of that raspberry syrup diluted with icy-cold spring-water.

They all heard Timmy barking excitedly as soon as they came near the caravans. He barked without ceasing, loudly and determinedly.

'He sounds cross,' said Dick. 'Poor old Tim! He must think we've quite deserted him.'

They came to the caravans and Timmy flung himself on George as if he hadn't seen her for a year. He pawed her and licked her, then pawed her again.

Barker and Growler were pleased to see him too, and as for Pongo, he was delighted. He shook hands with Timmy's tail several times, and was disappointed that Timmy took no notice of him.

'Hallo! What's Barker gnawing at?' suddenly said Dick. 'Raw meat! How did it come here? Do you suppose the farmer has been by and given Timmy some? Well, why didn't he eat it, then?'

They all looked at Barker, who was gnawing some meat on the ground. Growler ran to it too. But Timmy would not go near it. Nor would Pongo. Timmy put his tail down and Pongo hid his furry face behind his paws.

'Funny,' said the children, puzzled at the strange behaviour of the two animals. Then suddenly they understood – for poor Barker suddenly gave a terrible whine, shivered from head to foot, and rolled over on his side.

'Jiminy – it's poisoned!' yelled Nobby, and kicked Growler away from the meat. He picked Barker up, and to the children's utter dismay they saw that Nobby was crying.

'He's done for,' said the boy, in a choking voice. 'Poor old Barker.'

Carrying Barker in his arms, with Growler and Pongo behind him, poor Nobby stumbled down the hill. No one liked to follow him. Poisoned meat! What a terrible thing.

[13]

Julian thinks of a plan

George was trembling. Her legs felt as if they wouldn't hold her up, and she sank down on the ledge. She put her arms round Timmy.

'Oh, Timmy! That meat was meant for you! Oh, thank goodness, thank goodness you were clever enough not to touch it! Timmy, you might have been poisoned!'

Timmy licked his mistress soberly. The others stood round, staring, not knowing what to think. Poor Barker! Would he die? Suppose it had been old Timmy? They had left him all alone, and he might have eaten the meat and died.

'I'll never, never leave you up here alone again!' said George.

'Who threw him the poisoned meat, do you think?' said Anne, in a small voice.

'Who do you suppose?' said George, in a hard, scornful voice. 'Lou and Tiger Dan!'

'They want to get us away from here, that's plain,' said Dick. 'But again – why?'

'What can there be about this place that makes the men want to get rid of us all?' wondered Julian. 'They're real rogues. Poor Nobby. He must have an awful life with them. And now they've gone and poisoned his dog.'

Nobody felt like eating very much that evening. Anne got out the bread and the butter and a pot of jam. George wouldn't eat anything. What a horrid end to a lovely day!

They all went to bed early, and nobody objected when Julian said he was going to lock both the caravans. 'Not that I think either Lou or Dan will be up here tonight,' he said. 'But you never know!'

Whether they came or not the children didn't know, for although Timmy began to bark loudly in the middle of the night, and scraped frantically at the shut door of George's caravan, there was nothing to be seen or heard when Julian opened his door and flashed on his torch.

Timmy didn't bark any more. He lay quite quietly sleeping with one ear cocked. Julian lay in bed and thought hard. Probably Lou and Dan had come creeping up in the dark, hoping that Timmy had taken the meat and been poisoned. But when they heard him bark, they knew he was all right, and they must have gone away again. What plan would they make next?

'There's something behind all this,' Julian thought, again and again. 'But what can it be? Why do they want us out of this particular spot?'

He couldn't imagine. He fell asleep at last with a vague plan in his mind. He would tell it to the others tomorrow. Perhaps if he could make Lou and Dan think they had all gone off for the day – with Timmy – but really, he, Julian, would be left behind, in hiding – maybe he could find out something, if Lou and Dan came along . . .

Julian fell asleep in the middle of thinking out

his plan. Like the others, he dreamt of elephants squirting him with water, of Pongo chasing the monkeys, of the dogs playing football with excited yaps – and then into the dream came lumps of poisoned meat! Horrid.

Anne woke with a jump, having dreamt that someone had put poison into the hard-boiled eggs they were going to eat. She lay trembling in her bunk, and called to George in a small voice.

'George! I've been having an awful dream!'

George woke up, and Timmy stirred and stretched himself. George switched on her torch.

'I've been having beastly dreams, too,' she said. 'I dreamt that those men were after Timmy. I'll leave my torch on for a bit and we'll talk. I expect that with all the excitement we've had today, and the horrid end to it this evening, we're just in the mood for horrid dreams! Still – they are only dreams.'

'Woof,' said Timmy, and scratched himself.

'Don't,' said George. 'You shake the whole caravan when you do that, Timmy. Stop it.'

Timmy stopped. He sighed and lay down heavily. He put his head on his paws and looked sleepily at George, as if to say, 'Put that torch out. I want to go to sleep.'

The next morning was not so warm, and the sky was cloudy. Nobody felt very cheerful, because they kept thinking of Nobby and poor Barker. They ate their breakfast almost in silence, and then Anne and George began to stack the plates, ready to take them to the spring to rinse.

'*I'll* go to the farm this morning,' said Julian. 'You sit on the ledge and take the field-glasses, Dick. We'll see if Nobby goes out in his boat and waves. I've an idea that he won't want us down in the camp this morning. If he suspects his Uncle Dan and Lou of putting down the meat that poisoned Barker, he'll probably have had a frightful row with them.'

He went off to the farm with two empty baskets. Mrs Mackie was ready for him, and he bought a further supply of delicious-looking food. Her present this time was a round ginger cake, warm from the oven!

'Do the circus folk come up here often to buy food?' asked Julian, as he paid Mrs Mackie.

'They come sometimes,' said Mrs Mackie. 'I don't mind the women or the children – dirty though they are, and not above taking one of my chickens now and again – but it's the men I can't abide. There were two here last year, messing about in the hills, that my husband had to send off quickly.'

Julian pricked up his ears. 'Two men? What were they like?'

'Ugly fellows,' said Mrs Mackie. 'And one had the yellowest teeth I ever saw. Bad-tempered chaps, both of them. They came up here at night, and we were afraid our chickens would go. They swore they weren't after our chickens – but what else would they be up here at night for?'

'I can't imagine,' said Julian. He was sure that the two men Mrs Mackie spoke of were Lou and Tiger Dan. Why did they wander about in the hills at night?

He went off with the food. When he got near

the camping-place, Dick called to him excitedly.

'Hey, Julian! Come and look through the glasses. Nobby's out in his boat with Pongo, and I simply can't make out what it is they're both waving.'

Julian took the glasses and looked through them. Far down the hill, on the surface of the lake, floated Nobby's little boat. In it was Nobby, and with him was Pongo. Both of them were waving something bright red.

'Can't see what they're waving – but that doesn't matter,' said Julian. 'The thing is – what they're waving is red, not white. Red for danger. He's warning us.'

'Golly – I didn't think of that. What an idiot I am!' said Dick. 'Yes – red for danger. What's up, I wonder?'

'Well, it's clear we'd better not go down to the camp today,' said Julian. 'And it's also clear that whatever danger there is, is pretty bad – because both he *and* Pongo are waving red cloths – doubly dangerous!'

'Julian, you're jolly sharp,' said George, who was listening. 'You're the only one of us who worked that one out. Double-danger. What can it be?'

'Perhaps it means danger down at the camp, and danger here too,' said Julian, thoughtfully. 'I hope poor old Nobby is all right. Tiger Dan is so jolly beastly to him. I bet he's had a beating or two since last night.'

'It's a shame!' said Dick.

'Don't tell Anne we think there is double-danger about,' said Julian, seeing Anne coming back from the spring. 'She'll be scared. She was hoping we wouldn't have an adventure these hols – and now we seem to be plunged into the middle of one. Golly! I really think we ought to leave these hills and go on somewhere else.'

But he only said this half-heartedly, because he was burning to solve the curious mystery behind Lou's behaviour and Dan's. The others pounced on him at once.

'We can't leave! Don't be a coward, Ju!'

'I *won't* leave. Nor will Timmy.'

'Shut up,' said Julian. 'Here comes Anne.'

They said no more. Julian watched Nobby for a little while longer. Then the boy and the chimpanzee drew in to the shore and disappeared.

When they were all sitting together on the ledge, Julian proposed the plan he had been thinking out the night before.

'I'd like to find out what there is about this place that attracts Lou and Dan,' he said. 'There is *something* not far from here that makes the men want to get rid of us. Now suppose we four and Timmy go off down the hill and pass the camp, and yell out to Nobby that we're *all* – *all* of us – going to the town for the day – and you three do go, but I slip back up the hill – maybe Lou and Dan will come up here, and if I'm hiding I shall see what they're up to!'

'You mean, we'll all four pretend to go to town but really only three of us go, and you get back and hide,' said Dick. 'I see. It's a good idea.'

'And you'll hide somewhere and watch for the men to come,' said George. 'Well, for goodness' sake don't let them see you, Julian. You won't have Timmy, you know! Those men could make mincemeat of you if they wanted to.'

'Oh, they'd want to all right. I know that,' said Julian grimly. 'But you can be sure I'll be jolly well hidden.'

'I don't see why we can't have a good look round and see if we can't find the cave or whatever it is the men want to come to,' said Dick. 'If they can find it, we can, too!'

'We don't know that it *is* a cave,' said Julian. 'We haven't any idea at all what attracts the men up here. Mrs Mackie said they were up here last year, too, and the farmer had to drive them away. They thought the men were after the chickens – but I don't think so. There's *something* in these hills that makes the men want to get us away.'

'Let's have a good look round,' said George, feeling suddenly thrilled. 'I've gone all adventurous again!'

'Oh dear!' said Anne. But she couldn't help feeling rather thrilled, too. They all got up and Timmy followed, wagging his tail. He was pleased that his friends hadn't gone off and left him on guard by himself that morning.

'We'll all go different ways,' said Julian. 'Up, down and sideways. I'll go up.'

They separated and went off, George and Timmy together, of course. They hunted in the hillside for possible caves, or even for some kind of hiding-place. Timmy put his head down every rabbit-hole and felt very busy indeed.

After about half an hour the others heard Julian yelling. They ran back to the caravans, sure that he had found something exciting.

But he hadn't. He had simply got tired of hunting and decided to give it up. He shook his head when they rushed up to him, shouting to know what he had found.

'Nothing,' he said. 'I'm fed up with looking. There's not a cave anywhere here. I'm sure of that! Anyone else found anything?'

'Not a thing,' said everyone in disappointment. 'What shall we do now?'

'Put our plan into action,' said Julian, promptly. 'Let the men themselves show us what they're after. Off we go down the hills, and we'll yell out to Nobby that we're off for the day – and we'll hope that Lou and Tiger Dan will hear us!'

[14]

A very good hiding-place

They went down the hill with Timmy. Julian gave Dick some instructions. 'Have a meal in the town,' he said. 'Keep away for the day, so as to give the men a chance to come up the hill. Go to the post office and see if there are any letters for us – and buy some tins of fruit. They'll make a nice change.'

'Right, Captain!' said Dick. 'And just you be careful, old boy. These men will stick at nothing – bad-tempered brutes they are.'

'Look after the girls,' said Julian. 'Don't let George do anything mad!'

Dick grinned. 'Who can stop George doing what she wants to? Not me!'

They were now at the bottom of the hills. The circus camp lay nearby. The children could hear the barking of the dogs and the shrill trumpeting of Old Lady.

They looked about for Nobby. He was nowhere to be seen. Blow! It wouldn't be any good setting off to the town and laying such a good plan if they couldn't tell Nobby they were going!

Nobody dared to go into the camp. Julian thought of the two red cloths that Nobby and Pongo had waved. Double-danger! It would be wise not to go into the camp that morning. He stood still, undecided what to do.

Then he opened his mouth and yelled:

'Nobby! Nobby!'

No answer and no Nobby. The elephant man heard him shouting and came up. 'Do you want Nobby? I'll fetch him.'

'Thanks,' said Julian.

The little man went off, whistling. Soon Nobby appeared from behind a caravan, looking rather scared. He didn't come near Julian, but stood a good way away, looking pale and troubled.

'Nobby! We're going into the town for the

day,' yelled Julian at the top of his voice. 'We're—'

Tiger Dan suddenly appeared behind Nobby and grabbed his arm fiercely. Nobby put up a hand to protect his face, as if he expected a blow. Julian yelled again:

'We're going into the town, Nobby! We shan't be back till evening. Can you hear me? We're going to the town!'

The whole camp must have heard Julian. But he was quite determined that, whoever else didn't hear, Tiger Dan certainly should.

Nobby tried to shake off his uncle's hand, and opened his mouth to yell back something. But Dan roughly put his hand across Nobby's mouth and hauled him away, shaking him as a dog shakes a rat.

'How's barker?' yelled Julian. But Nobby had disappeared, dragged into his uncle's caravan by Dan. The little elephant man heard, however.

'Barker's bad,' he said. 'Not dead yet. But

nearly. Never saw a dog so sick in my life. Nobby's fair upset!'

The children walked off with Timmy. George had had to hold his collar all the time, for once he saw Dan he growled without stopping, and tried to get away from George.

'Thank goodness Barker isn't dead,' said Anne. 'I do hope he'll get better.'

'Not much chance,' said Julian. 'That meat must have been chock-full of poison. Poor old Nobby. How awful to be under the thumb of a fellow like Tiger Dan.'

'I just simply can't *imagine* him as a clown – Tiger Dan, I mean,' said Anne. 'Clowns are always so merry and lively and jolly.'

'Well, that's just acting,' said Dick. 'A clown needn't be the same out of the ring as he has to be when he's in it. If you look at photographs of clowns when they're just being ordinary men, they've got quite sad faces.'

'Well, Tiger Dan hasn't got a sad face. He's got a nasty, ugly, savage, cruel, fierce one,' said Anne, looking quite fierce herself.

That made the others laugh. Dick turned round to see if anyone was watching them walking towards the bus-stop, where the buses turned to go to the town.

'Lou the acrobat is watching us,' he said. 'Good! Can he see the bus-stop from where he is, Ju?'

Julian turned round. 'Yes, he can. He'll watch to see us all get into the bus – so I'd better climb in, too, and I'll get out at the first stop, double back, and get into the hills by some path he won't be able to see.'

'Right,' said Dick, enjoying the thought of playing a trick on Lou. 'Come on. There's the bus. We'll have to run for it.'

They all got into the bus. Lou was still watching, a small figure very far away. Dick felt inclined to wave cheekily to him, but didn't.

The bus set off. They took three tickets for the town and one for the nearest stop. Timmy had a ticket, too, which he wore proudly in his collar. He loved going in a bus.

Julian got out at the first stop. 'Well, see you

this evening!' he said. 'Send Timmy on ahead to the caravans when you come back – just in case the men are anywhere about. I may not be able to warn you.'

'Right,' said Dick. 'Goodbye – and good luck!'

Julian waved and set off back down the road he had come. He saw a little lane leading off up into the hills and decided to take it. It led him not very far from Mrs Mackie's farm, so he soon knew where he was. He went back to the caravans, and quickly made himself some sandwiches and cut some cake to take to his hiding-place. He might have a long wait!

'Now – where shall I hide?' thought the boy. 'I want somewhere that will give me a view of the track so that I can see when the men come up it. And yet it must be somewhere that gives me a good view of their doings, too. What would be the best place?'

A tree? No, there wasn't one that was near enough or thick enough. Behind a bush? No, the men might easily come round it and see him.

What about the middle of a thick gorse bush? That might be a good idea.

But Julian gave that up very quickly, for he found the bush far too prickly to force his way into the middle. He scratched his arms and legs terribly.

'Blow!' he said. 'I really must make up my mind, or the men may be here before I'm in hiding!'

And then he suddenly had a real brainwave, and he crowed in delight. Of course! The very place!

'I'll climb up on to the roof of one of the caravans!' thought Julian. 'Nobody will see me there – and certainly nobody would guess I was there! That really is a fine idea. I shall have a fine view of the track and a first-rate view of the men and where they go!'

It wasn't very easy to climb up on to the high roof. He had to get a rope, loop it at the end, and try to lasso the chimney in order to climb up.

He managed to lasso the chimney, and the

rope hung down over the side of the caravan, ready for him to swarm up. He threw his packet of food up on to the roof and then climbed up himself. He pulled up the rope and coiled it beside him.

Then he lay down flat. He was certain that nobody could see him from below. Of course, if the men went higher up the hill and looked down on the caravans, he could easily be spotted – but he would have to chance that.

He lay there quite still, watching the lake, and keeping eyes and ears open for anyone coming up the hillside. He was glad that it was not a very hot sunny day, or he would have been cooked up on the roof. He wished he had thought of filling a bottle with water in case he was thirsty.

He saw spires of smoke rising from where the circus camp lay, far below. He saw a couple of boats on the lake, a good way round the water – people fishing, he supposed. He watched a couple of rabbits come out and play on the hillside just below.

The sun came out from behind the clouds for about ten minutes and Julian began to feel uncomfortably hot. Then it went in again and he felt better.

He suddenly heard somebody whistling and stiffened himself in expectation – but it was only someone belonging to the farm, going down the hill some distance away. The whistle had carried clearly in the still air.

Then he got bored. The rabbits went in, and not even a butterfly sailed by. He could see no birds except a yellow-hammer that sat on the topmost spray of a bush and sang: 'Little-bit-of-bread-and-no-cheese', over and over again in a most maddening manner.

Then it gave a cry of alarm and flew off. It had heard something that frightened it.

Julian heard something, too, and glued his eyes to the track that led up the hill. His heart began to beat. He could see two men. Were they Lou and Dan?

He did not dare to raise his head to see them when they came nearer in case they spotted him. But he knew their voices when they came near enough!

Yes – it was Lou and Tiger Dan all right. There was no mistaking those two harsh, coarse voices. The men came right into the hollow, and Julian heard them talking.

'Yes, there's nobody here. Those kids have really gone off for the day at least – and taken that wretched dog with them!'

'I saw them get on the bus, dog and all, I told you,' growled Lou. 'There'll be nobody here for the day. We can get what we want to.'

'Let's go and get it, then,' said Dan.

Julian waited to see where they would go to. But they didn't go out of the hollow. They stayed there, apparently beside the caravans. Julian did not dare to look over the edge of the roof to see what they were up to. He was glad he fastened all the windows and locked the doors.

Then there began some curious scuffling sounds, and the men panted. The caravan on which Julian was lying began to shake a little.

'What *are* they doing?' thought Julian in bewilderment. In intense curiosity he slid quietly to the edge of the caravan roof and cautiously peeped over, though he had firmly made up his mind not to do this on any account.

He looked down on the ground. There was nobody there at all. Perhaps the men were the other side. He slid carefully across and peeped over the opposite side of the caravan, which was still shaking a little, as if the men were bumping against it.

There was nobody the other side either! How very extraordinary! 'Golly! They must be underneath the caravan!' thought Julian, going back to the middle of the roof. 'Underneath! What in the wide world for?'

It was quite impossible to see underneath the caravan from where he was, so he had to lie quietly and wonder about the men's doings. They grunted and groaned, and seemed to be scraping and scrabbling about, but nothing happened. Then Julian heard them scrambling out from underneath, angry and disappointed.

'Give us a cigarette,' said Lou in a disagreeable voice. 'I'm fed up with this. Have to shift this van. Those tiresome brats! What did they want to choose this spot for?'

Julian heard a match struck and smelt cigarette smoke. Then he got a shock. The caravan he was on began to move! Heavens! Were the men going to push it over the ledge and send it rolling down the hillside?

[15]

Several things happen

Julian was suddenly very scared. He wondered if he had better slide off the roof and run. He wouldn't have much chance if the caravan went hurtling down the hill! But he didn't move. He clung to the chimney with both hands, whilst the men shoved hard against the caravan.

It ran a few feet to the rocky ledge, and then stopped. Julian felt his forehead getting very damp, and he saw that his hands were trembling, but he couldn't stop them.

'Hey! Don't send it down the hill!' said Lou in alarm, and Julian's heart felt lighter. So they didn't mean to destroy the caravan in that way! They had just moved it to get at something underneath. But what could it be? Julian racked his brains to try and think what the floor of the hollow had been like when Dobby and Trotter pulled their caravans into it. As far as he could remember, it was just an ordinary heathery hollow.

The men were now scrabbling away again by the back steps of the caravan. Julian was absolutely eaten up with curiosity, but he did not dare even to move. He could find out the secret when the men had gone. Meantime he really must be patient or he would spoil everything.

There was some muttered talking, but Julian couldn't catch a word. Then, quite suddenly, there was complete and utter silence. Not a word. Not a bump against the caravan. Not a pant or even a grunt. Nothing at all.

Julian lay still. Maybe the men were still there. He wasn't going to give himself away. He lay for quite a long time, waiting and wondering. But he heard nothing.

Then he saw a robin fly to a nearby bramble spray. It flicked its wings and looked about for crumbs. It was a robin that came around when the children were having a meal – but it was not as tame as most robins, and would not fly down until the children had left the hollow.

Then a rabbit popped out of a hole on the hillside and capered about, running suddenly up to the hollow.

'Well,' thought Julian, 'it's plain the men aren't here now, or the birds and animals wouldn't be about like this. There's another rabbit. Those men have gone somewhere – though goodness knows where. I can peep over now and have a look, quite safely, I should think.'

He slid himself round and peered over the roof at the back end of the caravan. He looked down at the ground. There was absolutely nothing to be seen to tell him what the men had been doing, or where they had gone! The heather grew luxuriantly there as it did everywhere else. There was nothing to show what the men had been making such a disturbance about.

'This is really very strange,' thought Julian, beginning to wonder if he had been dreaming.

'The men are certainly gone – vanished into thin air, apparently! Dare I get down and explore a bit? No, I daren't. The men may appear at any moment, and it's quite on the cards they'll lose their temper if they find me here, and chuck both me and the caravans down the hill! It's pretty steep just here, too.'

He lay there, thinking. He suddenly felt very hungry and thirsty. Thank goodness he had been sensible enough to take food up to the roof! He could at least have a meal while he was waiting for the men to come back – if they ever did!

He began to eat his sandwiches. They tasted very good indeed. He finished them all and began on the cake. That was good, too. He had brought a few plums up as well, and was very glad of them because he was thirsty. He flicked the plum stones from the roof before he thought what he was doing.

'Dash! Why did I do that? If the men notice them they may remember they weren't there before. Still, they've most of them gone into the heather!'

The sun came out a little and Julian felt hot. He wished the men would come again and go down the hill. He was tired of lying flat on the hard roof. Also he was terribly sleepy. He yawned silently and shut his eyes.

How long he slept he had no idea – but he was suddenly awakened by feeling the caravan being moved again! He clutched the chimney in alarm, listening to the low voices of the two men.

They were pulling the caravan back into place again. Soon it was in the same position as before. Then Julian heard a match struck and smelt smoke again.

The men went and sat on the rocky ledge and took out food they had brought. Julian did not dare to peep at them, though he felt sure they had their backs to him. The men ate, and talked in low voices, and then, to Julian's dismay, they lay down and went to sleep! He knew that they were asleep because he could hear them snoring.

'Am I going to stay on this awful roof all day

long?' he thought. 'I'm getting so cramped, lying flat like this. I want to sit up!'

'R-r-r-r-r-r!' snored Lou and Dan. Julian felt that surely it would be all right to sit up now that the men were obviously asleep. So he sat up cautiously, stretching himself with pleasure.

He looked down on the two men, who were lying on their backs with their mouths open. Beside them were two neat sacks, strong and thick. Julian wondered what was inside them. They certainly had not had them when they came up the track.

The boy gazed down the hillside, frowning, trying to probe the mystery of where the men had been, and what they were doing up here – and suddenly he jumped violently. He stared as if he could not believe his eyes.

A squat and ugly face was peering out from a bramble bush there. There was almost no nose, and an enormous mouth. Who could it be? Was it someone spying on Lou and Dan? But what a face! It didn't seem human.

A hand came up to rub the face – and Julian

saw that it was hairy. With a start he knew who the face belonged to – Pongo the chimpanzee! No wonder he had thought it such an ugly, inhuman face. It was all right on a chimp, of course – quite a nice face – but not on a man.

Pongo stared at Julian solemnly, and Julian stared back, his mind in a whirl. What was Pongo doing there? Was Nobby with him? If so, Nobby was in danger, for at any moment the men might wake up. He couldn't think what to do. If he called out to warn Nobby, he would wake the men.

Pongo was pleased to see Julian, and did not seem to think the roof of a caravan a curious place to be in at all. After all, *he* often went up on the roofs of caravans. He nodded and blinked at the boy, and then scratched his head for a long time.

Then beside him appeared Nobby's face – a tear-stained face, bruised and swollen. He suddenly saw Julian looking over the roof of the caravan, and his mouth fell open in surprise. He seemed about to call out, and Julian shook his head frantically to stop him, pointing downwards to try and warn Nobby that somebody was there.

But Nobby didn't understand. He grinned and, to Julian's horror, began to climb up the hillside to the rocky ledge! The men were sleeping there, and Julian saw with dismay that Nobby would probably heave himself up right on top of them.

'Look out!' he said, in a low, urgent voice. 'Look out, you fathead!'

But it was too late. Nobby heaved himself up on to the ledge, and, to his utmost horror, found himself sprawling on top of Tiger Dan! He gave a yell and tried to slide away – but Dan, rousing suddenly, shot out a hand and gripped him.

Lou woke up, too. The men glared at poor Nobby, and the boy began to tremble and beg for mercy.

'I didn't know you were here, I swear it! Let me go, let me go! I only came up to look for my knife that I lost yesterday!'

Dan shook him savagely. 'How long have you been here? You been spying?'

'No, no! I've only just come! I've been at the camp all morning – you ask Larry and Rossy. I been helping them!'

'You been spying on us, that's what you've been doing!' said Lou, in a cold, hard voice that filled the listening Julian with dread. 'You've had plenty of beatings this week, but seemingly they aren't enough. Well, up here, there's nobody to hear your yells, see? So we'll show you what a real beating is! And if you can walk down to the camp after it, I'll be surprised.'

Nobby was terrified. He begged for mercy, he promised to do anything the men asked him, and tried to jerk his poor swollen face away from Dan's hard hands.

Julian couldn't bear it. He didn't want to give away the fact that it was he who had been spying, nor did he want to fight the men at all, for he was pretty certain he would get the worst of it. But nobody could lie in silence, watching two men treat a young boy in such a way. He made up his mind to leap off the roof right on to the men, and to rescue poor Nobby if he could.

Nobby gave an anguished yell as Lou gave him a flick with his leather belt – but before Julian could jump down to help him, somebody else bounded up! Somebody who bared his teeth and made ugly animal noises of rage, somebody whose arms were far stronger than either Lou's or Dan's – somebody who loved poor Nobby, and wasn't going to let him be beaten any more!

It was Pongo. The chimpanzee had been watching the scene with his sharp little eyes. He had still hidden himself in the bush, for he was afraid of Lou and Dan – but now, hearing Nobby's cries, he leapt out of the brambles and flung himself on the astonished men.

He bit Lou's arm hard. Then he bit Dan's leg. The men yelled loudly, much more loudly than poor Nobby had. Lou lashed out with his leather belt, and it caught Pongo on the shoulder. The chimpanzee made a shrill chattering noise, and leapt on Lou with his arms open, clasping the man to him, trying to bite his throat.

Tiger Dan rushed down the hill at top speed, terrified of the angry chimpanzee. Lou yelled to Nobby:

'Call him off! He'll kill me!'

'Pongo!' shouted Nobby. 'Stop it! Pongo! Come here.'

Pongo gave Nobby a look of the greatest surprise. 'What!' he seemed to say. 'You won't let me punish this bad man who beat you? Well, well – whatever you say must be right!'

And the chimpanzee, giving Lou one last vicious nip, let the man go. Lou followed Dan down the hill at top speed, and Julian heard him crashing through the bushes as if a hundred chimpanzees were after him.

Nobby sat down, trembling. Pongo, not quite sure if his beloved friend was angry with him or not, crept up to him putting a paw on the boy's knee. Nobby put his arm round the anxious animal, and Pongo chattered with joy.

Julian slid down from the roof of the caravan and went to Nobby. He, too, sat down beside him. He put his arm round the trembling boy and gave him a hug.

'I was just coming to give you a hand, when Pongo shot up the hill,' he said.

'Were you really?' said Nobby, his face lighting up. 'You're a real friend, you are. Good as Pongo, here.'

And Julian felt quite proud to be ranked in bravery with the chimpanzee!

[16]

A surprising discovery

'Listen – somebody's coming!' said Nobby, and Pongo gave an ugly growl. The sound of voices could be heard coming up the hill. Then a dog barked.

'It's all right. It's Timmy – and the others,' said Julian, unspeakably glad to welcome them back. He stood up and yelled.

'All right! Come along!'

George, Timmy, Dick and Anne came running up the track. 'Hallo!' shouted Dick. 'We thought it would be safe, because we saw Lou and Dan in the distance, running along at the bottom of the hill. I say – there's Pongo!'

Pongo shook hands with Dick, and then went to the back of Timmy, to shake hands with his tail. But Timmy was ready for him, and backing round, he held out his paw to Pongo instead. It was very funny to see the two animals solemnly shaking hands with one another.

'Hallo, Nobby!' said Dick. 'Goodness – what have you been doing to yourself? You look as if you've been in the wars.'

'Well, I have, rather,' said Nobby, with a feeble grin. He was very much shaken, and did not get up. Pongo ran to Anne and tried to put his arms round her.

'Oh, Pongo – you squeeze too hard,' said Anne. 'Julian, did anything happen? Did the men come? Have you any news?'

'Plenty,' said Julian. 'But what I want first is a jolly good drink. I've had none all day. Ginger-beer, I think.'

'We're all thirsty. I'll get five bottles – no, six, because I expect Pongo would like some.'

Pongo loved ginger-beer. He sat down with the children on the rocky ledge, and took his glass from Anne, just like a child. Timmy was a little jealous, but as he didn't like ginger-beer he couldn't make a fuss.

Julian began to tell the others about his day,

and how he had hidden on the caravan roof. He described how the men had come – and had gone under the caravan – and then moved it. They all listened with wide eyes. What a story!

Then Nobby told his part. 'I butted in and almost gave the game away,' he said, when Julian had got as far as the men falling asleep and snoring. 'But, you see, I had to come and warn you. Lou and Dan swear they'll poison Timmy somehow, even if they have to dope him, put him into a sack and take him down to the camp to do it. Or they might knock him on the head.'

'Let them try!' said George, in her fiercest voice, and put her arm round Timmy. Pongo at once put his arm round Timmy too.

'And they said they'd damage your caravans too – maybe put a fire underneath and burn them up,' went on Nobby.

The four children stared at him in horror. 'But they wouldn't do a thing like that, surely?' said Julian, at last. 'They'd get into trouble with the police if they did.'

'Well, I'm just telling you what they said,' Nobby went on. 'You don't know Lou and Tiger Dan like I do. They'll stick at nothing to get their way – or to get anybody *out* of their way. They tried to poison Timmy, didn't they? And poor old Barker got it instead.'

'Is – is Barker – all right?' asked Anne.

'No,' said Nobby. 'He's dying, I think. I've given him to Lucilla to dose. She's a marvel with sick animals. I've put Growler with the other dogs. He's safe with them.'

He stared round at the other children, his mouth trembling, sniffing as if he had a bad cold.

'I daren't go back,' he said, in a low voice, 'I daren't. They'll half-kill me.'

'You're not going back, so that's settled,' said Julian, in a brisk voice. 'You're staying here with us. We shall love to have you. It was jolly decent of you to come up and warn us – and bad luck to have got caught like that. You're our friend now – and we'll stick together.'

Nobby couldn't say a word, but his face

shone. He rubbed a dirty hand across his eyes, then grinned his old grin. He nodded his head, not trusting himself to speak, and the children all thought how nice he was. Poor old Nobby.

They finished their ginger-beer and then Julian got up. 'And now,' he said, 'we will do a little exploring and find out where those men went, shall we?'

'Oh yes!' cried George, who had sat still quite long enough. 'We *must* find out! Do we have to get under the caravan, Julian?'

''Fraid so,' said Julian. 'You sit there quietly, Nobby, and keep guard in case Lou or Dan come back.'

He didn't think for a moment that they would, but he could see that Nobby needed to sit quietly for a while. Nobby, however, had different ideas. He was going to share this adventure!

'Timmy's guard enough, and so is Pongo,' he said. 'They'll hear anyone coming half a mile away. I'm in on this!'

And he was. He went scrabbling underneath

the low-slung base of the caravan with the others, eager to find out anything he could.

But it was impossible to explore down in the heather, with the caravan base just over their heads. They had no room at all. Like Dan and Lou they soon felt that they would have to move the van.

It took all five of them, with Pongo giving a shove, too, to move the caravan a few feet away. Then down they dropped to the thick carpet of heather again.

The tufts came up easily by the roots, because the men had already pulled them up once that day and then replanted them. The children dragged up a patch of heather about five feet square, and then gave an exclamation.

'Look! Boards under the heather!'

'Laid neatly across and across. What for?'

'Pull them up!'

The boys pulled up the planks one by one and piled them on one side. Then they saw that the boards had closed up the entrance of a deep hole. 'I'll get my torch,' said Julian. He fetched it and flashed it on.

The light showed them a dark hole, going down into the hillside, with footholds sticking out of one side. They all sat and gazed down in excitement.

'To think we went and put our caravan *exactly* over the entrance of the men's hiding-place!' said Dick 'No wonder they were wild! No wonder they changed their minds and told us we could go down to the lake and camp there instead of here!'

'Gosh!' said Julian, staring into the hole. 'So that's where the men went! Where does it lead to? They were down there a mighty long time. They were clever enough to replace the planks and drag some of the heather over them, too, to hide them when they went down.'

Pongo suddenly took it into his head to go down the hole. Down he went, feeling for the footholds with his hairy feet, grinning up at the others. He disappeared at the bottom. Julian's torch could not pick him out at all.

'Hey, Pongo! Don't lose yourself down there!' called Nobby, anxiously. But Pongo had gone.

'Blow him!' said Nobby. 'He'll never find his way back, if he goes wandering about underground. I'll have to go after him. Can I have your torch, Julian?'

'I'll come too,' said Julian. 'George, get me your torch as well, will you?'

'It's broken,' said George. 'I dropped it last night. And nobody else has got one.'

'What an awful nuisance!' said Julian. 'I want us to go and explore down there – but we can't with only one torch. Well, I'll just go down with Nobby and get Pongo – have a quick look round and come back. I may see something worth seeing!'

Nobby went down first, and Julian followed, the others all kneeling round the hole, watching them enviously. They disappeared.

'Pongo!' yelled Nobby. 'Pongo! Come here, you idiot!'

Pongo had not gone very far. He didn't like

the dark down there very much, and he came to Nobby as soon as he saw the light of the torch. The boys found themselves in a narrow passage at the bottom of the hole, which widened as they went further into the hill.

'Must be caves somewhere,' said Julian, flashing his torch round. 'We know that a lot of springs run out of this hill. I daresay that through the centuries the water has eaten away the softer stuff and made caves and tunnels everywhere in the hill. And somewhere in a cave Lou and Dan store away things they don't want anyone to know about. Stolen goods, probably.'

The passage ended in a small cave that seemed to have no other opening out of it at all. There was nothing in it. Julian flashed his torch up and down the walls.

He saw footholds up one part, and traced them to a hole in the roof, which must have been made, years before, by running water. 'That's the way we go!' he said. 'Come on.'

'Wait!' said Nobby. 'Isn't your torch getting rather faint?'

'Goodness – yes!' said Julian in alarm, and shook his torch violently to make the light brighter. But the battery had almost worn out, and no better light came. Instead the light grew even fainter, until it was just a pin-prick in the torch.

'Come on – we'd better get back at once,' said Julian, feeling a bit scared. 'I don't want to wander about here in the pitch dark. Not my idea of fun at all.'

Nobby took firm hold of Pongo's hairy paw and equally firm hold of Julian's jersey. He didn't mean to lose either of them! The light in the torch went out completely. Now they must find their way back in black darkness.

Julian felt round for the beginning of the passage that led back to the hole. He found it and made his way up it, feeling the sides with his hands. It wasn't a pleasant experience at all, and Julian was thankful that he and Nobby had only gone a little way into the hill. It would have been like a nightmare if they had gone well in, and then found themselves unable to see the way back.

They saw a faint light shining further on and guessed it was the daylight shining down the entrance-hole. They stumbled thankfully towards it. They looked up and saw the anxious faces of the other three peering down at them, unable to see them.

'We're back!' called Julian, beginning to climb up. 'My torch went out, and we daren't go very far. We've got Pongo, though.'

The others helped to pull them out at the top of the hole. Julian told them about the hole in the roof of the little cave.

'That's where the men went,' he said. 'And tomorrow, when we've all bought torches, and matches and candles, that's where we're going, too! We'll go down to the town and buy what we want, and come back and do a Really Good Exploration!'

'We're going to have an adventure after all,' said Anne, in rather a small voice.

''Fraid so,' said Julian. 'But you can stay at

the farm with Mrs Mackie for the day, Anne dear. Don't you come with us.'

'If you're going on an adventure, I'm coming, too,' said Anne. 'So there! I wouldn't *dream* of not coming.'

'All right,' said Julian. 'We'll all go together. Golly, things are getting exciting!'

[17]

Another visit from Lou and Dan

Nobody disturbed the children that night, and Timmy did not bark once. Nobby slept on a pile of rugs in the boys' caravan, and Pongo cuddled up to him. The chimpanzee seemed delighted at staying with the caravanners. Timmy was rather jealous that another animal should be with them, and wouldn't take any notice of Pongo at all.

The next morning, after breakfast, the children discussed who was to go down to the town. 'Not Nobby and Pongo, because they wouldn't be allowed in the bus together,' said Julian. 'They had better stay behind.'

'Not by ourselves?' said Nobby, looking alarmed. 'Suppose Lou and Uncle Dan come up? Even if I've got Pongo I'd be scared.'

'Well, I'll stay here, too,' said Dick. 'We don't all need to go to buy torches. Don't forget to post that letter to Daddy and Mother, Julian.'

They had written a long letter to their parents, telling them of the exciting happenings. Julian put it into his pocket. 'I'll post it all right,' he said. 'Well, I suppose we might as well go now. Come on, girls. Keep a look-out, Dick, in case those rogues come back.'

George, Timmy, Anne and Julian went down the hill together, Timmy running on in front, his tail wagging nineteen to the dozen. Pongo climbed up to the roof of the red caravan to watch them go. Nobby and Dick sat down in the warm sun on the ledge, their heads resting on springy clumps of heather.

'It's nice up here,' said Nobby. 'Much nicer than down below. I wonder what everyone is thinking about Pongo and me. I bet Mr Gorgio, the head of the circus, is wild that the chimpanzee's gone. I bet he'll send up to fetch us.'

Nobby was right. Two people were sent up to get him – Lou and Tiger Dan. They came creeping up through the bracken and heather, keeping a sharp eye for Timmy or Pongo.

Pongo sensed them long before they could be seen and warned Nobby. Nobby went very pale. He was terrified of the two scoundrels.

'Get into one of the caravans,' said Dick in a low voice. 'Go on. I'll deal with those fellows – if it *is* them. Pongo will help me if necessary.'

Nobby scuttled into the green caravan and shut the door. Dick sat where he was. Pongo squatted on the roof of the caravan, watching.

Lou and Dan suddenly appeared. They saw Dick, but did not see Pongo. They looked all round for the others.

'What do you want?' said Dick.

'Nobby and Pongo,' said Lou with a scowl. 'Where are they?'

They're going to stay on with us,' said Dick.

'Oh, no, they're not!' said Tiger Dan. 'Nobby's in my charge, see? I'm his uncle.'

'Funny sort of uncle,' remarked Dick. 'How's that dog you poisoned, by the way?'

Tiger Dan went purple in the face. He looked

as if he would willingly have thrown Dick down the hill.

'You be careful what you say to me!' he said, beginning to shout.

Nobby, hidden in the caravan, trembled when he heard his uncle's angry yell. Pongo kept quite still, his face set and ugly.

'Well, you may as well say goodbye and go,' said Dick in a calm voice to Dan. 'I've told you that Nobby and Pongo are staying with us for the present.'

'Where *is* Nobby?' demanded Tiger Dan, looking as if he would burst with rage at any moment. 'Wait till I get my hands on him. Wait . . .'

He began to walk towards the caravans – but Pongo was not having any of that! He leapt straight off the roof on to the horrified man, and flung him to the ground. He made such a terrible snarling noise that Dan was terrified.

'Call him off!' he yelled. 'Lou, come and help.'

'Pongo won't obey *me*,' said Dick still sitting

down looking quite undisturbed. 'You'd better go before he bites big pieces out of you.'

Dan staggered to the rock ledge, looking as if he would box Dick's ears. But the boy did not move, and somehow Dan did not dare to touch him. Pongo let him go and stood glowering at him, his great hairy arms hanging down his sides, ready to fly at either of the men if they came near.

Tiger Dan picked up a stone – and as quick as lightning Pongo flung himself on him again and sent the man rolling down the hill. Lou fled in terror. Dan got up and fled, too, yelling furiously as he went. Pongo chased them in delight. He, too, picked up stones and flung them with a very accurate aim, so that Dick kept hearing yells of pain.

Pongo came back, looking extremely pleased with himself. He went to the green caravan, as Dick shouted to Nobby.

'All right, Nobby. They've gone. Pongo and I won the battle!'

Nobby came out. Pongo put his arm round

him at once and chattered nonsense in his ear. Nobby looked rather ashamed of himself.

'Bit of a coward, aren't I?' he said. 'Leaving you out here all alone.'

'I enjoyed it,' said Dick truthfully. 'And I'm sure Pongo did!'

'You don't know what dangerous fellows Lou and Dan are,' said Nobby, looking down the hillside to make sure the men were really gone. 'I tell you they'd stick at nothing. They'd burn your caravans, hurl them down the hill, poison your dog, and do what harm they could to you, too. You don't know them like I do!'

'Well, as a matter of fact, we've had some pretty exciting adventures with men just as tough as Dan and Lou,' said Dick. 'We always seem to be falling into the middle of some adventure or other. Now, last hols we went to a place called Smuggler's Top – and, my word, the adventures we had there! You wouldn't believe them!'

'You tell me and Pongo,' said Nobby, sitting

down beside Dick. 'We've plenty of time before the others come back.'

So Dick began to tell the tale of all the other thrilling adventures that the five of them had had, and the time flew. Both boys were surprised when they heard Timmy barking down the track, and knew that the others were back.

George came tearing up with Timmy at her heels. 'Are you all right? Did anything happen while we were away? Do you know, we saw Lou and Tiger Dan getting on the bus when we got off it! They were carrying bags as if they meant to go away and stay somewhere.'

Nobby brightened up at once. 'Did you really? Good! They came up here, you know, and Pongo chased them down the hill. They must have gone back to the camp, collected their bags, and gone to catch the bus. Hurrah!'

'We've got fine torches,' said Julian, and showed Dick his. 'Powerful ones. Here's one for you, Dick – and one for you, Nobby.'

'Oooh – thanks,' said Nobby. Then he went

red. 'I haven't got enough money to pay you for such a grand torch,' he said awkwardly.

'It's a present for you,' said Anne at once, 'a present for a friend of ours, Nobby!'

'Coo! Thanks awfully,' said Nobby, looking quite overcome. 'I've never had a present before. You're decent kids, you are.'

Pongo held out his hand to Anne and made a chattering noise as if to say: 'What about one for me, too?'

'Oh – we didn't bring one for Pongo!' said Anne. 'Why ever didn't we?'

'Good thing you didn't,' said Nobby. 'He would have put it on and off all day long and wasted the battery in no time!'

'I'll give him my old torch,' said George. 'It's broken, but he won't mind that!'

Pongo was delighted with it. He kept pressing down the knob that should make the light flash – and when there was no light he looked all about on the ground as if the light must have dropped out! The children roared at him. He liked them to laugh at him. He did a little dance all round them to show how pleased he was.

'Look here – wouldn't it be a jolly good time to explore underground now that we know Lou and Dan are safely out of the way?' asked Julian suddenly. 'If they've got bags with them, surely that means they're going to spend the night somewhere and won't be back till tomorrow at least. We'd be quite safe to go down and explore.'

'Yes, we would,' said George eagerly. 'I'm longing to get down there and Make Discoveries!'

'Well, let's have something to eat first,' said Dick. 'It's long past our dinner-time. It must be about half past one. Yes, it is!'

'George and I will get you a meal,' said Anne. 'We called at the farm on our way up and got a lovely lot of food. Come on, George.'

George got up unwillingly. Timmy followed her, sniffing expectantly. Soon the two girls were busy getting a fine meal ready, and they all sat on the rocky ledge to eat it.

'Mrs Mackie gave us this enormous bar of

chocolate for a present today,' said Anne, showing a great slab to Dick and Nobby. 'Isn't it lovely? No, Pongo, it's not for you. Eat your sandwiches properly, and don't grab.'

'I vote we take some food down into the hill with us,' said Julian. 'We may be quite a long time down there, and we shan't want to come back at tea-time.'

'Oooh – a picnic inside the hill!' said Anne. 'That would be thrilling. I'll soon pack up some food in the kit-bag. I won't bother to make sandwiches. We'll take a new loaf, butter, ham and a cake, and cut what we want. What about something to drink?'

'Oh, we can last out till we get back,' said Julian. 'Just take something to eat to keep us going till we have finished exploring.'

George and Nobby cleared up and rinsed the plates. Anne wrapped up some food in greased paper, and packed it carefully into the kit-bag for Julian to carry. She popped the big bar of chocolate into the bag, too. It would be nice to eat at odd moments.

At last they were all ready. Timmy wagged his tail. He knew they were going somewhere.

The five of them pushed the caravan back a few feet to expose the hole. They had all tugged the van back into place the night before, in case Lou and Dan came to go down the hole again. No one could get down it if the caravan was over it.

The boards had been laid roughly across the hole and the boys took them off, tossing them to one side. As soon as Pongo saw the hole he drew back, frightened.

'He's remembered the darkness down there,' said George. 'He doesn't like it. Come on, Pongo. You'll be all right. We've all got torches!'

But nothing would persuade Pongo to go down the hole again. He cried like a baby when Nobby tried to make him.

'It's no good,' said Julian. 'You'll have to stop up here with him.'

'What – and miss all the excitement!' cried Nobby indignantly. 'I jolly well won't. We can tie old Pongo up to a wheel of the van so that he won't wander off. Lou and Dan are away somewhere, and no one else is likely to tackle a big chimp like Pongo. We'll tie him up.'

So Pongo was tied firmly to one of the caravan wheels. 'You stay there like a good chimp till we come back,' said Nobby, putting a pail of water beside him in case he should want a drink. 'We'll be back soon!'

Pongo was sad to see them go – but nothing would have made him go down that hole again! So he sat watching the children disappear one by one. Timmy jumped down, too, and then they were all gone. Gone on another adventure. What would happen now?

[18]

Inside the hill

The children had all put on extra jerseys, by Julian's orders, for he knew it would be cold inside the dark hill. Nobby had been lent an old one of Dick's. They were glad of them as soon as they were walking down the dark passage that led to the first cave, for the air was very chilly.

They came to the small cave and Julian flashed his torch to show them where the footholds went up the wall to a hole in the roof.

'It's exciting,' said George, thrilled. 'I like this sort of thing. Where does that hole in the roof lead to, I wonder? I'll go first, Ju.'

'No, you won't,' said Julian firmly. 'I go first. You don't know what might be at the top!'

Up he went, his torch held in his mouth, for he needed both hands to climb. The footholds were strong nails driven into the rock of the cave-wall, and were fairly easy to climb.

He got to the hole in the roof and popped his head through. He gave a cry of astonishment.

'I say! There's a most enormous cavern here – bigger than six dance-halls – and the walls are all glittering with something – phosphorescence, I should think.'

He scrambled out of the hole and stood on the floor of the immense cave. Its walls twinkled in their weird light, and Julian shut off his torch. There was almost enough phosphorescent light in the cavern to see by!

One by one the others came up and stared in wonder. 'It's like Aladdin's cave!' said Anne. 'Isn't that an odd light shining from the walls – and from the roof, too, Julian?'

Dick and George had rather a difficulty in getting Timmy up to the cavern, but they managed it at last. Timmy put his tail down at once when he saw the curious light gleaming everywhere. But it went up again when George patted him.

'What an enormous place!' said Dick. 'Do you suppose this is where the men hide their stuff, whatever it is?'

Julian flashed his torch on again and swung it round and about, picking out the dark, rocky corners. 'Can't see anything hidden,' he said. 'But we'd better explore the cave properly before we go on.'

So the five children explored every nook and cranny of the gleaming cave, but could find nothing at all. Julian gave a sudden exclamation and picked something up from the floor.

'A cigarette end!' he said. 'That shows that Lou and Dan have been here. Come on, let's see if there's a way out of this great cave.'

Right at the far end, half-way up the gleaming wall was a large hole, rather like a tunnel. Julian climbed up to it and called to the others. 'This is the way they went. There's a dead match just at the entrance to the tunnel or whatever this is.'

It was a curious tunnel, no higher than their shoulders in some places, and it wound about as it went further into the hill. Julian thought that at one time water must have run through it. But it was quite dry now. The floor of the tunnel was worn very smooth, as if a stream had hollowed it out through many, many years.

'I hope the stream won't take it into its head to begin running suddenly again!' said George. 'We should get jolly wet!'

The tunnel went on for some way, and Anne was beginning to feel it must go on for ever. Then the wall at one side widened out and made a big rocky shelf. Julian, who was first, flashed his torch into the hollow.

'I say!' he shouted. 'Here's where those fellows keep their stores! There's a whole pile of things here!'

The others crowded up as closely as they could, each of them flashing their torch brightly. On the wide, rocky shelf lay boxes and packages, sacks and cases. The children stared at them. 'What's in them?' said Nobby, full of intense curiosity. 'Let's see!'

He put down his torch and undid a sack. He

slid in his hand – and brought it out holding a piece of shining gold plate!

'Coo!' said Nobby. 'So that's what the police were after last year when they came and searched the camp! And it was hidden safely here. Coo, look at all these things. Jumping Jiminy, they must have robbed the Queen herself!'

The sack was full of exquisite pieces of gold plate – cups, dishes, small trays. The children set them all out on the ledge. How they gleamed in the light of their torches!

'They're thieves in a very big way,' said Julian. 'No doubt about that. Let's look in this box.'

The box was not locked, and the lid opened easily. Inside was a piece of china, a vase so fragile that it looked as if it might break at a breath!

'Well, I don't know anything about china,' said Julian, 'but I suppose this is a very precious piece, worth thousands of pounds. A collector of china would probably give a very large sum for it. What rogues Lou and Dan are!'

'Look here!' suddenly said George, and she pulled leather boxes out of a bag. 'Jewellery!'

She opened the boxes. The children exclaimed in awe. Diamonds flashed brilliantly, rubies glowed, emeralds shone green. Necklaces, bracelets, rings, brooches – the beautiful things gleamed in the light of the five torches.

There was a tiara in one box that seemed to be made only of big diamonds. Anne picked it out of its box gently. Then she put it on her hair.

'I'm a princess! It's my crown!' she said.

'You look lovely,' said Nobby admiringly. 'You look as grand as Delphine the Bareback Rider when she goes into the ring on her horse, with jewels shining all over her!'

Anne put on necklaces and bracelets and sat there on the ledge like a little princess, shining brightly in the magnificent jewels. Then she took them off and put them carefully back into their satin-lined boxes.

'Well – what a haul those two rogues have made!' said Julian, pulling out some gleaming silver plate from another package. 'They must be very fine burglars!'

'*I* know how they work,' said Dick. 'Lou's a wonderful acrobat, isn't he? I bet he does all the climbing about up walls and over roofs and into windows – and Tiger Dan stands below and catches everything he throws down.'

'You're about right,' said Nobby, handling a beautiful silver cup. 'Lou could climb anywhere – up ivy, up pipes – even up the bare wall of a house, I shouldn't wonder! And jump! He can jump like a cat. He and Tiger Dan have been in this business for a long time, I expect. That's where Uncle Dan went at night, of course, when we were on tour, and I woke up and found him gone out of the caravan!'

'And I expect he stores the stolen goods in that wagon of his you showed us,' said Julian, remembering. 'You told us how angry he was with you once when you went and rummaged about in it. He probably stored it there, and then he and Lou came up here each year and hid the stuff underground – waiting till the police had given up the search for the stolen things – and then they come and get it and sell it somewhere safe.'

'A jolly clever plan,' said Dick. 'What a fine chance they've got – wandering about from place to place like that hearing of famous jewels or plate – slipping out at night – and Lou climbing up to bedrooms like a cat. I wonder how they found this place – it's a most wonderful hidy-hole!'

'Yes. Nobody would ever dream of it!' said George.

'And then we go and put our caravan bang on the top of the entrance – just when they want to put something in and take something out!' said Julian. 'I *must* have annoyed them.'

'What are we going to do about it?' said Dick.

'Tell the police, of course,' said Julian, promptly. 'What do you suppose? My word, I'd like to see the face of the policeman who first sees this little haul.'

They put everything back carefully. Julian

shone his torch up the tunnel. 'Shall we explore a bit further, or not?' he said. 'It still goes on. Look!'

'Better get back,' said Nobby. 'Now we've found this we'd better do something about it.'

'Oh, let's just see where the tunnel goes to,' said George. 'It won't take a minute!'

'All right,' said Julian, who wanted to go up the tunnel as much as she did. He led the way, his torch shining brightly.

The tunnel came out into another cave, not nearly as big as the one they had left behind. At one end something gleamed like silver, and seemed to move. There was a curious sound there, too.

'What is it?' said Anne, alarmed. They stood and listened.

'Water!' said Julian, suddenly. 'Of course! Can't you hear it flowing along? It's an underground stream, flowing through the hill to find an opening where it can rush out.'

'Like that stream we saw before we came to our caravan camping-place,' said George. 'It rushed out of the hill. Do you remember? This may be the very one!'

'I expect it is!' said Dick. They went over to it and watched it. It rushed along in its own hollowed out channel, close to the side of the cave-wall.

'Maybe at one time it ran across this cave and down the tunnel we came up by,' said Julian. 'Yes, look – there's a big kind of groove in the floor of the cave here – the stream must have run there once. Then for some reason it went a different way.'

'Let's get back,' said Nobby. 'I want to know if Pongo's all right. I don't somehow feel very comfortable about him. And I'm jolly cold, too. Let's go back to the sunshine and have something to eat. I don't want a picnic down here, after all.'

'All right,' said Julian, and they made their way back through the tunnel. They passed the rock shelf on which lay the treasure, and came at last to the enormous gleaming cavern. They went across it to the hole that led down into the small cave. Down they went, Julian and George trying to manage Timmy between them. But it was very awkward, for he was a big dog.

Then along the passage to the entrance-hole. They all felt quite pleased at the idea of going up into the sunshine again.

'Can't see any daylight shining down the hole,' said Julian puzzled. 'It would be near here.'

He came up against a blank wall, and was surprised. Where was the hole? Had they missed their way? Then he flashed his torch above him and saw the hole there – but there was no daylight shining in!

'I say!' said Julian, in horror. 'I say! What do you think's happened?'

'What?' asked everyone, in panic.

'The hole is closed!' said Julian. 'We can't get out! Somebody's been along and put those planks across – and I bet they've put the caravan over them, too. We can't get out!'

Everyone stared up at the closed entrance in dismay. They were prisoners.

'Whatever are we to do?' said George. 'Julian – what *are* we going to do?'

[19]

Prisoners underground

Julian didn't answer. He was angry with himself for not thinking that this might happen! Although Lou and Dan had been seen getting on the bus with bags, they might easily not have been spending the night away – the bags might contain things they wanted to sell – stolen goods of some kind.

'They came back quickly – and came up the hill, I suppose, to have another try at getting Nobby and Pongo back,' said Julian, out loud. 'What an idiot I am to leave things to chance like that. Well – I'll have a try at shifting these planks. I should be able to, with luck.'

He did his best, and did shift them to a certain extent – but, as he feared, the caravan had been run back over the hole, and even if he managed to shift some of the planks it was impossible to make a way out.

'Perhaps Pongo can help,' he said suddenly. He shouted loudly: 'Pongo! Pongo! Come and help!'

Everyone stood still, hoping that they would hear Pongo chattering somewhere near, or scraping at the planks above. But there was no sign or sound of Pongo.

Everyone called, but it was no use. Pongo didn't come. What had happened to him? Poor Nobby felt very worried.

'I wish I knew what has happened,' he kept saying. 'I feel as if something horrid has happened to poor old Pongo. Where can he be?'

Pongo was not very far away. He was lying on his side, his head bleeding. He was quite unconscious, and could not hear the frantic calls of the children at all. Poor Pongo!

What Julian had feared had actually happened. Lou and Dan had come back up the hill, bringing money with them to tempt Nobby and Pongo back. When they had got near to the hollow, they had stood still and called loudly.

'Nobby! Nobby! We've come to make friends, not to hurt you! We've got money for you. Be a sensible boy and come back to the camp. Mr Gorgio is asking for you.'

When there had been no reply at all, the men had gone nearer. Then they had seen Pongo and had stopped. The chimpanzee could not get at them because he was tied up. He sat there snarling.

'Where have those kids gone?' asked Lou. Then he saw that the caravan had been moved back a little, and he at once guessed.

'They've found the way underground! The interfering little brutes! See, they've moved one of the caravans off the hole. What do we do *now*?!'

'This first,' said Tiger Dan, in a brutal voice, and he picked up an enormous stone. He threw it with all his force at poor Pongo, who tried to leap out of the way. But the rope prevented him, and the stone hit him full on the head.

He gave a loud scream and fell down at once, lying quite still.

'You've gone and killed him,' said Lou.

'So much the better!' said Tiger Dan. 'Now let's go and see if the entrance-hole is open. Those kids want their necks wringing!'

They went to the hollow and saw at once that the hole had been discovered, opened, and that the children must have gone down it.

'They're down there now,' said Tiger Dan, almost choking with rage. 'Shall we go down and deal with them – and get our stuff and clear off? We meant to clear off tomorrow, anyway. We might as well get the stuff out now.'

'What – in the daylight – with any of the farm men about to see us!' said Lou with a sneer. 'Clever, aren't you?'

'Well, have you got a better idea?' asked Tiger Dan.

'Why not follow our plan?' said Lou. 'Go down when it's dark and collect the stuff. We can bring our wagon up as we planned to do tonight. We don't need to bother about forcing the children to go now – they're underground –

and we can make them prisoners till we're ready to clear off!'

'I see,' said Dan, and he grinned suddenly, showing his ugly teeth. 'Yes – we'll close up the hole and run the caravan back over it – and come up tonight in the dark with the wagon – go down – collect everything – and shut up the hole again with the children in it. We'll send a card to Gorgio when we're safe and tell him to go up and set the kids free.'

'Why bother to do that?' said Lou, in a cruel voice. 'Let 'em starve underground, the interfering little beasts. Serve 'em right.'

'Can't do that,' said Dan. 'Have the police after us worse than ever. We'll have to chuck some food down the hole, to keep them going till they're set free. No good starving them, Lou. There'd be an awful outcry if we do anything like that.'

The two men carefully put back the boards over the top of the hole and replaced the heather tufts. Then they ran the caravan back over the place. They looked at Pongo. The chimpanzee was still lying on his side, and the men could see what a nasty wound he had on his head.

'He ain't dead,' said Lou, and gave him a kick. 'He'll come round all right. Better leave him here. He might come to himself if we carried him back to camp, and fight us. He can't do us any harm tonight, tied up like that.'

They went away down the track. Not ten minutes afterwards the children came to the hole and found it blocked up! If only they hadn't stopped to explore that tunnel a bit further, they would have been able to get out and set Timmy on the two men.

But it was too late now. The hole was well and truly closed. No one could get out. No one could find poor Pongo and bathe his head. They were real prisoners.

They didn't like it at all. Anne began to cry, though she tried not to let the others see her. Nobby saw that she was upset, and put his arm round her.

'Don't cry, little Anne,' he said. 'We'll be all right.'

'It's no good staying here,' said Julian, at last. 'We might as well go somewhere more comfortable, and sit down and talk and eat. I'm hungry.'

They all went back down the passage, up through the hole in the roof, and into the enormous cavern. They found a sandy corner and sat down. Julian handed Anne the kit-bag and she undid it to get the food inside.

'Better only have one torch going,' said Julian. 'We don't know how long we'll be here. We don't want to be left in the dark!'

Everybody immediately switched off their torches. The idea of being lost in the dark inside the hill wasn't at all nice! Anne handed out slices of bread and butter, and the children put thin slices of Mrs Mackie's delicious ham on them.

They felt distinctly better when they had all eaten a good meal. 'That was jolly good,' said Dick. 'No, we won't eat that chocolate, Anne. We may want it later on. Golly, I'm thirsty!'

'So am I,' said Nobby. 'My tongue's hanging out like old Timmy's. Let's go and get a drink.'

'Where from?' asked Anne, in surprise.

'Well, there was a stream in that other cave beyond the tunnel, wasn't there?' said Nobby. 'We can drink from that. It'll be all right.'

'Well, I hope it will,' said Julian. 'We were told not to drink water that wasn't boiled while we were caravanning – but we didn't know this sort of thing was going to happen! We'll go through the tunnel and get some water to drink from the stream.'

They made their way through the long, winding tunnel, and passed the shelf of stolen goods. Then on they went and came out into the cave through which the stream rushed so quickly. They dipped in their hands and drank thirstily. The water tasted lovely – so clear and cold.

Timmy drank too. He was puzzled at this adventure, but so long as he was with George he was happy. If his mistress suddenly took it into her head to live underground like a worm, that was all right – so long as Timmy was with her!

'I wonder if this stream *does* go to that hole

in the hillside, and pours out there,' said Julian, suddenly. 'If it does, and we could follow it, we might be able to squeeze out.'

'We'd get terribly wet,' said George, 'but that wouldn't matter. Let's see if we can follow the water.'

They went to where the stream disappeared into a tunnel rather like the dry one they had come along. Julian shone his torch into it.

'We could wade along, I think,' he said. 'It is very fast but not very deep. I know – I'll go along it myself and see where it goes, and come back and tell you.'

'No,' said George, at once. 'If you go, we all go. You might get separated from us. That would be awful.'

'All right,' said Julian. 'I thought there was no sense in us all getting wet, that's all. Come on, we'll try now.'

One by one they waded into the stream. The current tugged at their legs, for the water ran very fast. But it was only just above the knees there. They waded along by the light of their torches, wondering where the tunnel would lead to.

Timmy half-waded, half-swam. He didn't like this water-business very much. It seemed silly to him. He pushed ahead of Julian and then, a little further down, jumped up to a ledge that ran beside the water.

'Good idea, Tim,' said Julian, and he got up on to it too. He had to crouch down rather as he walked because his head touched the roof of the tunnel if he didn't – but at least his legs were out of the icy-cold water! All the others did the same, and as long as the ledge ran along beside the stream they all walked along it.

But at times it disappeared and then they had to wade in the water again, which now suddenly got deeper. 'Gracious! It's almost to my waist,' said Anne. 'I hope it doesn't get any deeper. I'm holding my clothes up as high as I can, but they'll get soaked soon.'

Fortunately the water got no deeper, but it seemed to go faster. 'We're going downhill a bit,' said Julian at last. 'Perhaps we are getting near to where it pours out of the hill.'

They were! Some distance ahead of him Julian suddenly saw a dim light, and wondered whatever it could be. He soon knew! It was daylight creeping in through the water that poured out of the hole in the hillside – poured out in a torrent into the sunshine.

'We're almost there!' cried Julian. 'Come on.'

With light hearts the children waded along in the water. Now they would soon be out in the warm sunshine. They would find Pongo, and race down the hill in the warmth, catch the first bus, and go to the police station.

But nothing like that happened at all. To their enormous disappointment the water got far too deep to wade through, and Nobby stopped in fright. 'I daren't go no further,' he said. 'I'm almost off my feet now with the water rushing by.'

'I am, too,' said Anne, frightened.

'Perhaps I can swim out,' said Julian, and he struck out. But he gave it up in dismay, for the torrent of water was too much for him, and he was afraid of being hurled against the rocky sides and having his head cracked.

'It's no good,' he said, gloomily. 'No good at all. All that wading for nothing. It's far too dangerous to go any further – and yet daylight is only a few yards ahead. It's too sickening for words.'

'We must go back,' said George. 'I'm afraid Timmy will be drowned if we don't. Oh dear – we must go all that way back!'

[20]

More excitement

It was a very sad and disappointed little company that made their way back to the cave. Along the tunnel they went, painfully and slowly, for it was not so easy against the current. Julian shivered; he was wet through with trying to swim.

At last they were back in the cave through which the stream flowed so swiftly. 'Let's run round and round it to get warm,' said Julian. 'I'm frozen. Dick, let me have one of your dry jerseys. I must take off these wet ones.'

The children ran round and round the cave, pretending to race one another, trying to get warm. They did get warm in the end, and sank down in a heap on some soft sand in a corner, panting. They sat there for a little while to get their breath.

Then they heard something. Timmy heard it first and growled. 'Jumping Jiminy, what's up with Timmy?' said Nobby, in fright. He was the most easily scared of the children, probably because of the frights he had had the last few days.

They all listened, George with her hand on Timmy's collar. He growled again, softly. The noise they all heard was a loud panting coming from the stream over at the other side of the cave!

'Someone is wading up the stream,' whispered Dick, in astonishment. 'Did they get in at the place where we couldn't get out? They must have!'

'But who is it?' asked Julian. 'Can't be Lou or Dan. They wouldn't come that way when they could come the right way. Sh! Whoever it is, is arriving in the cave. I'll shut off my torch.'

Darkness fell in the cave as the light from Julian's torch was clicked off. They all sat and listened, and poor Nobby shook and shivered.

Timmy didn't growl any more, which was surprising. In fact, he even wagged his tail!

There was a sneeze from the other end of the cave – and then soft footsteps padded towards them. Anne felt as if she must scream. WHO was it?

Julian switched on his torch suddenly, and its light fell on a squat, hairy figure, halting in the bright glare. It was Pongo!

'It's *Pongo*!' everyone yelled, and leapt up at once. Timmy ran over to the surprised chimpanzee and sniffed round him in delight. Pongo put his arms round Nobby and Anne.

'Pongo! You've escaped! You must have bitten through your rope!' said Julian. 'How clever you are to find your way through the hole where the stream pours out. How did you know you would find us here! Clever Pongo.'

Then he saw the big wound on poor Pongo's head. 'Oh look!' said Julian. 'He's been hurt! I expect those brutes threw a stone at him. Poor old Pongo.'

'Let's bathe his head,' said Anne. 'I'll use my hanky.'

But Pongo wouldn't let anyone touch his wound, not even Nobby. He didn't snap or snarl at them but simply held their hands away from him, and refused to leave go. So nobody could bathe his head or bind it up.

'Never mind,' said Nobby at last, 'animals' wounds often heal up very quickly without any attention at all. He won't let us touch it, that's certain. I expect Lou and Dan hit him with a stone and knocked him unconscious when they came. They then shut up the hole and made us prisoners. Beasts!'

'I say,' suddenly said Dick. 'I say! I've got an idea. I don't know if it will work – but it really *is* an idea.'

'What?' asked everyone, thrilled.

'Well – what about tying a letter round Pongo's neck and sending him out of the hole again, to take the letter to the camp?' said Dick. 'He won't go to Lou or Dan because he's scared of them – but he'd go to any of the others all right, wouldn't he? Larry would be the best one. He seems to be a good fellow.'

'Would Pongo understand enough to do all that, though?' asked Julian, doubtfully.

'We could try him,' said Nobby. 'I do send him here and there sometimes, just for fun – to take the elephant's bat to Larry, for instance – or to put my coat away in my caravan.'

'Well, we could certainly try,' said Dick. 'I've got a notebook and a pencil. I'll write a note and wrap it up in another sheet, pin it together and tie it round Pongo's neck with a bit of string.'

So he wrote a note. It said:

'To whoever gets this note – please come up the hill to the hollow where there are two caravans. Under the red one is the entrance to an underground passage. We are prisoners inside the hill. Please rescue us soon.

Julian, Dick, George, Anne and Nobby.'

He read it out to the others. Then he tied the note round Pongo's neck. Pongo was surprised, but fortunately did not try to pull it off.

'Now, you give him his orders,' said Dick to Nobby. So Nobby spoke slowly and importantly to the listening chimpanzee.

'Where's Larry? Go to Larry, Pongo. Fetch Larry. Go. GO!'

Pongo blinked at him and made a funny little noise as if he was saying: 'Please, Nobby, I don't want to go.'

Nobby repeated everything again. 'Understand Pongo? I think you do. GO, then, GO. GO!'

And Pongo turned and went! He disappeared into the stream, splashing along by himself. The children watched him as far as they could by the light of their torches.

'He really is clever,' said Anne. 'He didn't want to go a bit, did he? Oh, I do hope he finds Larry, and that Larry sees the note and reads it and sends someone to rescue us.'

'I hope the note doesn't get all soaked and

pulpy in the water,' said Julian, rather gloomily. 'Gosh, I wish I wasn't so cold. Let's run round a bit again, then have a piece of chocolate.'

They ran about and played 'tag' for a time till they all felt warm again. Then they decided to sit down and have some chocolate, and play some sort of guessing game to while away the time. Timmy sat close to Julian, and the boy was very glad.

'He's like a big hot-water bottle,' he said. 'Sit closer, Tim. That's right. You'll soon warm me up!'

It was dull after a time, sitting in the light of one torch, for they dared not use them all. Already it seemed as if Julian's torch was getting a little dim. They played all the games they could think of and then yawned.

'What's the time? I suppose it must be getting dark outside now. I feel quite sleepy.'

'It's nine o'clock almost,' said Julian. 'I hope Pongo has got down to the camp all right and found someone. We could expect help quite soon, if so.'

'Well, then, we'd better get along to the passage that leads to the hole,' said Dick, getting up. 'It's quite likely that if Larry or anyone else comes they'll not see the footholds leading up the wall out of that first little cave. They might not know where we were!'

This seemed very likely. They all made their way down the tunnel that led past the hidden store of valuables, and came out into the enormous cave. There was a nice sandy corner just by the hole that led down into the first small cave, and the children decided to sit there, rather than in the passage or in the first rocky and uncomfortable little cave. They cuddled up together for warmth, and felt hungry.

Anne and Nobby dozed off to sleep. George almost fell asleep, too. But the boys and Timmy kept awake, and talked in low voices. At least, Timmy didn't talk, but wagged his tail whenever either Dick or Julian said anything. That was his way of joining in their conversation.

After what seemed a long while Timmy growled, and the two boys sat up straight. Whatever it was that Timmy's sharp ears had heard, they had heard nothing at all. And they continued to hear nothing. But Timmy went on growling.

Julian shook the others awake. 'I believe help has come,' he said. 'But we'd better not go and see in case it's Dan and Lou come back. So wake up and look lively!'

They were all wide awake at once. Was it Larry come in answer to their note – or was it those horrid men, Tiger Dan and Lou the acrobat?

They soon knew! A head suddenly poked out of the hole nearby, and a torch shone on them. Timmy growled ferociously and struggled to fly at the head, but George held on firmly to his collar, thinking it might be Larry.

But it wasn't! It was Lou the acrobat, as the children knew only too well when they heard his voice. Julian shone his torch on him.

'I hope you've enjoyed your little selves,'

came Lou's harsh voice. 'And you keep that dog under control, boy, or I'll shoot him. See? I'm not standing no nonsense from that dog this time. Have a look at this here gun!'

To George's horror she saw that Lou was pointing a gun at poor Timmy. She gave a scream and flung herself in front of him. 'Don't you dare to shoot my dog! I'll – I'll – I'll . . .'

She couldn't think of anything bad enough to do to the man who could shoot Timmy, and she stopped, choked by tears of rage and fear. Timmy, not knowing what the gun was, couldn't for the life of him understand why George wouldn't let him get at his enemy – such a nice position, too, with his head poking through a hole like that. Timmy felt he could deal with that head very quickly.

'Now, you kids, get up and go into that tunnel,' said Lou. 'Go on – go right ahead of me, and don't dare to stop. We've got work to do here tonight, and we're not going to have any more interference from kids like you. See?'

The children saw quite well. They began to walk towards the entrance of the tunnel. One by one they climbed into it. George first with Timmy. She dared not let his collar go for an instant. A few paces behind them came Lou with his revolver, and Dan with a couple of big sacks.

The children were made to walk right past the shelf on which were the hidden goods.

Then Lou sat down in the tunnel, his torch switched on fully so that he could pick out each child. He still pointed his revolver at Timmy.

'Now we'll get on,' he said to Tiger Dan. 'You know what to do. Get on with it.'

Tiger Dan began to stuff the things into one of the big sacks he had brought. He staggered off with it. He came back in about ten minutes and filled the other sack. It was plain that the men meant to take everything away this time.

'Thought you'd made a very fine discovery, didn't you?' said Lou, mockingly, to the children. 'Ho, yes – very smart you were! See what happens to little smarties like you – you're prisoners – and here you'll stay for two or three days!'

'What do you mean?' said Julian, in alarm. 'Surely you wouldn't leave us here to starve?'

'Not to starve. We're too fond of you,' grinned Lou. 'We'll chuck you down some food into the tunnel. And in two or three days maybe someone will come and rescue you.'

Julian wished desperately that Pongo would bring help before Lou and Dan finished their business in the tunnel and went, leaving them prisoners. He watched Tiger Dan, working quickly, packing everything, carrying it off, coming back again, and packing feverishly once more. Lou sat still with his torch and revolver, enjoying the scared faces of the girls and Nobby. Julian and Dick put on a brave show which they were far from feeling.

Tiger Dan staggered away with another sackful. But he hadn't been gone for more than half a minute before a wail echoed through the tunnel.

'Lou! Help! Help! Something's attacking me! HELP.'

Lou rose up and went swiftly down the tunnel. 'It's Pongo, I bet it's old Pongo,' said Julian thrilled.

[21]

Dick has a great idea!

'Listen,' said Dick in an urgent voice. 'It may be Pongo by himself – he may not have gone back to the camp at all – he may have wandered about and at last gone down the entrance-hole by the caravans, and come up behind Tiger Dan. If so he won't have much chance because Lou's got a gun and will shoot him. And we shan't be rescued. So I'm going to slip down the tunnel while there's a chance and hide in a big cave.'

'What good will that do?' said Julian.

'Well, idiot, I may be able to slip down into the passage that leads to the entrance-hole and hop out without the others seeing me,' said Dick, getting up. 'Then I can fetch help, see? You'd better all clear off somewhere and hide – find a good place, Julian, in case the men come after you when they find one of us is gone. Go on.'

Without another word the boy began to walk down the tunnel, past the rocky shelf on which now very few goods were left, and then came to the enormous cave.

Here there was a great noise going on, for Pongo appeared to have got hold of both men at once! Their torches were out, and Lou did not dare to shoot for fear of hurting Dan. Dick could see very little of this; he could only hear snarlings and shouting. He took a wide course round the heaving heap on the floor and made his way as quickly as he could in the dark to where he thought the hole was that led down into the first passage. He had to go carefully for fear of falling down it. He found it at last and let himself down into the cave below, and then, thinking it safe to switch on his torch in the passage, he flashed it in front of him to show him the way.

It wasn't long before he was out of the hole and was speeding round the caravans. Then he stopped. A thought struck him. He could fetch help all right – but the men would be gone by then! They had laid their plans for a getaway with all the goods; there was no doubt about that.

Suppose he put the boards over the hole, ramming them in with all his strength, and then rolled some heavy stones on top? He couldn't move the caravan over the boards, for it was far too heavy for a boy to push. But heavy stones would probably do the trick. The men would imagine that it was the caravan overhead again!

In great excitement Dick put back the boards, lugging them into place, panting and puffing. Then he flashed his torch round for stones. There were several small rocks nearby. He could not lift them, but he managed to roll them to the boards. Plonk! They went on to them one by one. Now nobody could move the boards at all.

'I know I've shut the others in with the men,' thought Dick. 'But I hope Julian will find a very safe hiding-place just for a time. Gosh, I'm hot! Now, down the hill I go – and I hope I don't lose my way in the darkness!'

Down below, the two men had at last freed themselves from the angry chimpanzee. They were badly bitten and mauled, but Pongo was not as strong and savage as usual because of his bad head-wound. The men were able to drive him off at last, and he went limping in the direction of the tunnel, sniffing out the children.

He would certainly have been shot if Lou could have found his revolver quickly enough. But he could not find it in the dark. He felt about for his torch, and found that although it was damaged, he could still put on the light by knocking it once or twice on the ground. He shone it on to Dan.

'We ought to have looked out for that ape when we saw he was gone,' growled Dan. 'He had bitten his rope through. We might have known he was somewhere about. He nearly did for me, leaping on me like that out of the darkness. It was lucky he flung himself on to my sack and not me.'

'Let's get the last of the things and clear out,' said Lou, who was badly shaken up. 'There's only one more load. We'll get back to the tunnel, scare the life out of those kids once more, shoot Pongo if we can, and then clear out. We'll chuck a few tins of food down the hole and then close it up.'

'I'm not going to risk meeting that chimp again,' said Dan. 'We'll leave the rest of the things. Come on. Let's go.'

Lou was not particularly anxious to see Pongo again either. Keeping his torch carefully switched on and his revolver ready, he followed Dan to the hole that led down to the first cave. Down they went, and then along the passage, eager to get out into the night and go with their wagon down the track.

They got a terrible shock when they found that the hole was closed. Lou shone his torch upwards, and gazed in amazement at the underside of the boards. Someone had put them back into place again. *They* were prisoners now!

Tiger Dan went mad. One of his furious rages overtook him, and he hammered against those boards like a madman. But the heavy stones held them down, and the raging man dropped down beside Lou.

'Can't budge the boards! Someone must have put the caravan overhead again. We're prisoners!'

'But who's made us prisoners? Who's put back those boards?' shouted Lou, almost beside himself with fury. 'Could those kids have slipped by us when we were having that fight with the chimp?'

'We'll go and see if the kids are still there,' said Tiger Dan grimly. 'We'll find out. We'll make them very, very sorry for themselves. Come on.'

The two men went back again to the tunnel. The children were not there. Julian had taken Dick's advice and had gone off to try and find a good hiding-place. He had suddenly thought that perhaps Dick might get the idea of shutting up the entrance-hole – in which case the two men would certainly be furious!

So up the tunnel the children went, and into the cave with the stream. It seemed impossible to find any hiding-place there at all.

'I don't see where we can hide,' said Julian, feeling rather desperate. 'It's no good wading down that stream again – we shall only get wet and cold – and we have no escape from there at all if the men should come after us!'

'I can hear something,' said George, suddenly. 'Put your light out, Julian – quick!'

The torch was snapped off, and the children waited in the darkness. Timmy didn't growl. Instead George felt that he was wagging his tail.

'It's someone friendly,' she whispered. 'Over there. Perhaps it's Pongo. Put the torch on again.'

The light flashed out, and picked out the chimpanzee, who was coming towards them across the cave. Nobby gave a cry of joy.

'Here's old Pongo again!' he said. 'Pongo, did you go to the camp? Did you bring help?'

'No – he hasn't been down to the camp,' said Julian, his eyes catching sight of the note still tied round the chimpanzee's neck. 'There's our letter still on him. Blow!'

'He's clever – but not clever enough to understand a difficult errand like that,' said George.

'Oh, Pongo – and we were depending on you! Never mind – perhaps Dick will escape and bring help. Julian, where *shall* we hide?'

'*Up* the stream?' suddenly said Anne. 'We've tried going *down* it. But we haven't tried going up it. Do you think it would be any good?'

'We could see,' said Julian, doubtfully. He didn't like this business of wading through water that might suddenly get deep. 'I'll shine my torch up the stream and see what it looks like.'

He went to the stream and shone his light up the tunnel from which it came. 'It seems as if we might walk along the ledge beside it,' he said. 'But we'd have to bend almost double – and the water runs so fast just here we must be careful not to slip and fall in.'

'I'll go first,' said Nobby. 'You go last, Julian. The girls can go in the middle with Pongo and Timmy.'

He stepped on to the narrow ledge inside the rocky tunnel, just above the rushing water. Then came Pongo. Then Anne, then George and Timmy – and last of all Julian.

But just as Julian was disappearing, the two men came into the cave, and by chance Lou's torch shone right on to the vanishing Julian. He gave a yell.

'There's one of them – look, over there! Come on!'

The men ran to where the stream came out of the tunnel, and Lou shone his torch up it. He saw the line of children, with Julian last of all. He grabbed hold of the boy and pulled him back.

Anne yelled when she saw Julian being pulled back. Nobby had a dreadful shock. Timmy growled ferociously, and Pongo made a most peculiar noise.

'Now look here,' came Lou's voice, 'I've got

a gun, and I'm going to shoot that dog and that chimp if they so much as put their noses out of here. So hang on to them if you want to save their lives!'

He passed Julian to Tiger Dan, who gripped the boy firmly by the collar. Lou shone his torch up the tunnel again to count the children. 'Ho, there's Nobby,' he said, 'You come on out here, Nobby.'

'If I do, the chimp will come out too,' said Nobby. 'You know that. And he may get *you* before you get him!'

Lou thought about that. He was afraid of the big chimpanzee. 'You stay up there with him, then,' he said. And the girl can stay with you, holding the dog. But the other boy can come out here.'

He thought that George was a boy. George didn't mind. She liked people to think she was a boy. She answered at once.

'I can't come. If I do the dog will follow me, and I'm not going to have him shot.'

'You come on out,' said Lou, threateningly.

'I'm going to show you two boys what happens to kids who keep spying and interfering. Nobby knows what happens, don't you, Nobby? He's had his lesson. And you two boys are going to have yours, too.'

Dan called to him. 'There ought to be another girl there, Lou. I thought Nobby said there were two boys and two girls. Where's the other girl?'

'Gone further up the tunnel, I suppose,' said Lou, trying to see. 'Now, you boy – come on out!'

Anne began to cry. 'Don't go, George, don't go. They'll hurt you. Tell them you're a—'

'Shut up,' said George, fiercely. She added, in a whisper: 'If I say I'm a girl they'll know Dick is missing, and will be all the angrier. Hang on to Timmy.'

Anne clutched Timmy's collar in her trembling hand. George began to walk back to the cave. But Julian was not going to let George be hurt. He began to struggle.

Lou caught hold of George as she came out

of the tunnel – and at the same moment Julian managed to kick high in the air, and knocked Lou's torch right out of his hand. It flew up into the roof of the cave and fell somewhere with a crash. It went out. Now the cave was in darkness.

'Get back into the tunnel, George, with Anne,' yelled Julian. 'Timmy, Timmy, come on! Pongo, come here!'

'I don't want Timmy to be shot!' cried out George, in terror, as the dog shot past her into the cave.

Even as she spoke a shot rang out. It was Lou, shooting blindly at where he thought Timmy was. George screamed.

'Oh, Timmy, Timmy! You're not hurt, are you?'

[22]

The end of the adventure

No, Timmy wasn't hurt. The bullet zipped past his head and struck the wall of the cave. Timmy went for Lou's legs. Down went the man with a crash and a yell, and the revolver flew out of his hand. Julian heard it slithering across the floor of the cave, and he was very thankful.

'Put on your torch, George, quickly!' he yelled. 'We must see what we're doing. Goodness, here's Pongo now!'

Tiger Dan gave a yell of fright when the torch flashed on and he saw the chimpanzee making straight for him. He dealt the ape a smashing blow on the face that knocked him down, and then turned to run. Lou was trying to keep Timmy off his throat, kicking frantically at the excited dog.

Dan ran to the tunnel – and then stopped in

astonishment. Four burly policemen were pushing their way out of the tunnel, led by Dick! One of them carried a revolver in his hand. Dan put his hands up at once.

'Timmy! Come off!' commanded George, seeing that there was now no need for the dog's delighted help. Timmy gave her a reproachful glance that said: 'Mistress! I'm really enjoying myself! Let me eat him all up!'

Then the dog caught sight of the four policemen and yelped furiously. More enemies! He would eat the lot.

'What's all this going on?' said the first man, who was an Inspector. 'Get up, you on the floor. Go on, get up!'

Lou got up with great difficulty. Timmy had nipped him in various places. His hair was over his eyes, his clothes were torn. He stared at the policemen, his mouth open in the utmost surprise. How had they come here? Then he saw Dick.

'So one of you kids slipped out – and shut the boards on us!' he said, savagely. 'I might have guessed. You—'

'Hold your tongue, Lewis Allburg,' rapped out the Inspector. 'You can talk when we tell you. You'll have quite a lot of talking to do, to explain some of the things we've heard about you.'

'Dick! How did you get here so soon?' cried Julian, going over to his brother. 'I didn't expect you for hours! Surely you didn't go all the way to the town and back?'

'No. I shot off to the farm, woke up the Mackies, used their telephone and got the police up here double-quick in their car,' said Dick, grinning. 'Everyone all right? Where's Anne? And Nobby?'

'There they are – just coming out of the tunnel, upstream,' said Julian, and swung his torch round. Dick saw Anne's white, scared face, and went over to her.

'It's all right,' he said. 'The adventure is over, Anne! You can smile again!'

Anne gave a watery sort of smile. Pongo took her hand and made little affectionate noises, and that made her smile a little more. George called Timmy to her, afraid that he might take a last nip at Lou.

Lou swung round and stared at her. Then he looked at Dick and Julian. Then at Anne.

'So there *was* only one girl!' he said. 'What did you want to tell me there were two boys and two girls for?' he said to Nobby.

'Because there were,' answered Nobby. He pointed to George. 'She's a girl, though she looks like a boy. And she's as good as a boy any day.'

George felt proud. She stared defiantly at Lou. He was now in the grip of a stout policeman, and Tiger Dan was being hustled off by two more.

'I think we'll leave this rather gloomy place,' said the Inspector, putting away the notebook he had been hastily scribbling in. 'Quick march!'

Julian led the way down the tunnel. He pointed out the shelf where the men had stored their things, and the Inspector collected the few things that were still left. Then on they went, Tiger Dan muttering and growling to himself.

'Will they go to prison?' whispered Anne to Dick.

'You bet,' said Dick. 'That's where they ought to have gone long ago. Their burglaries have been worrying the police for four years!'

Out of the tunnel and into the cave with gleaming walls. Then down the hole and into the small cave and along the narrow passage to the entrance-hole. Stars glittered over the black hole, and the children were very thankful to see them. They were tired of being underground!

Lou and Dan did not have a very comfortable journey along the tunnels and passages, for their guards had a very firm hold of them indeed. Once out in the open they were handcuffed and put into the large police car that stood a little way down the track.

'What are you children going to do?' asked the big Inspector, who was now at the wheel of the car. 'Hadn't you better come down into the town with us after this disturbing adventure?'

'Oh, no thanks,' said Julian politely. 'We're quite used to adventures. We've had plenty, you know. We shall be all right here with Timmy and Pongo.'

'Well, I can't say I'd like a chimpanzee for company myself,' said the Inspector. 'We'll be up here in the morning, looking round and asking a few questions, which I'm sure you'll be pleased to answer. And many thanks for your help in capturing two dangerous thieves!'

'What about the wagon of goods?' asked Dick. 'Are you going to leave it up here? It's got lots of valuables in it.'

'Oh, one of the men is driving down,' said the Inspector, nodding towards a policeman who stood nearby. 'He'll follow us. He can drive a horse all right. Well, look after yourselves. See you tomorrow!'

The car started up suddenly. The Inspector put her into gear, took off the brake and the car slid quietly down the hill, following the winding track. The policeman with the wagon followed slowly, clicking to the horse, which didn't seem at all surprised to have a new driver.

'Well, that's that!' said Julian thankfully. 'I must say we were well out of that. Gosh, Dick. I was glad to see you back with those bobbies so quickly. That was a brainwave of yours to telephone from the farm.'

Dick suddenly yawned. 'It must be frightfully late!' he said. 'Long past the middle of the night. But I'm so fearfully hungry that I simply must have something to eat before I fall into my bunk!'

'Got anything, Anne?' asked Julian.

Anne brightened up at once. 'I'll see,' she said. 'I can find something, I'm sure!'

And she did, of course. She opened two tins of sardines and made sandwiches, and she opened two tins of peaches, so they had a very nice meal in the middle of the night! They ate it sitting on the floor of George's caravan. Pongo had as good a meal as anyone, and Timmy crunched at one of his bones.

It didn't take them long to go to sleep that night. In fact they were all so sleepy when they had finished their meal that nobody undressed! They clambered into the bunks just as they were and fell asleep at once. Nobby curled up with Pongo, and Timmy, as usual, was on George's feet. Peace reigned in the caravans – and tonight no one came to disturb them!

All the children slept very late the next morning. They were awakened by a loud knocking on Julian's caravan. He woke up with a jump and yelled out:

'Yes! Who is it?'

'It's us,' said a familiar voice, and the door opened. Farmer Mackie and his wife peeped in, looking rather anxious.

'We wondered what had happened,' said the farmer. 'You rushed out of the farmhouse when you had used the phone last night and didn't come back.'

'I ought to have slipped back and told you,' said Dick, sitting up with his hair over his eyes.

He pushed it back. 'But I forgot. The police went down into the hills with us and got the two men. They're well-known burglars. The police got all the goods, too. It was a very thrilling night. Thanks most awfully for letting me use the phone.'

'You're very welcome,' said Mrs Mackie. 'And look – I've brought you some food.'

She had two baskets stacked with good things. Dick felt wide awake and very hungry when he saw them. 'Oh, thanks,' he said gratefully. 'You *are* a good sort!'

Nobby and Pongo suddenly uncurled themselves from their pile of rugs, and Mrs Mackie gave a squeal.

'Land-sakes, what's that? A monkey?'

'No, an ape, Mam,' said Nobby politely. 'He won't hurt you. Oi, take your hand out of that basket!'

Pongo, who had been hoping to find a little titbit unnoticed, covered his face with his hairy paw and looked through his fingers at Mrs Mackie.

'Look at that now – he's like a naughty child!' said Mrs Mackie. 'Isn't he, Ted?'

'He is that,' said the farmer. 'Strange sort of bedfellow, I must say!'

'Well, I must be getting along,' said Mrs Mackie, nodding and smiling at George and Anne, who had now come out of their caravan with Timmy to see who the visitors were. 'You come along to the farm if you want anything. We'll be right pleased to see you.'

'Aren't they nice?' said Anne as the two farm-folk went down the cart-track. 'And oh, my goodness – what a breakfast we're going to have! Cold bacon – tomatoes – fresh radishes – curly lettuces – and who wants new honey?'

'Marvellous!' said Julian. 'Come on – let's have it now, before we clean up.'

But Anne made them wash and tidy themselves first! 'You'll enjoy it much more if you're clean,' she said. 'We all look as black as sweeps! I'll give you five minutes – then you can come to a perfectly wonderful breakfast!'

'All right, Ma!' grinned Nobby, and he went

off with the others to wash at the spring. Then back they all went to the sunny ledge to feast on the good things kind Mrs Mackie had provided.

[23]

Goodbye, Nobby – goodbye, caravanners!

Before they had finished their breakfast the Inspector came roaring up the track in his powerful police car. There was one sharp-eyed policeman with him to take down notes.

'Hallo, hallo!' said the Inspector, eyeing the good things set out on the ledge. 'You seem to do yourselves well, I must say!'

'Have some new bread and honey,' said Anne in her best manner. 'Do! There's plenty!'

'Thanks,' said the Inspector, and sat down with the children. The other policeman wandered round the caravans, examining everything. The Inspector munched away at honey and bread, and the children talked to him, telling him all about their extraordinary adventure.

'It must have been a most unpleasant shock for those two fellows when they found that your caravan was immediately over the entrance to the place where they hid their stolen goods,' said the Inspector. 'Most unpleasant.'

'Have you examined the goods?' asked Dick eagerly. 'Are they very valuable?'

'Priceless,' answered the Inspector, taking another bit of bread and dabbing it thickly with honey. 'Quite priceless. Those rogues apparently stole goods they knew to be of great value, hid them here for a year or two till the hue and cry had died down, then got them out and quietly disposed of them to friends in Holland and Belgium.'

'Tiger Dan used to act in circuses in Holland,' said Nobby. 'He often told me about them. He had friends all over Europe – people in the circus line, you know.'

'Yes. It was easy for him to dispose of his goods abroad,' said the Inspector. 'He planned to go across to Holland today, you know – got everything ready with Lou – or, to give him his right name, Lewis Allburg – and was going to sell most of those things. You just saved them in time!'

'What a bit of luck!' said George. 'They almost got away with it. If Dick hadn't managed to slip out when Pongo was attacking them, we'd still have been prisoners down in the hill, and Lou and Dan would have been half-way to Holland!'

'Smart bit of work you children did,' said the Inspector approvingly, and looked longingly at the honey-pot. 'That's fine honey. I must buy some from Mrs Mackie.'

'Have some more,' said Anne, remembering her manners. 'Do. We've got another loaf.'

'Well, I will,' said the Inspector, and took another slice of bread, spreading it with the yellow honey. It looked as if there wouldn't even be enough left for Pongo to lick out! Anne thought it was nice to see a grown-up enjoying bread and honey as much as children did.

'You know, that fellow Lou did some very remarkable burglaries,' said the Inspector.

'Once he got across from the third floor of one house to the third floor of another *across the street* – and nobody knows how!'

'That would be easy for Lou,' said Nobby, suddenly losing his fear of the big Inspector. 'He'd just throw a wire rope across, lasso something with the end of it, top of a gutter-pipe, perhaps, draw tight, and walk across! He's wonderful on the tight-rope. There ain't nothing he can't do on the tight-rope.'

'Yes – that's probably what he did,' said the Inspector. 'Never thought of that! No, thanks, I really won't have any more honey. That chimpanzee will eat me if I don't leave some for him to lick out!'

Pongo took away the jar, sat himself down behind one of the caravans, and put a large pink tongue into the remains of the honey. When Timmy came running up to see what he had got, Pongo held the jar high above his head and chattered at him.

'Yarra-yarra-yarra-yarra!' he said. Timmy looked rather surprised and went back to

George. She was listening with great interest to what the Inspector had to tell them about the underground caves.

'They're very old,' he said. 'The entrance to them used to be some way down the hill, but there was a landslide and it was blocked up. Nobody bothered to unblock it because the caves were not particularly interesting.'

'Oh, but they *are*,' said Anne, 'especially the one with the gleaming walls.'

'Well, I imagine that quite by accident one day Dan and Lou found another way in,' said the Inspector. 'The way you know – a hole going down into the hill. They must have thought what a fine hiding-place it would make for any stolen goods – perfectly safe, perfectly dry, and quite near the camping-place here each year. What could be better?'

'And I suppose they would have gone on burgling for years and hiding the stuff if we hadn't just happened to put our caravan over the very spot!' said Julian. 'What a bit of bad luck for them!'

'And what a bit of good luck for us!' said the Inspector. 'We did suspect those two, you know, and once or twice we raided the circus to try and find the goods – but they must always have got warning of our coming and got them away in time – up here!'

'Have you been down to the camp, mister?' asked Nobby suddenly.

The Inspector nodded. 'Oh, yes. We've been down already this morning – seen everyone and questioned them. We created quite a stir!'

Nobby looked gloomy.

'What's the matter, Nobby?' said Anne.

'I shan't half cop it when I get back to the camp,' said Nobby. 'They'll say it's all my fault the coppers going there. We don't like the bobbies round the camp. I shall get into a whole lot of trouble when I go back. I don't want to go back.'

Nobody said anything. They all wondered what would happen to poor Nobby now his Uncle Dan was in prison.

Then Anne asked him: 'Who will you live with now in the camp, Nobby?'

'Oh, somebody will take me in and work me hard,' said Nobby. 'I wouldn't mind if I could be with the horses – but Rossy won't let me. I know that. If I could be with horses I'd be happy. I love them and they understand me all right.'

'How old are you, Nobby?' asked the Inspector, joining in the talk. 'Oughtn't you to be going to school?'

'Never been in my life, mister,' said Nobby. 'I'm just over fourteen, so I reckon I never will go now!'

He grinned. He didn't look fourteen. He seemed more like twelve by his size. Then he looked solemn again.

'Reckon I won't go down to the camp today,' he said. 'I'll be proper set on by them all – about you going there and snooping round like. And Mr Gorgio, he won't like losing his best clown and best acrobat!'

'You can stay with us as long as you like,' said Julian. 'We'll be here a bit longer, anyway.'

But he was wrong. Just after the Inspector

had left, taking his policeman with him, Mrs Mackie came hurrying up to them with a little orange envelope in her hand.

'The messenger boy's just been up,' she said. 'He was looking for you. He left this telegram for you. I hope it's not bad news.'

Julian tore the envelope open and read the telegram out loud.

'AMAZED TO GET YOUR LETTER ABOUT THE EXTRAORDINARY HAPPENINGS YOU DESCRIBE. THEY SOUND DANGEROUS. COME HOME AT ONCE. DADDY.'

'Oh dear,' said Anne. 'Now we shall have to leave. What a pity!'

'I'd better go down to the town and telephone Daddy and tell him we're all right,' said Julian.

'You can phone from my house,' said Mrs Mackie, so Julian thought he would. They talked as they went along and suddenly a bright idea struck Julian.

'I say – I suppose Farmer Mackie doesn't

want anyone to help him with his horses, does he?' he asked. 'He wouldn't want a boy who really loves and understands them and would work hard and well?'

'Well, now, I dare say he would,' said Mrs Mackie. 'He's a bit short-handed now. He was saying the other day he could do with a good lad, just leaving school.'

'Oh, *do* you think he'd try our friend Nobby from the circus camp?' said Julian. 'He's mad on horses. He can do anything with them. And he's been used to working very hard. I'm sure he'd do well.'

Before Julian had left the farmhouse after telephoning to his amazed parents, he had had a long talk with Farmer Mackie – and now he was running back with the good news to the caravans.

'Nobby!' he shouted as he got near. 'Nobby! How would you like to go and work for Farmer Mackie and help with the horses? He says you can start tomorrow if you like – and live at the farm!'

'Jumping Jiminy!' said Nobby, looking startled and disbelieving. 'At the farm? Work with the horses? Coo – I wouldn't half like that. But Farmer Mackie wouldn't have the likes of me.'

'He will. He says he'll try you,' said Julian. 'We've got to start back home tomorrow, and you can be with us till then. You don't need to go back to the camp at all.'

'Well – but what about Growler?' said Nobby. 'I'd have to have him with me. He's my dog. I expect poor old Barker's dead. Would the farmer mind me having a dog?'

'I shouldn't think so,' said Julian. 'Well, you'll have to go down to the camp, I suppose, to collect your few things – and to get Growler. Better go now, Nobby, and then you'll have the rest of the day with us.'

Nobby went off, his face shining with delight. 'Well, I never!' he kept saying to himself. 'Well, I never did! Dan and Lou gone, so they'll never hurt me again – and me not going to live in the camp any more – and going to have charge of them fine farm horses. Well, I never!'

The children had said good-bye to Pongo because he had to go back with Nobby to the camp. He belonged to Mr Gorgio, and Nobby could not possibly keep him. Anyway, it was certain that even if he could have kept him, Mrs Mackie wouldn't have let him live at the farm.

Pongo shook hands gravely with each one of them, even with Timmy. He seemed to know it was goodbye. The children were really sorry to see the comical chimpanzee go. He had shared in their adventure with them and seemed much more like a human being than an animal.

When he had gone down the hill a little way he ran back to Anne. He put his arms round her and gave her a gentle squeeze, as if to say: 'You're all nice, the lot of you, but little Anne's the nicest!'

'Oh, Pongo, you're really a dear!' said Anne, and gave him a tomato. He ran off with it, leaping high for joy.

The children cleared up everything, put the breakfast things away, and cleaned the caravans, ready for starting off the next day. At dinner-time they looked out for Nobby. Surely he should be back soon?

They heard him whistling as he came up the track. He carried a bundle on his back. Round his feet ran two dogs. Two!

'Why – one of them is Barker!' shouted George in delight. 'He must have got better! How simply marvellous!'

Nobby came up, grinning. They all crowded round him, asking about Barker.

'Yes, it's fine, isn't it?' said Nobby, putting down his bundle of belongings. 'Lucilla dosed him all right. He almost died – then he started to wriggle a bit, she said, and the next she knew he was as lively as could be – bit weak on his legs at first – but he's fine this morning.'

Certainly there didn't seem anything wrong with Barker. He and Growler sniffed round Timmy, their tails wagging fast. Timmy stood towering above them, but his tail wagged, too, so Barker and Growler knew he was friendly.

'I was lucky,' said Nobby. 'I only spoke to Lucilla and Larry. Mr Gorgio has gone off to answer some questions at the police station, and so have some of the others. So I just told Larry to tell Mr Gorgio I was leaving, and I got my things and hopped it.'

'Well, now we can really enjoy our last day,' said Julian. 'Everybody's happy!'

And they did enjoy that last day. They went down to the lake and bathed. They had a fine farmhouse tea at Mrs Mackie's, by special invitation. They had a picnic supper on the rocky ledge, with the three dogs rolling over and over in play. Nobby felt sad to think he would so soon say goodbye to his 'posh' friends – but he couldn't help feeling proud and pleased to have a fine job of his own on the farm – with the horses he loved so much.

Nobby, Barker, Growler, Farmer Mackie and his wife all stood on the cart-track to wave goodbye to the two caravans the next morning.

'Goodbye!' yelled Nobby. 'Good luck! See you again some time!'

'Goodbye!' shouted the others. 'Give our love to Pongo when you see him.'

'Woof! woof!' barked Timmy, but only Barker and Growler knew what *that* meant. It meant, 'Shake paws with Pongo for me!'

Goodbye, five caravanners . . . till your next exciting adventure!

FIVE ON KIRRIN ISLAND AGAIN

[1]

A letter for George

Anne was trying to do some of her prep in a corner of the common-room when her cousin George came bursting in.

George was not a boy; she was a girl called Georgina, but because she had always wanted to be a boy she insisted on being called George. So George she was. She wore her curly hair cut short, and her bright blue eyes gleamed angrily now as she came towards Anne.

'Anne! I've just had a letter from home – and what do you think? Father wants to go and live on my island to do some special work – and he wants to build a sort of tower or something in the castle yard!'

The other girls looked up in amusement, and Anne held out her hand for the letter that George was waving at her. Everyone knew about the little island off Kirrin Bay that belonged to George. Kirrin Island was a tiny place with an old ruined castle in the middle of it: the home of rabbits and gulls and jackdaws.

It had underground dungeons in which George and her cousins had had one or two amazing adventures. It had once belonged to George's mother, and she had given it to George – and George was very fierce where her precious Kirrin Island was concerned! It was *hers*. Nobody else must live there, or even land there without her permission.

And now, dear me, here was her father proposing to go to her island, and even build some sort of workshop there! George was red with exasperation.

'It's just like grown-ups; they go and give you things and then act as though the things were theirs all the time. I don't *want* Father living on my island, and building nasty messy sheds and things there.'

'Oh George – you know your father is a very famous scientist, who needs to work in peace,' said Anne, taking the letter. 'Surely you can lend him your island for a bit?'

'There are plenty of other places where he can work in peace,' said George. 'Oh dear – I was so hoping we could go and stay there in the Easter hols – take our boat there, and food and everything, just like we've done before. Now we shan't be able to if Father really does go there.'

Anne read the letter. It was from George's mother.

'My darling George,

'I think I must tell you at once that your father proposes to live on Kirrin Island for some little time in order to finish some very important experiments he is making. He will have to have some kind of building erected there – a sort of tower, I believe. Apparently he needs a place where he can have absolute peace and isolation, and also, for some reason, where there is water all around him. The fact of being

surrounded by water is necessary to his experiment.

'Now, dear, don't be upset about this. I know that you consider Kirrin Island is your very own, but you must allow your family to share it, especially when it is for something as important as your father's scientific work. Father thinks you will be very pleased indeed to lend him Kirrin Island, but I know your funny feelings about it, so I thought I had better write and tell you, before you arrive home and see him installed there, complete with his tower.'

The letter then went on about other things, but Anne did not bother to read these. She looked at George.

'Oh, George! I don't see why you mind your father borrowing Kirrin Island for a bit! I wouldn't mind *my* father borrowing an island from me – if I was lucky enough to have one!'

'*Your* father would talk to you about it first,

and ask your permission, and see if you minded,' said George, sulkily. 'My father never does anything like that. He just does exactly as he likes without asking anybody anything. I really do think he might have written to me himself. He just puts my back up.'

'You've got a back that is very easily put up, George,' said Anne, laughing. 'Don't scowl at me like that. *I'm* not borrowing your island without your gracious permission.'

But George wouldn't smile back. She took her letter and read it again gloomily. 'To think that all my lovely holiday plans are spoilt!' she said. 'You know how super Kirrin Island is at Easter time – all primroses and gorse and baby rabbits. And you and Julian and Dick were coming to stay, and we haven't stayed together since last summer when we went caravanning.'

'I know. It *is* hard luck!' said Anne. 'It would have been wizard to go and stay on the island these hols. But perhaps your father wouldn't mind if we did? We needn't disturb him.'

'As if living on Kirrin Island with Father

there would be the same as living there all by ourselves,' said George, scornfully. 'You know it would be horrid.'

Well yes – Anne didn't think on the whole that Kirrin Island would be much fun with Uncle Quentin there. George's father was such a hot-tempered, impatient man, and when he was in the middle of one of his experiments he was quite unbearable. The least noise upset him.

'Oh dear – how he will yell at the jackdaws to keep quiet, and shout at the noisy gulls!' said Anne, beginning to giggle. 'He won't find Kirrin quite so peaceful as he imagines!'

George gave a watery sort of smile. She folded up the letter and turned away. 'Well, I think it's just the limit,' she said. 'I wouldn't have felt so bad if only Father had asked my permission.'

'He'd never do that!' said Anne. 'It just wouldn't occur to him. Now George, don't spend the rest of the day brooding over your wrongs, for goodness' sake. Go down to the kennels and fetch Timmy. He'll soon cheer you up.'

Timothy was George's dog, whom she loved with all her heart. He was a big scruffy brown mongrel dog, with a ridiculously long tail, and a wide mouth that really seemed to smile. All the four cousins loved him. He was so friendly and loving, so lively and amusing, and he had shared so very many adventures with them all. The five of them had had many happy times together.

George went to get Timmy. Her school allowed the children to keep their own pets. If it hadn't allowed this, it is quite certain that George would not have gone to boarding-school! She could not bear to be parted from Timmy for even a day.

Timmy began to bark excitedly as soon as she came near. George lost her sulky look and smiled. Dear Timmy, dear trustable Timmy – he was better than any person! He was always on her side, always her friend whatever she did, and to Timmy there was no one in the world so wonderful as George.

They were soon going through the fields together, and George talked to Timmy as she always did. She told him about her father borrowing Kirrin Island. Timmy agreed with every word she said. He listened as if he understood everything, and not even when a rabbit shot across his path did he leave his mistress's side. Timmy always knew when George was upset.

He gave her hand a few little licks every now and again. By the time that George was back at school again she felt much better. She took Timmy into school with her, smuggling him in at a side door. Dogs were not allowed in the school building, but George, like her father, often did exactly as she liked.

She hurried Timmy up to her dormitory. He scuttled under her bed quickly and lay down. His tail thumped the floor gently. He knew what this meant. George wanted the comfort of his nearness that night! He would be able to jump on her bed, when lights were out, and snuggle into the crook of her knees. His green eyes gleamed with delight.

'Now, lie quiet,' said George, and went out of the room to join the other girls. She found Anne, who was busy writing a letter to her brothers, Julian and Dick, at their boarding-school.

'I've told them about Kirrin Island, and your father wanting to borrow it,' she said. 'Would you like to come and stay with *us*, George, these hols, instead of us coming to Kirrin? Then you won't feel cross all the time because your father is on your island.'

'No thanks,' said George, at once. 'I'm going home. I want to keep an eye on Father! I don't want him blowing up Kirrin Island with one of his experiments. You know he's messing about with explosives now, don't you?'

'Ooooh – atom bombs, or things like that?' said Anne.

'I don't know,' said George. 'Anyway, quite apart from keeping an eye on Father and my island, we ought to go and stay at Kirrin to keep

Mother company. She'll be all alone if Father's on the island. I suppose he'll take food and everything there.'

'Well, there's one thing, we shan't have to creep about on tiptoe and whisper, if your father isn't at Kirrin Cottage!' said Anne. 'We can be as noisy as we like. Do cheer up, George!'

But it took George quite a long time to get over the fit of gloom caused by her mother's letter. Even having Timmy on her bed each night, till he was discovered by an angry teacher, did not quite make up for her disappointment.

The term ran swiftly on to its end. April came in, with sunshine and showers. Holidays came nearer and nearer! Anne thought joyfully of Kirrin, with its lovely sandy beach, its blue sea, its fishing-boats and its lovely cliffside walks.

Julian and Dick thought longingly of them too. This term both they and the girls broke up on the same day. They could meet in London and travel down to Kirrin together. Hurrah!

The day came at last. Trunks were piled in the hall. Cars arrived to fetch some of the children who lived fairly near. The school coaches drew up to take the others down to the station. There was a terrific noise of yelling and shouting everywhere. The teachers could not make themselves heard in the din.

'Anyone would think that every single child had gone completely mad,' said one of them to another. 'Oh, thank goodness, they're getting into the coaches. George! *Must* you rush along the corridor at sixty miles an hour, with Timmy barking his head off all the time!'

'Yes, I must, I must!' cried George. 'Anne, where are you? Do come and get into the coach. I've got Timmy. He knows it's holidays now. Come on, Tim!'

Down to the station went the singing crowd of children. They piled into the train. 'Bags I this seat! Who's taken my bag? Get out, Hetty, you know you can't bring your dog in here with mine. They fight like anything. Hurrah, the guard's blowing his whistle! We're off!'

The engine pulled slowly out of the station, its long train of carriages behind it, filled to bursting with girls off for their holidays. Through the quiet countryside it went, through small towns and villages, and at last ran through the smoky outskirts of London.

'The boys' train is due in two minutes before ours,' said Anne, leaning out of the window, as the train drew slowly into the London station. 'If it was punctual, they might be on our platform to meet us. Oh look, George, look – there they are!'

George hung out of the window too. 'Hi, Julian!' she yelled. 'Here we are! Hi, Dick, Julian!'

[2]

Back at Kirrin Cottage

Julian, Dick, Anne, George and Timmy went straightaway to have buns and ginger-beer at the station tearoom. It was good to be all together again. Timmy went nearly mad with joy at seeing the two boys. He kept trying to get on to their knees.

'Look here, Timmy, old thing, I love you very much and I'm jolly glad to see you,' said Dick, 'but that's twice you've upset my ginger-beer all over me. Has he behaved himself this term, George?'

'Fairly well,' said George, considering. 'Hasn't he, Anne? I mean – he only got the joint out of the larder once – and he didn't do so *much* harm to that cushion he chewed – and if people *will* leave their goloshes all over the place nobody can blame Timmy for having a good old game with them.'

'And that was the end of the goloshes, I suppose,' said Julian, with a grin. 'On the whole, Timmy, you have a rather poor report. I'm afraid our Uncle Quentin will not award you the usual twenty-five pence we get for good reports.'

At the mention of her father, George scowled. 'I see George has not lost her pretty scowl,' said Dick, in a teasing voice. 'Dear old George! We shouldn't know her unless she put on that fearsome scowl half a dozen times a day!'

'Oh, she's better than she was,' said Anne hurrying to George's defence at once. George was not so touchy as she had once been, when she was being teased. All the same, Anne knew that there might be sparks flying over her father taking Kirrin Island these holidays, and she didn't want George to fly into a temper too soon!

Julian looked at his cousin. 'I say, old thing, you're not going to take this business of Kirrin Island too much to heart, are you?' he said.

'You've just got to realise that your father's a remarkably clever man, one of the finest scientists we've got – and *I* think that those kind of fellows ought to be allowed as much freedom as they like, for their work. I mean – if Uncle Quentin wants to work on Kirrin Island for some peculiar reason of his own, then you ought to be pleased to say "Go ahead, Father!"'

George looked a little mutinous after this rather long speech; but she thought a great deal of Julian, and usually went by what he said. He was older than any of them, a tall, good-looking boy, with determined eyes and a strong chin. George scratched Timmy's head, and spoke in a low voice.

'All right. I won't go up in smoke about it, Julian. But I'm frightfully disappointed. I'd planned to go to Kirrin Island ourselves these hols.'

'Well, we're all disappointed,' said Julian. 'Buck up with your bun, old thing. We've got to get across London and catch the train for Kirrin. We shall miss it if we don't look out.'

Soon they were in the train for Kirrin. Julian was very good at getting porters and taxis. Anne gazed admiringly at her big brother as he found them all corner-seats in a carriage. Julian did know how to tackle things!

'Do you think I've grown, Julian?' she asked him. 'I did hope I'd be as tall as George by the end of this term, but she grew too!'

'Well, I should think you might be a quarter of an inch taller than last term,' said Julian. 'You can't catch us up, Anne – you'll always be the smallest! But I like you small.'

'Look at Timmy, putting his head out of the window as usual!' said Dick. 'Timmy, you'll get grit in your eye. Then George will go quite mad with grief and think you're going blind!'

'Woof,' said Timmy, and wagged his tail. That was the nice part about Timmy. He always knew when he was being spoken to, even if his name was not mentioned, and he answered at once.

Aunt Fanny was at the station to meet them in the pony-trap. The children flung themselves on her, for they were very fond of her. She was kind and gentle, and did her best to keep her clever, impatient husband from finding too much fault with the children.

'How's Uncle Quentin?' asked Julian, politely, when they were setting off in the trap.

'He's very well,' said his aunt. 'And terribly excited. Really, I've never known him to be so thrilled as he has been lately. His work has been coming along very successfully.'

'I suppose you don't know what his latest experiment is?' said Dick.

'Oh no. He never tells me a word,' said Aunt Fanny. 'He never tells anyone anything while he is at work, except his colleagues, of course. But I do know it's very important – and I know, of course, that the last part of the experiment has to be made in a place where there is deep water all round. Don't ask me why! I don't know.'

'Look! There's Kirrin Island!' said Anne,

suddenly. They had rounded a corner, and had come in sight of the bay. Guarding the entrance to it was the curious little island topped by the old ruined castle. The sun shone down on the blue sea, and the island looked most enchanting.

George looked earnestly at it. She was looking for the building, whatever it was, that her father said he needed for his work. Everyone looked at the island, seeking the same thing.

They saw it easily enough! Rising from the centre of the castle, probably from the castle yard, was a tall thin tower, rather like a lighthouse. At the top was a glass-enclosed room, which glittered in the sun.

'Oh Mother! I don't like it! It spoils Kirrin Island,' said George, in dismay.

'Darling, it can come down when your father has finished his work,' said her mother. 'It's a very flimsy, temporary thing. It can easily be pulled down. Father promised me he would scrap it as soon as his work was done. He says you can go across and see it, if you like. It's really rather interesting.'

'Ooooh – I'd *love* to go and see it,' said Anne, at once. 'It looks so strange. Is Uncle Quentin all alone on Kirrin Island, Aunt Fanny?'

'Yes, I don't like him to be alone,' said her aunt. 'For one thing I am sure he doesn't get his meals properly, and for another, I'm always afraid some harm might come to him when he's experimenting – and if he's alone, how would I know if anything happened to him?'

'Well, Aunt Fanny, you could always arrange for him to signal to you each morning and night, couldn't you?' said Julian, sensibly. 'He could use that tower easily. He could flash a signal to you in the morning, using a mirror, you know – heliographing that he was all right – and at night he could signal with a lamp. Easy!'

'Yes. I did suggest that sort of thing,' said his aunt. 'I said I'd go over with you all tomorrow, to see him and perhaps, Julian dear, you could arrange something of the sort with your uncle? He seems to listen to you now.'

'Gracious! Do you mean to say Father wants us to invade his secret lair, and actually to see his strange tower?' asked George, surprised. 'Well – I don't think I want to go. After all, it's *my* island – and it's horrid to see someone else taking possession of it.'

'Oh, George, don't begin all that again,' said Anne, with a sigh. 'You and your island! Can't you even *lend* it to your own father! Aunt Fanny, you should have seen George when your letter came. She looked so fierce that I was quite scared!'

Everyone laughed except George and Aunt Fanny. She looked distressed. George was always so difficult! She found fault with her father, and got up against him time after time – but dear me, how very, very like him she was, with her scowls, her sudden temper, and her fierceness! If only George was as sweet-tempered and as easy-going as these three cousins of hers!

George looked at her mother's troubled face, and felt ashamed of herself. She put her hand on her knee. 'It's all right Mother! I won't make a fuss. I'll try and keep my feelings to myself, really I will. I know Father's work is important. I'll go with you to the island tomorrow.'

Julian gave George a gentle clap on the back. 'Good old George! She's actually learned, not only to give in, but to give in gracefully! George, you're more like a boy than ever when you act like that.'

George glowed. She liked Julian to say she was like a boy. But Anne looked a little indignant.

'It isn't *only* boys that can learn to give in decently, and things like that,' she said. 'Heaps of girls do. Well, I jolly well hope I do myself!'

'My goodness, here's another fire-brand!' said Aunt Fanny, smiling. 'Stop arguing now, all of you – here's Kirrin Cottage. Doesn't it look sweet with all the primroses in the garden, and the wallflowers coming out, and the daffodils peeping everywhere?'

It certainly did. The four children and Timmy tore in at the front gate, delighted to be back.

They clattered into the house, and, to their great delight, found Joanna, the old cook there. She had come back to help for the holidays. She beamed at the children, and fondled Timmy when he leapt round her barking.

'Well, there now! Haven't you all grown again? How big you are, Julian – taller than I am, I'd say. And little Anne, why, she's getting quite big.'

That pleased Anne, of course. Julian went back to the front door to help his aunt with the small bags in the trap. The trunks were coming later. Julian and Dick took everything upstairs.

Anne joined them, eager to see her old bedroom again. Oh, how good it was to be in Kirrin Cottage once more! She looked out of the windows. One looked on to the moor at the back. The other looked sideways on to the sea. Lovely! Lovely! She began to sing a little song as she undid her bag.

'You know,' she said to Dick, when he brought George's bag in, 'you know, Dick, I'm really quite pleased that Uncle Quentin has gone to Kirrin Island, even if it means we won't be able to go there much! I feel much freer in the house when he's away. He's a very clever man and he can be awfully nice – but I always feel a bit afraid of him.'

Dick laughed. 'I'm not afraid of him – but he's a bit of a wet blanket in the house, I must say, when we're here for the holidays. Funny to think of him on Kirrin Island all alone.'

A voice came up the stairs. 'Come down to tea, children, because there are hot scones for you, just out of the oven.'

'Coming, Aunt Fanny!' called Dick. 'Hurry, Anne. I'm awfully hungry. Julian, did you hear Aunt Fanny calling?'

George came up the stairs to fetch Anne. She was pleased to be home, and as for Timmy, he was engaged in going round every single corner of the house, sniffing vigorously.

'He always does that!' said George. 'As if he thought that there *might* be a chair or a table that didn't smell quite the same as it always did. Come on, Tim. Tea-time! Mother, as Father isn't here, can Timmy sit beside me on the floor? He's awfully well-behaved now.'

'Very well,' said her mother, and tea began. What a tea! It looked as if it was a spread for a party of twenty. Good old Joanna! She must have baked all day. Well, there wouldn't be much left when the Five had finished!

[3]

Off to Kirrin Island

Next day was fine and warm. 'We can go across to the island this morning,' said Aunt Fanny. 'We'll take our own food, because I'm sure Uncle Quentin will have forgotten we're coming.'

'Has he a boat there?' asked George. 'Mother – he hasn't taken *my* boat, has he?'

'No, dear,' said her mother. 'He's got another boat. I was afraid he would never be able to get it in and out of all those dangerous rocks round the island, but he got one of the fishermen to take him, and had his own boat towed behind, with all his stuff in.'

'Who built the tower?' asked Julian.

'Oh, he made out the plans himself and some men were sent down from the Ministry of Research to put the tower up for him,' said

Aunt Fanny. 'It was all rather hush-hush really. The people here were most curious about it, but they don't know any more than I do! No local man helped in the building, but one or two fishermen were hired to take the material to the island, and to land the men and so on.'

'It's all very mysterious,' said Julian. 'Uncle Quentin leads rather an exciting life, really, doesn't he? I wouldn't mind being a scientist myself. I want to be something really worthwhile when I grow up – I'm not just going into somebody's office. I'm going to be on my own.'

'I think I shall be a doctor,' said Dick.

'I'm off to get my boat,' said George, rather bored with this talk. She knew what *she* was going to do when she was grown-up – live on Kirrin Island with Timmy!

Aunt Fanny had got ready plenty of food to take across to the island. She was quite looking forward to the trip. She had not seen her husband for some days, and was anxious to know that he was all right.

They all went down to the beach, Julian

carrying the bag of food. George was already there with her boat. Alf, a fisher-boy friend of George's, was there too, ready to push the boat out for them.

He grinned at the children. He knew them all well. In the old days he had looked after Timmy for George when her father had said the dog must be given away. George had never forgotten Alf's kindness to Timmy, and always went to see him every holidays.

'Going off to the island?' said Alf. 'That's a strange thing in the middle of it, isn't it? Kind of lighthouse, it looks. Take my hand, and let me help you in.'

Anne took his hand and jumped into the boat. George was already there with Timmy. Soon they were all in. Julian and George took the oars. Alf gave them a shove and off they went on the calm, clear water. Anne could see every stone on the bottom!

Julian and George rowed strongly. They sent the boat along swiftly. George began to sing a rowing song and they all took it up. It was lovely to be on the sea in a boat again. Oh holidays, go slowly, don't rush away too fast!

'George,' said her mother nervously, as they came near to Kirrin Island, 'you *will* be careful of these awful rocks, won't you? The water's so clear today that I can see them all – and some of them are only just below the water.'

'Oh Mother! You know I've rowed hundreds of times to Kirrin Island!' laughed George. 'I simply *couldn't* go on a rock! I know them all, really I do. I could almost row blindfold to the island now.'

There was only one place to land on the island in safety. This was a little cove, a natural little harbour running up to a stretch of sand. It was sheltered by high rocks all round. George and Julian worked their way to the east side of the island, rounded a low wall of very sharp rocks, and there lay the cove, a smooth inlet of water running into the shore!

Anne had been looking at the island as the others rowed. There was the old ruined Kirrin

Castle in the centre, just the same as ever. Its tumbledown towers were full of jackdaws as usual. Its old walls were gripped by ivy.

'It's a lovely place!' said Anne, with a sigh. Then she gazed at the curious tower that now rose from the centre of the castle yard. It was not built of brick but some smooth, shiny material, that was fitted together in sections. Evidently the tower had been made in that way so that it might be brought to the island easily, and set up there quickly.

'Isn't it strange?' said Dick. 'Look at that little glass room at the top – like a look-out room! I wonder what it's for?'

'Can anyone climb up inside the tower?' asked Dick, turning to Aunt Fanny.

'Oh yes. There is a narrow spiral staircase inside,' said his aunt. 'That's about all there is inside the tower itself. It's the little room at the top that is important. It has got some extraordinary wiring there, essential to your uncle's experiments. I don't think he *does* anything with the tower – it just has to be there, doing something on its own, which has a certain effect on the experiments he is making.'

Anne couldn't follow this. It sounded too complicated. 'I should like to go up the tower,' she said.

'Well, perhaps your uncle will let you,' said her aunt.

'If he's in a good temper,' said George.

'Now George – you're not to say things like that,' said her mother.

The boat ran into the little harbour, and grounded softly. There was another boat there already – Uncle Quentin's.

George leapt out with Julian and they pulled it up a little further, so that the others could get out without wetting their feet. Out they all got, and Timmy ran up the beach in delight.

'Now, Timmy!' said George, warningly, and Timmy turned a despairing eye on his mistress. Surely she wasn't going to stop him looking to see if there were any rabbits? Only just *looking*! What harm was there in that?

Ah – there was a rabbit! And another and

another! They sat all about, looking at the little company coming up from the shore. They flicked their ears and twitched their noses, keeping quite still.

'Oh, they're as tame as ever!' said Anne in delight. 'Aunty Fanny, aren't they lovely? Do look at the baby one over there. He's washing his face!'

They stopped to look at the rabbits. They really were astonishingly tame. But then very few people came to Kirrin Island, and the rabbits multiplied in peace, running about where they liked, quite unafraid.

'Oh, that one is . . .' began Dick, but then the picture was spoilt. Timmy, quite unable to do nothing but look, had suddenly lost his self-control and was bounding on the surprised rabbits. In a trice nothing could be seen but white bobtails flashing up and down as rabbit after rabbit rushed to its burrow.

'*Timmy*!' called George, crossly, and poor Timmy put his tail down, looking round at George miserably. 'What!' he seemed to say.

'Not even a scamper after the rabbits? What a hard-hearted mistress!'

'Where's Uncle Quentin?' asked Anne, as they walked to the great broken archway that was the entrance to the old castle. Behind it were the stone steps that led towards the centre. They were broken and irregular now. Aunt Fanny went across them carefully, afraid of stumbling, but the children, who were wearing rubber shoes, ran over them quickly.

They passed through an old ruined doorway into what looked like a great yard. Once there had been a stone-paved floor, but now most of it was covered by sand, and by close-growing weeds or grass.

The castle had had two towers. One was almost a complete ruin. The other was in better shape. Jackdaws circled round it, and flew above the children's heads, crying 'chack, chack, chack'.

'I suppose your father lives in the little old room with the two slit-like windows,' said Dick to George. 'That's the only place in the castle that would give him any shelter. Everywhere else is in ruins except that one room. Do you remember we once spent a night there?'

'Yes,' said George. 'It was fun. I suppose that's where Father lives. There's nowhere else – unless he's down in the dungeons!'

'Oh, no one would live in the dungeons surely, unless they simply *had* to!' said Julian. 'They're so dark and cold. Where *is* your father, George? I can't see him anywhere.'

'Mother, where would Father be?' asked George. 'Where's his workshop – in that old room there?' She pointed to the dark, stone-walled, stone-roofed room, which was really all that was left of the part in which people had long ago lived. It jutted out from what had once been the wall of the castle.

'Well, really, I don't exactly know,' said her mother. 'I suppose he works over there. He's always met me down at the cove, and we've just sat on the sand and had a picnic and talked. He didn't seem to want me to poke round much.'

'Let's call him,' said Dick. So they shouted loudly.

'Uncle QUEN-tin! Uncle QUEN-tin! Where are you?'

The jackdaws flew up in fright, and a few gulls, who had been sitting on part of the ruined wall, joined in the noise, crying 'ee-oo, ee-oo, ee-oo' over and over again. Every rabbit disappeared in a trice.

No Uncle Quentin appeared. They shouted again.

'UNCLE QUENTIN! WHERE ARE YOU?'

'What a noise!' said Aunt Fanny, covering her ears. 'I should think that Joanna must have heard that at home. Oh dear – where is your uncle? This is most annoying of him. I *told* him I'd bring you across today.'

'Oh well – he must be somewhere about,' said Julian, cheerfully. 'If Mohammed won't come to the mountain, then the mountain must go to Mohammed. I expect he's deep in some book or other. We'll hunt for him.'

'We'll look in that little dark room,' said

Anne. So they all went through the stone doorway, and found themselves in a little dark room, lit only by two slits of windows. At one end was a space, or recess, where a fireplace had once been, going back into the thick stone wall.

'He's not here,' said Julian in surprise. 'And what's more – there's nothing here at all! No food, no clothes, no books, no stores of any sort. This is not his workroom, nor even his store!'

'Then he must be down in the dungeons,' said Dick. 'Perhaps it's necessary to his work to be underground – and with water all round! Let's go and find the entrance. We know where it is – not far from the old well in the middle of the yard.'

'Yes. He must be down in the dungeons. Mustn't he, Aunt Fanny?' said Anne. 'Are you coming down?'

'Oh no,' said her aunt. 'I can't bear those dungeons. I'll sit out here in the sun, in this sheltered corner, and unpack the sandwiches. It's almost lunch-time.'

'Oh good,' said everyone. They went towards the dungeon entrance. They expected to see the big flat stone that covered the entrance, standing upright, so that they might go down the steps underground.

But the stone was lying flat. Julian was just about to pull on the iron ring to lift it up when he noticed something peculiar.

'Look,' he said. 'There are weeds growing round the edges of the stone. Nobody has lifted it for a long time. Uncle Quentin isn't down in the dungeons!'

'Then where *is* he?' said Dick. 'Wherever *can* he be?'

[4]

Where is Uncle Quentin?

The four of them, with Timmy nosing round their legs, stood staring down at the big stone that hid the entrance to the dungeons. Julian was perfectly right. The stone could not have been lifted for months, because weeds had grown closely round the edges, sending their small roots into every crack.

'No one is down there,' said Julian. 'We need not even bother to pull up the stone and go down to see. If it had been lifted lately, those weeds would have been torn up as it was raised.'

'And anyway, we know that no one can get *out* of the dungeon once the entrance stone is closing it,' said Dick. 'It's too heavy. Uncle Quentin wouldn't be silly enough to shut himself in! He'd leave it open.'

'Of course he would,' said Anne. 'Well – he's not there, then. He must be somewhere else.'

'But *where*?' said George. 'This is only a small island, and we know every corner of it. Oh – would he be in that cave we hid in once? The only cave on the island.'

'Oh yes – he might be,' said Julian. 'But I doubt it. I can't see Uncle Quentin dropping down through the hole in the cave's roof – and that's the only way of getting into it unless you're going to clamber and slide about the rocks on the shore for ages. I can't see him doing that, either.'

They made their way beyond the castle to the other side of the island. Here there was a cave they had once lived in. It could be entered with difficulty on the seaward side, as Julian had said, by clambering over slippery rocks, or it could be entered by dropping down a rope through a hole in the roof to the floor some way below.

They found the hole, half hidden in old heather. Julian felt about. The rope was still there. 'I'll slide down and have a look,' he said.

He went down the rope. It was knotted at intervals so that his feet found holding-places and he did not slide down too quickly and scorch his hands.

He was soon in the cave. A dim light came in from the seaward side. Julian took a quick look round. There was absolutely nothing there at all, except for an old box that they must have left behind when they were last here themselves.

He climbed up the rope again, his head appearing suddenly out of the hole. Dick gave him a hand.

'Well?' he said. 'Any sign of Uncle Quentin?'

'No,' said Julian. 'He's not there, and hasn't been there either, I should think. It's a mystery! Where is he, and if he's really doing important work where is all his stuff? I mean, we know that plenty of stuff was brought here because Aunt Fanny told us so.'

'Do you think he's in the tower?' said Anne, suddenly. 'He might be in that glass room at the top.'

'Well, he'd see us at once, if he were!' said

Julian, scornfully. '*And* hear our yells too! Still, we might as well have a look.'

So back to the castle they went and walked to the peculiar tower. Their aunt saw them and called to them. 'Your lunch is ready. Come and have it. Your uncle will turn up, I expect.'

'But Aunt Fanny where is he?' said Anne, with a puzzled face. 'We've looked simply *everywhere*!'

Her aunt did not know the island as well as the children did. She imagined that there were plenty of places to shelter in, or to work in. 'Never mind,' she said, looking quite undisturbed. 'He'll turn up later. You come along and have your meal.'

'We think we'll go up the tower,' said Julian. 'Just in case he's up there working.'

The four children and Timmy went to where the tower rose up from the castle yard. They ran their hands over the smooth, shining sections, which were fitted together in curving rows. 'What's this stuff it's built of?' said Dick.

'Some kind of new plastic material, I should

think,' said Julian. 'Very light and strong, and easily put together.'

'I should be afraid it would blow down in a gale,' said George.

'Yes, so should I,' said Dick. 'Look – here is the door.'

The door was small, and rounded at the top. A key was in the keyhole. Julian turned it and unlocked the door. It opened outwards not inwards. Julian put his head inside and looked round.

There was not much room in the tower. A spiral staircase, made of the same shiny stuff as the tower itself, wound up and up and up. There was a space at one side of it, into which projected curious hook-like objects made of what looked like steel. Wire ran from one to the other.

'Better not touch them,' said Julian, looking curiously at them. 'Goodness, this is like a tower out of a fairy-tale. Come on – I'm going up the stairs to the top.'

He began to climb the steep, spiral stairway.

It made him quite giddy to go up and round, up and round so many, many times.

The others followed him. Tiny, slit-like windows, set sideways not downwards, were let into the side of the tower here and there, and gave a little light to the stairway. Julian looked through one, and had a wonderful view of the sea and the mainland.

He went on up to the top. When he got there he found himself in a small round room, whose sides were of thick, gleaming glass. Wires ran right into the glass itself, and then pierced through it, the free ends waving and glittering in the strong wind that blew round the tower.

There was nothing in the little room at all! Certainly Uncle Quentin was not there. It was clearly only a tower meant to take the wires up on the hook-like things, and to run them through the strange, thick glass at the top, and set them free in the air. What for? Were they catching some kind of wireless waves? Was it to do with radar? Julian wondered, frowning, what was the meaning of the tower and the thin, shining wires?

The others crowded into the little room. Timmy came too, having managed the spiral stairs with difficulty.

'Gracious! What a weird place!' said George. 'My goodness, what a view we've got from here. We can see miles and miles out to sea – and on this other side we can see miles and miles across the bay, over the mainland to the hills beyond.'

'Yes. It's lovely,' said Anne. 'But – *where* is Uncle Quentin? We still haven't found him. I suppose he *is* on the island.'

'Well, his boat was pulled up in the cove,' said George. 'We saw it.'

'Then he must be here somewhere,' said Dick. 'But he's not in the castle, he's not in the dungeons, he's not in the cave and he's not up here. It's a first-class mystery.'

'The Missing Uncle. Where is he?' said Julian. 'Look there's poor Aunt Fanny still down there, waiting with the lunch. We'd better go down. She's signalling to us.'

'I should like to,' said Anne. 'It's an awful squash in this tiny glass room. I say – did you feel the tower sway then, when that gust of wind shook it? I'm going down quickly, before the whole thing blows over!'

She began to go down the spiral stairs, holding on to a little hand-rail that ran down beside them. The stairs were so steep that she was afraid of falling. She nearly *did* fall when Timmy pushed his way past her, and disappeared below at a remarkably fast pace.

Soon they were all down at the bottom. Julian locked the door again. 'Not much good locking a door if you leave the key in,' he said. 'Still – I'd better.'

They walked over to Aunt Fanny. 'Well, I thought you were never coming!' she said. 'Did you see anything interesting up there?'

'Only a lovely view,' said Anne. 'Simply magnificent. But we didn't find Uncle Quentin. It's very mysterious, Aunt Fanny – we really have looked everywhere on the island – but he's just not here.'

'And yet his boat is in the cove,' said Dick. 'So he can't have gone.'

'Yes, it does sound odd,' said Aunt Fanny, handing round the sandwiches. 'But you don't know your uncle as well as I do. He always turns up all right. He's forgotten I was bringing you, or he would be here. As it is, we may not see him, if he's quite forgotten about your coming. If he remembers, he'll suddenly turn up.'

'But where from?' asked Dick, munching a potted meat sandwich. 'He's done a jolly good disappearing trick, Aunt Fanny.'

'Well, you'll see where he comes from, I've no doubt, when he arrives,' said Aunt Fanny. 'Another sandwich, George? No, *not* you, Timmy. You've had three already. Oh George, do keep Timmy's head out of that plate.'

'He's hungry too, Mother,' said George.

'Well, I've brought dog biscuits for him,' said her mother.

'Oh, Mother! As if Timmy would eat *dog* biscuits when he can have sandwiches,' said

George. 'He only eats dog biscuits when there's absolutely nothing else and he's so ravenous he can't help eating them.'

They sat in the warm April sunshine, eating hungrily. There was orangeade to drink, cool and delicious. Timmy wandered over to a rock pool he knew, where rain-water collected, and he could be heard lapping there.

'Hasn't he got a good memory?' said George proudly. 'It's ages since he was here – and yet he remembered that pool at once, when he felt thirsty.'

'It's funny Timmy hasn't found Uncle Quentin, isn't it?' said Dick, suddenly. 'I mean – when we were hunting for him, and got "Warm" you'd think Timmy would bark or scrape about or something. But he didn't.'

'I think it's jolly funny that Father can't be found anywhere,' said George. 'I do really. I can't think how you can take it so calmly, Mother.'

'Well, dear, as I said before, I know your father better than you do,' said her mother.

'He'll turn up in his own good time. Why, I remember once when he was doing some sort of work in the stalactite caves at Cheddar, he disappeared in them for over a week – but he wandered out all right when he had finished his experiments.'

'It's very strange,' began Anne, and then stopped suddenly. A curious noise came to their ears – a rumbling grumbling, angry noise, like a giant hidden dog, growling in fury. Then there was a hissing noise from the tower, and all the wires that waved at the top were suddenly lit up as if by lightning.

'There now – I knew your father was somewhere about,' said George's mother. 'I heard that noise when I was here before – but I couldn't make out where it came from.'

'Where *did* it come from?' said Dick. 'It sounded almost as if it was underneath us, but it couldn't have been. Gracious, this is most mysterious.'

No more noises came. They each helped themselves to buns with jam in the middle.

And then Anne gave a squeal that made them all jump violently.

'Look! *There's* Uncle Quentin! Standing over there, near the tower. He's watching the jackdaws! Wherever *did* he come from?'

[5]

A mystery

Everyone stared at Uncle Quentin. There he was, intently watching the jackdaws, his hands in his pockets. He hadn't seen the children or his wife.

Timmy leapt to his feet, and gambolled over to George's father. He barked loudly. Uncle Quentin jumped and turned round. He saw Timmy – and then he saw all the others, staring at him in real astonishment.

Uncle Quentin did not look particularly pleased to see anyone. He walked slowly over to them, a slight frown on his face. 'This *is* a surprise,' he said. 'I had no idea you were all coming today.'

'Oh *Quentin*!' said his wife, reproachfully. 'I wrote it down for you in your diary. You know I did.'

'Did you! Well, I haven't looked at my diary since, so it's no wonder I forgot,' said Uncle Quentin, a little peevishly. He kissed his wife, George and Anne, and shook hands with the boys.

'Uncle Quentin – where did you come from?' asked Dick, who was eaten up with curiosity. 'We've looked for you for ages.'

'Oh, I was in my workroom,' said Uncle Quentin, vaguely.

'Well, but where's that?' demanded Dick. 'Honestly, Uncle, we can't imagine where you hid yourself. We even went up the tower to see if you were in that funny glass room at the top.'

'*What*!' exploded his uncle, in a sudden surprising fury. 'You dared to go up there? You might have been in great danger. I've just finished an experiment, and all those wires in there were connected with it.'

'Yes, we saw them acting a bit strangely,' said Julian.

'You've no business to come over here, and interfere with my work,' said his uncle, still looking furious. 'How did you get into that tower? I locked it.'

'Yes, it was locked all right,' said Julian. 'But you left the key in, you see, Uncle – so I thought it wouldn't matter if . . .'

'Oh, that's where the key is, is it?' said his uncle. 'I thought I'd lost it. Well, don't you ever go into that tower again. I tell you, it's dangerous.'

'Uncle Quentin, you haven't told us yet where your workroom is,' said Dick, who was quite determined to know. 'We can't imagine where you suddenly came from.'

'I told them you would turn up, Quentin,' said his wife. 'You look a bit thin, dear. Have you been having regular meals? You know, I left you plenty of good soup to heat up.'

'Did you?' said her husband. 'Well, I don't know if I've had it or not. I don't worry about meals when I'm working. I'll have some of those sandwiches now, though, if nobody else wants them.'

He began to devour the sandwiches, one

after another, as if he was ravenous. Aunt Fanny watched him in distress.

'Oh Quentin – you're starving. I shall come over here and stay and look after you!'

Her husband looked alarmed. 'Oh no! Nobody is to come here. I can't have my work interfered with. I'm working on an extremely important discovery.'

'Is it a discovery that nobody else knows about?' asked Anne, her eyes wide with admiration. How clever Uncle Quentin was!

'Well – I'm not sure about that,' said Uncle Quentin, taking two sandwiches at once. 'That's partly why I came over here – besides the fact that I wanted water round me. I have a feeling that somebody knows a bit more than I want them to know. But there's one thing – they can't come here unless they're shown the way through all those rocks that lie round the island. Only a few of the fishermen know that, and they've been given orders not to bring anyone here at all. I think you're the only other person that knows the way, George.'

'Uncle Quentin – please do tell us where your workroom is,' begged Dick, feeling that he could not wait a single moment more to solve the mystery.

'Don't keep bothering your uncle,' said his aunt, annoyingly. 'Let him eat his lunch. He can't have had anything for ages!'

'Yes, but Aunt Fanny, I—' began Dick and was interrupted by his uncle.

'You obey your aunt, young man. I don't want to be pestered by any of you. What does it matter where I work?'

'Oh, it doesn't really matter a bit,' said Dick, hurriedly. 'It's only that I'm awfully curious to know. You see, we looked for you simply everywhere.'

'Well, you're not quite so clever as you thought you were then,' said Uncle Quentin, and reached for a jammy bun. 'George, take this dog of yours away from me. He keeps breathing down my neck, hoping I shall give him a tit-bit. I don't approve of tit-bits at meal-times.'

George pulled Timmy away. Her mother watched her father gobbling up the rest of the food. Most of the sandwiches she had saved for tea-time had gone already. Poor Quentin! How very hungry he must be.

'Quentin, you don't think there's any danger for you here, do you?' she said. 'I mean – you don't think anyone would try to come spying on you, as they did once before?'

'No. How could they?' said her husband. 'No plane can land on this island. No boat can get through the rocks unless the way through is known, and the sea's too rough round the rocks for any swimmer.'

'Julian, see if you can make him promise to signal to me night and morning,' said Aunt Fanny, turning to her nephew. 'I feel worried about him somehow.'

Julian tackled his uncle manfully. 'Uncle, it wouldn't be too much of a bother to you to signal to Aunt Fanny twice a day, would it?'

'If you don't, Quentin, I shall come over every single day to see you,' said his wife.

'And we might come too,' said Anne mischievously. Her uncle looked most dismayed at the idea.

'Well, I could signal in the morning and in the evening when I go up to the top of the tower,' he said. 'I have to go up once every twelve hours to readjust the wires. I'll signal then. Half past ten in the morning and half past ten at night.'

'How will you signal?' asked Julian. 'Will you flash with a mirror in the morning?'

'Yes – that would be quite a good idea,' said his uncle. 'I could do that easily. And I'll use a lantern at night. I'll shine it out six times at half past ten. Then perhaps you'll all know I'm all right and will leave me alone! But don't look for the signal tonight. I'll start tomorrow morning.'

'Oh Quentin dear, you do sound cross,' said his wife. 'I don't like you being all alone here, that's all. You look thin and tired. I'm sure you're not . . .'

Uncle Quentin put on a scowl exactly like George sometimes put on. He looked at his wrist-watch. 'Well I must go,' he said. 'Time to get to work again. I'll see you to your boat.'

'We're going to stay to tea here, Father,' said George.

'No, I'd rather you didn't,' said her father, getting up. 'Come on – I'll take you to your boat.'

'But Father – I haven't been on my island for ages!' said George, indignantly. 'I want to stay here a bit longer. I don't see why I shouldn't.'

'Well, I've had enough interruption to my work,' said her father. 'I want to get on.'

'We shan't disturb you, Uncle Quentin,' said Dick, who was still terribly curious to know where his uncle had his workroom. Why wouldn't he tell them! Was he just being annoying? Or didn't he want them to know?

Uncle Quentin led them all firmly towards the little cove. It was plain that he meant them to go and to go quickly.

'When shall we come over and see you again, Quentin?' asked his wife.

'Not till I say so,' said her husband. 'It won't

take me long now to finish what I'm on. My word, that dog's got a rabbit at last!'

'Oh *Timmy*!' yelled George in distress. Timmy dropped the rabbit he had actually managed to grab. It scampered away unhurt. Timmy came to his mistress looking very sheepish.

'You're a very bad dog. Just because I took my eye off you for half a second! No, it's no good licking my hand like that. I'm cross.'

They all came to the boat. 'I'll push her off,' said Julian. 'Get in, all of you. Well, good-bye, Uncle Quentin. I hope your work goes well.'

Everyone got into the boat. Timmy tried to put his head on George's knee, but she pushed it away.

'Oh, be kind to him and forgive him,' begged Anne. 'He looks as if he's going to cry.'

'Are you ready?' cried Julian. 'Got the oars, George? Dick, take the other pair.'

He shoved the boat off and leapt in himself. He cupped his hands round his mouth. 'Don't forget to signal! We'll be watching out morning and evening!'

'And if you forget, I shall come over the very next day!' called his wife.

The boat slid away down the little inlet of water, and Uncle Quentin was lost to sight. Then round the low wall of rocks went the boat, and was soon on the open sea.

'Ju, watch and see if you can make out where Uncle Quentin is, when we're round these rocks,' said Dick. 'See what direction he goes in.'

Julian tried to see his uncle, but the rocks just there hid the cove from sight, and there was no sign of him at all.

'*Why* didn't he want us to stay? Because he didn't want us to know his hiding-place!' said Dick. 'And *why* doesn't he want us to know? Because it's somewhere *we* don't know, either!'

'But I thought we knew every single corner of my island,' said George. 'I think it's mean of Father not to tell me, if it's somewhere I don't know. I can't think *where* it can be!'

Timmy put his head on her knee again. George was so absorbed in trying to think where her father's hiding-place could be that she absent-mindedly stroked Timmy's head. He was almost beside himself with delight. He licked her fingers lovingly.

'Oh Timmy – I didn't mean to pet you for ages,' said George. 'Stop licking my hands. You make them feel wet and horrid. Dick, it's very mysterious, isn't it – where *can* Father be hiding?'

'I can't imagine,' said Dick. He looked back at the island. A cloud of jackdaws rose up into the air calling loudly, 'Chack, chack, chack!'

The boy watched them. What had disturbed them? Was it Uncle Quentin? Perhaps his hiding-place was somewhere about that old tower then, the one the jackdaws nested in? On the other hand, the jackdaws often rose into the air together for no reason at all.

'Those jackdaws are making a bit of fuss,' he said. 'Perhaps Uncle's hiding-place is not far from where they roost together, by that tower.'

'Can't be,' said Julian. 'We went all round there today.'

'Well, it's a mystery,' said George, gloomily, 'and I think it's horrible having a mystery about my very own island – and to be forbidden to go to it, and solve it. It's really *too* bad!'

[6]

Up on the cliff

The next day was rainy. The four children put on their macintoshes and sou'westers and went out for a walk with Timmy. They never minded the weather. In fact Julian said that he really *liked* the feel of the wind and rain buffeting against his face.

'We forgot that Uncle Quentin couldn't flash to us if the weather wasn't sunny!' said Dick. 'Do you suppose he'll find some way to signal instead?'

'No,' said George. 'He just won't bother. He thinks we're awful fussers anyway, I'm sure. We'll have to watch at half past ten tonight to see if he signals.'

'I say! Shall I be able to stay up till then?' said Anne, pleased.

'I shouldn't think so,' said Dick. 'I expect

Julian and I will stay up - but you kids will have to buzz off to bed!'

George gave him a punch. 'Don't call us "*kids*"! I'm almost as tall as you are now.'

'It's not much use waiting about till half past ten now to see if Uncle signals to us in any way, is it?' said Anne. 'Let's go up on the cliff – it'll be lovely and blowy. Timmy will like that. I love to see him racing along in the wind, with his ears blown back straight!'

'Woof,' said Timmy.

'He says he likes to see you with yours blown back too,' said Julian, gravely. Anne gave a squeal of laughter.

'You really are an idiot, Ju! Come on – let's take the cliff-path!'

They went up the cliff. At the top it was very windy indeed. Anne's sou'wester was blown to the back of her head. The rain stung their cheeks and made them gasp.

'I should think we must be about the only people out this morning!' gasped George.

'Well, you're wrong,' said Julian. 'There are two people coming towards us!'

So there was. They were a man and a boy, both well wrapped up in macintoshes and sou'westers. Like the children, they too wore high rubber boots.

The children took a look at them as they passed. The man was tall and well built, with shaggy eyebrows and a determined mouth. The boy was about sixteen, also tall and well built. He was not a bad-looking boy, but he had rather a sullen expression.

'Good morning,' said the man, and nodded.

'Good morning,' chorused the children, politely. The man looked them over keenly, and then he and the boy went on.

'Wonder who they are?' said George. 'Mother didn't say there were any new people here.'

'Just walked over from the next village, I expect,' said Dick.

They went on for some way. 'We'll walk to the coastguard's cottage and then go back,' said Julian. 'Hey, Tim, don't go so near the cliff!'

The coastguard lived in a little whitewashed cottage on the cliff, facing the sea. Two other cottages stood beside it, also whitewashed. The children knew the coastguard well. He was a red-faced, barrel-shaped man, fond of joking.

He was nowhere to be seen when they came to his cottage. Then they heard his enormous voice singing a sea-shanty in the little shed behind. They went to find him.

'Hallo,' said Anne.

He looked up and grinned at the children. He was busy making something. 'Hallo to you!' he said. 'So you're back again are you? Bad pennies, the lot of you – always turning up when you're not wanted!'

'What are you making?' asked Anne.

'A windmill for my young grandson,' said the coastguard, showing it to Anne. He was very clever at making toys.

'Oh, it's *lovely*,' said Anne, taking it in her hands. 'Does the windmill part go round – oh yes – it's super!'

'I've been making quite a bit of money out of

my toys,' said the old fellow, proudly. 'I've got some new neighbours in the next cottage – man and a boy – and the man's been buying all the toys I make. Seems to have a lot of nephews and nieces! He gives me good prices too.'

'Oh – would that be the man and the boy we met, I wonder?' said Dick. 'Both tall, and well built – and the man had shaggy eyebrows.'

'That's right,' said the coastguard, trimming a bit of his windmill. 'Mr Curton and his son. They came here some weeks ago. You ought to get to know the son, Julian. He's about your age, I should think. Must be pretty lonely for him up here!'

'Doesn't he go to any school?' asked Julian.

'No. He's been ill, so his father said. Got to have plenty of sea-air and that sort of thing. Not a bad sort of boy. He comes and helps me with my toys sometimes. And he likes to mess about with my telescope.'

'I do too,' said George. 'I love looking through your telescope. Can I look through it now? I'd like to see if I can spot Kirrin Island.'

'Well, you won't see much in this weather,' said the coastguard. 'You wait a few minutes. See that break in the clouds? Well, it'll clear in a few minutes, and you'll be able to see your island easily. That's a funny thing your father's built there, isn't it? Part of his work, I suppose.'

'Yes,' said George. 'Oh Timmy – look what he's done – he's upset that tin of paint. Bad boy, Timmy!'

'It's not my tin,' said the coastguard. 'It's a tin belonging to that young fellow next door. I told you he comes in to help me sometimes. He brought in that tin to help paint a little dolls' house I made for his father.'

'Oh dear,' said George, in dismay. 'Do you think he'll be cross when he knows Timmy spilt it?'

'Shouldn't think so,' said the coastguard. 'He's a funny boy though – quiet and a bit sulky. Not a bad boy, but doesn't seem very friendly like.'

George tried to clear up the mess of paint. Timmy had some on his paws, and made a little pattern of green paw-marks as he pattered about the shed.

'I'll tell the boy I'm sorry, if I meet him on the way back,' she said. 'Timmy if you dare to go near any more tins of paint you shan't sleep on my bed tonight.'

'The weather's a bit clearer now,' said Dick. 'Can we have a squint through the telescope?'

'Let *me* see my island first,' said George at once. She tilted the telescope in the direction of Kirrin Island. She looked through it earnestly, and a smile came over her face.

'Yes, I can see it clearly. There's the tower Father has had built. I can even see the glass room quite clearly, and there's nobody in it. No sign of Father anywhere.'

Everyone had a turn at looking through the telescope. It was fascinating to see the island appearing so close. On a clear day it would be even easier to see all the details. 'I can see a rabbit scampering,' said Anne, when her turn came.

'Don't you let that dog of yours squint

through the telescope then,' said the coastguard at once. 'He'll try to get down it after that rabbit!'

Timmy cocked his ears up at the mention of the word rabbit. He looked all round and sniffed. No, there was no rabbit. Then why did people mention them?

'We'd better go now,' said Julian. 'We'll be up here again sometime, and we'll come and see what toys you've done. Thanks for letting us look through the telescope.'

'You're welcome!' said the old fellow. 'You're not likely to wear it out through looking! Come along any time you want to use it.'

They said goodbye and went off, Timmy capering round them. 'Couldn't we see Kirrin Island well!' said Anne. 'I wished I could see where your father was, George. Wouldn't it be fun if we spotted him just coming out of his hiding-place?'

The four children had discussed this problem a good deal since they had left the island. It puzzled them very much indeed.

How did it happen that George's father knew a hiding-place that they didn't know? Why, they had been over every inch of the island! It must be quite a big hiding-place too, if he had got all his stuff for his experiments with him. According to George's mother, there had been quite a lot of this, to say nothing of stores of food.

'If Father knew a place I didn't know, and never told me about it, I think he's jolly mean,' George said half a dozen times. 'I do really. It's *my* island!'

'Well, he'll probably tell you when he's finished the work he's on,' said Julian. 'Then you'll know. We can all go and explore it then, wherever it is.'

After they left the coastguard's cottage they turned their steps home. They made their way along the cliff, and then saw the boy they had met before. He was standing on the path looking out to sea. The man was not with him.

He turned as they came up and gave them a

pale kind of smile. 'Hallo! Been up to see the coastguard?'

'Yes,' said Julian. 'Nice old fellow, isn't he?'

'I say,' said George, 'I'm so sorry but my dog upset a tin of green paint, and the coastguard said it was yours. Can I pay you for it, please?'

'Goodness, no!' said the boy. 'I don't mind. There wasn't much of it left anyway. That's a nice dog of yours.'

'Yes, he is,' said George, warmly. 'Best dog in the world. I've had him for years, but he's still as young as ever. Do you like dogs?'

'Oh yes,' said the boy, but he made no move to pat Timmy or fuss him, as most people did. And Timmy did not run round the boy and sniff at him as he usually did when he met anyone new. He just stood by George, his tail neither up nor down.

'That's an interesting little island,' said the boy, pointing to Kirrin. 'I wish I could go there.'

'It's *my* island,' said George, proudly. 'My very own.'

'Really?' said the boy, politely. 'Could you let me go over one day then?'

'Well – not just at present,' said George. 'You see, my father's there – working – he's a scientist.'

'Really?' said the boy again. 'Er – has he got some new experiment on hand, then?'

'Yes,' said George.

'Ah – and that weird tower is something to do with it, I suppose,' said the boy, looking interested for the first time. 'When will his experiment be finished?'

'What's that to do with you?' said Dick, suddenly. The others stared at him in surprise. Dick sounded rather rude, and it was not like him.

'Oh nothing!' said the boy, hastily. 'I only thought that if his work will soon be finished, perhaps your brother would take me over to his island!'

George couldn't help feeling pleased. This boy thought *she* was a boy! George was always gracious to people who made the mistake of thinking she was a boy.

'Of *course* I'll take you!' she said. 'It shouldn't be long before I do – the experiment is nearly done.'

[7]

A little squabble

A sound made them turn. It was the boy's father coming up. He nodded to the children. 'Making friends?' he said, amiably. 'That's right. My boy's pretty lonely here. I hope you'll come up and see us some time. Finished your conversation, son?'

'Yes,' said the boy. 'This boy here says that island is his, and he's going to take me over it when his father has finished his work there – and that won't be long.'

'And do you know the way through all those wicked rocks?' said the man. '*I* shouldn't care to try it. I was talking to the fishermen the other day, and not one of them appeared to know the way!'

This was rather astonishing. Some of the fishermen *did* know it. Then the children remembered that the men had all been forbidden to take anyone to the island while Uncle Quentin was at work there. It was clear that they had pretended not to know the way, in loyalty to their orders.

'Did you want to go to the island then?' asked Dick, suddenly.

'Oh no! But my boy here would love to go,' said the man. '*I* don't want to be seasick, bobbing up and down on those waves near the island. I'm a poor sailor. I never go on the sea if I can help it!'

'Well, we must go,' said Julian. 'We've got to do some shopping for my aunt. Goodbye!'

'Come and see us as soon as you can,' said the man. 'I've a fine television set that Martin here would like to show you. Any afternoon you like!'

'Oh thanks!' said George. She seldom saw television. 'We'll come!'

They parted, and the four children and Timmy went on down the cliff-path.

'Whatever made you sound so rude, Dick?'

said George. 'The way you said "What's that to do with you?" sounded quite insulting.'

'Well – I just felt suspicious, that's all,' said Dick. 'That boy seemed to be so jolly interested in the island and in your father's work, and when it would be finished.'

'Why shouldn't he be?' demanded George. 'Everyone in the village is interested. They all know about the tower. And all the boy wanted to know was when he could go to my island – that's why he asked when Father's work would be finished. I liked him.'

'You only liked him because he was ass enough to think you were a boy,' said Dick. 'Jolly girlish-looking boy you are, that's all I can say.'

George flared up at once. 'Don't be mean! I'm *not* girlish-looking. I've far more freckles than you have, for one thing, and better eyebrows. *And* I can make my voice go deep.'

'You're just silly,' said Dick, in disgust. 'As if freckles are boyish! Girls have them just as much as boys. I don't believe that boy thought you were a boy at all. He was just sucking up to you. He must have heard how much you like playing at being what you aren't.'

George walked up to Dick with such a furious look on her face that Julian hastily put himself in between them. 'Now, no brawls,' he said. 'You're both too old to begin slapping each other like kids in the nursery. Let me tell you, you're both behaving like babies, not like boys *or* girls!'

Anne was looking on with scared eyes. George didn't go off the deep end like this usually. And it *was* funny of Dick to have spoken so rudely to the boy on the cliff. Timmy gave a sudden little whine. His tail was down, and he looked very miserable.

'Oh George – Timmy can't *bear* you to quarrel with Dick!' said Anne. 'Look at him! He's just miserable!'

'He didn't like that boy a bit,' said Dick. 'That was another thing I thought was funny. If Timmy doesn't like a person, *I* don't like him either.'

'Timmy doesn't *always* rush round new people,' said George. 'He didn't growl or snarl, anyway. All right, all right, Julian; I'm not going to start brawling. But I do think Dick is being silly. Making a mountain out of a molehill – just because someone was interested in Kirrin Island and Father's work, and just because Timmy didn't caper all round him. He was such a solemn sort of boy that I'm not surprised Timmy wasn't all over him. He probably knew the boy wouldn't like it. Timmy's clever like that.'

'Oh, do stop,' said Dick. 'I give in – gracefully! I may be making a fuss. Probably am. I couldn't help my feelings, though.'

Anne gave a sigh of relief. The squabble was over. She hoped it wouldn't crop up again. George had been very touchy since she had been home. If only Uncle Quentin would hurry up and finish his work, and they could all go to the island as much as they liked, things would be all right.

'I'd rather like to see that television set,' said George. 'We might go up some afternoon.'

'Right,' said Julian. 'But on the whole, I think it would be best if we steered clear of any talk about your father's work. Not that we know much. Still, we do know that once before there were people after one of his theories. The secrets of the scientists are very, very important these days, you know, George. Scientists are VIP!'

'What's VIP?' asked Anne.

'Very Important People, baby!' said Julian, with a laugh. 'What did you think it meant? Violet, Indigo, Purple? I guess those are the colours Uncle Quentin would go if he knew anyone was trying to snoop into his secrets!'

Everyone laughed, even George. She looked affectionately at Julian. He was always so sensible and good-tempered. She really would go by what he said.

The day passed swiftly. The weather cleared and the sun came out strongly. The air smelt of gorse and primroses and the salt of the sea. Lovely! They went shopping for Aunt Fanny, and stopped to talk with Alf, the fisher-boy.

'Your father's got the island, I see,' he said to George with a grin. 'Bad luck, you won't be going over there so often. And nobody else will, either, so I've heard.'

'That's right,' said George. 'Nobody is allowed to go over there for some time. Did you help to take some of the stuff over, Alf?'

'Yes. I know the way, you see, because I've been with you,' said Alf. 'Well, how did you find your boat when you went across yesterday? I got her all ship-shape for you, didn't I?'

'Yes, you did, Alf,' said George, warmly. 'You made her look beautiful. You must come across to the island with us next time we go.'

'Thanks,' said Alf, his ready grin showing all his white teeth. 'Like to leave Timmy with me for a week or two? See how he wants to stay!'

George laughed. She knew Alf was only joking. He was very fond of Timmy, though, and Timmy adored Alf. He was now pushing himself hard against the fisher-boy's knees, and trying to put his nose into his brown hand.

Timmy had never forgotten the time when Alf looked after him so well.

The evening came, and the bay was softly blue. Little white horses flecked it here and there. The four gazed across to Kirrin Island. It always looked so lovely at this time of the evening.

The glass top of the tower winked and blinked in the sun. It looked almost as if someone was signalling. But there was no one in the little glass room. As the children watched they heard a faint rumbling sound, and suddenly the top of the tower was ablaze with a curious glare.

'Look! That's what happened yesterday!' said Julian, in excitement. 'Your father's at work all right, George. I do wonder what he's doing!'

Then there came a throbbing sound, almost like the noise of an aeroplane, and once more the glass top of the tower shone and blazed, as the wires became full of some curious power.

'Weird,' said Dick. 'A bit frightening too.

Where's your father at this very moment? I wonder, George. How I'd like to know!'

'I bet he's forgotten all about meals again,' said George. 'Didn't he wolf our sandwiches – he must have been starving. I wish he'd let Mother go over there and look after him.'

Her mother came in at that moment. 'Did you hear the noise?' she said. 'I suppose that was your father at work again. Oh dear, I hope he doesn't blow himself up one of these days!'

'Aunt Fanny, can I stay up till half past ten tonight?' asked Anne, hopefully. 'To see Uncle Quentin's signal, you know?'

'Good gracious, no!' said her aunt. 'No one needs to stay up. I am quite capable of watching for it myself!'

'Oh Aunt Fanny! Surely Dick and I can stay up!' said Julian. 'After all, we're not in bed till ten at school.'

'Yes – but this is *half past* ten, and you wouldn't even be in bed then,' said his aunt.

'There's no reason why you shouldn't lie in bed and watch for it though, if you want to – providing you haven't fallen asleep!'

'Oh yes – I can do that,' said Julian. 'My window looks across to Kirrin Island. Six flashes with a lantern? I shall count them carefully.'

So the four went to bed at the usual time. Anne was asleep long before half past ten, and George was so drowsy that she could not make herself get up and go into the boys' room. But Dick and Julian were both wide awake. They lay in their beds and looked out of the window. There was no moon, but the sky was clear, and the stars shone down, giving a faint light. The sea looked very black. There was no sign of Kirrin Island. It was lost in the darkness of the night.

'Almost half past ten,' said Julian, looking at his watch which had luminous hands. 'Now then, Uncle Quentin, what about it?'

Almost as if his uncle was answering him, a light shone out in the glass top of the tower. It was a clear, small light, like the light of a lantern.

Julian began to count. 'One flash.' There was a pause. 'Two flashes.' Another pause. 'Three . . . four . . . five . . . six!'

The flashes stopped. Julian snuggled down into bed. 'Well, that's that. Uncle Quentin's all right. I say, it's weird to think of him climbing that spiral stairway right to the top of the tower, in the dark of night, isn't it? – just to mess about with those wires.'

'Mmmmm,' said Dick sleepily. 'I'd rather he did it, than I! You can be a scientist if you like, Ju – but *I* don't want to climb towers in the dead of night on a lonely island. I'd like Timmy there, at least!'

Someone knocked on their door and it opened. Julian sat up at once. It was Aunt Fanny.

'Oh Julian dear – did you see the flashes? I forgot to count them. Were there six?'

'Oh yes, Aunt Fanny! I'd have rushed down to tell you if anything was wrong. Uncle's all right. Don't you worry!'

'I wish I'd told him to do an *extra* flash to tell me if he's had some of that nice soup,' said his aunt. 'Well, good night, Julian. Sleep well!'

[8]

Down in the quarry

The next day dawned bright and sunny. The four tore down to breakfast, full of high spirits. 'Can we bathe? Aunt Fanny, it's *really* warm enough! Oh do say we can!'

'Of course not! Whoever heard of bathing in April!' said Aunt Fanny. 'Why, the sea is terribly cold. Do you want to be in bed for the rest of the holiday with a chill?'

'Well, let's go for a walk on the moors at the back of Kirrin Cottage,' said George. 'Timmy would love that. Wouldn't you, Tim?'

'Woof,' said Timmy, thumping his tail hard on the ground.

'Take your lunch with you if you like,' said her mother. 'I'll pack some for you.'

'You'll be glad to be rid of us for a little while, I expect, Aunt Fanny,' said Dick, with a grin. 'I know what we'll do. We'll go to the old quarry and look for prehistoric weapons! We've got a jolly good museum at school, and I'd like to take back some stone arrow-heads or something like that.'

They all liked hunting for things. It would be fun to go to the old quarry, and it would be lovely and warm in the hollow there.

'I hope we shan't find a poor dead sheep there, as we once did,' said Anne, with a shudder. 'Poor thing! It must have fallen down and baa-ed for help for ages.'

'Of course we shan't,' said Julian. 'We shall find stacks of primroses and violets though, growing down the sides of the quarry. They are always early there because it's sheltered from every wind.'

'And Timmy, of course, will hunt for rabbits, and will hope to bring home enough for you to decorate the larder from top to bottom,' said Dick, solemnly. Timmy looked thrilled and gave an excited little woof.

They waited for Uncle Quentin's signal at

half past ten. It came – six flashes of a mirror in the sun. The flashes were quite blinding.

'Nice little bit of heliographing!' said Dick. 'Good morning and goodbye, Uncle! We'll watch for you tonight. Now, everybody ready?'

'Yes! Come on, Tim! Who's got the sandwiches? I say, isn't the sun hot!'

Off they all went. It was going to be a really lovely day!

The quarry was not really very far – only about a quarter of a mile. The children went for a walk beforehand, for Timmy's sake. Then they made for the quarry.

It was a strange place. At some time or other it had been deeply quarried for stone, and then left to itself. Now the sides were covered with small bushes and grass and plants of all kinds. In the sandy places heather grew.

The sides were very steep, and as few people came there, there were no paths to follow. It was like a huge rough bowl, irregular in places, and full of colour now where primroses opened their pale petals to the sky. Violets grew there by the thousands, both white and purple. Cowslips were opening too, the earliest anywhere.

'Oh, it's lovely!' said Anne, stopping at the top and looking down. 'Simply super! I never in my life saw so many primroses – nor such huge ones!'

'Be careful how you go, Anne,' said Julian. 'These sides are very steep. If you lose your footing you'll roll right down to the bottom – and find yourself with a broken arm or leg!'

'I'll be careful,' said Anne. 'I'll throw my basket down to the bottom, so that I can have two hands to cling to bushes with, if I want to.'

She flung the basket down, and it bounced all the way to the bottom of the quarry. The children climbed down to where they wanted to go – the girls to a great patch of big primroses, the boys to a place where they thought they might find stone weapons.

'Hallo!' said a voice, suddenly, from much lower down. The four stopped in surprise, and Timmy growled.

'Why – it's you!' said George, recognising the boy they had met the day before.

'Yes. I don't know if you know my name. It's Martin Curton,' said the boy.

Julian told him their names too. 'We've come to picnic here,' he said, 'And to see if we can find stone weapons. What have you come for?'

'Oh – to see if I can find stone weapons too,' said the boy.

'Have you found any?' asked George.

'No. Not yet.'

'Well, you won't find any just there,' said Dick. 'Not in heather! You want to come over here, where the ground is bare and gravelly.'

Dick was trying to be friendly, to make up for the day before. Martin came over and began to scrape about with the boys. They had trowels with them, but he had only his hands.

'Isn't it hot down here?' called Anne. 'I'm going to take off my coat.'

Timmy had his head and shoulders down a rabbit-hole. He was scraping violently, sending up heaps of soil behind him in a shower.

'Don't go near Timmy unless you want to be buried in earth!' said Dick. 'Hey, Timmy – is a rabbit really worth all that hard work?'

Apparently it was, for Timmy, panting loudly, went on digging for all he was worth. A stone flew high in the air and hit Julian. He rubbed his cheek. Then he looked at the stone that lay beside him. He gave a shout. 'Look at this – a jolly fine arrow-head! Thanks, Timmy, old fellow. Very good of you to go digging for me. What about a hammer-head next?'

The others came to see the stone arrow-head. Anne thought she would never have known what it was – but Julian and Dick exclaimed over it in admiration.

'Jolly good specimen,' said Dick. 'See how it's been shaped, George? To think that this was used thousands of years ago to kill the enemies of a cave-man!' Martin did not say much. He just looked at the arrow-head, which certainly was a very fine unspoilt specimen, and then turned away. Dick thought he was a strange fellow. A bit dull and boring. He wondered if they ought to ask him to their picnic. He didn't want to in the least.

But George did! 'Are you having a picnic here too?' she said. Martin shook his head.

'No. I haven't brought any sandwiches.'

'Well, we've plenty. Stay and have some with us when we eat them,' said George, generously.

'Thanks. It's very nice of you,' said the boy. 'And will you come and see my television this afternoon in return? I'd like you to.'

'Yes, we will,' said George. 'It would be something to do! Oh Anne – just look at those violets! I've never seen such big white ones before.'

The boys went deeper down, scraping about with their trowels in any likely place. They came to where a shelf of stone projected out a good way. It would be a nice place to have their lunch. The stone would be warm to sit on, and was flat enough to take ginger-beer bottles and cups in safety.

At half past twelve they all had their lunch. They were very hungry. Martin shared their sandwiches, and became quite friendly over them.

'Best sandwiches I've ever tasted,' he said. 'I do like those sardine ones. Does your mother make them for you? I wish I had a mother. Mine died ages ago.'

There was a sympathetic silence. The four could not think of any worse thing to happen to a boy or girl. They offered Martin the nicest buns, and the biggest piece of cake immediately.

'I saw your father flashing his signals last night,' said Martin, munching a bun.

Dick looked up at once. 'How do you know he was signalling?' he asked. 'Who told you?'

'Nobody,' said the boy. 'I just saw the six flashes, and I thought it must be George's father.' He looked surprised at Dick's sharp tone. Julian gave Dick a nudge, to warn him not to go off the deep end again.

George scowled at Dick. 'I suppose you saw my father signalling this morning too,' she said to Martin. 'I bet scores of people saw the flashes. He just heliographs with a mirror at half past ten to signal that he's all right – and flashes a lantern at the same time at night.'

Now it was Dick's turn to scowl at George. Why give away all this information? It wasn't necessary. Dick felt sure she was doing it just to pay him back for his sharp question. He tried to change the subject.

'Where do you go to school?' he asked.

'I don't,' said the boy. 'I've been ill.'

'Well, where did you go to school before you were ill?' asked Dick.

'I – I had a tutor,' said Martin. 'I didn't go to school.'

'Bad luck!' said Julian. He thought it must be terrible not to go to school and have all the fun, the work and the games of school-life. He looked curiously at Martin. Was he one of these rather stupid boys who did no good at school, but had to have a tutor at home? Still he didn't *look* stupid. He just looked rather sullen and dull.

Timmy was sitting on the warm stone with

the others. He had his share of the sandwiches, but had to be rationed, as Martin had to have some too.

He was funny with Martin. He took absolutely no notice of him at all. Martin might not have been there!

And Martin took no notice of Timmy. He did not talk to him, or pat him. Anne was sure he didn't really like dogs, as he had said. How could anyone be with Timmy and not give him even *one* pat?

Timmy did not even look at Martin, but sat with his back to him, leaning against George. It was really rather amusing, if it wasn't so odd. After all, George was talking in a friendly way to Martin; they were all sharing their food with him – and Timmy behaved as if Martin simply wasn't there at all!

Anne was just about to remark on Timmy's odd behaviour when he yawned, shook himself, and leapt down from the rock. 'He's going rabbiting again,' said Julian. 'Hey, Tim – find me another arrow-head will you, old fellow?'

Timmy wagged his tail. He disappeared under the shelf of rock, and there came the sound of digging. A shower of stones and soil flew into the air.

The children lay back on the stone and felt sleepy. They talked for some minutes, and then Anne felt her eyes closing. She was awakened by George's voice.

'Where's Timmy? Timmy! Timmy! Come here! Where have you got to?'

But no Timmy came. There was not even an answering bark. 'Oh blow,' said George. 'Now he's gone down some extra-deep rabbit-hole, I suppose. I must get him. Timmy! Wherever are you?'

[9]

George makes a discovery – and loses her temper

George slipped down from the rock. She peered under it. There was a large opening there, scattered with stones that Timmy had loosened in his digging.

'Surely you haven't at last found a rabbit-hole big enough to go down!' said George. 'TIMMY! Where are you?'

Not a bark, not a whine came from the hole. George wriggled under the shelf of rock, and peered down the burrow. Timmy had certainly made it very big. George called up to Julian.

'Julian! Throw me down your trowel, will you?'

The trowel landed by her foot. George took it and began to make the hole bigger. It might be big enough for Timmy, but it wasn't big enough for her!

She dug hard and soon got very hot. She crawled out and looked over on to the rock to see if she could get one of the others to help her. They were all asleep.

'Lazy things!' thought George, quite forgetting that she too would have been dozing if she hadn't wondered where Timmy had gone.

She slipped down under the rock again and began to dig hard with her trowel. Soon she had made the hole big enough to get through. She was surprised to find quite a large passage, once she had made the entrance big enough to take her. She could crawl along on hands and knees!

'I say – I wonder if this is just some animal's runway – or leads somewhere!' thought George. 'TIMMY! Where *are* you?'

From somewhere deep in the quarry side there came a faint whine. George felt thankful. So Timmy *was* there, after all. She crawled along, and then quite suddenly the tunnel became high and wide and she realised that she must be in a passage. It was perfectly dark, so she could not see anything, she could only feel.

Then she heard the sound of pattering feet, and Timmy pressed affectionately against her legs, whining. 'Oh Timmy – you gave me a bit of a fright!' said George. 'Where have you been? Is this a real passage – or just a tunnel in the quarry, made by the old miners, and now used by animals?'

'Woof,' said Timmy, and pulled at George's jeans to make her go back to the daylight.

'All right, I'm coming!' said George. 'Don't imagine I want to wander alone in the dark! I only came to look for you.'

She made her way back to the shelf of rock. By this time Dick was awake, and wondered where George had gone. He waited a few minutes, blinking up into the deep blue sky, and then sat up.

'George!' There was no answer. So, in his turn Dick slipped down from the rock and looked around. And, to his very great astonishment he saw first Timmy, and then George on hands and knees, appearing out of the hole under the rock. He stared open-mouthed, and George began to giggle.

'It's all right. I've only been rabbiting with Timmy!'

She stood beside him, shaking and brushing soil from her jersey and trousers. 'There's a passage behind the entrance to the hole under the rock,' she said. 'At first it's just a narrow tunnel, like an animal's hole – then it gets wider – and then it becomes a proper high wide passage! I couldn't see if it went on, of course, because it was dark. Timmy was a long way in.'

'Good gracious!' said Dick. 'It sounds exciting.'

'Let's explore it, shall we?' said George. 'I expect Julian's got a torch.'

'No,' said Dick. 'We won't explore today.'

The others were now awake, and listening with interest. 'Is it a secret passage?' said Anne, thrilled. 'Oh do let's explore it!'

'No, not today,' said Dick again. He looked at Julian. Julian guessed that Dick did not want Martin to share this secret. Why should he? He was not a real friend of theirs, and they had only just got to know him. He nodded back to Dick.

'No, we won't explore today. Anyway, it may be nothing – just an old tunnel made by the quarrymen.'

Martin was listening with great interest. He went and looked into the hole. 'I wish we could explore,' he said. 'Maybe we could plan to meet again with torches and see if there really is a passage there.'

Julian looked at his watch. 'Nearly two o'clock. Well, Martin, if we're going to see that half past two programme of yours, we'd better be getting on.'

The girls began to climb up the steep side of the quarry. Julian took Anne's basket from her, afraid she might slip and fall. Soon they were all at the top. The air felt quite cool there after the warmth of the quarry.

They made their way to the cliff-path and before long were passing the coastguard's cottage. He was out in his garden, and he waved to them.

They went in the gateway of the next-door cottage. Martin pushed the door open. His father was sitting at the window of the room inside, reading. He got up with a broad, welcoming smile.

'Well, well, well! This *is* nice! Come along in, do. Yes, the dog as well. I don't mind dogs a bit. I like them.'

It seemed rather a crowd in the small room. They all shook hands politely. Martin explained hurriedly that he had brought the children to see a television programme.

'A good idea,' said Mr Curton, still beaming. Anne stared at his great eyebrows. They were very long and thick. She wondered why he didn't have them trimmed – but perhaps he liked them like that. They made him look very fierce, she thought.

The four looked round the little room. There

was a television set standing at the far end, on a table. There was also a magnificent radio – and something else that made the boys stare with interest.

'Hallo! You've got a transmitting set, as well as a receiving set,' said Julian.

'Yes,' said Mr Curton. 'It's a hobby of mine. I made that set.'

'Well! You must be brainy!' said Dick.

'What's a transmitting set?' asked Anne. 'I haven't heard of one before.'

'Oh, it just means a set to send out messages by radio – like police cars have, when they send back messages to the police stations,' said Dick. 'This is a very powerful one, though.'

Martin was fiddling about with the television switches. Then the programme began.

It was great fun seeing the television programme. When it was over Mr Curton asked them to stay to tea.

'Now don't say no,' he said. 'I'll ring up and ask your aunt, if you like, if you're afraid she might be worried.'

'Well – if you'd do that, sir,' said Julian. 'I think she *would* wonder where we'd gone!'

Mr Curton rang up Aunt Fanny. Yes, it was quite all right for them to stay, but they mustn't be too late back. So they settled down to an unexpectedly good tea. Martin was not very talkative, but Mr Curton made up for it. He laughed and joked and was altogether very good company.

The talk came round to Kirrin Island. Mr Curton said how beautiful it looked each evening. George looked pleased.

'Yes,' she said. '*I* always think that. I do wish Father hadn't chosen this particular time to work on my island. I'd planned to go and stay there.'

'I suppose you know every inch of it!' said Mr Curton.

'Oh yes!' said George. 'We all do. There are dungeons there, you know – real dungeons that go deep down – where we once found gold ingots.'

'Yes – I remember reading about that,' said

Mr Curton. 'That must have been exciting. Fancy *finding* the dungeons too! And there's an old well too you once got down, isn't there?'

'Yes,' said Anne, remembering. 'And there is a cave where we once lived – it's got an entrance through the roof, as well as from the sea.'

'And I suppose your father is conducting his marvellous experiments down in the dungeons?' said Mr Curton. 'Well, what a strange place to work in!'

'No – we don't—' began George, when she got a kick on the ankle from Dick. She screwed up her face in pain. It had been a very sharp kick indeed.

'What were you going to say?' said Mr Curton, looking surprised.

'Er – I was just going to say that – er – er – we don't know which place Father has chosen,' said George, keeping her legs well out of the way of Dick's feet.

Timmy gave a sudden sharp whine. George

looked down at him in surprise. He was looking up at Dick, with a very hurt expression.

'What's the matter, Timmy?' said George anxiously.

'He's finding the room too hot, I think,' said Dick. 'Better take him out, George.'

George, feeling quite anxious, took him out. Dick joined her. She scowled at him. 'What did you want to kick me for like that? I shall have a frightful bruise.'

'You know jolly well why I did,' said Dick. 'Giving away everything like that! Can't you see the chap's very interested in your father being on the island? There may be nothing in it at all, but you might at least keep your mouth shut. Just like a girl, can't help blabbing. I had to stop you somehow. I don't mind telling you I trod jolly hard on poor old Timmy's tail too, to make him yelp, so that you'd stop talking!'

'Oh – you beast!' said George, indignantly. 'How *could* you hurt Timmy?'

'I didn't want to. It was a shame,' said Dick,

stopping to fondle Timmy's ears. 'Poor old Tim. I didn't want to hurt you, old fellow.'

'I'm going home,' said George, her face scarlet with anger. 'I hate you for talking to me like that – telling me I blab like a girl – and stamping on poor Timmy's tail. You can go back and say I'm taking Timmy home.'

'Right,' said Dick. 'And a jolly good thing too. The less you talk to Mr Curton the better. *I'm* going back to find out exactly what he is and what he does. I'm getting jolly suspicious. You'd better go before you give anything else away!'

Almost choking with rage, George went off with Timmy. Dick went back to make her apologies. Julian and Anne, sure that something was up, felt most uncomfortable. They rose to go, but to their surprise, Dick became very talkative and appeared to be suddenly very much interested in Mr Curton and what he did.

But at last they said good-bye and went. 'Come again, do,' said Mr Curton, beaming at the three of them. 'And tell the other boy –

what's his name, George – that I hope his dog is quite all right again now. Such a nice, well-behaved dog! Well goodbye! See you again, soon, I hope!'

[10]

A surprising signal

'What's up with George?' demanded Julian, as soon as they were safely out of earshot. 'I know you kicked her at tea-time, for talking too much about the island – that was idiotic of her – but why has she gone home in a huff?'

Dick told them how he had trodden on poor Timmy's tail to make him whine, so that George would turn her attention to him and stop talking. Julian laughed, but Anne was indignant.

'That was *horrid* of you, Dick.'

'Yes, it was,' said Dick. 'But I couldn't think of any other way to head George off the island. I really honestly thought she was giving away to that fellow all the things he badly wanted to know. But now I think he wanted to know them for quite another reason.'

'What do you mean?' said Julian puzzled.

'Well, I thought at first he must be after Uncle Quentin's secret, whatever it is,' said Dick, 'and that was why he wanted to know all the ins and outs of everything. But now that he's told me he's a journalist – that's a man who writes for the newspapers, Anne – I think after all he only wants the information so that he can use it for his paper and make a splash when Uncle has finished his work.'

'Yes, I think that too,' said Julian thoughtfully. 'In fact, I'm pretty sure of it. Well, there's no harm in that but I don't see why we should sit there and be pumped all the time. He could easily say, "Look here, I'd be obliged if you'd spill the beans about Kirrin Island – I want to use it in a newspaper story." But he didn't say that.'

'No. So I was suspicious,' said Dick. 'But I see now he'd want all sorts of tit-bits about Kirrin Island to put in his newspaper, whatever it is. Blow! Now I shall have to explain to George I was wrong – and she really is in a temper!'

'Let's take the road to Kirrin Village and go to get some bones for Timmy at the butcher's,' said Julian. 'A sort of apology to Tim!'

This seemed a good idea. They bought two large meaty bones at the butcher's, and then went to Kirrin Cottage. George was up in her bedroom with Timmy. The three went up to find her.

She was sitting on the floor with a book. She looked up sulkily as they came in.

'George, sorry I was such a beast,' said Dick. 'I did it in a good cause, if you only knew it. But I've discovered that Mr Curton isn't a spy, seeking out your father's secret – he's only a journalist, smelling out a story for his paper! Look – I've brought these for Timmy – I apologise to him too.'

George was in a very bad temper, but she tried to respond to Dick's friendliness. She gave him a small smile.

'All right. Thanks for the bones. Don't talk to me tonight anybody. I feel mad, but I'll get over it.'

They left her sitting on the floor. It was always best to leave George severely alone when she was in one of her tempers. As long as Timmy was with her, she was all right, and he certainly would not leave her while she was cross and unhappy.

George did not come down to supper. Dick explained. 'We had a bit of a row, Aunt Fanny, but we've made it up. George still feels sore about it though. Shall I take her supper up?'

'No, I will,' said Anne, and she took up a tray of food.

'I'm not hungry,' said George, so Anne prepared to take it away again. 'Well, you can leave it,' said George hurriedly. 'I expect Timmy will like it.'

So Anne, with a secret smile to herself, left the tray. All the dishes were empty by the time she climbed the stairs to fetch the tray again!

'Dear me – Timmy *was* hungry!' she said to George, and her cousin smiled sheepishly. 'Aren't you coming down now? We're going to play Monopoly.'

'No thanks. You leave me alone this evening, and I'll be all right tomorrow,' said George. 'Really I will.'

So Julian, Dick, Anne and Aunt Fanny played Monopoly without George. They went up to bed at the usual time and found George in bed, fast asleep, with Timmy curled up on her toes.

'I'll look out for Uncle Quentin's signal,' said Julian, as he got into bed. 'Gosh, it's a dark night tonight.'

He lay in bed and looked out of the window towards Kirrin Island. Then, at exactly half past ten, the six flashes came – flash, flash, flash, through the darkness. Julian buried his head in his pillow. Now for a good sleep!

He was awakened by a throbbing noise some time later. He sat up and looked out of the window, expecting to see the top of the tower ablaze with light, as it sometimes was when his uncle conducted a special experiment. But nothing happened. There was no flare of light. The throbbing died away and Julian lay down again.

'I saw Uncle's signals all right last night, Aunt Fanny,' he said next morning. 'Did you?'

'Yes,' said his aunt. 'Julian, do you think you would watch for them this morning, dear? I have to go and see the vicar about something, and I don't believe I would be able to see the tower from the vicarage.'

'Yes, of course I will, Aunt Fanny,' said Julian. 'What's the time now? Half past nine. Right. I'll write some letters sitting by the window in my room – and at half past ten I'll watch for the signals.'

He wrote his letters interrupted first by Dick, then by George, Anne and Timmy, who wanted him to go on the beach with them. George had quite recovered herself now, and was trying to be specially nice to make up for yesterday's temper.

'I'll come at half past ten,' said Julian. 'After I've seen the signals from the tower. They're due in ten minutes.'

At half past ten he looked at the glass top of the tower. Ah – there was the first signal, blazing brightly as the sun caught the mirror held by his uncle in the tower.

'One flash,' counted Julian. 'Two – three – four – five – six. He's all right.'

He was just about to turn away when another flash caught his eyes. 'Seven!' Then another came. Eight. Nine. Ten. Eleven. Twelve.

'How strange,' said Julian. 'Why twelve flashes? Hallo here we go again!'

Another six flashes came from the tower, then no more at all. Julian wished he had a telescope, then he could see right into the tower! He sat and thought for a moment, puzzled. Then he heard the others come pounding up the stairs. They burst into the room.

'Julian! Father flashed eighteen times instead of six!'

'Did you count them, Ju?'

'Why did he do that? Is he in danger of some sort?'

'No. If he was he'd flash the SOS signal,' said Julian.

'He doesn't know Morse code!' said George.

'Well, I expect he just wants to let us know that he needs something,' said Julian. 'We must go over today and find out what it is. More food perhaps.'

So, when Aunt Fanny came home they suggested they should all go over to the island. Aunt Fanny was pleased.

'Oh yes! That would be nice. I expect your uncle wants a message sent off somewhere. We'll go this morning.'

George flew off to tell Alf she wanted her boat. Aunt Fanny packed up plenty of food with Joanna's help. Then they set off to Kirrin Island in George's boat.

As they rounded the low wall of rocks and came into the little cove, they saw Uncle Quentin waiting for them. He waved his hand, and helped to pull in the boat when it ran gently on to the sand.

'We saw your treble signal,' said Aunt Fanny. 'Did you want something, dear?'

'Yes, I did,' said Uncle Quentin. 'What's that you've got in your basket, Fanny? More of those delicious sandwiches. I'll have some!'

'Oh Quentin – haven't you been having your meals properly again?' said Aunt Fanny. 'What about that lovely soup?'

'What soup?' said Uncle Quentin, looking surprised. 'I wish I'd known about it. I could have done with some last night.'

'But *Quentin*! I told you about it before,' said Aunt Fanny. 'It will be bad by now. You must pour it away. Now don't forget – pour it away! Where is it? Perhaps I had better pour it away myself.'

'No. I'll do it,' said Uncle Quentin. 'Let's sit down and have our lunch.'

It was much too early for lunch, but Aunt Fanny at once sat down and began to unpack the food. The children were always ready for a meal at any time, so they didn't in the least mind lunch being so early.

'Well, dear – how is your work getting on?' asked Aunt Fanny, watching her husband devour sandwich after sandwich. She began to wonder if he had had anything at all to eat since she had left him two days ago.

'Oh very well indeed,' said her husband. 'Couldn't be better. Just got to a most tricky and interesting point. I'll have another sandwich, please.'

'Why did you signal eighteen times, Uncle Quentin?' asked Anne.

'Ah, well – it's difficult to explain, really,' said her uncle. 'The fact is – I can't help feeling there's somebody else on this island besides myself!'

'*Quentin*! What in the world do you mean?' cried Aunt Fanny, in alarm. She looked over her shoulder as if she half expected to see somebody there. All the children stared in amazement at Uncle Quentin.

He took another sandwich. 'Yes, I know it sounds mad. Nobody else could possibly have got here. But I know there *is* someone!'

'Oh don't, Uncle!' said Anne, with a shiver. 'It sounds horrid. And you're all alone at night too!'

'Ah, that's just it! I wouldn't mind a bit if I *was* all alone at night!' said her uncle. 'What worries me is that I don't think I *shall* be all alone.'

'Uncle, what makes you think there's somebody here?' asked Julian.

'Well, when I had finished the experiment I was doing last night – about half past three in the early morning it would be – but pitch dark, of course,' said Uncle Quentin, 'I came into the open for a breath of fresh air. And I could swear I heard somebody cough – yes, cough twice!'

'Good gracious!' said Aunt Fanny, startled. 'But Quentin – you might have been mistaken. You do imagine things sometimes, you know, when you're tired.'

'Yes, I know,' said her husband. 'But I couldn't imagine *this*, could I?'

He put his hand into his pocket and took something out. He showed it to the others. It was a cigarette end, quite crisp and fresh.

'Now, I don't smoke cigarettes. Nor do any of you! Well then – who smoked that cigarette?

And how did he come here? No one would bring him by boat – and that's the only way here.'

There was a silence. Anne felt scared. George stared at her father, puzzled. Who could be here? And why? And how had they got there?

'Well, Quentin – what are you going to do?' said his wife. 'What would be best?'

'I'll be all right if George will give her consent to something,' said Uncle Quentin. 'I want Timmy here, George! Will you leave him behind with me?'

[11]

George makes a hard choice

There was a horrified silence. George stared at her father in complete dismay. Everyone waited to see what she would say.

'But Father – Timmy and I have never been separated once,' she said at last, in a pleading voice. 'I do see you want him to guard you – and you *can* have him – but I'll have to stay here too!'

'Oh no!' said her father at once. 'You can't possibly stay, George. That's out of the question. As for never being separated from Timmy, well surely you wouldn't mind that for once? If it was to ensure my safety?'

George swallowed hard. This was the most difficult decision she had ever had to make in her life. Leave Timmy behind on the island – where there was some unknown hidden enemy, likely to harm him if he possibly could!

And yet there was Father too – he might be in danger if there was no one to guard him.

'I shall just *have* to stay here, Father,' she said. 'I can't leave Timmy behind unless I stay too. It's no good.'

Her father began to lose his temper. He was like George – he wanted his own way, and if he didn't have it he was going to make a fuss!

'If I'd asked Julian or Dick or Anne this same thing, and they'd had a dog, they would all have said yes, at once!' he raged. 'But you, George, you must always make things difficult if you can! You and that dog – anyone would think he was worth a thousand pounds!'

'He's worth much more than that to me,' said George, in a trembling voice. Timmy crept nearer to her and pushed his nose into her hand. She held his collar as if she would not let him go for a moment.

'Yes. That dog's worth more to you than your father or mother or anyone,' said her father, in disgust.

'No, Quentin, I can't have you saying things

like that,' said his wife, firmly. 'That's just silly. A mother and father are quite different from a dog – they're loved in different ways. But you are perfectly right, of course – Timmy *must* stay behind with you – and I shall certainly not allow George to stay with him. I'm not going to have *both* of you exposed to danger. It's bad enough to worry about *you*, as it is.'

George looked at her mother in dismay.

'Mother! Do tell Father I must stay here with Timmy.'

'Certainly not,' said her mother. 'Now George, be unselfish. If it were left to Tim to decide, you know perfectly well that he would stay here – and stay *without* you. He would say to himself, "I'm needed here – my eyes are needed to spy out enemies, my ears to hear a quiet footfall – and maybe my teeth to protect my master. I shall be parted from George for a few days – but she, like me, is big enough to put up with that!" That's what Timmy would say, George, if it were left to him.'

Everyone had been listening to this

unexpected speech with great attention. It was about the only one that could persuade George to give in willingly!

She looked at Timmy. He looked back at her, wagging his tail. Then he did an extraordinary thing – he got up, walked over to George's father, and lay down beside him, looking at George as if to say 'There you are! Now you know what *I* think is right!'

'You see?' said her mother. 'He agrees with me. You've always said that Timmy was a good dog, and this proves it. He knows what his duty is. You ought to be proud of him.'

'I am, said George, in a choky voice. She got up and walked off. 'All right,' she said over her shoulder. 'I'll leave him on the island with Father. I'll come back in a minute.'

Anne got up to go after poor George, but Julian pulled her down again. 'Leave her alone! She'll be all right. Good old Timmy – you know what's right and what's wrong, don't you? Good dog, splendid dog!'

Timmy wagged his tail. He did not attempt

to follow George. No – he meant to stay by her father now, even though he would much rather be with his mistress. He was sorry that George was unhappy – but sometimes it was better to do a hard thing and be unhappy about it, than try to be happy without doing it.

'Oh Quentin dear, I don't like this business of you being here and somebody else spying on you,' said his wife, 'I really don't. How long will it be before you've finished your work?'

'A few days more,' said her husband. He looked at Timmy admiringly. 'That dog might almost have known what you were saying, Fanny, just now. It was remarkable the way he walked straight over to me.'

'He's a very clever dog,' said Anne warmly. 'Aren't you, Tim? You'll be quite safe with him, Uncle Quentin. He's terribly fierce when he wants to be!'

'Yes. I shouldn't care to have him leaping at *my* throat,' said her uncle. 'He's so big and powerful. Are there any more pieces of cake?'

'Quentin, it's really too bad of you to go

without your meals,' said his wife. 'It's no good telling me you haven't, because you wouldn't be as ravenous as this if you had had your food regularly.'

Her husband took no notice of what she was saying. He was looking up at his tower. 'Do you ever see those wires at the top blaze out?' he asked. 'Wonderful sight, isn't it?'

'Uncle, you're not inventing a new atom bomb, or anything are you?' asked Anne.

Her uncle looked at her scornfully. 'I wouldn't waste my time inventing things that will be used to kill and maim people! No – I'm inventing something that will be of the greatest use to mankind. You wait and see!'

George came back. 'Father,' she said, 'I'm leaving Timmy behind for you – but please will you do something for me?'

'What?' asked her father. 'No silly conditions now! I shall feed Timmy regularly, and look after him, if that's what you want to ask me. I may forget my own meals, but you ought to know me well enough to know I shouldn't neglect any animal dependent on me.'

'Yes – I know, Father,' said George, looking a bit doubtful all the same. 'What I wanted to ask you was this – when you go up in the tower to signal each morning, will you please take Timmy with you? I shall be up at the coast-guard's cottage, looking through his telescope at the glass room in the tower – and I shall be able to see Timmy then. If I catch just a glimpse of him each day and know he's all right, I shan't worry so much.'

'Very well,' said her father. 'But I don't suppose for a moment that Timmy will be able to climb up the spiral stairway.'

'Oh, he can, Father – he's been up it once already,' said George.

'Good heavens!' said her father. 'Has the dog been up there too? All right, George – I promise I'll take him up with me each morning that I signal, and get him to wag his tail at you. There! Will that satisfy you?'

'Yes. Thank you,' said George. 'And you'll

give him a few kind words and a pat occasionally, Father, won't you . . . and . . .?'

'And put his bib on for him at meal-times, I suppose, and clean his teeth for him at night!' said her father, looking cross again. 'I shall treat Timmy like a proper grown-up dog, a friend of mine, George – and believe me, that's the way he wants me to treat him. Isn't it, Timmy? You like all those frills to be kept for your mistress, don't you, not for me?'

'Woof,' said Timmy, and thumped his tail. The children looked at him admiringly. He really was a very sensible clever dog. He seemed somehow much more grown-up than George.

'Uncle, if anything goes wrong, or you want help or anything, flash eighteen times again,' said Julian. 'You ought to be all right with Timmy. He's better than a dozen policemen – but you never know.'

'Right. Eighteen flashes if I want you over here for anything,' said his uncle. 'I'll remember. Now you'd better all go. It's time I got on with my work.'

'You'll pour that soup away, won't you, Quentin?' said his wife, anxiously. 'You don't want to make yourself ill by eating bad soup. It must be green by now! It would be so like you to forget all about it while it was fresh and good – and only remember when it was bad!'

'What a thing to say!' said her husband, getting up. 'Anyone would think I was five years old, without a brain in my head, the way you talk to me!'

'You've plenty of brains dear, we all know that,' said his wife. 'But you don't seem very old sometimes! Now look after yourself – and keep Timmy by you all the time.'

'Father won't need to bother about *that*,' said George. 'Timmy will keep by *him*! You're on guard, Timmy, aren't you? And you know what *that* means!'

'Woof,' said Timmy, solemnly. He went with them all to the boat, but he did not attempt to get in. He stood by George's father and watched the boat bob away over the water.

'Goodbye, Timmy!' shouted George, in a funny fierce voice. 'Look after yourself!'

Her father waved, and Timmy wagged his tail. George took one of the pairs of oars from Dick and began to row furiously, her face red with the hard work.

Julian looked at her in amusement. It was hard work for him, too, to keep up with the furious rowing, but he didn't say anything. He knew all this fury in rowing was George's way of hiding her grief at parting with Timmy. Funny old George! She was always so intense about things – furiously happy or furiously unhappy, in the seventh heaven of delight or down in the very depths of despair or anger.

Everyone talked hard so that George would think they were not noticing her feelings at parting with Timmy. The talk, of course, was mostly about the unknown man on the island. It seemed very mysterious indeed that he should suddenly have arrived.

'How did he get there? I'm sure not one of the fishermen would have taken him,' said Dick.

'He must have gone at night, of course, and I doubt if there is anyone but George who would know the way in the dark – or even dare to try and find it. These rocks are so close together, and so near the surface; one yard out of the right course and any boat would have a hole in the bottom!'

'No one could reach the island by swimming from the shore,' said Anne. 'It's too far, and the sea is too rough over these rocks. I honestly do wonder if there *is* anyone on the island after all. Perhaps that cigarette end was an old one.'

'It didn't look it,' said Julian. 'Well, it just beats me how anyone got there!'

He fell into thought, puzzling out all the possible and impossible ways. Then he gave an exclamation. The others looked at him.

'I've just thought – would it be possible for an aeroplane to parachute anyone down on the island? I did hear a throbbing noise one night – was it last night? It must have been a plane's engine, of course! *Could* anyone be dropped on the island?'

'Easily,' said Dick. 'I believe you've hit on the explanation, Ju! Good for you! But I say – whoever it is must be in deadly earnest, to risk being dropped on a small island like that in the dark of night!'

In deadly earnest! That didn't sound at all nice. A little shiver went down Anne's back. 'I *am* glad Timmy's there,' she said. And everyone felt the same – yes even George!

[12]

The old map again

It was only about half past one when they arrived back, because they had had lunch so very early, and had not stayed long on the island. Joanna was most surprised to see them.

'Well, here you are again!' she said. 'I hope you don't all want another lunch, because there's nothing in the house till I go to the butcher's!'

'Oh no, Joanna – we've had our picnic lunch,' said George's mother, 'and it was a good thing we packed so much, because my husband ate nearly half the lunch! He still hasn't had that nice soup we made for him. Now it will be bad of course.'

'Oh, the men! They're as bad as children!' said Joanna.

'*Well!*' said George. 'Do you really think any

of *us* would let your good soup go bad, Joanna? You know jolly well we'd probably eat it up before we ought to!'

'That's true – I wouldn't accuse any of you four – or Timmy either – of playing about with your food,' said Joanna. 'You make good work of it, the lot of you. But where is Timmy?'

'I left him behind to look after Father,' said George. Joanna stared at her in surprise. She knew how passionately fond of Timmy George was.

'You're a very good girl – sometimes!' she said. 'See now – if you're still hungry because your father has eaten most of your lunch, go and look in the biscuit tin. I made you some of your favourite ginger biscuits this morning. Go and find them.'

That was always Joanna's way! If she thought anyone was upset, she offered them her best and freshest food. George went off to find the biscuits.

'You're a kind soul, Joanna,' said George's

mother. 'I'm so thankful we left Timmy there. I feel happier about my husband now.'

'What shall we do this afternoon?' said Dick, when they had finished munching the delicious ginger biscuits. 'I say, aren't these good? You know, I do think good cooks deserve some kind of decoration, just as much as good soldiers or scientists, or writers. I should give Joanna the OBCBE.'

'Whatever's that?' said Julian.

'Order of the Best Cooks of the British Empire,' said Dick grinning. 'What did you think it was? "Oh Be Careful Before Eating"?'

'You really are an absolute donkey,' said Julian. 'Now, what *shall* we do this afternoon?'

'Go and explore the passage in the quarry,' said George.

Julian cocked an eye at the window. 'It's about to pour with rain,' he said. 'I don't think that clambering up and down the steep sides of that quarry in the wet would be very easy. No – we'll leave that till a fine day.'

'I'll tell you what we'll do,' said Anne

suddenly. 'Do you remember that old map of Kirrin Castle we once found in a box? It had plans of the castle in it – a plan of the dungeons, and of the ground floor, and of the top part. Well, let's have it out and study it! Now we know there is another hiding-place somewhere, we might be able to trace it on that old map. It's sure to be on it somewhere – but perhaps we didn't notice it before!'

The others looked at her, thrilled. 'Now that really is a brilliant idea of yours, Anne,' said Julian, and Anne glowed with pleasure at his praise. 'A very fine idea indeed. Just the thing for a wet afternoon. Where's the map? I suppose you've got it somewhere safe, George?'

'Oh yes,' said George. 'It's still in that old wooden box, inside the tin lining. I'll get it.'

She disappeared upstairs and came down again with the map. It was made of thick parchment, and was yellow with age. She laid it out on the table. The others bent over it, eager to look at it once more.

'Do you remember how frightfully excited

we were when we first found the box?' said Dick.

'Yes, and we couldn't open it, so we threw it out of the top window down to the ground below, hoping it would burst open!' said George.

'And the crash woke up Uncle Quentin,' said Anne, with a giggle. 'And he came out and got the box and wouldn't let us have it!'

'Oh dear yes – and poor Julian had to wait till Uncle Quentin was asleep, and creep in and get the box to see what was in it!' finished Dick. 'And we found this map – and how we pored over it!'

They all pored over it again. It was in three parts, as Anne had said – a plan of the dungeons, a plan of the ground floor and a plan of the top part.

'It's no good bothering about the top part of the castle,' said Dick. 'It's all fallen down and ruined. There's practically none of it left except for that one tower.'

'I say!' said Julian, suddenly putting his

finger on a certain spot in the map, 'do you remember there were *two* entrances to the dungeons? One that seemed to start somewhere about that little stone room – and the other that started where we did at last find the entrance? Well – we never found the other entrance, did we?'

'No! We didn't!' said George, in excitement. She pushed Julian's finger away from the map. 'Look – there are steps shown here – somewhere where that little room is – so there *must* be an entrance there! Here's the *other* flight of steps – the ones we did find, near the well.'

'I remember that we hunted pretty hard for the entrance in the little room,' said Dick. 'We scraped away the weeds from every single stone, and gave it up at last. Then we found the other entrance, and forgot all about this one.'

'And *I* think Father has found the entrance we *didn't* find!' said George, triumphantly. 'It leads underground, obviously. Whether or not it joins up with the dungeons we know I can't make out from this map. It's a bit blurred here. But it's quite plain that there *is* an entrance here, with stone steps leading underground somewhere! Look, there's some sort of passage or tunnel marked, leading from the steps. Goodness knows where it goes, it's so smeared.'

'It joins up with the dungeons, I expect,' said Julian. 'We never explored the whole of them, you know – they're so vast and weird. If we explored the whole place, we should probably come across the stone steps leading from somewhere near that little room. Still, they may be ruined or fallen in now.'

'No, they can't be,' said George. 'I'm perfectly *sure* that's the entrance Father has found. And I'll tell you something that seems to prove it, too.'

'What?' said everyone.

'Well, do you remember the other day when we first went to see Father?' said George. 'He didn't let us stay long, and he came to see us off at the boat. Well, we tried to see where he went, but we couldn't – but Dick said he saw the jackdaws rising up in a flock, as if they had been suddenly disturbed – and he wondered if Father had gone somewhere in that direction.'

Julian whistled. 'Yes – the jackdaws build in the tower, which is by the little room – and anyone going into the room would disturb them. I believe you're right, George.'

'It's been puzzling me awfully where Uncle Quentin could be doing his work,' said Dick. 'I simply could *not* solve the mystery – but now I think we have!'

'I wonder how Father found his hiding-place,' said George, thoughtfully. 'I still think it was mean of him not to tell me.'

'There must have been some reason,' said Dick, sensibly. 'Don't start brooding again!'

'I'm not,' said George. 'I'm puzzled, that's all. I wish we could take the boat and go over to the island at once, and explore!'

'Yes. I bet we'd find the entrance all right now,' said Dick. 'Your father is sure to have left some trace of where it is – a stone a bit cleaner than the rest – or weeds scraped off – or something.'

'Do you suppose the unknown enemy on the island knows Uncle Quentin's hiding-place?' said Anne, suddenly. 'Oh, I do hope he doesn't! He could so easily shut him in if he did.'

'Well, he hasn't gone there to shut Uncle up – he's gone there to steal his secret, or find it out,' said Julian. 'Golly, I'm thankful he's got Timmy. Timmy could tackle a dozen enemies.'

'Not if they had guns,' said George, in a small voice. There was a silence. It was not a nice thought to think of Timmy at the wrong end of a gun. This had happened once or twice before in their adventures, and they didn't want to think of it happening again.

'Well, it's no good thinking silly things like that,' said Dick, getting up. 'We've had a jolly interesting half-hour. I think we've solved *that* mystery. But I suppose we shan't know for certain till your father's finished his experiment, George, and left the island – then we can go over and have a good snoop round.'

'It's still raining,' said Anne, looking out of

the window. 'But it's a bit clearer. It looks as if the sun will be out soon. Let's go for a walk.'

'I shall go up to the coastguard's cottage,' said George, at once. 'I want to look through his telescope to see if I can just get a glimpse of Timmy.'

'Try the field-glasses,' suggested Julian. 'Go up to the top of the house with them.'

'Yes, I will,' said George. 'Thanks for the idea.'

She fetched the field-glasses, where they hung in the hall, and took them out of their leather case. She ran upstairs with them. But she soon came down again, looking disappointed.

'The house isn't high enough for me to see much of the island properly. I can see the glass top of the tower easily, of course – but the telescope would show it much better. It's more powerful. I think I'll go up and have a squint. You don't need to come if you don't want to.' She put the glasses back into their case.

'Oh, we'll all come and have a squint for old Timmy dog,' said Dick, getting up. 'And I don't mind telling you what we'll see!'

'What?' said George, in surprise.

'We'll see Timmy having a perfectly wonderful time, chasing every single rabbit on the island!' said Dick with a grin. 'My word – you needn't worry about Timmy not having his food regularly! He'll have rabbit for breakfast, rabbit for dinner, rabbit for tea – and rainwater from his favourite pool. Not a bad life for old Timmy!'

'You know perfectly well he'll do nothing of the sort,' said George. 'He'll keep close to Father and not think of rabbits once!'

'You don't know Timmy if you think that,' said Dick dodging out of George's way. She was turning red with exasperation. 'I bet that's why he wanted to stay. *Just* for the rabbits!'

George threw a book at him. It crashed to the floor. Anne giggled. 'Oh stop it, you two. We'll never get out. Come on Ju – we won't wait for the squabblers!'

[13]

Afternoon with Martin

By the time they reached the coastguard's cottage the sun was out. It was a real April day, with sudden showers and then the sun sweeping out, smiling. Everything glittered, especially the sea. It was wet underfoot, but the children had on their rubber boots.

They looked for the coastguard. As usual he was in his shed, singing and hammering.

'Good-day to you,' he said, beaming all over his red face. 'I was wondering when you'd come and see me again. How do you like this railway station I'm making?'

'It's better than any I've ever seen in the shops,' said Anne in great admiration. The coastguard certainly had made it well, down to the smallest detail.

He nodded his head towards some small

wooden figures of porters and guards and passengers. 'Those are waiting to be painted,' he said. 'That boy Martin said he'd come in and do them for me – very handy with his paints he is, a proper artist – but he's had an accident.'

'*Has* he? What happened?' said Julian.

'I don't quite know. He was half-carried home this morning by his father,' said the coastguard. 'Must have slipped and fallen somewhere. I went out to ask, but Mr Curton was in a hurry to get the boy on a couch. Why don't you go in and ask after him? He's a funny sort of boy – but he's not a bad boy.'

'Yes, we will go and ask,' said Julian. 'I say – would you mind if we looked through your telescope again?'

'Now you go and look at all you want to!' said the old fellow. 'I tell you, you won't wear it out by looking! I saw the signal from your father's tower last night, George – just happened to be looking that way. He went on flashing for a long time, didn't he?'

'Yes,' said George. 'Thank you. I'll go and have a look now.'

She went to the telescope and trained it on her island. But no matter where she looked she could not see Timmy, or her father. They must be down in his workroom, wherever it was. She looked at the glass room in the top of the tower. That was empty too, of course. She sighed. It would have been nice to see Timmy.

The others had a look through as well. But nobody saw Timmy. It was plain that he was keeping close to his master – a proper little guard!

'Well – shall we go in and see what's happened to Martin?' said Julian, when they had finished with the telescope. 'It's just about to pour with rain again – another April shower! We could wait next door till it's over.'

'Right. Let's go,' said Dick. He looked at George. 'Don't be afraid I shall be rude, George. Now that I know Mr Curton is a journalist, I shan't bother about him.'

'All the same – I'm not "blabbing" any

more,' said George, with a grin. 'I see your point now – even if it doesn't matter, I still shan't "blab" any more.'

'Good for you!' said Dick, pleased. 'Spoken like a boy!'

'Ass!' said George, but she was pleased all the same.

They went through the front gateway of the next cottage. As they filed in, they heard an angry voice.

'Well, you can't! Always wanting to mess about with a brush and paint. I thought I'd knocked that idea out of your head. You lie still and get that ankle better. Spraining it just when I want your help!'

Anne stopped, feeling frightened. It was Mr Curton's voice they could hear through the open window. He was giving Martin a good talking to about something, that was plain. The others stopped too, wondering whether to go in or not.

Then they heard a bang, and saw Mr Curton leaving the cottage from the back entrance. He walked rapidly down the garden, and made for the path, that led to the back of the cliff. There was a road there that went to the village.

'Good. He's gone. *And* he didn't see us!' said Dick. 'Who would have thought that such a genial, smiling fellow could have such a rough brutal voice when he loses his temper? Come on – let's pop in and see poor Martin while there's a chance.'

They knocked on the door. 'It's us!' called Julian, cheerfully. 'Can we come in?'

'Oh yes!' shouted Martin from indoors, sounding pleased. Julian opened the door and they all went in.

'I say! We heard you'd had an accident,' said Julian. 'What's up? Are you hurt much?'

'No. It's just that I twisted my ankle, and it was so painful to walk on that I had to be half-carried up here,' said Martin. 'Silly thing to do!'

'Oh – it'll soon be right if it's just a twist,' said Dick. 'I've often done that. The thing is to walk on it as soon as you can. Where were you when you fell?'

Martin went suddenly red, to everyone's surprise. 'Well – I was walking on the edge of the quarry with my father – and I slipped and rolled a good way down,' he said.

There was a silence. Then George spoke. 'I say,' she said, 'I hope you didn't go and give away our little secret to your father? I mean – it's not so much fun when grown-ups share a secret. They want to go snooping about themselves – and it's much more fun to discover things by ourselves. You didn't tell him about that hole under the shelf of rock, did you?'

Martin hesitated. 'I'm afraid I did,' he said at last. 'I didn't think it would matter. I'm sorry.'

'Blow!' said Dick. 'That was our own little discovery. We wanted to go and explore it this afternoon, but we thought it would be so wet we'd fall down the steep slope.'

Julian looked at Martin sharply. 'I suppose that's what happened to *you*?' he said. 'You tried clambering down and slipped!'

'Yes,' said Martin. 'I'm really sorry if you thought it was your secret. I just mentioned it to my father out of interest – you know – something to say – and he wanted to go down and see for himself.'

'I suppose journalists are always like that,' said Dick. 'Wanting to be on the spot if there's anything to be ferreted out. It's their job. All right, Martin – forget it. But do try and head your father off the quarry. We *would* like to do a bit of exploring, before he butts in. Though there may be nothing to be found at all!'

There was a pause. Nobody knew quite what to say. Martin was rather difficult to talk to. He didn't talk like any ordinary boy – he never made a joke, or said anything silly.

'Aren't you bored, lying here?' said Anne feeling sorry for him.

'Yes, awfully. I wanted my father to go in and ask the coastguard to bring in some little figures I said I'd paint for him,' said Martin. 'But he wouldn't let me. You know I simply love painting – even doing a little thing like that – painting clothes on toy porters and guards –

so long as I can have a brush in my hand and colours to choose from!'

This was the longest speech Martin had ever made to the four children! His face lost its dull, bored look as he spoke, and became bright and cheerful.

'Oh – you want to be an artist, I suppose?' said Anne. 'I would like that too!'

'Anne! You can't even draw a cat that looks like one!' said Dick, scornfully. 'And when you drew a cow I thought it was an elephant.'

Martin smiled at Anne's indignant face. 'I'll show you some of my pictures,' he said. 'I have to keep them hidden away, because my father can't bear me to want to be an artist!'

'Don't get up if you don't want to,' said Julian. 'I'll get them for you.'

'It's all right. If it's good for me to try and walk, I will,' said Martin, and got off the couch. He put his right foot gingerly to the floor and then stood up. 'Not so bad after all!' he said. He limped across the room to a bookcase. He put his hand behind the second row of books and brought out a cardboard case, big and flat. He took it to the table. He opened it and spread out some pictures.

'Gracious!' said Anne. 'They're *beautiful*! Did you really do these?'

They were strange pictures for a young person to draw, for they were of flowers and trees, birds and butterflies – all drawn and coloured most perfectly, every detail put in lovingly.

Julian looked at them in surprise. This boy was certainly gifted. Why, these drawings were as good as any he had ever seen in exhibitions! He picked a few up and took them to the window.

'Do you mean to say your father doesn't think these are good – doesn't think it's worthwhile to let you train as an artist?' he said, in surprise.

'He hates my pictures,' said Martin, bitterly. 'I ran away from school, and went to an art-school to train – but he found me and forbade me to think of drawing any more. He thinks it's a weak, feeble thing for a man to do. So I only do it in secret now.'

The children looked at Martin with sympathy. It seemed an awful thing to them that a boy who had no mother, should have a father who hated the thing his son most loved. No wonder he always looked dull and miserable and sullen!

'It's very bad luck,' said Julian at last. 'I wish we could do something to help.'

'Well – get me those figures and the paint tins from the coastguard,' said Martin, eagerly. 'Will you? Father won't be back till six. I'll have time to do them. And do stay and have tea with me. It's so dull up here. I hate it.'

'Yes, I'll get the things for you,' said Julian. 'I can't for the life of me see why you shouldn't have something to amuse yourself with if you want to. And we'll ring up my aunt and tell her we're staying here to tea – so long as we don't eat everything you've got!'

'Oh, that's all right,' said Martin, looking very cheerful indeed. 'There's plenty of food in the house. My father has an enormous appetite. I say, thanks most awfully.'

Julian rang up his aunt. The girls and Dick

went to fetch the figures and the paint from the coastguard. They brought them back and arranged them on a table beside Martin. His eyes brightened at once. He seemed quite different.

'This is grand,' he said. 'Now I can get on! It's a silly little job, this, but it will help the old man next door, and I'm always happy when I'm messing about with a brush and paints!'

Martin was very, very clever at painting the little figures. He was quick and deft, and Anne sat watching him, quite fascinated. George went to hunt in the larder for the tea-things. There was certainly plenty of food! She cut some bread and butter, found some new honey, brought out a huge chocolate cake and some ginger buns, and put the kettle on to boil.

'I say, this is really grand,' said Martin again. 'I wish my father wasn't coming back till eight. By the way – where's the dog? I thought he always went everywhere with you! Where's Timmy?'

[14]

A shock for George

Dick looked at George. He didn't think it would matter telling Martin where Timmy was, so long as George didn't give the *reason* why he had been left on the island.

But George was going to hold her tongue now. She looked at Martin and spoke quite airily. 'Oh, Timmy? We left him behind today. He's all right.'

'Gone out shopping with your mother, I suppose, hoping for a visit to the butcher's!' said Martin. This was the first joke he had ever made to the children, and though it was rather a feeble one they laughed heartily. Martin looked pleased. He began to try and think of another little joke, while his deft hands put reds and blues and greens on the little wooden figures.

They all had a huge tea. Then, when the clock said a quarter to six the girls carried the painted figures carefully back to the coastguard, who was delighted with them. Dick took back the little tins of paint, and the brush stuck in a jar of turpentine.

'Well now, he's clever that boy, isn't he?' said the coastguard, eyeing the figures in delight. 'Looks sort of miserable and sulky – but he's not a bad sort of boy!'

'I'll just have one more squint through your telescope,' said George, 'before it gets too dark.'

She tilted it towards her island. But once more there was no sign of Timmy, or of her father either. She looked for some time, and then went to join the others. She shook her head as they raised their eyebrows inquiringly.

They washed up the tea-things, and cleared away neatly. Nobody felt as if they wanted to wait and see Mr Curton. They didn't feel as if they liked him very much, now they knew how hard he was on Martin.

'Thanks for a lovely afternoon,' said Martin, limping to the door with them. 'I enjoyed my spot of painting, to say nothing of your company.'

'You stick out for your painting,' said Julian. 'If it's the thing you've *got* to do, and you know it, you must go all out for it. See?'

'Yes,' said Martin, and his face went sullen again. 'But there are things that make it difficult – things I can't very well tell you. Oh well – never mind! I dare say it will all come right one day, and I'll be a famous artist with pictures in the Academy!'

'Come on, quickly,' said Dick, in a low voice to Julian. 'There's his father coming back!'

They hurried off down the cliff-path, seeing Mr Curton out of the corner of their eyes, coming up the other path.

'Horrid man!' said Anne. 'Forbidding Martin to do what he really longs to do. And he seemed so nice and jolly and all-over-us, didn't he?'

'Very all-over-us,' said Dick, smiling at Anne's new word. 'But there are a lot of people like that – one thing at home and quite another outside!'

'I hope Mr Curton hasn't been trying to explore that passage in the side of the quarry,' said George, looking back, and watching the man walk up to his back door. 'It would be too bad if he butted in and spoilt our fun. I mean – there may be nothing to discover at all – but it will be fun even finding there *is* nothing.'

'Very involved!' said Dick, with a grin. 'But I gather what you mean. I say, that was a good tea, wasn't it?'

'Yes,' said George, looking all round her in an absent-minded manner.

'What's up?' said Dick. 'What are you looking like that for?'

'Oh – how silly of me – I was just looking for Timmy,' said George. 'You know, I'm so used to him always being at my heels or somewhere near that I just can't get used to him not being here.'

'Yes, I feel a bit like that too,' said Julian. 'As

if there was something missing all the time. Good old Tim! We shall miss him awfully, all of us – but you most of all, George.'

'Yes. Especially on my bed at night,' said George. 'I shan't be able to go to sleep for ages and ages.'

'I'll wrap a cushion up in a rug and plonk it down on your feet when you're in bed,' said Dick. 'Then it will feel like Timmy!'

'It won't! Don't be silly,' said George, rather crossly. 'And anyway it wouldn't *smell* like him. He's got a lovely smell.'

'Yes, a Timmy-smell,' agreed Anne. 'I like it too.'

The evening went very quickly, playing the endless game of Monopoly again. Julian lay in bed later, watching for his uncle's signal. Needless to say, George was at the window too! They waited for half past ten.

'Now!' said Julian. And just as he spoke there came the first flash from the lantern in the tower.

'One,' counted George, 'two – three – four –

five – six!' She waited anxiously to see if there were any more, but there weren't.

'Now you can go to bed in peace,' said Julian to George. 'Your father is all right, and that means that Timmy is all right too. Probably he has remembered to give Timmy a good supper and has had some himself as well!'

'Well, Timmy would soon remind him if he forgot to feed him, that's one thing,' said George, slipping out of the room. 'Good-night, Dick; good-night, Ju! See you in the morning.'

And back she went to her own bed and snuggled down under the sheets. It was strange not to have Timmy on her feet. She tossed about for a while, missing him, and then fell asleep quite suddenly. She dreamed of her island. She was there with Timmy – and they were discovering ingots of gold down in the dungeon. What a lovely dream!

Next morning dawned bright and sunny again. The April sky was as blue as the forget-me-nots coming out in the garden. George gazed out of the dining-room window at breakfast time wondering if Timmy was running about her island.

'Dreaming about Tim?' said Julian, with a laugh. 'Never mind – you'll soon see him, George. Another hour or so and you'll feast your eyes on him through the coastguard's telescope!'

'Do you really think you'll be able to make out Tim, if he's in the tower with your father at half past ten?' asked her mother. 'I shouldn't have thought you would be able to.'

'Yes, I shall, Mother,' said George. 'It's a very powerful telescope, you know. I'll just go up and make my bed, then I'll go up the cliff-path. Anyone else coming?'

'I want Anne to help me with some turning out,' said her mother. 'I'm looking out some old clothes to give to the vicar's wife for her jumble sale. You don't mind helping me, Anne, do you?'

'No, I'd like to,' said Anne at once. 'What are the boys going to do?'

'I think I must do a bit of my holiday work

this morning,' said Julian, with a sigh. 'I don't want to – but I've kept on putting it off. You'd better do some too, Dick. You know what you are like – you'll leave it all to the last day if you're not careful!'

'All right. I'll do some too,' said Dick. 'You won't mind scooting up to the coastguard's cottage alone, will you, George?'

'Not a bit,' said George. 'I'll come back just after half past ten, as soon as I've spotted Timmy and Father.'

She disappeared to make her bed. Julian and Dick went to fetch some books. Anne went to make her bed too, and then came down to help her aunt. In a few minutes George yelled goodbye and rushed out of the house.

'What a hurricane!' said her mother. 'It seems as if George never walks if she can possibly run. Now Anne, put the clothes in three piles – the very old, the not so old, and the quite nice.'

Just before half past ten Julian went up to his window to watch for the signal from his uncle.

He waited patiently. A few seconds after the half-hour the flashes came – one, two, three, four, five, six – good! Now George would settle down for the day. Perhaps they could go to the quarry in the afternoon. Julian went back to his books and was soon buried in them, with Dick grunting by his side.

At about five minutes to eleven there was the sound of running feet and panting breath. George appeared at the door of the sitting-room where the two boys were doing their work. They looked up.

George was red in the face, and her hair was windblown. She fought to get her breath enough to speak. 'Julian! Dick! Something's happened – Timmy wasn't there!'

'What do you mean?' said Julian in surprise. George slumped down on a chair, still panting. The boys could see that she was trembling too.

'It's serious, Julian! I tell you Timmy wasn't in the tower when the signals came!'

'Well, it only means that your absent-minded father forgot to take him up with him,' said

Julian, in his most sensible voice. 'What *did* you see?'

'I had my eye glued to the telescope,' said George, 'and suddenly I saw someone come into the little glass room at the top. I looked for Timmy, of course, at once – but I tell you, he wasn't there! The six flashes came, the man disappeared – and that was all. No Timmy! Oh I do feel so dreadfully worried, Julian.'

'Well, don't be,' said Julian, soothingly. 'Honestly, I'm sure that's what happened. Your father forgot about Timmy. Anyway, if you saw *him*, obviously things are all right.'

'I'm not thinking about Father!' cried George. 'He must be all right if he flashed his signals – I'm thinking about Timmy. Why, even if Father forgot to take him, he'd go with him. You know that!'

'Your father might have shut the door at the bottom and prevented Timmy from going up,' said Dick.

'He might,' said George, frowning. She hadn't thought of that. 'Oh dear – now I shall worry all day long. *Why* didn't I stay with Timmy? What shall I do now?'

'Wait till tomorrow morning,' said Dick. 'Then probably you'll see old Tim all right.'

'Tomorrow morning! Why, that's *ages* away!' said poor George. She put her head in her hands and groaned. 'Oh, nobody understands how much I love Timmy. You would perhaps if you had a dog of your own, Julian. It's an awful feeling, really. Oh Timmy, are you all right?'

'Of course he's all right,' said Julian, impatiently. 'Do pull yourself together, George.'

'I *feel* as if something's wrong,' said George, looking obstinate. 'Julian – I think I'd better go across to the island.'

'No,' said Julian at once. 'Don't be idiotic, George. Nothing is wrong, except that your father's been forgetful. He's sent his OK signal. That's enough! You're not to go and create a scene over there with him. That would be disgraceful!'

'Well – I'll try and be patient,' said George,

unexpectedly meek. She got up, looking worried. Julian spoke in a kinder voice.

'Cheer up, old thing! You do like to go off the deep end, don't you?'

[15]

In the middle of the night

George did not moan any more about her worries. She went about with an anxious look in her blue eyes, but she had the sense not to tell her mother how worried she was at not seeing Timmy in the glass room, when her father signalled.

She mentioned it, of course, but her mother took the same view as Julian did. 'There! I knew he'd forget to take Timmy up! He's so very forgetful when he's at work.'

The children decided to go to the quarry that afternoon and explore the tunnel under the shelf of rock. So they set off after their lunch. But when they came to the quarry, they did not dare to climb down the steep sides. The heavy rain of the day before had made them far too dangerous.

'Look,' said Julian, pointing to where the bushes and smaller plants were ripped up and crushed. 'I bet that's where old Martin fell down yesterday! He might have broken his neck!'

'Yes. I vote we don't attempt to go down till it's as dry as it was the other day,' said Dick.

It was very disappointing. They had brought torches, and a rope, and had looked forward to a little excitement. 'Well, what shall we do?' asked Julian.

'I'm going back home,' said George, unexpectedly. 'I'm tired. You others go for a walk.'

Anne looked at George. She did seem rather pale.

'I'll come back with you, George,' said Anne slipping her hand through her cousin's arm. But George shook it off.

'No thanks, Anne. I want to be alone.'

'Well – we'll go over to the cliff then,' said Julian. 'It'll be nice and blowy up there. See you later, George!'

They went off. George turned and sped back

to Kirrin Cottage. Her mother was out. Joanna was upstairs in her bedroom. George went to the larder and took several things from it. She bundled them into a bag and then fled out of the house.

She found Alf the fisher-boy. 'Alf! You're not to tell a soul. I'm going over to Kirrin Island tonight – because I'm worried about Timmy. We left him there. Have my boat ready at ten o'clock!'

Alf was always ready to do anything in the world for George. He nodded and asked no questions at all. 'Right. It'll be ready. Anything you want put in it?'

'Yes, this bag,' said George. 'Now don't split on me, Alf. I'll be back tomorrow if I find Tim's all right.'

She fled back to the house. She hoped Joanna would not notice the things she had taken from the larder shelf.

'I can't help it if what I'm doing is wrong,' she kept whispering to herself. 'I know something isn't right with Timmy. And I'm not at all sure about Father, either. He *wouldn't* have forgotten his solemn promise to me about taking Timmy up with him. I'll have to go across to the island. I can't help it if it's wrong!'

The others wondered what was up with George when they came back from their walk. She was so fidgety and restless. They had tea and then did some gardening for Aunt Fanny. George did some too, but her thoughts were far away, and twice her mother had to stop her pulling up seedlings instead of weeds.

Bedtime came. The girls got into bed at about a quarter to ten. Anne was tired and fell asleep at once. As soon as George heard her regular breathing she crept quietly out of bed and dressed again. She pulled on her warmest jersey, got her raincoat, rubber boots and a thick rug, and tiptoed downstairs.

Out of the side door she went and into the night. There was a bit of a moon in the sky, so it was not as dark as usual. George was glad. She would be able to see her way through the rocks a little now – though she was sure she could guide the boat even in the dark!

Alf was waiting for her. Her boat was ready. 'Everything's in,' said Alf. 'I'll push off. Now you be careful – and if you do scrape a rock, row like anything in case she fills and sinks. Ready?'

Off went George, hearing the lap-lap of the water against the sides of the boat. She heaved a sigh of relief, and began to row strongly away from the shore. She frowned as she rowed. Had she brought everything she might want? Two torches. Plenty of food. A tin-opener. Something to drink. A rug to wrap herself in tonight.

Back at Kirrin Cottage Julian lay in bed watching for his uncle's signal. Half past ten. Now for the signal. Ah, here they were! One – two – three – four – five – six! Good. Six and no more!

He wondered why George hadn't come into his and Dick's room to watch for them. She had last night. He got up, padded to the door of George's room and put his head in. 'George!' he said softly. 'It's OK. Your father's signals have just come again.'

There was no reply. Julian heard regular breathing and turned to go back to bed. The girls must be asleep already! Well, George couldn't really be worrying much about Timmy now, then! Julian got into his bed and soon fell asleep himself. He had no idea that George's bed was empty – no idea that even now George was battling with the waves that guarded Kirrin Island!

It was more difficult than she had expected, for the moon did not really give very much light, and had an annoying way of going behind a cloud just when she badly needed every scrap of light she could get. But, deftly and cleverly, she managed to make her way through the passage between the hidden rocks. Thank goodness the tide was high so that most of them were well below the surface!

At last she swung her boat into the little cove. Here the water was perfectly calm. Panting a little, George pulled her boat up as far as she could. Then she stood in the darkness and thought hard.

What was she going to do? She did not know where her father's hiding-place was – but she felt certain the entrance to it must be somewhere in or near the little stone room. Should she make her way to that?

Yes, she would. It would be the only place to shelter in for the night, anyway. She would put on her torch when she got there, and hunt round for any likely entrance to the hiding-place. If she found it, she would go in – and what a surprise she would give her father! If old Timmy was there he would go mad with delight.

She took the heavy bag, draped the rug over her arm, and set off. She did not dare to put on her torch yet, in case the unknown enemy was lurking near. After all, her father had heard him cough at night!

George was not frightened. She did not even think about being frightened. All her thoughts were set on finding Timmy and making sure he was safe.

She came to the little stone room. It was pitch-dark in there, of course – not even the faint light of the moon pierced into its blackness. George had to put on her torch.

She put down her bundle by the wall at the back, near the old fireplace recess. She draped the rug over it and sat down to have a rest, switching off her torch.

After a while she got up cautiously and switched on her torch again. She began to search for the hiding-place. Where *could* the entrance be? She flashed her torch on to every flagstone in the floor of the room. But not one looked as if it had been moved or lifted. There was nothing to show where there might be an entrance underground.

She moved round the walls, examining those too in the light of her torch. No – there was no sign that a hidden way lay behind any of those stones either. It was most tantalising. If she only knew!

She went to wrap the rug round her, and to sit and think. It was cold now. She was shivering, as she sat there in the dark, trying to puzzle out where the hidden entrance could be.

And then she heard a sound! She jumped and then stiffened all over, holding her breath painfully. What was it?

There was a curious grating noise. Then a slight thud. It came from the recess where people long ago had built their big log fires! George sat perfectly still, straining her eyes and ears.

She saw a beam of light in the fireplace recess. Then she heard a man's cough!

Was it her father? He had a cough at times. She listened hard. The beam of light grew brighter. Then she heard another noise – it sounded as if someone had jumped down from somewhere! And then – a voice!

'Come on!'

It was not her father's voice! George grew cold with fear then. Not her father's voice! Then what had happened to him – and to Timmy?

Someone else jumped down into the recess,

grumbling. 'I'm not used to this crawling about!'

That wasn't her father's voice either. So there were *two* unknown enemies! Not one. And they knew her father's secret workroom. George felt almost faint with horror. Whatever had happened to him and Timmy?

The men walked out of the little stone room without seeing George at all. She guessed they were going to the tower. How long would they be? Long enough for her to search for the place they had appeared from?

She strained her ears again. She heard their footsteps going into the great yard. She tiptoed to the doorway and looked out. Yes – there was the light of their torch near the tower! If they were going up, there would be plenty of time to look round.

She went back into the little stone room. Her hands were trembling and she found it difficult to switch on her torch. She went to the fireplace recess and flashed the light in it.

She gave a gasp! Half-way up the recess at

the back was a black opening! She flashed the light up there. Evidently there was a movable stone half-way up that swung back and revealed an entrance behind. An entrance to what? Were there steps such as were shown in the old map?

Feeling quite breathless, George stood on tiptoe and flashed her light into the hole. Yes – there were steps! They went down into the wall at the back. She remembered that the little stone room backed on to one of the immensely thick old walls still left.

She stood there, uncertain what to do. Had she better go down and see if she could find Timmy and her father? But if she did, she might be made a prisoner too. On the other hand, if she stayed outside, and the men came back and shut up the entrance, she might not be able to open it. She would be worse off than ever!

'I'll go down!' she suddenly decided. 'But I'd better take my bag and the rug, in case the men come back and see them. I don't want them to know I'm on the island if I can help it! I could hide them somewhere down there, I expect. I wonder if this entrance leads to the dungeons.'

She lifted up the rug and the bag and pushed them into the hole. She heard the bag roll down the steps, the tins inside making a muffled noise.

Then she climbed up herself. Gracious, what a long dark flight of steps! Wherever did they lead to?

[16]

Down to the caves

George went cautiously down the stone steps. They were steep and narrow. 'I should think they run right down in the middle of the stone wall,' thought George. 'Goodness, here's a narrow bit!'

It was so narrow that she had to go sideways. 'A fat man would never get through there!' she thought to herself. 'Hallo – the steps have ended!'

She had got the rug round her shoulders, and had picked up her bag on the way down. In her other hand she held her torch. It was terribly dark and quiet down there. George did not feel scared because she was hoping to see Timmy at any moment. No one could feel afraid with Timmy just round the corner, ready to welcome them!

She stood at the bottom of the steps, her torch showing her a narrow tunnel. It curved sharply to the left. 'Now will it join the dungeons from here?' she wondered, trying to get her sense of direction to help her. 'They can't be far off. But there's no sign of them at the moment.'

She went down the narrow tunnel. Once the roof came down so low she almost had to crawl. She flashed her torch on it. She saw black rock there, which had evidently been too hard to be removed by the tunnel-builders long ago.

The tunnel went on and on and on. George was puzzled. Surely by now she must have gone by all the dungeons! Why – she must be heading towards the shore of the island! How very strange! Didn't this tunnel join the dungeons then? A little further and she would be under the bed of the sea itself.

The tunnel took a deep slope downwards. More steps appeared, cut roughly from rock. George climbed down them cautiously. Where in the world was she going?

At the bottom of the steps the tunnel seemed to be cut out of solid rock – or else it was a natural passage, not made by man at all. George didn't know. Her torch showed her black, rocky walls and roof, and her feet stumbled over an irregular rocky path. How she longed for Timmy beside her!

'I must be very deep down,' she thought, pausing to flash her torch round her once more. 'Very deep down and very far from the castle! Good gracious – whatever's that awful noise?'

She listened. She heard a muffled booming and moaning. Was it her father doing one of his experiments? The noise went on and on, a deep, never-ending boom.

'Why – I believe it's the sea!' said George, amazed. She stood and listened again. 'Yes – it *is* the sea – over my head! I'm under the rocky bed of Kirrin Bay!'

And now poor George did feel a bit scared! She thought of the great waves surging above her, she thought of the restless, moving water scouring the rocky bed over her head, and felt frightened in case the sea should find a way to leak down into her narrow tunnel!

'Now don't be silly,' she told herself sternly. 'This tunnel has been here under the sea-bed for hundreds of years – why should it suddenly become unsafe just when *you* are in it, George?'

Talking to herself like this, to keep up her spirits, she went on again. It was very weird indeed to think she was walking under the sea. So this was where her father was at work! Under the sea itself.

And then George suddenly remembered something he had said to them all, the first time they had visited him on the island. What was it now? 'Oh yes! He said he had to have water *above* and *around* him!' said George. '*Now* I see what he meant! His workroom is somewhere down here – so the sea-water is *above* him – and it's all *round* the tower, because it's built on an island!'

Water above and water around – so that was why her father had chosen Kirrin Island for his experiment. How had he found the secret passage under the sea, though? 'Why, even I didn't know of that,' said George. 'Hallo – what am I coming to?'

She stopped. The passage had suddenly widened out into an enormous dark cave, whose roof was unexpectedly high, lost in dark shadows. George stared round. She saw strange things there that she didn't understand at all – wires, glass boxes, little machines that seemed to be at work without a sound, whose centres were alive with funny, gleaming, shivering light.

Sudden sparks shot up now and again, and when that happened a funny smell crept round the cave. 'How weird all this is!' thought George. 'How ever can Father understand all these machines and things! I wonder where he is. I do hope those men haven't made him prisoner somewhere!'

From this strange Aladdin's cave another tunnel led. George switched on her torch again and went into it. It was much like the other one, but the roof was higher.

She came to another cave, smaller this time, and crammed with wires of all kinds. There was a curious humming sound here, like thousands of bees in a hive. George half-expected to see some flying round.

'It must be these wires making the noise,' she said. There was nobody in the cave at all, but it led into another one, and George hoped that soon she would find Timmy and her father.

She went into the next cave, which was perfectly empty and very cold. She shivered. Then down another passage, and into a small cave. The first thing she saw beyond this tiny cave was a light!

A light! Then perhaps she was coming to the cave her father must be in! She flashed her torch round the little cave she was now standing in and saw tins of food, bottles of beer, tins of sweets, and a pile of clothes of some sort. Ah, this was where her father kept his stores. She went on to the next cave, wondering why Timmy had not heard her and come to greet her.

She looked cautiously into the cave where the light came from. Sitting at a table, his head in his hands, perfectly still, was her father! There was no sign of Timmy.

'Father!' said George. The man at the table jumped violently and turned round. He stared at George as if he really could not believe his eyes. Then he turned back again, and buried his face in his hands.

'*Father!*' said George again, quite frightened because he did not say anything to her.

He looked round again, and this time he got up. He stared at George once more, and then sat down heavily. George ran to him. 'What's the matter? Oh Father, what's the matter? Where's Timmy?'

'George! Is it *really* you, George? I thought I must be dreaming when I looked up and saw you!' said her father. 'How did you get here? Good gracious, it's impossible that you should be here!'

'Father are you all right? What's happened – and where's Timmy?' said George, urgently.

She looked all round, but could see no sign of him. Her heart went cold. Surely nothing awful had happened to Timmy?

'Did you see two men?' asked her father. 'Where were they?'

'Oh Father – we keep asking each other questions and not answering them!' said George. 'Tell me first – where is Timmy?'

'I don't know,' said her father. 'Did those two men go to the tower?'

'Yes,' said George. 'Father, what's happened?'

'Well, if they've gone to the tower, we've got about an hour in peace,' said her father. 'Now listen to me, George, very carefully. This is terribly important.'

'I'm listening,' said George. 'But do hurry up and tell me about Timmy.'

'These two men were parachuted down on to the island, to try and find out my secret,' said her father. 'I'll tell you what my experiments are for, George – they are to find a way of replacing all coal, coke and oil – an idea to give the world all the heat and power it wants, and to do away with mines and miners.'

'Good gracious!' said George. 'It would be one of the most wonderful things the world has ever known.'

'Yes,' said her father. 'And I should *give* it to the whole world – it shall not be in the power of any one country, or collection of men. It shall be a gift to the whole of mankind. But, George, there are men who want my secret for themselves, so that they may make colossal fortunes out of it.'

'How hateful!' cried George. 'Go on, Father – how did they hear of it?'

'Well, I was at work on this idea with some of my colleagues, my fellow-workers,' said her father. 'And one of them betrayed us, and went to some powerful businessmen to tell them of my idea. So when I knew this I decided to come away in secret and finish my experiments by myself. Then nobody could betray me.'

'And you came here!' said George. 'To my island.'

'Yes, because I needed water over me and water around me,' said her father. 'Quite by chance I looked at a copy of that old map, and thought that if the passage shown there – the one leading from the little stone room, I mean – if the passage there *really* did lead under the sea, as it seemed to show, that would be the ideal place to finish my experiments.'

'Oh Father – and I made such a fuss!' said George, ashamed now, to remember how cross she had been.

'Did you?' said her father, as if he had forgotten all about that. 'Well, I got all my stuff and came here. And now these fellows have found me, and got hold of me!'

'Poor Father! Can't I help?' said George. 'I could go back and bring help over here, couldn't I?'

'Yes, you could!' said her father. 'But you mustn't let those men see you, George.'

'I'll do anything you want me to, Father, anything!' said George. 'But first do tell me what's happened to Timmy?'

'Well, he kept by me all the time,' said her father. 'Really, he's a wonderful dog, George. And then, this morning, just as I was coming out of the entrance in that little room to go up into the tower with Timmy to signal, the two men pounced on me and forced me back here.'

'But what happened to Timmy?' asked George, impatiently. Would her father *never* tell her what she wanted to know?

'He flew at the men, of course,' said her father. 'But somehow or other one of them lassoed him with a noose of rope and caught him. They pulled the rope so tight round his neck that he almost choked.'

'Oh poor, poor Timmy,' said George, and the tears ran down her cheeks. 'Is he – do you think – he's all right, Father?'

'Yes. From what I heard the men saying afterwards I think they've taken him to some cave and shut him in there,' said her father. 'Anyway, I saw one of them getting some dog biscuits out of a bag this evening, so that looks as if he's alive and kicking – and hungry!'

George heaved a great sigh of relief. So long as Timmy was alive and all right! She took a few steps towards what she thought must be another cave. 'I'm going to find Timmy, Father,' she said. 'I *must* find him!'

[17]

Timmy at last

'No, George!' called her father sharply. 'Come back. There is something very important I want to say. Come here!'

George went over to him, filled with impatience to get to Timmy, wherever he was. She *must* find him!

'Now listen,' said her father. 'I have a book in which I have made all my notes of this great experiment. The men haven't found it! I want you to take it safely to the mainland, George. Don't let it out of your sight! If the men get hold of it they would have all the information they needed!'

'But don't they know everything just by looking at your wires and machines and things?' asked George.

'They know a very great deal,' said her

father, 'and they've found out a lot more since they've been here – but not quite enough. I daren't destroy my book of notes, because if anything should happen to me, my great idea would be completely lost. So, George, I must entrust it to you and you must take it to an address I will give you, and hand it to the person there.'

'It's an awful responsibility,' said George, a little scared of handling a book which meant so much, not only to her father, but possibly to the whole of the world. 'But I'll do my best, Father. I'll hide in one of the caves till the men come back, and then I'll slip back up the passage to the hidden entrance, get out, go to my boat and row back to the mainland. Then I'll deliver your book of notes without fail, and get help sent over here to you.'

'Good girl,' said her father, and gave her a hug. 'Honestly, George, I am proud of you.'

George thought that was the nicest thing her father had ever said to her. She smiled at him. 'Well, Father, I'll go and see if I can find Timmy now. I simply must see that he's all right before I go to hide in one of the other caves.'

'Very well,' said her father. 'The man who took the biscuits went in that direction – still further under the sea, George. Oh, by the way, how is it you're here, in the middle of the night?'

It seemed to strike her father for the first time that George also might have a story to tell. But George felt that she really couldn't waste any more time – she *must* find Timmy!

'I'll tell you later, Father,' she said. 'Oh, where's that book of notes?'

Her father rose and went to the back of the cave. He took a box and stood on it. He ran his hand along a dark ridge of rock, and felt about until he had found what he wanted.

He brought down a slim book, whose pages were of very thin paper. He opened the book and George saw many beautifully drawn diagrams, and pages of notes in her father's small neat handwriting.

'Here you are,' said her father, handing her

the book, 'do the best you can. If anything happens to me, this book will still enable my fellow-workers to give my idea to the world. If I come through this all right, I shall be glad to have the book, because it will mean I shall not have to work out all my experiments again.'

George took the precious book. She stuffed it into her macintosh pocket, which was a big one. 'I'll keep it safe, Father. Now I must go and find Timmy, or those two men will be back before I can hide in one of the other caves.'

She left her father's cave and went into the next one. There was nothing there at all. Then on she went down a passage that twisted and turned in the rock.

And then she heard a sound she longed to hear. A whine! Yes, really a whine!

'Timmy!' shouted George, eagerly. 'Oh Timmy! I'm coming!'

Timmy's whine stopped suddenly. Then he barked joyously. 'Woof, woof, woof, woof!' George almost fell as she tried to run down the narrow tunnel. Her torch showed her a big boulder that seemed to be blocking up a small cave in the side of the tunnel. Behind the boulder Timmy barked, and scraped frantically!

George tugged at the stone with all her strength. 'Timmy!' she panted. 'Timmy! I'll get you out! I'm coming! Oh, Timmy!'

The stone moved a little. George tugged again. It was almost too heavy for her to move at all, but despair made her stronger than she had ever been in her life. The stone quite suddenly swung to one side, and George just got one of her feet out of its way in time, or it would have been crushed.

Timmy squeezed out of the space left. He flung himself on George, who fell on the ground with her arms tight round him. He licked her face and whined, and she buried her nose in his thick fur in joy. 'Timmy! What have they done to you? Timmy, I came as soon as I could!'

Timmy whined again and again in joy, and tried to paw and lick George as if he couldn't have enough of her. It would have been difficult to say which of the two was the happier.

At last George pushed Timmy away firmly. 'Timmy we've got work to do! We've got to escape from here and get across to the mainland and bring help.'

'Woof,' said Timmy. George stood up and flashed her torch into the tiny cave where Timmy had been. She saw that there was a bowl of water there and some biscuits. The men had not ill-treated him, then, except to lasso him and half-choke him when they caught him. She felt round his neck tenderly, but except for a swollen ridge there, he seemed none the worse.

'Now hurry up – we'll go back to Father's cave – and then find another cave beyond his to hide in till the two men come back from the tower. Then we'll creep out into the little stone room and row back to the mainland,' said George. 'I've got a very, very important book here in my pocket, Timmy.'

Timmy growled suddenly, and the hairs on

the back of his neck rose up. George stiffened, and stood listening.

A stern voice came down the passage. 'I don't know who you are or where you've come from, but if you have dared to let that dog loose he'll be shot! And, to show you that I mean what I say, here's something to let you know I've a revolver!'

Then there came a deafening crash, as the man pulled the trigger, and a bullet hit the roof somewhere in the passage. Timmy and George almost jumped out of their skins. Timmy would have leapt up the passage at once, but George had her hand on his collar. She was very frightened, and tried hard to think what was best to do.

The echoes of the shot went on and on. It was horrid. Timmy stopped growling, and George stayed absolutely still.

'Well?' said the voice. 'Did you hear what I said? If that dog is loose, he'll be shot. I'm not having my plans spoilt now. And you, whoever you are, will please come up the tunnel and let me see you. But I warn you, if the dog's with you, that's the end of him!'

'Timmy! Timmy, run away and hide somewhere!' whispered George suddenly. And then she remembered something else that filled her with despair. She had her father's precious book of notes with her – in her pocket! Suppose the man found it on her? It would break her father's heart to know that his wonderful secret had been stolen from him after all.

George hurriedly took the thin, flat little book from her pocket. She pushed it at Timmy. 'Put it in your mouth. Take it with you, Tim. And go and hide till it's safe to come. Quick! Go, Timmy, go! I'll be all right.'

To her great relief Timmy, with the book in his mouth, turned and disappeared down the tunnel that led further under the sea. How she hoped he would find a safe hiding-place! The tunnel must end soon – but maybe before it did, Timmy would settle down in some dark corner and wait for her to call him again.

'Will you come up the passage or not?'

shouted the voice angrily. 'You'll be sorry if I have to come and fetch you, because I shall shoot all the way along!'

'I'm coming!' called George, in a small voice, and she went up the passage. She soon saw a beam of light, and in a moment she was in the flash of a powerful torch. There was a surprised exclamation.

'Good heavens! A boy! What are *you* doing here, and where did you come from?'

George's short curly hair made the man with the torch think she was a boy, and George did not tell him he was wrong. The man held a revolver, but he let it drop as he saw George.

'I only came to rescue my dog, and to find my father,' said George, in a meek voice.

'Well, you can't move that heavy stone!' said the man. 'A kid like you wouldn't have the strength. And you can't rescue your father either! We've got him prisoner, as you no doubt saw.'

'Yes,' said George, delighted to think that the man was sure she had not been strong enough to move the big stone. She wasn't going to say a word about Timmy! If the man thought he was still shut up in that tiny cave, well and good!

Then she heard her father's voice, anxiously calling from somewhere beyond the man. 'George! Is that you? Are you all right?'

'Yes, Father!' shouted back George, hoping that he would not ask anything about Timmy. The man beckoned her to come to him. Then he pushed her in front of him and they walked to her father's cave.

'I've brought your boy back,' said the man. 'Silly little idiot, thinking he could set that savage dog free! We've got him penned up in a cave with a big boulder in front!'

Another man came in from the opposite end of the cave. He was amazed to see George. The first man explained.

'When I got down here, I heard a noise out beyond this cave, the dog barking and someone talking to him and found this kid there, trying to set the dog free. I'd have shot the dog, of course, if he *had* been freed.'

'But, how did this boy get here?' asked the other man, still amazed.

'Maybe *he* can tell us that!' said the other. And then, for the first time, George's father heard how George had got there and why.

She told them how she had watched for Timmy in the glass room of the tower and hadn't seen him, and that had worried her and made her suspicious. So she had come across to the island in her boat at night, and had seen where the men came from. She had gone down the tunnel, and kept on till she came to the cave, where she had found her father.

The three men listened in silence. 'Well, you're a tiresome nuisance,' one of the men said to George, 'but my word, you're a son to be proud of. It's not many boys would have been brave enough to run so much risk for anyone.'

'Yes. I'm really proud of you, George,' said her father. He looked at her anxiously. She knew what he was thinking – what about his precious book? Had she been sensible enough to hide it? She did not dare to let him know anything while the men were there.

'Now, this complicates matters,' said the other man, looking at George. 'If you don't go back home you'll soon be missed, and there will be all kinds of search-parties going on – and maybe someone will send over to the island here to tell your father you have disappeared! We don't want anyone here at present, not till we know what we want to know!'

He turned to George's father. 'If you will tell us what we want to know, and give us all your notes, we will set you free, give you whatever sum of money you ask us for, and disappear ourselves.'

'And if I still say I won't?' said George's father.

'Then I am afraid we shall blow up the whole of your machines and the tower – and possibly you will never be found again because you will be buried down here,' said the man, in a voice that was suddenly very hard.

There was a dead silence. George looked at

her father. 'You couldn't do a thing like that,' he said at last. 'You would gain nothing by it at all!'

'It's all or nothing with us,' said the man. 'All or nothing. Make up your mind. We'll give you till half past ten tomorrow morning – about seven hours. Then either you tell us everything, or we blow the island sky-high!'

They went out of the cave and left George and her father together. Only seven hours! And then, perhaps, the end of Kirrin Island!

[18]

Half past four in the morning

As soon as the men were out of earshot, George's father spoke in a low voice.

'It's no good. I'll have to let them have my book of notes. I can't risk having you buried down here, George. I don't mind anything for myself – workers of my sort have to be ready to take risks all their lives – but it's different now you're here!'

'Father, I haven't got the book of notes,' whispered George, thankfully. 'I gave them to Timmy. I *did* manage to get that stone away from the entrance to his little prison, though the men think I didn't! I gave the book to Timmy and told him to go and hide till I fetched him.'

'Fine work, George!' said her father. 'Well, perhaps if you got Timmy now and brought him here, he could deal with these two men before they suspect he is free! He is quite capable of getting them both down on the ground at once.'

'Oh yes! It's our only chance,' said George. 'I'll go and get him now. I'll go a little way along the passage and whistle. Father, why didn't *you* go and try and rescue Timmy?'

'I didn't want to leave my book,' said her father. 'I dared not take it with me, in case the men came after me and found it. They've been looking in all the caves for it. I couldn't bear to leave it here, and go and look for the dog. I was sure he was all right, when I saw the men taking biscuits out of the bag. Now do go, George, and whistle to Timmy. The men may be back at any moment.'

George took her torch and went into the passage that led to the little cave where Timmy had been. She whistled loudly, and then waited. But no Timmy came. She whistled again, and then went farther along the passage. Still no Timmy.

She called him loudly. 'TIMMY! TIMMY!

COME HERE!' But Timmy did not come. There was no sound of scampering feet, no joyful bark.

'Oh bother!' thought George. 'I hope he hasn't gone so far away that he can't hear me. I'll go a little farther.'

So she made her way along the tunnel, past the cave where Timmy had been, and then on down the tunnel again. Still no Timmy.

George rounded a corner and then saw that the tunnel split into three. Three different passages, all dark, silent and cold. Oh dear! She didn't in the least know which to take. She took the one on the left.

But that also split into three a little way on! George stopped. 'I shall get absolutely lost in this maze of passages under the sea if I go on,' she thought. 'I simply daren't. It's too frightening. TIMMY! TIMMY!'

Her voice went echoing along the passage and sounded very strange indeed. She retraced her steps and went right back to her father's cave, feeling miserable.

'Father, there's no sign of Timmy at all. He must have gone along one of the passages and got lost! Oh dear, this is awful. There are lots of tunnels beyond this cave. It seems as if the whole rocky bed of the sea is mined with tunnels!' George sat down and looked very down-hearted.

'Quite likely,' said her father. 'Well, that's a perfectly good plan gone wrong. We must try and think of another.'

'I do wonder what Julian and the others will think when they wake up and find me gone,' said George, suddenly. 'They might even come and try to find me here.'

'That wouldn't be much good,' said her father. 'These men will simply come down here and wait, and nobody will know where we are. The others don't know of the entrance in the little stone room, do they?'

'No,' said George. 'If they came over here I'm sure they'd never find it! We've looked before. And that would mean they'd be blown up with the island. Father, this is simply dreadful.'

'If only we knew where Timmy was,' said her father, 'or if we could get a message to Julian to tell him not to come. What's the time? My word, it's half past three in the early morning! I suppose Julian and the others are fast asleep.'

Julian *was* fast asleep. So was Anne. Dick was in a deep sleep as well, so nobody guessed that George's bed was empty.

But, about half past four Anne awoke, feeling very hot. 'I really must open the window!' she thought. 'I'm boiling!'

She got up and went to the window. She opened it, and stood looking out. The stars were out and the bay shone faintly.

'George,' whispered Anne. 'Are you awake?'

She listened for a reply. But none came. Then she listened more intently. Why, she couldn't even hear George's breathing! Surely George was there?

She felt over George's bed. It was flat and empty. She switched on the light and looked at it. George's pyjamas were still on the bed. Her clothes were gone.

'George has gone to the island!' said Anne, in a fright. 'All in the dark by herself!'

She went to the boys' room. She felt about Julian's bed for his shoulder, and shook him hard. He woke up with a jump. 'What is it? What's up?'

'Julian! George is gone. Her bed's not been slept in,' whispered Anne. Her whisper awoke Dick, and soon both boys were sitting up wide awake.

'Blow! I might have guessed she'd do a stupid thing like that,' said Julian. 'In the middle of the night too – and all those dangerous rocks to row round. *Now* what are we going to do about it? I *told* her she wasn't to go to the island – Timmy would be quite all right! I expect Uncle Quentin forgot to take him up to the tower with him yesterday, that's all. She might have waited till half past ten this morning, then she would probably have seen him.'

'Well, we can't do anything now, I suppose, can we?' said Anne, anxiously.

'Not a thing,' said Julian. 'I've no doubt she's

safely on Kirrin Island by now, making a fuss of Timmy, and having a good old row with Uncle Quentin. Really George is the limit!'

They talked for half an hour and then Julian looked at his watch. 'Five o'clock. We'd better try and get a bit more sleep. Aunt Fanny will be worried in the morning when she hears of George's latest escapade!'

Anne went back to her room. She got into bed and fell asleep. Julian could not sleep – he kept thinking of George and wondering where exactly she was. Wouldn't he give her a talking-to when she came back!

He suddenly heard a peculiar noise downstairs. Whatever could it be? It sounded like someone climbing in at a window. Was there one open? Yes, the window of the little wash-place might be open. Crash! What in the world was that? It couldn't be a burglar – no burglar would be foolish enough to make such a noise.

There was a sound on the stairs, and then the bedroom door was pushed open. In alarm Julian put out his hand to switch on the light, but before he could do something heavy jumped right on top of him!

He yelled and Dick woke up with a jump. He put on the light, then Julian saw what was on his bed – Timmy!

'Timmy! How did you get here? Where's George! Timmy, is it really you?'

'Timmy!' echoed Dick, amazed. 'Has George brought him back then? Is she here too?'

Anne came in, woken by the noise. 'Why, *Timmy*! Oh Julian, is George back too, then?'

'No, apparently not,' said Julian, puzzled. 'I say, Tim, what's this you've got in your mouth? Drop it, old chap, drop it!'

Timmy dropped it. Julian picked it up from the bed. 'It's a book of notes – all in Uncle's handwriting! What *does* this mean? How did Timmy get hold of it – and why did he bring it here? It's most extraordinary!'

Nobody could imagine why Timmy had suddenly appeared with the book of notes – and no George.

'It's very odd,' said Julian. 'There's something

I don't understand here. Let's go and wake Aunt Fanny.'

So they went and woke her up, telling her all they knew. She was very worried indeed to hear that George was gone. She picked up the book of notes and knew at once that it was very important.

'I must put this into the safe,' she said. 'I know this is valuable. How *did* Timmy get hold of it?'

Timmy was acting strangely. He kept pawing at Julian and whining. He had been very pleased to see everyone, but he seemed to have something on his mind.

'What is it, old boy?' asked Dick. 'How did you get here? You didn't swim, because you're not wet. If you came in a boat, it must have been with George – and yet you've left her behind!'

'*I* think something's happened to George,' said Anne, suddenly. 'I think Timmy keeps pawing you to tell you to go with him and find her. Perhaps she brought him back in the boat, and then was terribly tired and fell asleep on the beach or something. We ought to go and see.'

'Yes, I think we ought,' said Julian. 'Aunt Fanny, would you like to wake Joanna and get something hot ready, in case we find George is tired out and cold? We'll go down to the beach and look. It will soon be daylight now. The eastern sky is just beginning to show its first light.'

'Well go and dress then,' said Aunt Fanny, still looking very worried indeed. 'Oh, what a dreadful family I've got – always in some scrape or other!'

The three children began to dress. Timmy watched them, waiting patiently till they were ready. Then they all went downstairs and out of doors. Julian turned towards the beach, but Timmy stood still. He pawed at Dick and then ran a few steps in the opposite direction.

'Why, he doesn't *want* us to go the beach! He wants us to go another way!' cried Julian, in surprise. 'All right, Timmy, you lead the way and we'll follow!'

[19]

A meeting with Martin

Timmy ran round the house and made for the moor behind. It was most extraordinary. Wherever was he going?

'This is awfully strange,' said Julian. 'I'm sure George can't be anywhere in this direction.'

Timmy went on swiftly, occasionally turning his head to make sure everyone was following him. He led the way to the quarry!

'The quarry! Did George come here then?' said Dick. 'But why?'

The dog disappeared down into the middle of the quarry, slipping and sliding down the steep sides as he went. The others followed as best they could. Luckily it was not as slippery as before, and they reached the bottom without accident.

Timmy went straight to the shelf of rock and

disappeared underneath it. They heard him give a short sharp bark as if to say 'Come on! This is the way! Hurry up!'

'He's gone into the tunnel under there,' said Dick. 'Where we thought we might explore and didn't. There must be a passage or something there, then. But is George there?'

'I'll go first,' said Julian, and wriggled through the hole. He was soon in the wider bit and then came out into the part where he could almost stand. He walked a little way in the dark, hearing Timmy bark impatiently now and then. But in a moment or two Julian stopped.

'It's no good trying to follow you in the dark, Timmy!' he called. 'We'll have to go back and get torches. I can't see a foot in front of me!'

Dick was just wriggling through the first part of the hole. Julian called to him to go back.

'It's too dark,' he said. 'We must go and get torches. If George for some reason is up this passage, she must have had an accident, and we'd better get a rope, and some brandy.'

Anne began to cry. She didn't like the idea of George lying hurt in that dark passage. Julian put his arm round her as soon as he was in the open air again. He helped her up the sides of the quarry, followed by Dick.

'Now don't worry. We'll get her all right. But it beats me why she went there – and I still can't imagine how Tim and she came from the island, if they are here, instead of on the beach!'

'Look – there's Martin!' suddenly said Dick in surprise. So there was! He was standing at the top of the quarry, and seemed just as surprised to see them as they were to see him!

'You're up early,' called Dick. 'And goodness me – are you going gardening or something? Why the spades?'

Martin looked sheepish and didn't seem to know what to say. Julian suddenly walked up to him and caught hold of his shoulder. 'Look here, Martin! There's some funny business going on here! What are you going to do with those spades? Have you seen George? Do you know where she is, or anything about her? Come on, tell me!'

Martin shook his shoulder away from Julian's grip looking extremely surprised.

'George? No! What's happened to him?'

'George isn't a him – she's a her,' said Anne, still crying. 'She's disappeared. We thought she'd gone to the island to find her dog – and Timmy suddenly appeared at Kirrin Cottage, and brought us here!'

'So it looks as if George might be somewhere near here,' said Julian. 'And I want to know if you've seen her or know anything of her whereabouts?'

'No, Julian. I swear I don't!' said Martin.

'Well, tell me what you're doing here so early in the morning, with spades,' said Julian, roughly. 'Who are you waiting for? Your father?'

'Yes,' said Martin.

'And what are you going to do?' asked Dick. 'Going exploring up the hole there?'

'Yes,' said Martin again, sullen and worried. 'No harm in that, is there?'

'It's all – very – strange!' said Julian, eyeing him and speaking slowly and loudly. 'But – let me tell you this – *we're* going exploring – not you! If there's anything odd up that hole, *we'll* find it! We shall not allow you or your father to get through the hole. So go and find him and tell him that!'

Martin didn't move. He went very white, and stared at Julian miserably. Anne went up to him, tears still on her face, and put her hand on his arm.

'Martin, what is it? Why do you look like that? What's the mystery?'

And then, to the dismay and horror of everyone, Martin turned away with a noise that sounded very like a sob! He stood with his back to them, his shoulders shaking.

'Good gracious! What *is* up?' said Julian, in exasperation. 'Pull yourself together, Martin! Tell us what's worrying you.'

'Everything, everything!' said Martin, in a muffled voice. Then he swung round to face them. 'You don't know what it is to have no mother and no father – nobody who cares about you – and then—'

'But you *have* got a father!' said Dick at once.

'I haven't. He's not my father, that man. He's only my guardian, but he makes me call him father whenever we're on a job together.'

'A job? What sort of job?' said Julian.

'Oh any kind – all beastly,' said Martin. 'Snooping round and finding things out about people, and then getting money from them if we promise to say nothing – and receiving stolen goods and selling them – and helping people like the men who are after your uncle's secret—'

'*Oho*!' said Dick at once. 'Now we're coming to it. I *thought* you and Mr Curton were both suspiciously interested in Kirrin Island. What's this present job, then?'

'My guardian will half-kill me for telling all this,' said Martin. 'But, you see, they're planning to blow up the island – and it's about the worst thing I've ever been mixed up in – and I know your uncle is there – and perhaps George too now, you say. I can't go on with it!'

A few more tears ran down his cheeks. It was awful to see him crying like that, and the three felt sorry for Martin now. They were also full of horror when they heard him say that the island was to be blown up!

'How do you know this?' asked Julian.

'Well, Mr Curton's got a radio receiver and transmitter as you know,' explained Martin, 'and so have the fellows on the island – the ones who are after your uncle's secret – so they can easily keep in touch with one another. They mean to get the secret if they can – if not, they are going to blow the whole place sky-high so that *nobody* can get the secret. But they can't get away by boat because they don't know the way through those rocks—'

'Well, how will they get away then?' demanded Julian.

'We feel sure this hole that Timmy found the other day, leads down to the sea, and under the sea-bed to Kirrin Island,' said Martin. 'Yes, I know it sounds too mad to be true, but Mr Curton's got an old map which clearly shows there was once a passage under the sea-bed. If there is – well, the fellows across on the island can escape down it, after making all preparations for the island to be blown up. See?'

'Yes,' said Julian, taking a long breath. 'I *do* see. I see it all very clearly now. I see something else too! *Timmy* has found his way from the island, using that same passage you have just told us about, and *that's* why he's led us back here – to take us to the island and rescue Uncle Quentin and George.'

There was a deep silence. Martin stared at the ground. Dick and Julian thought hard. Anne sobbed a little. It all seemed quite unbelievable to her. Then Julian put his hand on Martin's arm.

'Martin! You did right to tell us. We may be able to prevent something dreadful. But you must help. We may need those spades of yours and I expect you've got torches too. We haven't. We don't want to waste time going back and getting them, so will you come with us and help us? Will you lend us those spades and torches?'

'Would you trust me?' said Martin, in a low voice. 'Yes, I want to come and help you. And if we get in now, my guardian won't be able to follow, because he won't have a torch. We can get to the island and bring your uncle and George safely back.'

'Good for you!' said Dick. 'Well, come on then. We've been talking far too long. Come on down again, Ju. Hand him a spade and torch, Martin.'

'Anne, you're not to come,' said Julian to his little sister. 'You're to go back and tell Aunt Fanny what's happened. Will you do that?'

'Yes. I don't want to come,' said Anne. 'I'll go back now. Do be careful, Julian!'

She climbed down with the boys and then stood and watched till all three had disappeared into the hole. Timmy, who had been waiting impatiently during the talking, barking now and again, was glad to find that at last they were going to make a move. He ran ahead in the tunnel, his eyes gleaming green every time he turned to see if they were following.

Anne began to climb up the steep side of the quarry again. Then, thinking she heard a cough, she stopped and crouched under a bush. She peered through the leaves and saw Mr Curton. Then she heard his voice.

'Martin! Where on earth are you?'

So he had come to look for Martin and go up the tunnel with him! Anne hardly dared to breathe. Mr Curton called again and again, then made an impatient noise and began to climb down the side of the quarry.

Suddenly he slipped! He clutched at a bush as he passed, but it gave way. He rolled quite near Anne, and caught sight of her. He looked astonished, but then his look became one of fear as he rolled more and more quickly to the bottom of the deep quarry. Anne heard him give a deep groan as at last he came to a stop.

Anne peered down in fright. Mr Curton was

sitting up, holding one of his legs and groaning. He looked up to see if he could spy Anne.

'Anne!' he called. 'I've broken my leg, I think. Can you fetch help? What are you doing here so early? Have you seen Martin?'

Anne did not answer. If he had broken his leg, then he couldn't go after the others! And Anne could get away quickly. She climbed carefully, afraid of rolling down to the bottom, and having to lie beside the horrid Mr Curton.

'Anne! Have you seen Martin? Look for him and get help for me, will you?' shouted Mr Curton, and then groaned again.

Anne climbed to the top of the quarry and looked down. She cupped her hands round her mouth and shouted loudly:

'You're a very wicked man. I shan't fetch help for you. I simply can't *bear* you!'

And, having got all that off her chest, the little girl shot off at top speed over the moor.

'I must tell Aunt Fanny. She'll know what to do! Oh I hope the others are safe. What shall we do if the island blows up? I'm glad, glad, glad I told Mr Curton he was a very wicked man.'

And on she ran, panting. Aunt Fanny would know what to do!

[20]

Everything boils up!

Meanwhile the three boys and Timmy were having a strange journey underground. Timmy led the way without faltering, stopping every now and again for the others to catch up with him.

The tunnel at first had a low roof and the boys had to walk along in a stooping position, which was very tiring indeed. But after a bit the roof became higher and Julian, flashing his torch round, saw that the walls and floor, instead of being made of soil, were now made of rock. He tried to reckon out where they were.

'We've come practically straight towards the cliff,' he said to Dick. 'That's allowing for a few turns and twists. The tunnel has sloped down so steeply the last few hundred yards that I think we must be very far underground indeed.'

It was not until the boys heard the curious booming noise that George had heard in the caves, that they knew they must be under the rocky bed of the sea. They were walking under the sea to Kirrin Island. How strange, how unbelievably astonishing!

'It's like a peculiarly vivid dream,' said Julian. 'I'm not sure I like it very much! All right Tim, we're coming. Hallo – what's this?'

They all stopped. Julian flashed his torch ahead and saw a pile of fallen rocks. Timmy had managed to squeeze himself through a hole in them and go through to the other side, but the boys couldn't.

'This is where the spades come in, Martin!' said Dick, cheerfully. 'Take a hand!'

By dint of pushing and shovelling, the boys at last managed to move the pile of fallen rocks enough to make a way past. 'Thank goodness for the spades!' said Julian.

They went on, and were soon very glad of the spades again, to move another heap of rock. Timmy barked impatiently when they kept him waiting. He was very anxious to get back to George.

Soon they came to where the tunnel forked into two. But Timmy took the right-hand passage without hesitation, and when that one forked into three, he again chose one without stopping to think for a moment.

'Marvellous, isn't he?' said Julian. 'All done by smell! He's been this way once, so he knows it again. We should be completely lost under here if we came by ourselves.'

Martin was not enjoying this adventure at all. He said very little, but laboured on after the others. Dick guessed he was worrying about what was going to happen when the adventure was over. Poor Martin. All he wanted to do was to draw, and instead of that he had been dragged into one horrible job after another, and used as a cat's-paw by his evil guardian.

'Do you think we're anywhere near the island?' said Dick, at last. 'I'm getting tired of this!'

'Yes, we must be,' said Julian. 'In fact I think

we'd better be as quiet as we can, in case we come suddenly on the enemy!'

So, without speaking again, they went as quietly as they could – and then suddenly they saw a faint light ahead of them. Julian put out his hand to stop the others.

They were nearing the cave where George's father had his books and papers – where George had found him the night before. Timmy stood in front of them, listening too. He was not going to run headlong into danger!

They heard voices, and listened intently to see whose they were. 'George's – and Uncle Quentin's,' said Julian at last. And as if Timmy had also satisfied himself that those were indeed the two voices, the dog ran ahead and went into the lighted cave, barking joyfully.

'Timmy!' came George's voice, and they heard something overturn as she sprang up. 'Where have you been?'

'Woof,' said Timmy, trying to explain. 'Woof!'

And then Julian and Dick ran into the cave

followed by Martin! Uncle Quentin and George stared in the very greatest amazement.

'Julian! Dick! And *Martin*! How did *you* get here?' cried George, while Timmy jumped and capered round her.

'I'll explain,' said Julian. 'It was Timmy that fetched us!' And he related the whole story of how Timmy had come into Kirrin Cottage in the early morning and had jumped on his bed, and all that had happened since.

And then, in their turn, Uncle Quentin and George told all that had happened to *them*!

'Where are the two men?' asked Julian.

'Somewhere on the island,' said George. 'I went scouting after them some time ago, and followed them up to where they get out into the little stone room. I think they're there until half past ten, when they'll go up and signal, so that people will think everything is all right.'

'Well, what are our plans?' said Julian. 'Will you come back down the passage under the sea with us? Or what shall we do?'

'Better not do that,' said Martin, quickly.

'My guardian may be coming– and he's in touch with other men. If he wonders where I am, and thinks something is up, he may call in two or three others, and we might meet them making their way up the passage.'

They did not know, of course, that Mr Curton was even then lying with a broken leg at the bottom of the quarry. Uncle Quentin considered.

'I've been given seven hours to say whether or not I will give the fellows my secret,' he said. 'That time will be up just after half past ten. Then the men will come down again to see me. I think between us we ought to be able to capture them – especially as we've got Timmy with us!'

'Yes, that's a good idea,' said Julian. 'We could hide somewhere till they come and then set Timmy on them before they suspect anything!'

Almost before he had finished these words the light in the cave went out! Then a voice spoke out of the blackness.

'Keep still! One movement and I'll shoot.'

George gasped. What was happening? Had the men come back unexpectedly? Oh, why hadn't Timmy given them warning? She had been fondling his ears, so probably he had been unable to hear anything!

She held Timmy's collar, afraid that he would fly at the man in the darkness and be shot. The voice spoke again.

'Will you or will you not give us your secret?'

'Not,' said Uncle Quentin in a low voice.

'You will have this whole island, and all your work, blown up then, and yourself too and the others.'

'Yes! You can do what you like!' suddenly yelled George. 'You'll be blown up yourself too. You'll never be able to get away in a boat – you'll go on the rocks!'

The man in the darkness laughed. 'We shall be safe,' he said. 'Now keep at the back of the cave. I have you covered with my revolver.'

They all crouched at the back. Timmy growled, but George made him stop at once.

She did not know if the men knew he was free or not.

Quiet footsteps passed across the cave in the darkness. George listened, straining her ears. Two pairs of footsteps! Both men were passing through the cave. She knew where they were going! They were going to escape by the undersea passage – and leave the island to be blown up behind them!

As soon as the footsteps had died away, George switched on her torch. 'Father! Those men are escaping now, down the sea-tunnel. We must escape too – but not that way. My boat is on the shore. Let's get there quickly and get away before there's any explosion.'

'Yes, come along,' said her father. 'But if only I could get up into my tower, I could stop any wicked plan of theirs! They mean to use the power there, I know – but if I could get up to the glass room, I could undo all their plans!'

'Oh do be quick then, Father!' cried George, getting in quite a panic now. 'Save my island if you can!'

They all made their way through the cave up to the passage that led to the stone flight of steps from the little stone room. And there they had a shock!

The stone could not be opened from the inside! The men had altered the mechanism so that it could now only be opened from the outside.

In vain Uncle Quentin swung the lever to and fro. Nothing happened. The stone would not move.

'It's only from outside it can be opened,' he said in despair. 'We're trapped!'

They sat down on the stone steps in a row, one above the other. They were cold, hungry and miserable. What could they do now? Make their way back to the cave, and then go on down the under-sea tunnel?

'I don't want to do that,' said Uncle Quentin. 'I'm so afraid that if there is an explosion, it may crack the rocky bed of the sea, which is the roof of the tunnel – and then water would pour in. It wouldn't be pleasant if we happened to be there at that moment.'

'Oh no. Don't let's be trapped like that,' said George with a shudder. 'I couldn't bear it.'

'Perhaps I could get something to explode this stone away,' said her father, after a while. 'I've got plenty of stuff if only I've time to put it together.'

'Listen!' said Julian, suddenly. 'I can hear something outside this wall. Sh!'

They all listened intently. Timmy whined and scratched at the stone that would not move.

'It's voices!' cried Dick. 'Lots of them. Who can it be?'

'Be *quiet*,' said Julian, fiercely. 'We *must* find out!'

'I know, I know!' said George, suddenly. 'It's the fishermen who have come over in their boats! *That's* why the men didn't wait till half past ten! *That's* why they've gone in such a hurry! They saw the fisherboats coming!'

'Then Anne must have brought them!' cried Dick. 'She must have run home to Aunt Fanny, told her everything and given the news to the fishermen – and they've come to rescue us! Anne! ANNE! WE'RE HERE!'

Timmy began to bark deafeningly. The others encouraged him, because they felt certain that Timmy's bark was louder than their shouts!

'WOOF! WOOF! WOOF!'

Anne heard the barking and the shouting as soon as she ran into the little stone room. 'Where are you? Where are you?' she yelled.

'HERE! HERE! MOVE THE STONE!' yelled Julian, shouting so loudly that everyone near him jumped violently.

'Move aside, Miss – I can see which stone it is,' said a man's deep voice. It was one of the fishermen. He felt round and about the stone in the recess, sure it was the right one because it was cleaner than the others through being used as an entrance.

Suddenly he touched the right place, and found a tiny iron spike. He pulled it down – and the lever swung back behind it, and pulled the stone aside!

Everyone hurried out, one on top of the other! The six fishermen standing in the little room stared in astonishment. Aunt Fanny was there too, and Anne. Aunt Fanny ran to her husband as soon as he appeared – but to her surprise he pushed her away quite roughly.

He ran out of the room, and hurried to the tower. Was he in time to save the island and everyone on it? Oh hurry, hurry!

[21]

The end of the adventure

'Where's he gone?' said Aunt Fanny, quite hurt. Nobody answered. Julian, George and Martin were watching the tower with anxious intensity. If only Uncle Quentin would appear at the top. Ah – there he was!

He had taken up with him a big stone. As everyone watched he smashed the glass round the tower with the stone. Crash! Crash! Crash!

The wires that ran through the glass were broken and split as the glass crashed into pieces. No power could race through them now. Uncle Quentin leaned out of the broken glass room and shouted exultantly.

'It's all right! I was in time! I've destroyed the power that might have blown up the island – you're safe!'

George found that her knees were suddenly

shaking. She had to sit down on the floor. Timmy came and licked her face wonderingly. Then he too sat down.

'What's he doing, smashing the tower up?' asked a burly fisherman. 'I don't understand all this.'

Uncle Quentin came down the tower and rejoined them. 'Another ten minutes and I should have been too late,' he said. 'Thank goodness, Anne, you all arrived when you did.'

'I ran all the way home, told Aunt Fanny, and we got the fishermen to come over as soon as they could get out their boats,' explained Anne. 'We couldn't think of any other way of rescuing you. Where are the wicked men?'

'Trying to escape down the under-sea tunnel,' said Julian. 'Oh – you don't know about that, Anne!' And he told her, while the fishermen listened open-mouthed.

'Look here,' said Uncle Quentin, when he had finished. 'As the boats are here, the men might as well take all my gear back with them.

I've finished my job here. I shan't want the island any more.'

'Oh! Then *we* can have it!' said George, delighted. 'And there's plenty of the holidays left. We'll help to bring up what you want, Father.'

'We ought to get back as quickly as we can, so as to catch those fellows at the other end of the tunnel,' said one of the fishermen.

'Yes. We ought,' said Aunt Fanny.

'Gracious! They'll find Mr Curton there with a broken leg,' said Anne, suddenly remembering.

The others looked at her in surprise. This was the first they had heard of Mr Curton being in the quarry. Anne explained.

'And I told him he was a very wicked man,' she ended triumphantly.

'Quite right,' said Uncle Quentin, with a laugh. 'Well, perhaps we'd better get my gear another time.'

'Oh, two of us can see to that for you now,' said the burly fisherman. 'George here, she's got her boat in the cove, and you've got yours. The others can go back with you, if you like – and Tom and me, we'll fix up your things and bring them across to the mainland later on. Save us coming over again.'

'Right,' said Uncle Quentin, pleased. 'You do that then. It's down in the caves through that tunnel behind the stone.'

They all went down to the cove. It was a beautiful day and the sea was very calm, except just round the island where the waters were always rough. Soon the boats were being sailed or rowed to the mainland.

'The adventure is over!' said Anne. 'How strange – I didn't think it was one while it was happening – but now I see it was!'

'Another to add to our long list of adventures,' said Julian. 'Cheer up, Martin, don't look so blue. Whatever happens, we'll see you don't come out badly over this. You helped us, and you threw in your lot with us. We'll see that you don't suffer – won't we, Uncle Quentin? We'd never have got through those falls of rock if we hadn't had Martin and his spades!'

'Well, thanks,' said Martin. 'If you can get me away from my guardian – and never let me see him again – I'll be happy!'

'It's quite likely that Mr Curton will be put somewhere safe where he won't be able to see his friends for quite a long time,' said Uncle Quentin dryly. 'So I don't think you need worry.'

As soon as the boats reached shore, Julian, Dick, Timmy and Uncle Quentin went off to the quarry to see if Mr Curton was still there and to wait for the other two men to come out of the tunnel!

Mr Curton was there all right, still groaning and calling for help. Uncle Quentin spoke to him sternly.

'We know your part in this matter, Curton. You will be dealt with by the police. They will be along in a short while.'

Timmy sniffed round Mr Curton, and then walked away, nose in air, as if to say 'What a nasty bit of work!' The others arranged themselves at the mouth of the hole and waited.

But nobody came. An hour went by – two hours. Still nobody. 'I'm glad Martin and Anne didn't come,' said Uncle Quentin. 'I do wish we'd brought sandwiches.'

At that moment the police arrived, scrambling down the steep sides of the quarry. The police doctor was with them and he saw to Mr Curton's leg. Then, with the help of the others, he got the man to the top with great difficulty.

'Julian, go back and get sandwiches,' said Uncle Quentin at last. 'It looks as if we've got a long wait!'

Julian went back, and was soon down the quarry with neat packets of ham sandwiches and a thermos of hot coffee. The two policemen who were still left offered to stay and watch, if Uncle Quentin wanted to go home.

'Dear me, no!' he said. 'I want to see the faces of these two fellows when they come out. It's going to be one of the nicest moments of my life!

The island is not blown up. My secret is safe. My book is safe. My work is finished. And I just want to tell these things to my two dear friends!'

'You know, Father, I believe they've lost their way underground,' said George. 'Julian said there were many different passages. Timmy took the boys through the right ones, of course – but they would have been quite lost if they hadn't had him with them!'

Her father's face fell at the thought of the men being lost underground. He did so badly want to see their dismayed faces when they arrived in the quarry!

'We could send Timmy in,' said Julian. 'He would soon find them and bring them out. Wouldn't you, Tim?'

'Woof,' said Timmy, agreeing.

'Oh yes, that's a good idea,' said George. 'They won't hurt him if they think he can show them the way out! Go in, Timmy. Find them boy; find them! Bring them here!'

'Woof,' said Timmy, obligingly, and disappeared under the shelf of rock.

Everyone waited, munching sandwiches and sipping coffee. And then they heard Timmy's bark again, from underground!

There was a panting noise, then a scraping sound as somebody came wriggling out from under the rock. He stood up – and then he saw the silent group watching him. He gasped.

'Good morning, Johnson,' said Uncle Quentin, in an amiable voice. 'How are you?'

Johnson went white. He sat down on the nearby heather. 'You win!' he said.

'I do,' said Uncle Quentin. 'In fact, I win handsomely. Your little plan went wrong. My secret is still safe – and next year it will be given to the whole world!'

There was another scraping sound and the second man arrived. He stood up too – and then he saw the quietly watching group.

'Good morning, Peters,' said Uncle Quentin. 'So nice to see you again. How did you like your underground walk? We found it better to come by sea.'

Peters looked at Johnson, and he too sat

down suddenly. 'What's happened?' he said to Johnson.

'It's all up,' said Johnson. Then Timmy appeared, wagging his tail, and went to George.

'I bet they were glad when Timmy came up to them!' said Julian.

Johnson looked at him. 'Yes. We were lost in those hateful tunnels. Curton said he'd come to meet us, but he never came.'

'No. He's probably in the prison hospital by now, with a broken leg,' said Uncle Quentin. 'Well, constable – do your duty.'

Both men were at once arrested. Then the whole company made their way back over the moor. The two men were put into a police car and driven off. The rest of the company went into Kirrin Cottage to have a good meal.

'I'm most terribly hungry,' said George. 'Joanna, have you got anything nice for breakfast?'

'Not much,' said Joanna, from the kitchen. 'Only bacon and eggs and mushrooms!'

'Ooooh!' said Anne, 'Joanna, you shall have the OBCBE!'

'And what may that be?' cried Joanna, but Anne couldn't remember.

'It's a decoration!' she cried.

'Well, I'm not a Christmas tree!' shouted back Joanna. 'You come and help with the breakfast!'

It was a very jolly breakfast that the seven of them – no eight, for Timmy must certainly be counted – sat down to. Martin, now that he was free of his guardian, became quite a different boy.

The children made plans for him. 'You can stay with the coastguard, because he likes you – he kept on and on saying you weren't a bad boy! And you can come and play with us and go to the island. And Uncle Quentin will see if he can get you into an art-school. He says you deserve a reward for helping to save his wonderful secret!'

Martin glowed with pleasure. It seemed as if a load had fallen away from his shoulders. 'I've never had a chance till now,' he said. 'I'll make good. You see if I don't!'

'Mother! Can we go and stay on Kirrin Island and watch the tower being taken down tomorrow?' begged George. 'Do say yes! And can we stay there a whole week? We can sleep in that little room as we did before.'

'Well – I suppose you can!' said her mother, smiling at George's eager face. 'I'd rather like to have your father to myself for a few days and feed him up a bit.'

'Oh, that reminds me, Fanny,' said her husband, suddenly. 'I tried some soup you left for me, the night before last. And my dear, it was horrible! Quite bad!'

'Oh *Quentin*! I told you to pour it away! You know I did,' said his wife, distressed. 'It must have been completely bad. You really are dreadful.'

They all finished their breakfast at last, and went out into the garden. They looked across Kirrin Bay to Kirrin Island. It looked lovely in the morning sun.

'We've had a lot of adventures together,' said

Julian. 'More than most children. They *have* been exciting, haven't they?'

Yes, they have, but now we must say goodbye to the Five, and to Kirrin Island too. Goodbye, Julian, Dick, George, Anne – and Timmy. But only Timmy hears our goodbye, for he has such sharp ears.

'Woof! Goodbye!'

Enid Blyton

The Famous Five's Survival Guide

Packed with useful information on surviving outdoors and solving mysteries, here is the one mystery that the Famous Five never managed to solve. See if you can follow the trail to discover the location of the priceless Royal Dragon of Siam.

The perfect book for all fans of mystery, adventure and the Famous Five!

ISBN 9780340970836

Read the next exciting collection of Secret Seven adventures:

The Secret Seven

The Secret Seven super sleuths are on the trail of a mystery. Dressed in disguise they follow a lead to a spooky old house in the snow . . .

Secret Seven Adventure

When a priceless pearl necklace goes missing the Secret Seven are first off the mark to catch the thief!

Well Done, Secret Seven

The gang have a new meeting place – a treehouse! But someone else is using it too. The Secret Seven are furious, until they learn that the intruder desperately needs their help.

Read the next exciting collection of Secret Seven adventures:

Secret Seven On The Trail

Something mysterious is going on at Tigger's Barn and the Secret Seven are intrigued. Peter thinks it's just gossip, but Jack isn't so sure when he overhears a strange conversation.

Go Ahead Secret Seven

When a sinister-looking man gets George in to trouble with the police, the gang are outraged! Will spying on him shed any light on his motives?

Good Work, Secret Seven

When Peter and Janet realise they are the only witnesses to a car theft, they decide to investigate. However, they are tracking a dangerous gang. Have they taken on too much this time?

READ THE NEXT EXCITING COLLECTION OF SECRET SEVEN ADVENTURES:

Secret Seven Win Through

The gang have a new meeting place, but someone else is using it too. How dare they? They are determined to catch this cheeky intruder, no matter what it takes!

Three Cheers, Secret Seven

When Peter and Jack go looking for their model aeroplane in an old abandoned house, they find a lit fire in one of the rooms. So, who is living there, and why?

Secret Seven Mystery

A girl has mysteriously run away from home and her parents are frantic with worry. Can the gang follow the clues and catch up with her?

READ THE NEXT EXCITING COLLECTION OF FAMOUS FIVE ADVENTURES:

Five Go Off To Camp

Spook-trains in the dead of night! They seem to vanish into thin air – sounds like another case for the Famous Five.

Five Get Into Trouble

Dick's been mistaken for somebody else and been kidnapped! When the remaining gang go to check things out, they are imprisoned too. How will they escape?

Five Fall Into Adventure

George and Timmy the dog have disappeared – and someone has broken into Kirrin cottage! There must be a connection – but can the remaining three uncover it?